University Scholarships, Awards & Bursaries

Brian Heap

8th edition
University Scholarships, Awards & Bursaries

The ONLY guide to all the extra financial assistance available from higher education institutions

University Scholarships, Awards & Bursaries
This eighth edition published in 2009 by
Trotman Publishing, an imprint of Crimson Publishing
Westminster House, Kew Road, Richmond, Surrey TW9 2ND
www.crimsonpublishing.co.uk

© Brian Heap 2009

Editions 6 and 7 published by Trotman Publishing in 2006 and 2007
Editions 2–5 published as *University Scholarships & Awards* in 1999, 2000, 2002 and 2005
Edition 1 published as *A Guide to University Scholarships & Awards* in 1998

Author Brian Heap

British Library Cataloguing in Publication Data
A catalogue record for this book is available from the British Library.

ISBN 978 1 84455 183 5

Typeset by RefineCatch Ltd, Bungay, Suffolk.

Printed and bound in the UK by CPI Antony Rowe, Chippenham, Wiltshire

CONTENTS

erasmus

Erasmus, the European exchange programme for higher education students, enables you to study or do a work placement in one of 30 other countries in Europe. Students from all subject areas participate - as it isn't just for language students - and typically go for three to 12 months.

All eligible students get a grant to help cover the extra costs that might arise from living abroad. You do not pay any tuition fees to the university you are visiting and if you go for a full academic year, you do not pay any tuition fees to your home university or college for that year either.

"Moving to a decidedly cheaper country like the Czech Republic made a world of difference to my livelihood. I could afford to buy organic vegetables by the cart load and ride the public transport system for virtually. Good accommodation was also much cheaper to come by. Without having to fret about the price of nutritious food, rent or transportation, I knew I could genuinely concentrate on my studies."

Jennifer Draxlbauer, Film & Moving Image Production course, Leeds Metropolitan University/FAMU, Prague

If you are nervous of studying abroad for part of your degree because of fears over language skills you can still take part in the programme because many universities run courses in English. Even if you aren't studying languages but are keen to go abroad and need some help with learning the language, you could go on an intensive language course in some countries, with a grant from the European Commission.

Erasmus students don't just come back from their time abroad with some academic credits, a great network of friends and some fantastic memories, they return highly motivated, with more life experience and new skills. So if you want to discover a different culture, make new friends from all over Europe, learn a foreign language and do something different that will look great on your CV with the support of an EU grant, make sure you take part in the Erasmus programme.

Find out more at www.britishcouncil.org/erasmus

ABOUT THIS BOOK

The cost of higher education has always been a serious issue for many students and parents – more so now with the added expense of tuition fees. To try to assist students in need, however, universities and colleges have introduced a range of bursary schemes to help those with financial problems. In addition, there are also other forms of financial assistance for both home and EU students and for those from overseas, in the form of scholarships (which are usually awarded on a competitive basis).

University Scholarships, Awards & Bursaries aims to provide the reader with information on the range of awards available. **Chapter 2** lists those universities and colleges offering scholarships to home and overseas students, with additional information on the tuition fees for non-EU students and the cost of living outlay in various locations. (Bursaries are being made available to eligible UK and EU students by all institutions charging fees for their courses, although it is important to check their websites and also www.bursarymap.direct.gov.uk, since new schemes are being introduced at the time of going to press.)

Details of the tuition fee bursaries offered by each institution are also provided in this chapter – however, universities and colleges advise that such bursaries are constantly under review and could change annually. Please check websites for the most up-to-date information. A further section of the book provides some information for non-EU students, and gives details of approximate tuition fees (for one year) and annual living costs.

Chapters 3, 4 and 6 give details of awards and bursaries available to students irrespective of where they are studying, including those for people from specified geographical areas, and **Chapter 4** provides information on scholarships awarded by professional, commercial and other organisations. **Chapter 5** lists those institutions offering sandwich courses, many of which enable students to receive full pay during their year out when working with various employers. Finally, for ease of reference, the remaining chapters list subject- and university-specific awards for home and EU students.

With a huge number of awards on offer, at both university and department level, *University Scholarships, Awards & Bursaries* cannot hope to list them all. However, my aim is simply to point you in the right direction and to provide some of the answers to help you through your course.

Good Luck!
Brian Heap

Most of the information in Chapter 2 has been provided by universities and colleges to whom I extend my grateful thanks.

INSTITUTIONAL ABBREVIATIONS

AA	Architectural Association
BGC	Bishop Grosseteste College
CAD	College of Art and Design
CAFRE	College of Agriculture, Food and Rural Enterprise
CM	College of Music
CMD	College of Music and Drama
Coll	College
CSM	Camborne School of Mines
CSSD	Central School of Speech and Drama
DMU	De Montfort University
EBS	European Business School
GSA	Guildford School of Acting
IHE	Institute of Higher Education
Inst	Institute
IPA	Institute of Performing Arts
LIPA	Liverpool Institute of Performing Arts
LSE	London School of Economics and Political Science
Marjon	University College Plymouth St Mark and St John
RBS	Regents Business School
RCM	Royal College of Music
RCN	Royal College of Nursing
RNCM	Royal Northern College of Music
RSAMD	Royal Scottish Academy of Music and Drama
SOAS	School of Oriental and African Studies
TVU	Thames Valley University
UC	University College
UCAS	Universities and Colleges Admissions Service
UCL	University College London
UCLan	University of Central Lancashire
UWE	University of the West of England
UWIC	University of Wales Institute, Cardiff

OTHER ABBREVIATIONS

ACU	Association of Commonwealth Universities
AfPP	Association for Perioperative Practice
AHRC	Arts and Humanities Research Council
ALF	Access to Learning Fund
ALG	Assembly Learning Grant
ATI	Associateship of the Textile Institute
BBSRC	Biotechnology and Biological Sciences Research Council
BFWG	British Federation of Women Graduates
CCETSA	Canon Collins Educational Trust for Southern Africa
CF	Conditional firm choice
CIES	Council for International Exchange of Scholars
CIMA	Chartered Institute of Management Accountants
CIOB	Chartered Institute of Building
CSFP	Commonwealth Scholarship and Fellowship Programme
CUSA	Crichton University Scholarship Agreement
CVCP	Committee of Vice-Chancellors and Principals
DARO	Development and Alumni Relations Office
DCSF	Department for Children, Schools and Families
DfID	Department for International Development
DHPA	Dorothy Hodgkin Postgraduate Awards
DRC	Disability Resource Centre
ECS	School of Electronics and Computer Science
EO	Employers Organisation
EPSRC	Engineering and Physical Sciences Research Council
ESRC	Economic and Social Research Council
FCO	Foreign and Commonwealth Office
FTE	Full-time Equivalent
GBCET	Great Britain–China Educational Trust
GSP	Graduate School of Pan-Pacific International Studies
HEFCE	Higher Education Funding Council for England
HEMGs	Higher Education Maintenance Grants
HTI	Higher Technical Institute
IB	International Baccalaureate
ICE	Institution of Civil Engineers
ICNA	Infection Control Nurses Association
IEE	Institution of Electrical Engineers
IET	Institution of Engineering and Technology
IFIC	International Fire Investigators & Consultants
IFS	International Family Scholarships
IIE	Institute of International Education
IMechE	Institute of Mechanical Engineers
IOP	Institute of Physics
KRSF	Karim Rida Said Foundation
MRC	Medical Research Council
NAFUM	North American Foundation Awards for Postgraduate Study at the University of Manchester
NERC	National Environment Research Council
NHSBSA	NHS Business Services Authority

NLIAH	National Leadership and Innovation Agency for Healthcare
NUT	National Union of Teachers
OCSKET	Oxford and Cambridge Society, Karachi, Educational Trust
ODI	Overseas Development Institute
ODPM	Office of the Deputy Prime Minister
ORS	Overseas Research Student
ORSAS	Overseas Research Student Award Scheme
PGCE	Postgraduate (or Professional Graduate) Certificate in Education
PPARC	Particle Physics and Astronomy Research Council
PPE	Politics, Philosophy and Economics
QUEST	Queen's Jubilee Scholarship Trust
RandA	Royal and Ancient (Golf Club)
RADAR	Royal Association for Disability and Rehabilitation
RASE	Royal Agricultural Society of England
RCN	Royal College of Nursing
RHS	Royal Horticultural Society
SAAS	Student Awards Agency for Scotland
SEAS	School of Engineering and Applied Science (Aston University)
SPS	Social and Political Sciences
SYHEDT	South Yorkshire Higher Education and Development Trust
TASS	Talented Athlete Scholarship Scheme
TCTP	Technical Cooperation and Training Programme
TI	Tube Investment
UCAS	Universities and Colleges Admissions Service
UCCE	Universities Centre of Cricketing Excellence
UF	Unconditional firm choice
URS	University Research Studentships
WCCC	Worcestershire County Cricket Club
WUAP	Warwick Undergraduate Aid Programme
YLCE	Yorkshire Ladies' Council of Education

1 | FINANCING YOUR COURSE

Going to university or college can be expensive. Initially there are costs involving books and course materials and for many who will be living away from home, there are the added costs of accommodation, food, travel and other day-to-day expenses, not forgetting the annual tuition fee. Universities can set their own fees for degree courses and for 2009/10 the majority will set the maximum fee of £3,225. However depending on various individual circumstances, financial help is available by way of grants, loans, bursaries and scholarships although different financial arrangements apply in Scotland, Wales and Northern Ireland (see below).

GRANTS
Maintenance Grants
Maintenance grants are available to students towards their living costs depending on their household income. These grants are set on a sliding scale and are not repayable. For household incomes less than £25,000 the maximum grant payable is £2,906 and between £25,001 and £50,020, partial grants can be claimed. Applications for maintenance grants are made through your local authority and should be made as soon as possible after submitting your university or college applications.

Special Support Grants
These grants are for full-time students who can claim income-related benefits including lone single parents and disabled students. The maximum is again £2,906 and is non-repayable. Students eligible for this grant cannot receive the maintenance grant.

Disabled Students Allowances
These allowances are for students with disabilities, special learning difficulties or mental health conditions. The payments are not related to household income and include up to £5,161 for special equipment throughout the course and up to £20,520 per year for a non-medical helper's allowance. In addition £1,724 is payable as a general allowance and with a travel allowance to cover extra travel costs.

Childcare Grants
These grants are to help with childcare costs for dependent children under the age of 15 and are related to household income.

Parents Learning Allowances
These allowances are offered to help with course related costs for those with dependent children and are again set against income. The maximum amount payable is £1,508.

Adult Dependent Grant
For those who are responsible financially for a dependent adult the maximum grant set against income is £2,642 per year.

Access to Learning Fund
All universities and colleges can also provide help in cases of financial hardship.

LOANS
Tuition Fee Loans
Loans of up to £3,225 can be borrowed which are only repayable when the student has left the course and is earning over £15,000 per year.

Maintenance Loan

The purpose of this loan, which is also repayable as above, is to assist with living costs, the amount payable depending on household income. Maximum amounts are as follows:

* £3,838: Students living at their parents' home.
* £6,928: Living elsewhere or at home and studying in London.
* £4,950: Living elsewhere or in their own home and studying elsewhere.
* £5,895: Studying abroad for at least one academic term.

Loans are administered by the Student Loans Company (SLC) at ww.direct.gov.uk/studentfinance.

BURSARIES AND OTHER AWARDS

In addition to any grants you may receive universities and colleges charging the maximum tuition fee also provide bursaries. The amounts vary between institutions and range between a minimum of £319 to over £3,000 for students on the full grant. Check the universities and colleges in Chapter 2 to see what is on offer.

Universities have always offered bursaries and scholarships to home students and those from EU countries. Also there are other awards to non-EU (overseas) students and to postgraduates (see Chapters 8 and 9). Some universities also offer progression bursaries to encourage students to complete their course increasing the annual amount each year. These are usually awarded irrespective of personal financial circumstances. NHS bursaries for health professional courses are also offered irrespective of financial need.

Bursaries also vary in size depending on the institution and recent research suggests that they are not always necessarily linked to financial need, 25% of them being based exclusively on merit.

The majority of scholarships, however are normally linked to academic or other personal achievements such as high grades at A-level, sporting, music or choral awards and in some cases a person's contribution to school or community activities. At some institutions awards may be 'open' or 'closed', the former being open to any, applicant whilst the latter may be restricted to students residing in certain locations or who are applying for courses in specific subjects.

Scottish and Scottish-resident students studying in Scotland

Students domiciled in Scotland receive free tuition. Young student bursaries of up to £2,575 are payable depending on family income and student loans are also available. Tuition fees are however payable by English, Welsh and Northern Irish students studying in Scotland and in 2008/09 these were £1,775, or for medical courses £2,825. The fees for 2009/10 will be published prior to the commencement of courses. See also www.student-support-saas.gov.uk.

Welsh and Welsh-resident students studying in Wales

Tuition fees in 2009/10 will be £3,225 with a non-means tested, non-repayable fee grant of up to £1,940. Student loans are also available. Welsh students studying outside Wales pay the tuition fee of their university or college of choice and may be eligible for a means-tested grant of up to £2,906. Non-Welsh home students studying in Wales will pay fees of up to £3,225 in 2009/10. Contact www.studentfinancewales.co.uk.

The tuition-fee grant of £1,940 above, which is provided regardless of background, is to be phased out for new students from September 2010. In its place more help is to be directed to those from lower income backgrounds.

Northern Irish and Northern Irish-resident students

Means-tested grant and loans are available. All UK home students will pay tuition fees of up to £3,225 in 2009/10 in Northern Ireland or in other parts of the UK. Contact www.studentfinanceni.co.uk or www.direct.gov.uk/studentfinance.

You should start to consider possible degree courses and universities no later than March of the year prior to entry and preferably earlier. The university and college listings in the next chapter will give you some idea of the degree subjects being offered, although changes are constantly taking place so it's important to check prospectuses and websites. Similarly it's also worth checking your chosen subject department for any awards on offer since these are often made at the discretion of the departmental head and may not be annual awards.

Whilst early applications are usually required, some can only be made once you have been offered or have accepted a place and some can only be submitted after starting the course. Finally whatever the award, you should realise that there will be stiff competition so plan your application form with care. Here are a few rules of engagement

1. Read through the form carefully before you put pen to paper.
2. Plan your answers beforehand.
3. Only answer exactly what is asked.
4. Write neatly.
5. And check your spelling.

Full details of the financial help for students are published in 'A Guide to Financial Support for Higher Education Students 2009/10' available by phoning 0800 731 9133 and for more information go to www.direct.gov.uk/studentfinance.

Important note
Many universities and colleges are constantly reviewing their financial arrangements. Some scholarships are offered every year whilst others are introduced for one year only, similarly application arrangements and dates may also change. Readers therefore are advised to check with institutions for up-to-date information. The level of tuition fees is currently being reviewed by the government. At present there is a cap of £3,500 on all fees.

The level of tution fees is currently being reviewed by the government. At present there is a cap of £3,500 on all fees.

2 | UNIVERSITIES AND UNIVERSITY COLLEGES IN THE UK

All publicly funded institutions, or those privately funded but running individual courses receiving public funding charge tuition fees (eg Universities, University Colleges, Colleges of Agriculture, Art, Drama, Music etc). Courses include First degrees (BA, Bsc, BEd, etc), Foundation degrees (FdA, FdSc, FdEng) Higher National Diplomas and Certificates, Diplomas of Higher Education and the Postgraduate Certificate in Education.

The following chapter lists all the Universities and University Colleges in the UK, and the awards on offer at the time of publication. **However changes are constantly taking place and applicants are advised to contact the university department in their chosen subject to obtain details of any awards, before accepting a place firmly or provisionally.**

ABERDEEN UNIVERSITY

The University of Aberdeen is the most northerly of all universities in the UK. It is one of the UK's ancient universities, dating back to 1495, with most teaching taking place on the main King's College campus. There are 14,000 students following courses in a wide range of subjects.

Exchanges take place with 15 North American universities, five Hong Kong universities, one university in Korea and one Japanese university, in addition to which there are links with over 170 universities across the EU and European Economic Area.

DEGREE SUBJECTS OFFERED

Accountancy; Animal Ecology; Anthropology; Archaeology; Artificial Intelligence; Biochemistry; Biotechnology; Celtic Studies; Chemistry; Computing; Cultural History; Divinity; Ecology; Economics; Education; Engineering (Chemical; Civil; Electrical/Electronic; Integrated; Mechanical; Petroleum); English; Entrepreneurship; Environmental Microbiology; Environmental Science; European Business; European Languages; Film and Visual Culture; Finance; Forestry; French; Gaelic Studies; Genetics; Geography; Geology; Geoscience; German; Health Science; Hispanic Studies; History; History of Art; Immunology; Language and Linguistics; Law; Legal Studies; Management Studies; Marine and Coastal Resource Management; Mathematics; Medicinal Chemistry; Mental Philosophy; Microbiology; Natural Philosophy; Neuroscience; Parasitology; Pharmacology; Physics; Physiology; Plant Science; Politics; Primary Education; Property; Psychology; Religious Studies; Rural Surveying; Scottish Studies; Social Science; Sociology; Spatial Planning; Sports and Exercise Science; Theology; Tropical Environmental Sciences; Wildlife Management; Zoology.

TUITION FEES (2009/10)

Students domiciled in Scotland receive free tuition; See www.saas.gov.uk and **Chapter 1 'Financing Your Course'.**

BURSARIES AND OTHER AWARDS

See www.abdn.ac.uk/sras/undergraduate/bursaries_scholarships.shtml.

Entrance Scholarships

The University of Aberdeen is currently offering Entrance Scholarships of £1,000 for each year of study to students of outstanding academic merit undertaking undergraduate degrees at the university, for students who might be deterred from taking a university place for financial reasons.

Applicants must have applied to the university for a place starting in September. To be awarded a scholarship they must receive and firmly accept an offer, either conditional or unconditional, of a place. Scholarships are available to all, regardless of gender, race, religion, ethnic or national origin, but all applicants must be living in the UK. Scholarships will be available for all full time undergraduate degree courses. Applications must be submitted by April prior to entry. Full information can be obtained from www.abdn.ac.uk/sras/undergraduate/bursaries_scholarships.shtml.

Choral, Organ and Music Scholarships

There are several awards made each year to outstanding musicians, including Organ, Choral and Instrumental Scholarships. For further information on any of these, contact Professor Pete Stollery in the University Music Department on p.stollery@abdn.ac.uk. There is also a further award (the Derek Ogston Music Scholarship) worth £1,250, awarded for one year in the first instance.

Golf Bursaries

The aim of the University of Aberdeen Golf Bursary Scheme is to assist young men and young women of exceptional golfing ability to improve and develop their game during their full-time study at the University of Aberdeen. Full information can be obtained from www.abdn.ac.uk/sportandrec/glfburs.hti.

Sports Bursaries

The Alumni Annual Fund Sports Bursary Scheme is funded each year by the University of Aberdeen Alumni department. The Alumni raise funds for many causes across the University, through the generosity of former students of the University of Aberdeen. Full information can be obtained from www.abdn.ac.uk/sportandrec/sprtburs.hti.

Elizabeth Wilson Scholarship

Agriculture students can apply for the Elizabeth Wilson Scholarship which awards up to £1,000. To be eligible, students must have been resident in the North East of Scotland for five years. It is open to both undergraduates and postgraduates. For further information contact the Department of Agriculture and Forestry or email bioscience@abdn.ac.uk.

Charles Sutherland Scholarship for Agriculture, Engineering and Economics

This scholarship is also open to both undergraduates and postgraduates. For further information contact the Department of Agriculture and Forestry or email bioscience@abdn.ac.uk.

European Union Student Awards

EU students taking a complete degree course at the University are eligible to apply for tuition fee awards from the Student Awards Agency for Scotland (SAAS), Gyleview House, 3 Redheughs Rigg, Edinburgh EH12 9HH.

Department of Agriculture Scholarships

The Sir Maitland Mackie Scholarship worth up to £1,000 is available to undergraduates showing promise in the field of animal production for the food industry in relation to dairy science and practice.

The Johnston and Carmichael Land Management Scholarship.

This award worth up to £1,000 is awarded to undergraduates showing promise in the field of farm estate or other rural land management in relation to accountancy and business methods.

Engineering Scholarships
About six industrial sponsorships, each worth £1,000 or more, are made available each year in Engineering to students who have already completed at least one year. Contact the School of Engineering for further information.

AWARDS FOR NON-EU STUDENTS
Scholarships and grants are available for overseas students including several department awards for postgraduate students. For further information see www.abdn.ac.uk/sras/postgraduate/bursaries.shtml.

POSTGRADUATE AWARDS
Chemistry
The department has a number of endowments which are used to assist postgraduate students. Email chemistry@abdn.ac.uk.

Computing Science
Research Council studentships are normally available to UK and EU (fees-only) research students. Research assistantships leading to award of research degrees may also be available in specific research areas. For details email pgstudy@csd.abdn.ac.uk.

Engineering
EPSRC Master's Training Awards, the TotalFinaElf Bursary and the Mike Marnie Bursary are available for the MSc Programme in Safety Engineering, Reliability and Risk Management. For further details about funding possibilities for this course contact c.croydon@abdn.ac.uk.

Fraser Joseph Scholarships
The Fraser Joseph Scholarships are open to postgraduate research students but preference will be given to Sri Lankan nationals. Email s.skilling@abdn.ac.uk for further details.

Geology and Petroleum Geology
The department offers scholarships each year. Email the department at geology@abdn.ac.uk for information about funding opportunities.

Health Services and Public Health Research
The Department of Public Health has four studentships – two MSc and two PhDs. For further details contact the Postgraduate Coordinator, Dr Edwin Van Teijlingen, on van.teijlingen@abdn.ac.uk or refer to the Department of Public Health website.

Mathematics
Milner Scholarships are available to postgraduate research students in the field of mathematics – also available for research in bacteriology or pathology. For more information, contact maths@maths.abdn.ac.uk.

Music
There are scholarships available for musicians including the Ogston Postgraduate Scholarship, Nora Bently Scholarship, the Scottish Students' Songbook Award, five Principal's Scholarships and 10 Chapel Choir Scholarships. Email p.stollery@abdn.ac.uk for more information on any of the above funding opportunities.

Plant and Soil Science
The Robert Carrick Memorial Trust for Zulu students to study Environmental Sciences. Available for taught Master's courses only, not research. Awards are not necessarily made every year, and beneficiaries should be of the Zulu race, be domiciled in KwaZulu, and be likely to make a distinct contribution to the development of the Zulu lands.

See Chapters 2, 4 and 6 for additional awards, applicable to all universities

Dr RJ Colley Bursary

The bursary is currently valued at £1,500 per year, and will be offered for two years only. Postgraduate students who have enrolled for a degree programme at the University of Aberdeen are eligible to apply. Preference will be given to students from Christian missionary families, or who may be a member of, or in sympathy with, a mainstream Christian Church. Applicants must be able to demonstrate academic potential and that they face financial difficulties. For more information contact Susan Maclennan at susan.maclennan@abdn.ac.uk.

There are also other awards including the BTCO/Aberdeen Scholarship for Taiwan students to study Environmental Science and the British Council/Swire Group Scholarship for students from Thailand. Several other awards are available from the British Council (Bridgwater House, Manchester M1 6BB).

See also under **Charles Sutherland Scholarships** (above).

INFORMATION AND APPROXIMATE FEES FOR NON-EU STUDENTS

Students from overseas make up 19% of the student body, and there are 120 nationalities. **English language entry requirement:** IELTS 6.0 (or equivalent); Medicine IELTS 7.0 (or equivalent). A four week English course is available in August before the start of the academic year. **Fees:** arts courses £9,250; science courses £11,500; Medicine £22,500. **Living costs:** £6,000.

University of Aberdeen, King's College, Aberdeen AB24 3FX; tel: 01224 272090; www. abdn.ac.uk.

ABERTAY DUNDEE UNIVERSITY

The University of Abertay Dundee was founded in 1888 and is located in the centre of Dundee. There is a student population of over 4,000 following vocational courses in a wide range of subjects to degree and Diploma of Higher Education levels. Most of the courses are taught on a modular basis, which provides greater flexibility of course content and enables courses to be tailored to individual needs.

DEGREE SUBJECTS OFFERED

Accountancy; Behavioural Sciences; Biomedical Sciences; Biotechnology; Business Administration; Business Portfolio; Civil Engineering; Computer Arts; Computer Games Technology; Computing; Criminological Studies; Engineering; European Economy and Management; Finance and Business; Food and Consumer Sciences; Forensic Psychobiology; Forensic Sciences; Game Production Management; Health Sciences; Information Systems; Law; Marketing and Business; Media, Culture and Society; Mental Health and Counselling; Multimedia Development; Natural Resources Management; Nursing; Psychology; Social Science; Sociology; Sports Coaching and Development; Sports, Health and Exercise; Tourism; Web Design and Development.

TUITION FEES (2009/10)

Students domiciled in Scotland receive free tuition. See www.saas.gov.uk and **Chapter 1 'Financing Your Course'.**

BURSARIES AND OTHER AWARDS

Angus Educational Trust Awards

The Angus Educational Trust may award bursaries to persons resident in Angus to assist them in following a course of study at the university. Further information regarding eligibility for an award may be obtained form the Clerk to the Angus Education Department, County Buildings, Forfar.

City of Dundee Educational Trust Awards

The City of Dundee Educational Trust may award bursaries to persons resident in Dundee to assist them in following a course of study leading to 'responsible employment in industry, commerce or a profession'. Further information regarding eligibility for an award may be obtained from the Clerk to the Governors of the City of Dundee Educational Trust, Miller Hendry, 13 Ward Road, Dundee.

Margaret Parkinson Scholarships

These awards worth £1,000, are open to undergraduate students following courses in Health subjects.

Educational Endowments

The Student Awards Agency for Scotland maintains a register of educational endowments. Application forms may be obtained from the SAAS. See also **Chapter 10**.

Financial assistance for mature students

Mature Scottish students may be eligible for support from the Student Awards Agency for Scotland. Mature students from elsewhere in the UK should contact their local authority (or in the case of Northern Ireland the Library Board) for details of financial assistance. Some mature students may be eligible for additional support in the form of non-repayable supplementary grants.

Mature Student Bursaries

Eligible full-time undergraduate students from Scotland can apply for a non-repayable Mature Student Bursary. The bursary is means tested on personal and financial circumstances. These bursaries are administered by the institution, and institutions may not always be able to pay the maximum limits under the scheme; the aim is to reimburse costs such as childcare, housing or excess travel costs. There will be a maximum overall limit of bursary for each student.

Norman Fraser Design Trust Award

This is an undergraduate scholarship open to students following Civil Engineering courses.

Trust Funds and Bursaries

The university operates a number of trusts on behalf of the trustees:

* The Carnegie Trust
* The Robert Reid Fund
* The Donald Stewart Bursary
* The Sutherland Page Trust.

Nine Incorporated Trades of Dundee

The Nine Incorporated Trades of Dundee offer small awards for part-time students undertaking management courses at the university who can demonstrate links to the City of Dundee. Awards are made towards fees, books and equipment.

Opportunities Bursaries

The university has introduced Opportunities Bursaries for first-year students who can demonstrate good academic achievement. Bursaries of £500 will be awarded to those students who can satisfy the criterion.

See Chapters 2, 4 and 6 for additional awards, applicable to all universities

AWARDS FOR NON-EU STUDENTS
Abertay Achievers Scholarship

Overseas students (those from outside the EU and identified as liable to pay the overseas student fee) commencing the study of a full-time undergraduate honours degree, and intending to complete all four years of the programme, can apply to be considered for the Abertay Achievers Scholarship. This scholarship will cover the difference between the overseas tuition fee (currently £7,750) and the 'home' students tuition fee (currently £1,175) in the final (fourth) year of an undergraduate degree programme, for those who have successfully completed their studies of the first three years of the programme at Abertay.

Applicants must intend to commence study on a full-time undergraduate honours degree programme and complete Years 1, 2 and 3. This award is not available to those students who have been permitted to enter a degree programme 'with advanced standing'. Applicants must also have achieved an academic performance to allow them to progress to the honours year of the under-graduate degree programme, have paid all university fees required of them and have no outstanding debt to the university prior to commencing the final (fourth) year of study.

Overseas Students' Scholarship Scheme

Students from the undermentioned countries intending to enrol on full-time, undergraduate or postgraduate courses can apply to the Overseas Students' Scholarship Scheme. Ten scholarships for each of the following countries are provided as a contribution towards the payment of tuition fees and are to the value of £1,000 per year of study: Bangladesh; Canada; China; India; Malaysia; Pakistan; Russia; Singapore; Sri Lanka; Thailand; UAE/Oman; USA; Vietnam.

POSTGRADUATE AWARDS

Some awards are available. Contact the university.

INFORMATION AND APPROXIMATE FEES FOR NON-EU STUDENTS

International students make up 10% of the student body. **English language entry requirement:** IELTS 5.5 (or equivalent). A pre-sessional English course is available, as is a full-time English course from September to May and free English tuition throughout the degree course. **Fees:** all courses £8,150. **Living costs:** £5,000–£6,000.

University of Abertay Dundee, Bell Street, Dundee DD1 1HG; tel: 01382 308080; www.abertay.ac.uk.

ABERYSTWYTH (University of Wales)

The University of Wales, Aberystwyth is located on a hillside overlooking the town and Cardigan Bay. A wide range of subjects is offered at degree level, in the Faculties of Arts, Economic and Social Studies and Science, as single, joint and major/minor schemes. A small number of HND courses and foundation degrees in science are also available in land-based studies. Students number over 7,500 with some 48% in university accommodation (hall of residence places are guaranteed for all first-year students including those who apply through Clearing).

DEGREE SUBJECTS OFFERED

Accounting and Finance; Agriculture; American Studies; Animal Science; Art; Art History; Artificial Intelligence and Robotics; Behavioural Biology; Biochemistry; Biological Sciences; Biology and Sport Science; Business and Management; Business Information Technology; Celtic Studies; Computer

Graphics, Vision and Games; Computer Science; Countryside Management; Creative Writing and English; Criminology; Drama; Economics; Education; English; Environmental Earth Science; Environmental Science; Equine and Human Sport Science; Equine Studies/Science; European History; European Languages: French, German, Spanish; Film and Television Studies; Genetics; Genetics and Human Health; Geography; History; Information and Library Studies; Information Management; International Politics; Internet Computing; Internet Engineering; Irish; Law; Marketing; Mathematics; Media and Communication Studies; Medieval and Early Modern History; Microbiology; Mobile and Wearable Computing; Modern and Contemporary History; Modern German Studies; Museum and Gallery Studies; Performance Studies; Physics; Psychology; Politics; Scenographic Studies; Software Engineering; Space Science and Robotics; Sport and Exercise Science; Sustainable Rural Development; Tourism Management; Welsh; Welsh History; Zoology.

TUITION FEES (2009/10)
See www.studentfinancewales.co.uk and also **Chapter 1 'Financing your course'**.

BURSARIES AND OTHER AWARDS
Entrance Scholarships
The university assists many students by way of some 300 Entrance Scholarships and Merit Awards which are awarded each year. Examinations for this competition are held in February of each year for students wishing to enter in the following autumn. Two two-hour examinations are taken in two different subjects. Usually these are subjects being taken at A-level. The Scholarships are worth £1,000 to £1,200 per year, and all are tenable for the normal length of the course. Merit Awards are worth £1,000, which is payable during the first year. All Scholars and Merit Award holders receive an unconditional offer – provided they have taken papers appropriate for the degree course they wish to study.

Financial Contingency Funds
These funds are available through the university for students who face hardship during the course. Assistance may be provided on a selective basis in the form of grants and loans. Contact www.aber.ac.uk/student finance.

Year in Employment
Students can opt to take a year in paid employment. Contact the University Careers Advisory Service.

Care Leavers Bursaries
Students who have previously been in care can claim a care leavers bursary valued between £1,000–£1,800.

Senior Scholarships
A minimum of two awards (£1,200 per year) are made each year to candidates who achieve the highest aggregate marks in the Entrance Scholarship Examination.

Evan Morgan Scholarships
Eighteen Evan Morgan Scholarships with an annual value of £1,000 each are offered each year. The scholarships are awarded on the basis of performance in the Entrance Scholarship Examinations. Students must be resident in Wales with a knowledge of Welsh and English and have attended a school or college in Wales for a minimum of two years. GCSE Maths or Science is required.

Open Entrance Awards
Eighteen Scholarships with an annual value of £1,000 each are offered. The scholarships are awarded on the basis of performance in the Entrance Scholarship Examinations. The scholarships do not require residential or other qualifications.

See Chapters 2, 4 and 6 for additional awards, applicable to all universities

Bryn Terfel Scholarship

Value: £1,000 per year. The scholarship is awarded on the basis of performance in the Entrance Scholarship Examination and is open to candidates born in Wales who are eligible for admission as mature entrants, and who intend to read for a degree within the Faculty of Arts at the University of Wales, Aberystwyth. The scholarship will be available every fourth year and will be tenable for three years.

Excellence Bursaries

These bursaries are available to students pursuing single and joint honours and major programmes in the Sciences, European Languages, Welsh and defined Welsh-medium schemes. They are valued at £2,000 for a three-year course, £2,667 for a four-year course, and £3,334 for a five-year course (£1,400 for two-year foundation degrees).

Excellence Bursaries are available to UK/EU students who have no previous experience of Higher Education, who can show high levels of academic achievement before entering university and who accept Aberystwyth as their Firm choice preference via UCAS. There are no entrance examinations – the normal academic standard required is a minimum of 300 points from the best full three A-levels or equivalent. Any specific A-level prerequisites for the proposed course must also be met at the level specified in the offer. The normal academic standard required for HNDs/foundation degrees is 160 points including two A-level passes or equivalent and any specified level of performance at A-level or equivalent.

Aberystwyth Bursaries

These form part of the Wales National Bursary Scheme but are unique to Aberystwyth. They are means-tested and non-repayable and range from £200 to £1,000 per year. Aberystwyth Bursaries are open to UK and EU students.

Residential Bursaries

The university is offering a £500 discount from the relevant first-year residential fee for all full-time undergraduate UK/EU students residing in a Hall of Residence or University Managed property. The £500 is set against the full academic year's accommodation fee (and will be reduced pro rata in the event of withdrawal). Students must have placed Aberystwyth as their Firm choice through UCAS by the specified deadline.

Music Bursaries

Value: £400 per year. Number available: variable. Open to students who hold any kind of offer (including insurance offers) at the time of the closing date. You need not apply for the Entrance Scholarship Examination in order to be considered for a Music Bursary.

The Music Bursaries are intended for experienced players of orchestral instruments who can actively contribute to the university's wide range of orchestras, bands etc. They are awarded on the basis of competitive audition to new entrants in any discipline (undergraduate and postgraduate) for a period of up to three years. The closing date for applications is 20 April in the year in which entry to the university is proposed.

Application forms, regulations and further details are available from the Director of Music, University of Wales, Aberystwyth, 10 Laura Place, Aberystwyth SY23 2AU.

Sports Bursaries

Ten awards of £500 are offered each year to students who can demonstrate recent achievement of a high standard in sport and commitment to performance development.

Other Open Awards

* **Edward Hamer Scholarship:** £1,000 – Once every three years.
* **Elizabeth Richards Scholarship:** £1,000 – Once every three years.
* **Hudson-Williams Scholarship:** £1,000 – Applicants to the Faculty of Arts.
* **John Hughes Scholarship:** £1,000.

Other Closed Awards

* **Richard and Anne Roberts Aberdovey Scholarships:** £1,000 – For natives of Aberdovey educated at Aberdovey Primary School or Tywyn Secondary School.
* **Elizabeth Anne Davies Scholarship:** £1,000 – For Welsh-speaking candidates.
* **Pembrokeshire Scholarship:** £1,000 – Candidates living in Pembrokeshire.
* **Evan Bolle-Jones Scholarship:** £1,000 – Applicants for degree schemes in the Institute of Biological, Environmental and Rural Sciences.
* **Dewi and Annie Williams Scholarships:** £1,000 – Applicants for Geography or courses in the Department of Welsh.
* **The Loveluck Scholarship:** £1,000 – Applicants for a degree in Biological Sciences.
* **Miss S.A. Davis Scholarship:** £1,000 – For Welsh-speaking girls whose parents reside or who are rate-payers in the Parish of Llandysul.
* **Thomas Davies Scholarship:** £1,000 – Applicants for degree schemes in Chemistry and Agriculture.
* **Sir Alfred Jones Scholarship:** £1,000 – Applicants whose parents or guardians reside in the Borough of Carmarthen and in every other year in any part of Wales including Monmouthshire other than the Borough of Carmarthen.
* **Thomas Lewis Scholarship:** £1,000 – Candidates who have been residents for at least three year within three miles of the Parish Church of Pennal or in the Parish of Isygarreg in the Country of Montgomery.
* **David Morgan Thomas of Caterham Memorial Scholarship:** £1,000 – For sons of Noncomformist Ministers.
* **Joseph Thomas Scholarship:** £1,000 – For male candidates born in the counties of Pembrokeshire, Carmarthenshire, or Ceredigion or in the town and county of Haverfordwest.
* **Mrs Clarke's Scholarships:** £1,000 – For male candidates, born in Edeyrn, Caernarfonshire or in Pwllheli or if no candidates any school in Wales.
* **Reverend Herbert Morgan Scholarship:** £1,000 – For Welsh candidates or a student in residence.
* **Richard Davies Mynyddog Scholarship:** £1,000 – For candidates born and resident in Wales with preference given to natives of Montgomeryshire.

University of Wales Scholarships

* **The Aberfan Children's Scholarship:** £800 – For candidates whose parents were living in Aberfan at the time of the disaster or to a person of school age living in Merthyr Tydfil.
* **D. Lloyd Thomas Memorial Scholarship:** £600 – For Welsh-speaking applicants born or resident in the County of Mid-Glamorgan with preference to those who have been resident in the Maesteg area (as defined by the boundaries of the borough or Ogwr).
* **Dr Howell Rees Scholarship:** £500 – Awarded every third year (alternatively to Cardiff and Swansea universities) for candidates born in Carmarthenshire.
* **Price Davies Scholarship:** £400 – Open to applicants for degrees in Arts and Sciences.
* **Dr Vaughan Roberts Scholarship:** £40 – For pupils of Ysgol y Moelwyn, Blaenau Ffestiniog.

Institute of Geography and Earth Sciences – Human Geography Excellence Bursaries

Value: £2,000 (£667 per year over a three-year period). A minimum of five awards per year are awarded to single honours, joint honours or major/minor applicants who choose Aberystwyth as their firm choice and achieve a top five ranking by points.

Institute of Mathematical and Physical Sciences Scholarships to pursue studies in Mathematics

To qualify for an Institute Scholarship an applicant must either be in receipt of an Entrance Scholarship, or achieve three (or more) A grades at A-level, including Mathematics. Applicants must attend an interview to receive the award. The level of the award is £500 per year; the award is retained providing an exam average of 70% (or more) is achieved each year. Joint honours students are eligible for £250.

See Chapters 2, 4 and 6 for additional awards, applicable to all universities

Institute of Mathematical and Physical Sciences Scholarships to pursue studies in Physics

To qualify for an Institute Scholarship an applicant must either be in receipt of an Entrance Scholarship, or achieve three (or more) A grades at A-level, including Physics or Mathematics. Applicants must attend an interview to receive the award. The level of the award is £500 per year; the award is retained providing an exam average of 65% (or more) is achieved each year. Joint honours students are eligible for £250.

Institute of Physics Bursaries

The Institute of Physics (IOP) runs an Undergraduate Bursary Scheme which has awards with a value of up to £1,000 per year. The IOP bursaries aim to encourage applications for physics degrees from non-standard applicants such as mature students and from under represented groups. These bursaries are open to students who attend a UCAS visit and will be based on performance during the interview at the visit.

School of Management and Business Scholarships for international students on undergraduate programmes

£2,000 tuition fee discount, awarded on a competitive basis for academic merit.

POSTGRADUATE AWARDS

For details on the range of awards available to postgraduate students, contact the Postgraduate Admissions Office.

INFORMATION AND APPROXIMATE FEES FOR NON-EU STUDENTS

There is a large number of international students. **English language entry requirement:** IELTS 6.5 (or equivalent). Full-time courses in English tuition are available. **Fees:** arts courses £8,000; joint courses: £9,500. **Living costs:** £5,000–£6,000.

University of Wales Aberystwyth, The Old College, King Street, Aberystwyth, Ceredigion SY23 2AX; tel: 01970 622021; www.aber.ac.uk

---

ANGLIA RUSKIN UNIVERSITY

Anglia Ruskin University was founded in 1989 and has two main sites, at Cambridge and at Chelmsford. There is a student population of over 7,500. Degree and Higher National Diploma courses are offered in a wide range of subjects.

DEGREE SUBJECTS OFFERED

Accounting; Animal Behaviour; Architecture; Art and Design; Art History; Audio Technology; Biological Science; Biology; Biomedical Science; Building Surveying; Business; Cell and Molecular Biology; Chemistry; Childhood Studies; Civil Engineering; Communication Studies; Computer Aided Engineering; Computer Science; Construction Management; Countryside Management; Criminology; Drama; Earth Science; Ecology and Conservation; Economics; Education (Primary/Secondary); Electronics; English; Environmental Science; Estate Management; European Business; Facilities Management; Film Studies; Forensic Science; French; Geochemistry; Geography; Geology; German; Health and Gender Studies; Hispanic Cultural Studies; History; Housing; Information Systems; Italian; Law; Leisure Planning; Mathematics; Medical Chemistry; Microbiology; Midwifery; Multimedia; Music; Natural History; Nursing; Ophthalmic Dispensing; Optical Management; Performing Arts; Philosophy; Photographic and Digital Media; Planning; Politics; Printmaking; Property Management; Psychology; Quantity Surveying; Social Policy; Software Engineering; Spanish; Sports Science/Studies; Surveying; Tourism and Leisure; Wildlife Biology.

TUITION FEES (2009/10)
£3,225.

BURSARIES AND OTHER AWARDS
There is a £319 bursary for each year of the course, for all students in receipt of the full mainte-nance grant.

Anglia Ruskin Aspire Scheme
The Scheme offers an award of £500 to eligible students subject to successful progression from the first to the second semester.

Anglia Ruskin Foundation Scholarships
The Anglia Trust offers a maximum of 12 Foundation Scholarships worth between £250 and £750. They are intended to assist Foundation Scholars to spend a period of time outside the UK under-taking a study visit in connection with their chosen programme.

Chelmsford Rotary Club Academic Year Ambassadorial Scholarship
This is available to students on the Chelmsford Campus whose family home is in the UK. It is intended to fund a year of study abroad and in addition the Rotary Foundation will provide a round-trip airfare.

Sports Scholarships
A number of selective Sports Scholarships and Bursaries are offered to students of high potential. Awards are available in the core sports of cricket, rowing, athletics and swimming (other sports are considered on a case-to-case basis). Awards are made each year, subject to availability. The schol-arships, which are available to students who are competing at national level in their sport, equate to £500–1,000 per year to a maximum of three years' full-time study. Students are expected to use the money for training, equipment and travel expenses for their sport. Bursaries are available to students who have previously achieved national ranking and/or who have the potential to do so. Bursaries are valued at £500 per year to a maximum of three years' full-time study; all awards are reviewed annually. Applicants for awards must possess the appropriate admissions requirements.

POSTGRADUATE AWARDS
Anglia Trust Foundation Scholarships (see above). Funding is also available for students following courses in English, Communication Studies, Film and Media, and Radiography.

INFORMATION AND APPROXIMATE FEES FOR NON-EU STUDENTS
International students make up 21% of the student body. **English language entry requirement:** IELTS 5.5 (or equivalent). A one-year international foundation course is available. **Fees:** Classroom-based £9,500; Laboratory-based £10,925. **Living costs:** £5,000–£6,000.

Anglia Ruskin University, East Road, Cambridge CB1 1PT; tel: 08542 713333; www.anglia.ac.uk.

ARCHITECTURAL ASSOCIATION SCHOOL OF ARCHITECTURE

The Architectural Association School (AA) is an independent School of Architecture with an interna-tional character – its 570 students are drawn from over 60 countries. The AA's independence allows it to devise open and constantly evolving architectural programmes, and to explore new ways of thinking about architecture. Throughout the 150 years since the founding of the Architectural Association its principal aim has remained the same: to open up architectural education and practice to critical debate at all levels. Summer School Programmes are held in July/August each year.

See Chapters 2, 4 and 6 for additional awards, applicable to all universities

DEGREE SUBJECT OFFERED

Courses are divided into two main areas: the five-year ARB/RIBA-recognised undergraduate programme leading to AA Intermediate (ARB/RIBA Part 1), AA Finals (ARB/RIBA Part 2) and the AA Diploma; and the graduate programmes, which grant MA (validated by the Open University), MArch and PhD degrees. These programmes are supplemented by the one-year foundation course, one-year and 15-week visiting students' programmes, and part-time postgraduate courses in Building Conservation (AA Graduate Diploma) and Professional Practice (ARB/RIBA Part 3). Launching in January 2009, the AA Inter-professional Studio (AAIS) is a new course for those who wish to step outside of their existing working life or studies and develop their abilities and experience in an innovative, multidisciplinary academic setting.

TUITION FEES (2009/10)

Private fees. Check with the school.

BURSARIES AND OTHER AWARDS

AA Scholarships and Bursaries

More than 13% of all students studying at the AA, and who demonstrate academic excellence and financial need, receive financial assistance from the school's scholarship and bursary programme.

Scholarships are offered to new first-, second- and fourth-year undergraduate applicants, for two or three years, subject to continuing progress. Bursaries are offered to existing AA students and new Graduate School students, and must be applied for on a yearly basis. There is also an AA Eden Scholarship which is awarded to one British (home) MA student on the AA master's course in Environment and Energy – for further details contact the AA.

Most scholarships are equivalent to one-third or two-thirds of the fees, although there are also some full-fee scholarships available to British Diploma students. Bursary assistance covers a student's fees for a period ranging from half a term to one-and-a-half terms per year.

Undergraduate applicants wishing to apply for a scholarship must be recommended in the first instance by the interview panel upon application to the AA, and will be asked to submit a portfolio and financial information to a scholarship committee in June. New graduate applicants wishing to apply for a bursary must first have been offered a place on an AA graduate course. The bursary committee meets in July.

INFORMATION AND APPROXIMATE FEES FOR NON-EU STUDENTS

Fees: Foundation course £12,200; undergraduate course £13,700; 12-month MA/MSc £15,900; 16-month MArch £21,000. **Living costs:** £10,000.

Architectural Association, 34–36 Bedford Square, London WC1B 3ES; tel: 020 7887 4051; www.aaschool.ac.uk.

ASTON UNIVERSITY

Aston University was founded over 100 years ago and became a university in 1966. The campus is in Birmingham city centre. Modern buildings comprise the academic departments, library, sports centres, Students' Guild and student accommodation in high- and low-rise residence blocks. Aston is able to guarantee all its overseas fee-paying students campus accommodation for the duration of their programme, subject to certain deadlines and conditions. UK students are guaranteed accommodation for the first year with many places available for final year students. There are around 9,000 students in total at Aston, 7,500 of whom are undergraduates.

DEGREE SUBJECTS OFFERED

Accounting; Audiology; Automotive Design; Biochemistry; Biology; Business; Business and Engineering foundation programmes; Cell and Molecular Biology; Combined Honours and Interdisciplinary Programmes; Computing Science; Construction Management; Engineering (Chemical/Communications/Electrical/Electromechanical/Electronic/Mechanical); Engineering Product Design; English Language; French; German; Human Resource Management; Industrial Product Design; Infection and Immunity; International Business; International Relations; Internet Systems; Law; Logistics; Marketing; Mathematics; Medical Product Design; Optometry; Pharmacy; Politics; Psychology; Public Policy; Sociology; Spanish; Translation Studies; Transport Management; Technology and Enterprise Management.

TUITION FEES (2009/10)

£3,225.

BURSARIES AND OTHER AWARDS

The university will offer means-tested bursaries of up to £800 to students with family incomes of less that £18,000, then on a sliding scale for students with family incomes of between £18,000–£39,000. Students on placement year will receive an Aston Placement Allowance of £1,000.

Aston Placement Allowances and Placement Bursaries

Aston University is committed to the concept of integrated sandwich placement years and year abroad programmes. In recognition of this, the university will offer a Placement Allowance of £1,000 to every home/EU student who undertakes a sandwich placement year. Home/EU students who undertake an unpaid sandwich work/study placement or a placement outside of the United Kingdom for a whole academic year will receive an additional Placement Bursary of £500. This includes language students on their year abroad. The Tuition Fee for the placement year is £1,610. Placement bursaries and awards are only available to students who are required to pay this fee.

The Placement Allowance and the Placement Bursaries can be used to pay tuition fees or to help support students on their placement year/year abroad. Many Aston students are also paid a salary on their placement year.

BSc Audiology

This programme is NHS-funded and fees are normally paid by the NHS for home/EU students who do not qualify for Aston or Placement Bursaries.

AWARDS FOR NON-EU STUDENTS
School of Engineering and Applied Science International Scholarship Scheme

The School of Engineering and Applied Science (SEAS) offers an automatic entrance scholarship of £1,500 to all international students who undertake a SEAS undergraduate bachelor's degree programme.

Note that the scholarship does not apply to the foundation or placement year.

An additional award may be available (dependent on subject), based on academic merit, which will enhance the basic scholarship from £1,500 up to a maximum of £3,000 in the year of enrolment. For subsequent years, a scholarship of between £1,500 and £3,000 may be available based on academic merit. When a student is successfully awarded one of these scholarships, the amount awarded will be deducted from his or her tuition fees.

See Chapters 2, 4 and 6 for additional awards, applicable to all universities

School of Engineering and Applied Science International Scholarship Scheme for Combined Honours

The SEAS offers an automatic entrance scholarship of £750 to all international students who undertake a combined honours undergraduate degree programme involving any of the following subjects: Biochemistry, Chemical Process Design, Chemistry, Computer Science, Environmental Science and Technology, Geographical Information Systems, or Mathematics.

Note that the scholarship does not apply to the foundation or placement year. For subsequent years, the scholarship may be renewed depending on satisfactory academic performance.

POSTGRADUATE AWARDS
MBA Scholarships

In order to help facilitate this mix of nationalities on the programme, Aston University is offering several scholarship programmes for the MBA course starting in the autumn term 2009.

Scholarships may be available to students from EU countries, EU candidate countries, Latin American countries, African countries, Russia, Japan and South Korea.

A scholarship of £5,000 is available for qualifying applicants to help with the cost of tuition fees. Scholarships of the value of 50% of the tuition fees are available to students exclusively from African countries to help with the cost of study.

Up to six scholarships are available to students exclusively from African countries through the Ferguson Trust Scholarship. The university offers a scholarship of £5,000 for qualifying applicants to help with the cost of tuition fees.

Students wishing to be considered for a scholarship have to submit an application form and an essay of 2–3,000 words on one of the topics below.

* What do you consider to be your major strengths and weaknesses? How might the Aston MBA help you to address them?
* A significant proportion of the MBA involves working in syndicate groups. What would you be able to contribute to other students in your group?
* Describe a significant success or failure from your professional experience and explain what you discovered as a result.

Contact mba@aston.ac.uk for further information.

INFORMATION AND APPROXIMATE FEES FOR NON-EU STUDENTS

Students from over 80 countries (15% of the total student population) are taking degree courses at Aston. **English language entry requirement:** IELTS 6.0 (or equivalent) as a minimum for most courses. An international foundation course is offered as a bridge to degree courses. **Fees:** non-science courses £10,500; semi-laboratory-based courses (Computer Science, Psychology etc) £11,200; Engineering and science courses £12,300. **Living costs:** £7,000.

Aston University, Aston Triangle, Birmingham B4 7ET; tel: 0121 204 3000; www.aston.ac.uk.

BANGOR (University of Wales)

The University of Wales, Bangor is situated between Snowdon and the sea and throughout its 114-year history has always placed great emphasis on maintaining high-quality teaching. With a population of 9,000 students, it is large enough to offer a wide range of academic courses, and social and sporting activities. The main university campus is situated in Bangor with other teaching locations in Wrexham.

DEGREE SUBJECTS OFFERED

Accounting and Finance; Administration and Management; Agriculture; Applied Marine Biology; Applied Physics; Banking and Finance; Biblical Studies; Biology; Biomedical Science; Business and Social Administration; Business Economics; Business Studies; Chemistry; Childhood Studies; Communications; Community Development; Computer Science; Computer Systems Engineering; Conservation and Forest Ecosystems; Criminology; Design and Technology; Diagnostic Radiography and Imaging; Ecology; Economics; Education (Primary/Secondary); Electronic Engineering; English; Environmental Chemistry; Environmental Conservation; Environmental Science; Forestry; French; Geography; Geological Oceanography; German; Health Studies; Heritage Management; History; Italian; Journalism and Media Studies; Law: Leisure and Tourism; Linguistics; Management; Marine Environmental Studies; Marketing; Medieval History; Midwifery; Modern History; Molecular Biology; Music; Nursing; Ocean Sciences; Physical Education; Plant Biology and Conservation; Political and Social Sciences; Psychology; Radiography; Religious Studies; Social Work; Sociology; Spanish; Sport, Health and Physical Education; Sports Science; Sustainable Development; Theatre and Media Studies; Theology; Tourism; Welsh; Welsh History; Zoology.

TUITION FEES (2009/10)

See www.studentfinancewales.co.uk and **Chapter 1 'Financing your course'.**

BURSARIES AND OTHER AWARDS

Bangor Bursaries

Bursaries between £500 and £1,000 are offered to those students with a household income below £39,300.

Parry Williams Scholarships

These awards are worth £1,000 each and are given to the three students with the best entry qualifications.

Drapers Scholarships

Ten scholarships are offered worth £1,000 per year each, and are open to Electronic Engineering and Computer Science candidates studying a four-year course. The primary considerations for the awards are financial need and semester one examination results in Year 1. Continuation of the bursary in successive years depends on satisfactory academic performance and attendance.

David Crystal Scholarship

The scholarship is worth £600 (£200 per year) for three years and is open to all those candidates who apply for a place on a single honours degree course in Linguistics, English Language or Linguistics with English Language and who put Bangor as their first choice for any unconditional or conditional offer made by the university.

Organ Scholarships

Two scholarships are offered, one at £300 per year and one at £200 per year. Candidates are usually applicants for a Music degree. Accompanying cathedral services is one of the conditions of these awards.

Choral Scholarships

There is at least one Choral Scholarship offered at Bangor Cathedral each year. The choral scholar is required to attend rehearsals and sing in the regular services held at the cathedral. Each scholarship is worth £70 per year. Assistance will also be granted to those who are required to remain in Bangor for part of the vacation. Further information and application forms may be obtained from the School of Music.

See Chapters 2, 4 and 6 for additional awards, applicable to all universities

Excellence Scholarships
These awards are valued at £5,000 and may be available in some subject areas, based on students achieving the highest academic attainment in the relevant subject areas. Contact the Head of Department.

Entrance and Merit Scholarships
Approximately 40 Merit Scholarships of up to £3,000 are available to those who excel in the University's annual Entrance Scholarship examinations (Closing date November).

TOP Scholarships
Bangor's Talent Opportunities Programme is a widening access programme which operates across North Wales. The schools involved are located in areas which have been identified as having socially-disadvantaged or deprived communities under the Welsh Assembly Government's Communities First programme. Details of the TOP Scholarships are sent directly to the schools and pupils involved in Year 12 and 13.

Dr William Jones Williams Scholarships
Two scholarships of £500 each. One is open to all candidates and the other is restricted to natives of Wales who have been educated at secondary schools in Wales.

Dr ET Davies Scholarship
Value: £1,500. Open to candidates who are natives of Wales, educated at secondary schools in Wales.

John Hughes Scholarship
Value: £1,500. Open to candidates born in or resident in the counties of Anglesey, Conwy and Gwynedd.

Richard Hughes Scholarship
Value: £1,500. Open to candidates born in or resident in the counties of Anglesey, Conwy and Gwynedd.

Thomas Hughes Scholarship
Value: £1,500. Open to candidates born in or resident in the counties of Anglesey, Conwy and Gwynedd.

William Pritchard Scholarship
Value: £1,500. Open to candidates born in or resident in the counties of Anglesey, Conwy and Gwynedd.

Lady Gladstone Scholarship
Value: £1,500. Open to candidates born in or resident in the counties of Conwy, Denbighshire, Flintshire and Wrexham Maelor.

Piercy Scholarship
Value: £1,500. Open to candidates born in or resident in Conwy, Denbighshire, Flintshire and Wrexham Maelor.

Anna Boyd Scholarship
Value: £300. Preference is given to those from Criccieth.

Bay of Colwyn Scholarship
Value: £500. Open to candidates resident in the area represented by the Town Council (Colwyn Bay, Rhos-on-Sea and Old Colwyn).

Denbighshire Scholarship
Value: £500. Open to candidates resident within the County of Denbighshire.

Gwynedd Scholarships
Two scholarships of £1,500. Open to candidates resident within the County of Gwynedd.

Isle of Anglesey Scholarship
Value: £1,500. Open to candidates resident and attending a secondary school in Anglesey.

Welsh Medium Studies Scholarship
Value: £1,500. Offered to candidates who provide proof of their ability to follow a university course through the medium of Welsh.

Rosa Hovey Memorial Scholarships
Value: approximately £1,500 per year. May be awarded on the recommendation of the college as a result of the College Entrance Scholarship Examination, to female pupils at a secondary school in the former counties of Caernarvonshire and Denbighshire, with preference given to those who received their secondary education in whole or in part in the present Borough of Colwyn or adjacent parishes. It is a condition that the holders of these scholarships reside in a hall of residence.

Schools of Computer Science and Electronic Engineering Scholarships
Three scholarships of £1,500 each, open to all candidates.

Gold Scholarship
Value £1,000. Based on academic excellence. Subjects: computing, mathematics and IT.

School of Theology and Religious Studies Scholarships
Value: £600 over three years. The Hywel D Lewis Memorial Scholarship and three other scholarships all of £600 over three years to those who wish to study Religious Studies.

Sports Scholarships
The university is now offering Sports Scholarships for new undergraduate students. Worth a minimum of £500 a year for three years, they will be offered this year in a scheme designed to recognise sporting potential and develop sporting excellence. Maesglas Bursaries allow free access to the training rooms in the Maesglas Sports Centre, and a new major university award, the Llew Rees Memorial Prize (£750), is awarded annually to the most successful sportsperson in the university.

The scholarships are not restricted to any particular sport and will be awarded to those who, in the judgement of the university, have already displayed excellence in their chosen sport or show promise of excellence in the future.

Normal Fund Scholarship
The Normal Fund Scholarship is open to applicants wishing to study any undergraduate degree course within the School of Education. The prize of £500 will be paid after registration in the first year of the course.

Start-up Bursaries
Bursaries of £300 are available to those entering university from care homes or mature students.

AWARDS FOR NON-EU STUDENTS
The International Office is offering applicants scholarships of up to £1,000 per year. Some individual academic schools offer further bursaries on a competitive basis. For further details on available funding and eligibility, contact the International Office.

See Chapters 2, 4 and 6 for additional awards, applicable to all universities

POSTGRADUATE AWARDS

A number of funded master's opportunities are currently available from individual academic schools, from partial bursaries to full scholarships. The university also offers a number of doctoral research studentships, which are advertised at points throughout the year on the university website and at www.jobs.ac.uk. Further information is available at postgraduate.bangor.ac.uk or www.scholarship-search.org.uk.

Price Davies Postgraduate Scholarships

Scholarships are awarded from time to time of the same value as a University Postgraduate Studentship. They are tenable for one academic year from the date of the award but may be renewed for a second and third academic year. Applications should be submitted to the Registrar of the University of Wales, Bangor, not later than 22 June.

INFORMATION AND APPROXIMATE FEES FOR NON-EU STUDENTS

International students make up 10% of the student body and come from 70 different countries. **English language entry requirement:** IELTS 6.0 (or equivalent). The university offers a pre-study English language course, starting in September, January or April (depending on your level of English proficiency), leading to an international foundation course. One-, two- or three-month pre-sessional courses are also available immediately prior to starting your degree course. **Fees:** undergraduate courses: £8,500–9,500; postgraduate courses: £9,000–11,000. **Living costs:** £5,700.

University of Wales, Bangor, Gwynedd LL57 2DG; tel: 01248 382017; www.bangor.ac.uk.

BATH UNIVERSITY

The University of Bath was founded in 1966 and is located on a spacious purpose-built campus site south of Bath. It is one of the 'technological' universities with many courses containing a practical element and sandwich course options in which students spend time in employment in industry and commerce. Some Higher National Diploma courses are offered. There is a student population of over 9,000.

DEGREE SUBJECTS OFFERED

Applied Biology; Architectural Studies; Biochemistry; Biology; Business Administration; Chemistry; Computer Science; Economics; Education; Engineering (Aerospace; Automotive; Biochemical; Chemical; Civil; Civil and Architectural; Communications; Electrical/Electronic; Environmental Chemical; Information; Innovation and Engineering Design; Manufacturing; Mechanical; Sports); French; German; International Management; Italian; Materials Science; Mathematics; Natural Sciences; Pharmacology; Pharmacy; Physics; Politics; Psychology; Russian; Social Policy and Administration; Social Sciences; Social Work; Sociology; Sport and Exercise Science; Statistics.

TUITION FEES (2009/10)

£3,225.

BURSARIES AND OTHER AWARDS

University of Bath Bursaries will be paid to all those receiving a government maintenance grant. The level of award according to family household income (level of family income will be taken from the local authority assessment for government support) will be as follows:

Up to £25,000: £1,200 bursary; £25,001–£30,000: £900 bursary; £30,001–£35,000: £600 bursary; £35,001–£50,000: £300 bursary. The rate is reduced during placement years.

These bursaries are unlimited and will be provided to every student assessed as eligible for government support within the above income bands. Bursaries will be paid directly into your bank account in instalments and will normally be available for each year of full-time study.

PGCE students are also eligible for Bath Bursaries according to income.

Alumni Merit Scholarships
£1,000 is awarded to selected high-achieving undergraduate entrants studying Chemistry, Chemical Engineering or Modern Languages and European Studies.

RB and SE Whorrod Bursary
Up to £6,000 (£1,500 per year) is on offer for exceptional Mechanical Engineering or Electronic and Electrical Engineering students with limited financial resources. For further information see the Faculty of Engineering and Design area of the university website.

Sports Scholarships
Support costs worth up to £3,000 are available under the Talented Athlete Scholarship Scheme (see www.tass.gov.uk).

Free coaching and support facilities worth up to £2,000 are available to selected students through TeamBath Performance Membership. For further information see www.teambath.com.

Choral Scholarships
Up to £1,800 per year is on offer for students who sing in Bath Abbey Choir. Contact music@bathabbey.org for more information.

Jeremy Fry Memorial Scholarship
Donated by the James Dyson Foundation, the scholarship is worth £5,000 over four years to support a talented South-West region undergraduate engineering faculty student.

Mechanical Engineering
See under **Whorrod Bursary** and **Jeremy Fry Memorial Scholarship** above.

Institute of Physics Undergraduate Bursary
£1,000 is available to undergraduates recommended by the department to The Institute of Physics (merit and needs assessed). Apply to ugphys.admissions@bath.ac.uk.

AWARDS FOR NON-EU STUDENTS
International Student Scholarships
The International Office is offering 75 undergraduate scholarships each year to new international students. The scholarships are worth £3,000 each and are awarded purely on the basis of academic merit. They are open to applicants who are paying 'overseas' tuition fees and all eligible applicants are automatically considered for the scholarship.

Chemical Engineering
Overseas fee-paying undergraduates who are self-financing are offered scholarships of between £500 and £3,000 during their first year of study, according to academic merit.

POSTGRADUATE AWARDS
Alumni discount
There is a 10% fee reduction for all Bath alumni returning to the University of Bath for a postgraduate degree. This applies to all alumni (including UK/EU students and those on part-time and distance learning programmes), provided that they are privately funded, ie not already in receipt of a full scholarship.

University and Departmental Scholarships
These cover home tuition fees, training support fees where applicable and, normally, maintenance for up to three years for students registered for research degrees.

Santander-Abbey Masters Scholarships
Open to students from Latin America, Spain and Portugal.

Alumni Fund Scholarships
These are offered to American students and are worth £3,000.

Steve Huckvale Scholarships
These are open to African students studying Engineering.

Commonwealth Scholarships
These cover tuition fees and living expenses for full-time taught and research courses. See www.acu.ac.uk.

PGCEs
PGCE students liable for variable fees will be eligible for Bath Bursaries ranging from £300 to £1,500 per year according to family income.

For more information on all postgraduate funding opportunities at the university, visit www.bath.ac.uk/grad-office.

INFORMATION AND APPROXIMATE FEES FOR NON-EU STUDENTS
There are 1,500 international students from around 100 countries. **English language entry requirement:** IELTS 6.0 (or equivalent). Pre-degree language courses are offered, ranging from one month to one year. **Fees:** arts and social science courses £10,000; Engineering and science courses £12,700. **Living costs:** £7,000–£8,000.

University of Bath, Claverton Down, Bath BA2 7AY; tel: 01225 383019; www.bath.ac.uk.

BATH SPA UNIVERSITY

Bath Spa University gained its university title in 2005, having been a university college since 1997. BA and BSc single honours and combined honours courses are offered as well as foundation degrees and Diploma of Higher Education (DipHE) courses. There are around 5,000 students in total, following a wide range of courses. The university is based on two sites: the main Newton Park campus, and the Sion Hill campus housing the School of Art and Design.

DEGREE SUBJECTS OFFERED
Art; Biology; Business and Management; Ceramics; Commercial Music; Creative Arts; Creative Music Technology; Creative Studies in English; Cultural Studies; Dance; Diet and Health; Education: Early Years; Education Studies; English Literature; Environmental Science; Fashion and Textile Design; Fine Art; Food, Nutrition and Consumer Protection; Food Studies; Geographic Information Systems; Geography; Graphic Design; Health Studies; History; Media Communications; Music; Performing Arts; Psychology; Sociology; Study of Religions; Textile Design Studies; Tourism Management.

TUITION FEES (2009/10)
£3,225.

BURSARIES AND OTHER AWARDS

Bursaries of up to £1,200 are available for all eligble full-time students on undergraduate courses. Payments are dependent on family income. Students with family income below £16,999 will receive the full amount of £1,200; those with a family income over £38,330 will receive no bursary; those with family incomes between £17,910 and £38,330 will receive a bursary on a sliding scale.

Scholarships (not means-tested) worth £1,000 per year are open to students on the following courses:

* BSc (Hons) Biology
* BSc (Hons) Diet and Health
* BSc (Hons) Environmental Science
* BSc (Hons) Food, Nutrition and Consumer Protection
* BSc (Hons) Geographic Information Systems
* BSc Human Nutrition
* FDSc Development Geography.

POSTGRADUATE AWARDS
PGCEs
The tuition fee of £3,145 will be reimbursed for all students. For further details call 01225 875548.

INFORMATION AND APPROXIMATE FEES FOR NON-EU STUDENTS

Students come from 40 countries. **English language entry requirement:** IELTS 5.5–6.0 (or equivalent). Foundation courses are available for applicants with lower scores. **Fees:** £9,000–£9,580. **Living costs:** £7,000–£8,000.

Bath Spa University, Newton St Loe, Bath BA2 9BN; tel: 01225 875875; www.bathspa.ac.uk.

BEDFORDSHIRE UNIVERSITY

The University of Bedfordshire was established in August 2006 from the merger of the University of Luton and De Montfort University's Bedford campus. Full-time and sandwich courses are offered for over 8,000 students, of whom over 500 are from overseas.

DEGREE SUBJECTS OFFERED

Accounting; Animation; Architecture; Artificial Intelligence; Biochemistry; Biology; Biomedical Science; Biotechnology; Business Studies; Computer Science; Creative Writing; Criminology; Film Studies; Health Studies; Law; Leisure Management; Marketing; Media Studies; Microbiology; Midwifery; Nursing; Nutrition; Pharmacology; Photography; Psychology; Social Policy; Social Science; Software Engineering; Sport; Television Studies; Travel and Tourism.

TUITION FEES (2009/10)
£3,225.

BURSARIES AND OTHER AWARDS

Bedfordshire bursaries are awarded to students on a sliding scale dependent on residual income. Below £18,360 the means-tested bursary is £820; up to £27,800, the award is £615 and to £39,290, students will receive £460. From £39,290 and above the mandatory bursary is £319.

Development Fund Bursaries

These awards are based on financial need.

* **The Steel Charitable Trust Final Year Bursary** – 25 bursaries at £1,000 each.
* **The Neville Group Bursary** – One award of £1,000 per year for three years.
* **The Ludlow Group Bursaries** – Five awards of £1,000 for Business School students.

Partnership Scholarships

£300 is given on entry to students from partner colleges who register at the university on an honours degree.

Dallow Ward Bursary

This bursary is open to students who are resident in Dallow Ward, Luton.

University of Bedfordshire Scholarship

Academic Scholarship
£1,025 is awarded to students who enter with a score greater than 280 UCAS points of which 200 points must be at A2 level.

EU Scholarships
Scholarships valued at £1,000 are open to EU students and based on academic excellence.

Sporting Scholarships
£1,025 per year is awarded to students who have reached international standard in their chosen sport. £310 is awarded to students who have reached county level.

POSTGRADUATE AWARDS
The Alumni Discount Bursary

This is open to Bedfordshire University graduates who progress to a full-time postgraduate course at the university.

INFORMATION AND APPROXIMATE FEES FOR NON-EU STUDENTS

There are approximately 500 international students who are at present enrolled on courses at the university. **English Language entry requirement:** IELTS 6.0 (or equivalent). English programmes are offered including a summer school. **Fees:** £8,000–£8,200. **Living costs:** £5,000–£6,000.

University of Bedfordshire, Park Square, Luton, Bedfordshire, LU1 3JU; tel 01582 48286; www.beds.ac.uk

BIRKBECK (University of London)

Birkbeck is a teaching and research institution offering part-time degrees, certificates and short courses. Most of the 19,000 students fall into the 25–45 age range and above and those who lack conventional educational qualifications are welcomed. There are a number of study centres in the Gower Street area and also in Stratford.

DEGREE COURSES OFFERED

Accounting, Archaeology, Art and Architecture, Biology, Botany, Business Studies, Chemistry, Classical Studies, Community Studies, Computer Science, Conservation Studies, Counselling, Creative Writing, Cultural Studies, Development Studies, Distance Learning, Drama and Theatre

Studies, Earth Science, Ecology, Economics, English, Environmental Studies, European Studies, Film and Media, Finance, Forensic Science, French Studies, Geography, Geology, German, Greek, Health Studies, History and Archaeology, Humanities, Human Rights, Information Systems, Information Technology, International Studies, Japanese, Journalism, Latin, Latin American Studies, Law and Legal Studies, Linguistics, London Studies, Management, Mathematics, Media Studies, Molecular Biology, Philosophy, Planetary Science, Politics, Portuguese Studies, Psychology, Public Sector Studies, Science, Social Policy, Social Science, Sociology, South American Studies, Spanish, Statistics, Theatre Studies.

TUITION FEES (2009/10)
Vary between subjects. Contact the College.

BURSARIES AND OTHER AWARDS
Eligibility for financial support for home and EU students varies depending on single, married or partnered status including the numbers of dependent children and the incomes (single or joint) of the applicants. There is also a Birkbeck Student Opportunity Fund, Stratford Opportunity Bursaries (for those living in East London) and Disability Allowances available.

INFORMATION AND APPROXIMATE FEES FOR INTERNATIONAL STUDENTS
English Language entry requirements: IELTS 6.5 (or equivalent); **Fees:** See above. **Living costs:** £9,000–£10,000.

Birkbeck, University of London, Malet Street, London WC1E 7HX; tel 020 7631 6000; www.bbk.ac.uk

BIRMINGHAM UNIVERSITY

The University of Birmingham is one of the 'red-brick' universities, founded in 1900 and located on a spacious campus two-and-a-half miles from the centre of Birmingham, with a student population of over 26,000. Research intensive and a member of the Russell Group, the university consists of five colleges with a range of state-of-the-art facilities, research centres and institutes and welcoming over 9,000 new students every year.

DEGREE SUBJECTS OFFERED
Accounting and Finance; African Studies; American and Canadian Studies; Ancient History; Anthropology; Archaeology; Artificial Intelligence; Astrophysics; Biochemistry; Biological Sciences; Biomedical Materials Science; Biotechnology; Business Management; Business Studies; Chemistry; Childhood, Culture and Education; Classical Literature; Computer Science; Culture, Society and Communication; Dentistry; Drama and Theatre Arts; East Mediterranean History; Economics; Engineering (Biomedical; Chemical; Civil; Communications; Computer; Electronic; Energy; Mathematical; Mechanical; Metallurgy/Materials; Software; Systems); English; Environmental Science; European Studies; Events Management; Film Studies; French; Genetics; Geography; Geology; German; Hispanic Studies; History; History of Art; International Business/Relations/ Studies; Italian; Law; Materials Science; Mathematics; Media, Culture and Society; Medical Science; Medicine; Modern Languages; Money, Banking and Finance; Music; Natural Sciences; Nursing; Philosophy; Physics; Physiotherapy; Planning; Political Science; Portuguese; Psychology; Public Policy; Resource and Applied Geology; Russian; Social Policy; Social Science; Social Work; Sociology; Spanish; Sport and Exercise Science; Sport, Physical Education and Community; Sports Management; Statistics; Technology; Theatre Studies; Theology; War Studies; Zoology.

TUITION FEES (2009/10)
£3,225.

BURSARIES AND OTHER AWARDS
The Birmingham Grant offers £860 in additional support to all students whose household income is less than £35,460 and who are in receipt of a maintenance grant. The Birmingham Scholarship, worth £1,290 each year, is available to students who are awarded the Birmingham Grant and who get at least AAB in their highest three A-levels, 34 IB points or DDD BTEC. Other examinations may be considered but award of a scholarship is not based on UCAS tariff points.

Excellence Scholarships
The College of Engineering and Physical Sciences will be offering 10 Excellence Scholarships for new undergraduate students joining the University in September 2009. The Scholarships will be for £5,000 per annum and are available in the following subject areas:

* Chemistry
* Chemical Engineering
* Civil Engineering
* Computer Science
* Electrical, Electronic and Computer Engineering
* Mathematics
* Metallurgy and Materials
* Mechanical Engineering
* Physics and Astronomy

Scholarships will be renewed for each year of undergraduate study, provided that the recipient is performing to first class degree level.

Subject-based scholarships
Subject-based scholarships are also available and can be awarded in addition to a Birmingham Scholarship.

Abbeydale and Haworth Scholarships
Awards of £1,000 are available to entrants to the School of Chemistry with a further £1,000 per year for continuing academic excellence.

School of Physics and Astronomy
The school offers financial scholarships to students receiving excellent results at A-level, who make Birmingham their firm-choice by the end of April in the year of entry. Scholarships and prizes are also awarded throughout the degree programme. In addition, in collaboration with the Birmingham Conservatoire, the school offers Physics students Music Scholarships each year in instrument, dance or voice. Students must have received either Grade 7 with merit or Grade 8, and intend to continue their music tuition. They must also meet the usual entry requirements for Physics.

School of Computer Science
The Paul and Yuanbi Ramsay Undergraduate Bursary is offered to encourage excellent students to study Computer Science. It provides £1,000 per year over a three-year undergraduate programme. The bursary is tenable for three years and eligibility is based on financial need. The school also offers a number of scholarships of £1,000 each, tenable for one year. These are awarded according to criteria based on academic performance. Additionally, a number of scholarships are available for international students.

School of Law
The Benussi Law Bursary was established from a donation made by a Law School alumna, Diane Benussi. The £1,000 bursary is offered to a student starting an LLB Law (single honours) programme, on the basis of financial need.

Music Scholarships

In recognition of the role that music plays within the university, five Music Scholarships a year are offered. These are for applicants to disciplines other than Music, and provide access to specialist facilities and musical tuition of 20 hours per year. The scholarships are open to candidates who have already achieved Grade 8 in instrumental or vocal studies.

Sports Scholarships

Sport is an important part of life at Birmingham, in terms of both its world-leading School of Sport and Exercise Sciences and its successful university sports teams. In recognition of this, University Sport Birmingham offers around 30 scholarships each year to international-level performers from any academic department and of any nationality. Scholarship support consists of facility membership (gym and swimming pool), strength and conditioning work, sport science and medicine services (including physiotherapy), lifestyle workshops and help with sports-specific expenditure.

For more details of Sports Scholarships contact 0121 414 4519 or see www.sport.bham.ac.uk/scholarships.

Whittaker Ellis Bullock Bursaries Fund

Grants from the fund may be made to undergraduate and postgraduate students in the School of Civil Engineering for the purpose of either providing assistance in the case of severe financial hardship, or helping them to undertake some specific educational but extracurricular activity. Grants from the fund are awarded by the academic board on the recommendation of the head of the School of Civil Engineering, to whom applications should be made.

Brockhouse Scholarships

A number of scholarships are offered to first-year undergraduates up to the limit of available funds. Children or grandchildren of Brockhouse Forgings Ltd employees take priority in the award of these scholarships. Awards may be renewed for subsequent years subject to continued satisfactory performance. Scholarships are awarded on the basis of A-level results and candidates will also be interviewed.

Engineering Awards

A number of scholarships may be offered, subject to the availability of funds, to undergraduate students in the School of Engineering on the basis of their performance in their programmes. Each award is tenable for one year only, but the holder of an award in his or her second year will be eligible for a further award tenable in the third year. Students registered in the first or second year of a scheme of study leading to the degree of BEng/MEng will be eligible for these awards.

John Avins Scholarships

Up to four John Avins Scholarships may be awarded in any science year and they will be open to undergraduates in the College of Engineering and Physical Sciences who have attended any secondary school in Birmingham. Such undergraduates who are registered in the first or second year of a scheme of study leading to the degree of BSc or BEng/MEng will be eligible to be considered for the award. Each scholarship will be tenable for one year and may be renewable for a further year.

Allen and Elizabeth Murray Centenary Scholarships

Established by Professor Sir Kenneth Murray in memory of his mother and father, the Allen and Elizabeth Murray Scholarships scheme provides awards to the value of £2,000 to full-time home undergraduate students entering their second year of study. Candidates must be from a low-income background and be of outstanding academic ability. Each scholar will have their scholarship renewed in their third year provided they maintain a 2:1 standard of progression.

The Allen Murray Centenary Scholarship is available to students in the schools of Biosciences, Chemistry, Computer Science, Mathematics and Physics and Astronomy. The Elizabeth Murray Centenary Scholarship is available to students in the School of Health and Population Sciences and the Institute of Applied Social Sciences.

See Chapters 2, 4 and 6 for additional awards, applicable to all universities

GE Foundation Scholar Leaders Programme

This scholarship is provided by the General Electric Company, a philanthropic organisation who seek to identify and recognise students based on academic merit and financial need. In order to qualify, you must be a first year undergraduate pursuing a degree in the field of engineering, technology, economics or management. Students must have high academic attainment, as demonstrated by their tutor assessment, first term university results, A-level and GSCE results. Applicants must also be receiving a full Maintenance Grant. The scholarship is worth £6,000 split into two instalments of £3,000 spread over your second and third years of bachelors' studies.

The MISYS Award for Information Technology subjects

The MISYS Charitable Foundation was created in 1997 with the goal of furthering education in information and communications technology worldwide. Its work focuses on three key areas: university scholarships, in the UK and overseas; funding for information technology (IT) equipment in UK state schools; and IT-related support for charities working in communities. The Foundation is funded directly through donations from MISYS plc, the global software company.

Scholarships are available to undergraduate home/EU students entering their 2nd year of a programme with a strong computing element (Computer Science, Artificial Intelligence, etc), who are academically strong (averaging 2:1 or above) who are not in receipt of the Maintenance Grant or a Birmingham Grant. On average scholarships are worth £1,000 per year, tenable for 2 years. Application forms are available at the end of January.

The University will short list candidates to be put forward to the Foundation. All applicants will be notified of the outcome of their application by the University.

The Leverhulme Trade Charities Bursary

In order to be eligible for this bursary, you must be an undergraduate student who is the son or daughter, spouse, widow or widower of a commercial traveller, chemist, or grocer, who has been engaged in this occupation in the UK for at least five years in the recent past. A parent or spouse who is unemployed (or deceased) but who fell within one of these three categories when their employment ceased is also included. Funds are intended for those who are experiencing financial hardship. The maximum value of the bursary is £3,000 per annum, however the award will be adjusted according to the circumstances of the candidate, and will be dependent on satisfactory academic performance.

Charles Brotherton Trust

Awards from the Charles Brotherton Trust are non repayable and they typically range between £200 and £1,000. The trust fund was set up in order to assist British undergraduate and postgraduate students experiencing financial hardship and who are studying scientific subjects in particular, with priority going to students studying Chemistry and other related subjects. The committee will also consider applications from students studying other subjects.

Wellcome Trust Vacation Scholarships

The Wellcome Trust provides scholarships to undergraduate students seeking to take up a summer research placement in the field of Biomedicine. The deadline for applications is usually February/March each year – please visit www.wellcome.ac.uk for further details.

BP Summer Internship Scholarships

BP is committed to supporting individuals who will be the future talent in industry throughout their education. The scholarships recognise, reward and support academic excellence and support the potential for future achievement in the workplace. Students who are awarded one of the scholarships will not only receive a financial reward but will also get the opportunity to gain an insight into the exciting careers available in BP and will be able to forge strong relationships with industry experts. Successful applicants will also receive a guaranteed place at a BP assessment centre in their final year. Please visit www.bp.com/sectiongenericarticle.do?categoryId=9025000and contentId=7046591 for details.

Whitworth Scholarship Awards
Whitworth Scholarship Awards are for prospective or current undergraduates or postgraduates of any engineering discipline who have completed a 2 year engineering apprenticeship. The scholarships are valued up to £18,000 (for full time study up to £4,500 pa is available over 4 years, for part time study up to £3,000 pa). The closing date for applications is 30th June each year.

Alderman Frederick Smith Bequest/Holt Education Trust
The Alderman Frederick Smith Bequest provides a small number of scholarships each year for **male** undergraduates whose normal residence is in the City of Liverpool and are currently in receipt of statutory support via Liverpool Education Authority.

The Holt Education Trust provides a small number of scholarships each year for **female** undergraduates whose normal residence is in the City of Liverpool and are currently in receipt of statutory support via Liverpool Education Authority.

The Alderman Frederick Smith Bequest also provides travelling scholarships awarded to male and female undergraduates currently whose normal residence is in the City of Liverpool. The scholarship will be granted towards the cost of travel abroad during vacations, with applicants required to live abroad for more than four weeks and to state in their application the details of the proposed travel. These scholarships are granted only once, and are intended to assist in exceptional circumstances, which are not adequately covered by the present award regulations.

Applicants will be required to state the specific circumstances that they wish the trustees to consider and include details of any extra expenditure in connection to their particular course of study. Application forms are available from Student Support (Trusts), PO Box 2013, Liverpool, L69 2DY or by calling 0151 233 3006.

The Ridgeway Scholarship
The Ridgeway Scholarship provides the opportunity for students who are normally resident in Lincolnshire or Huntingdonshire, who are 1st or 2nd year undergraduates the opportunity to undertake a year's study in the United States of America.

The scholarship is for one academic year at the University of Evansville, Indiana, USA. The Scholarship offers return air fare, tuition fees and room and board in University accommodation.

Applications are to be made to the College Secretary at Harlaxton College, Harlaxton Manor, Grantham, Lincs, NG32 1AG before February each year.

Bowater Trust
The income from the trust is used to provide travel grants to engineers to enable them to broaden their education by, for example, attending programmes, conferences, meetings of learned societies, exhibitions etc. Preference will be given to activities that fall outside the normal requirements of the applicant's degree programme. Grants will not be made to enable students to travel to the USA or to Canada.

Andy Ozimek Travel Bursaries
One bursary will be available annually for award to a first- or second-year full-time registered undergraduate student in one of the Schools of Chemistry, Biochemistry or Chemical Engineering, for travel either abroad or within the UK.

TI Group Scholarships
Scholarships of £1,000 may be awarded, up to the limit of available funds, to undergraduate students who intend to pursue a scientific or technological career in the manufacturing industry. Children of Tube Investment employees take priority, up to a maximum of two new undergraduate awards each session. Awards will not normally be made to students who hold any other scholarships or who are sponsored by industry. Awards may be renewed for subsequent years subject to

continued satisfactory performance. Nominations, based on candidates' qualifications for entry, should be made by the head of the relevant engineering department in the first term of the academic year. Further details can be obtained from Student Funding Office.

Armourers and Brasiers Entry Scholarship
One scholarship each year may be awarded to an outstanding new undergraduate entrant to the School of Metallurgy and Materials, to the value of £1,000. The scholarship may be renewed for the second year depending on the availability of funds and the academic performance of the holder, but not normally for any later years.

Alumni Awards
A number are offered to full-time students of the university to assist undergraduates to undertake worthwhile and original vacation projects in the UK or abroad.

Ede and Ravenscroft Travel Bursary
One bursary is offered to full-time undergraduate students in their second year of study to enable them to undertake travel for academic or cultural purposes, not necessarily connected with their course of study.

Francis Brett Young Scholarships
A number are offered annually to undergraduates, not in their final year, to assist long vacation projects connected with their studies. Awards are also offered by the Birmingham Chamber of Commerce for the purpose of travel abroad, for students following courses in Business, Public Policy and Social Science.

AWARDS FOR NON-EU STUDENTS
Awards are valued at £2,000 for up to three years, for students from China, Hong Kong, India, Kenya, Mauritius, Singapore, Sri Lanka and the Maldives.

A number of awards are made to international students on the basis of outstanding academic achievement. Many of these awards are made by specific schools and departments from which further details may be obtained. These departments include Bioscience, Computer Science, Earth Science, Law, Psychology and Sport Science.

The School of Engineering also offers scholarships to students from a group of colleges in Malaysia (Taylors College, PRIME College and the INTI College). In order to be considered for one of the above awards, applicants need to:

* Have applied for, and been offered, a place at the university through UCAS;
* Have chosen Birmingham as their conditional firm ('CF') or unconditional firm ('UF') choice;
* Be eligible for overseas fees status at the university.

Note: There is no application form for all of the above awards except those applying specifically for Law (see below); the university will consider applicants automatically when they have made their choice of university.

The university will make the decision on who receives the awards on the basis of the applicant's UCAS application, examination results and a recommendation by the applicant's head of school/college. The decisions will be made in August at the latest, when the university has received all examination results. In the case of no candidates being suitable, the university reserves the right not to award the scholarship.

No individual student is able to win more than one award for entry in September and the continuation of each scholarship throughout the duration of a student's studies is dependent upon them at least passing each year of their course.

Applicants for the Law Scholarships will be requested to write a short essay on an issue of legal interest. When they are made an offer of a place they will be given more information about how to apply for these awards.

POSTGRADUATE AWARDS

Region-specific scholarships are offered to students commencing one-year taught master's degrees from Asia and Pacific Region, Middle East, Latin America, Pakistan, Sri Lanka/Maldives, Russia and Turkey.

In addition, other awards are available through the Ford Foundation International Fellowship Programme. There are also Queen Elizabeth Scholarships, Research and Hong Kong Scholarships.

Postgraduate Scholarships are also offered for graduates from Universitas 21 (www.universitas 21.com) member institutions and for graduates of the University of Birmingham.

In addition, scholarships are offered for students entering the School of Education and MSc scholarships in International Business. See also Whittaker Ellis Bullock Bursaries Fund above.

INFORMATION AND APPROXIMATE FEES FOR NON-EU STUDENTS

There are 4,000 international students from 152 countries. **English language entry requirement:** IELTS 6.0 (or equivalent). Six-, 10- and 20-week English language programmes are available, depending on language proficiency, ranging from IELTS 4.5 to 5.5 (or equivalent). **Fees:** non-laboratory-based courses £8,700; laboratory-based courses £10,900; clinical courses £20,200. **Living costs:** £7,500.

University of Birmingham, Edgbaston, Birmingham B15 2TT; tel: 0121 414 3344;www. bham.ac.uk.

BIRMINGHAM CITY UNIVERSITY

Birmingham City University is made up of six faculties, spread across eight locations in and around the city centre, including the main City North Campus at Perry Barr and Edgbaston Campus, home to its Faculty of Health with plans afoot to invest around £150m in a new City Centre Campus. Around 23,000 students attend Birmingham City University on full- and part-time undergraduate and postgraduate courses.

DEGREE SUBJECTS OFFERED

Accountancy; Advertising; Animation; Architectural Technology; Architecture; Acting; Art; Broadcasting; Business; Computer-aided Design; Computing and IT; Construction; Criminology; Design; Diagnostic Radiography; Economics; Education and Teacher Training; Engineering (Automotive; Communications and Networks; Electronic; Mechanical; Software); English and Drama; Fashion; Finance; Fine Art; Gemmology; Graphic Design; Health Studies; Horology; Housing; Human Resources; Interior Design; Landscape Architecture; Law; Management; Marketing; Midwifery; Multimedia; Music; Nursing; Photography; Psychology; Public Relations; Radiography and Radiotherapy; Real Estate; Retail Management; Social Work; Sociology; Software Engineering; Speech and Language Therapy; Surveying; Textiles; Town and Country Planning; Visual Communication.

TUITION FEES (2009/10)
£3,225

BURSARIES AND OTHER AWARDS
A £525 bursary (2008/09) is available for all students in receipt of full and partial state support. Check with the university.

Each year Birmingham City University provides a number of bursaries and scholarships to students to cover a proportion of the tuition fees for the first year of study. In general, each faculty offers five scholarships equivalent to a maximum reduction of 20% in annual tuition fees and a number of bursaries equivalent to a reduction of 10% in annual tuition fees.

Birmingham Conservatoire
A national conservatoire and part of UCE Birmingham, Birmingham Conservatoire offers a variety of scholarships at undergraduate and postgraduate level.

Entrance Scholarships (UK/EU candidates)
A number of Entrance Scholarships of between £400 and £1,000 are awarded each year to UK and European Union candidates on the recommendation of auditions panels. Exceptionally, these scholarships may be renewed in subsequent years of a student's course.

AWARDS FOR NON-EU STUDENTS
Birmingham Conservatoire Bursaries
A number of tuition fee bursaries of up to £2,000 are awarded each year to overseas candidates. These bursaries are normally renewed for each subsequent year of the student's course.

University Scholarships
A number of University Scholarships are awarded to students to cover a proportion of their tuition fees and they may apply for a scholarship if they are offered a place to study at UCE Birmingham. Scholarships are generally awarded on academic excellence, leadership qualities, personal and financial circumstances and contribution to the life of the community.

INFORMATION AND APPROXIMATE FEES FOR NON-EU STUDENTS
There is a large number of international students. **English language entry requirement:** IELTS 6.0 (or equivalent). There are pre-sessional language courses and in-session language support. There is also an orientation programme for all students. **Fees:** £8,400–£12,000. **Living costs:** £7,000.

Birmingham City University, City North Campus, Perry Barr, Birmingham B42 2SU. Tel: 0121 331 5595 or visit www.bcu.ac.uk.

BIRMINGHAM UNIVERSITY COLLEGE

The college was formerly the Birmingham College of Food, Tourism and Creative Studies and is situated in central Birmingham. It offers a range of full-time and sandwich courses to over 3,000 students, some of whom are on paid industrial placements or study periods.

DEGREE SUBJECTS OFFERED
Adventure Tourism Management, Culinary Arts Management, Early Childhood Studies, Education and ICT, Events Management, Food Management, Hospitality Management, Marketing Management, Retail Business Management, Salon Business Management, Ports Management, Tourism Business Management.

TUITION FEES (2009/10)
£3,225

BURSARIES AND OTHER AWARDS
For 2008/09, students from low income households under £25,000 will be eligible for a college bursary of £1,050. Between £32,5001 and £42,500 the award will be £630 and from £42,501 a bursary of £315. Students receiving a disabled living allowance will receive a bursary of £1,575. Check with university for bursaries for 2009/10.

UCB does not charge a tuition fee for students on industrial placement however bursaries are not offered for this period.

AWARDS FOR NON-EU STUDENTS
International Scholarships
The college offers a strictly limited number of scholarships for new international students each year. The scholarships are available for one year of a programme only and are awarded on the basis of an applicant's ability to show sustained effort and/or excellence in study, commitment to an employment sector relevant to the college's programmes, or commitment to a community. Successful applicants are awarded a scholarship in the form of a reduction in their tuition fees for their first year of study only. The scholarships are as follows:

* A limited number of International Scholarships for programmes of one year's duration worth up to £1,500, in the categories of:
  * five James Liu Scholarships (for students from the continent of Asia studying hospitality or tourism)
  * two Midconsort Scholarships (for international students studying at bachelor's degree level).
* A limited number of International Scholarships worth up to £1,500 for students in the first year of their study at the college, undertaking a two-, three- or four-year taught programme, in the categories of:
  * two International Academic Excellence Scholarships (for students whose main residence is in a non-European country)
  * two European Academic Excellence Scholarships (for students whose main residence is in a European country)
  * two Gill Boydol Scholarships (for international students studying hospitality subjects);
  * two Tim Brighouse Scholarships (for international students studying childcare or care subjects).

INFORMATION AND APPROXIMATE FEES FOR NON-EU STUDENTS
There are 650 students from 63 countries following courses at the college. **English language entry requirement:** IELTS 6.0 (or equivalent). For those students with a lower score, summer and intensive language programmes are arranged. **Fees:** £7,100. **Living costs:** £6,000–£7,000.

Birmingham (UC), Summer Row, Birmingham B3 1JB; tel: 0121 604 1040; www.ucb. ac.uk.

BISHOP GROSSETESTE
UNIVERSITY COLLEGE LINCOLN

The College was established in 1862 and enjoys a long-standing reputation as an independent higher education Anglican institution. The campus is situated in historic uphill Lincoln and draws students from Lincoln itself and surrounding areas.

DEGREE SUBJECTS OFFERED

Drama in the Community, Early Childhood Studies, Education Studies, English Literature, Heritage Studies, Primary Education.

TUITION FEES (2009/10)

£3,225.

BURSARIES AND OTHER AWARDS

The BGC Bursary Scheme provides non-repayable bursary support of £1,075 each year to all new undergraduate students eligible to receive a full or partial HE Grant (household income below around £39,333).

You can choose to receive £1,000 as cash (paid directly into your bank account) or use it all or part of it to pay for goods and services, for example college accommodation or a computer.

Prospective students are encouraged to make enquiries direct to the Student Support Team at BGC, or pick up a leaflet at Open Days for more information about the scheme.

Organ and Choral Scholarships

One Organ Scholarship (open to men and women) and three Choral Scholarships (one each for counter-tenor, tenor and bass voices) are offered annually. Scholarships are tenable for the duration of the college course, subject to satisfactory performance of duties at both cathedral and college. Students accepted for any course (not necessarily a Music course) at the college may apply for a scholarship. Scholarship fees are regularly reviewed and are related to payments to regular choir members.

Scholars become full-time members of the cathedral music establishment so far as their other duties allow. They are required to attend the college chapel choir, which rehearses on Tuesdays from 6.10–7.10pm, and sing Evensong on Wednesday afternoons. In view of this, they are allowed to miss one cathedral Evensong per week. Organ/vocal tuition is provided by the college, at no cost to the scholar.

The cathedral choir sings Evensong every day except Wednesday, and two services on Sunday mornings. There is a rehearsal before each service. Extra services, broadcasts, recordings etc arise from time to time and additional payments are sometimes made for these. Scholars are required to sing at the cathedral at Christmas and Easter. Accommodation out of college term is provided.

Scholars who are following a teacher training course may be unable to sing at the cathedral during certain teaching practices.

INFORMATION AND APPROXIMATE FEES FOR NON-EU STUDENTS

English language entry requirement: IELTS 6.0 (or equivalent). **Fees:** £7,725. **Living costs:** £7,500.

Bishop Grosseteste College, Lincoln LN1 3DY; tel: 01522 583658; www.bishopg.ac.uk.

BOLTON UNIVERSITY

University of Bolton, originally Bolton Institute, was founded in 1982 from colleges of education and technology, and became a university in 2005. It offers a full range of degree and diploma courses. The university is located close to Bolton town centre some 15 miles north of Manchester.

DEGREE SUBJECTS OFFERED

Accountancy; Architectural Technology; Art and Design; Automobile Engineering; Automotive Product Design; Biology; Building Surveying; Business Information Systems; Business Studies; Civil Engineering; Community Studies; Computer-Aided Engineering; Computing; Construction; Creative Writing; Education; Electronic Engineering; English; Environmental Studies; Film Studies; Graphic Design; History; Human Resource Management; Human Science; Law joint courses; Marketing; Mathematics; Mechanical Engineering; Philosophy; Photography; Psychology; Quantity Surveying; Sociology; Sport Sciences; Textile Design; Textile Technology; Theatre Studies; Visual Arts.

TUITION FEES (2009/10)

£3,225

BURSARIES AND OTHER AWARDS

Bolton Bursary

The means-tested bursary will provide support for course related costs to Full Time Undergraduate UK students who will be paying £3,225 per annum towards Tuition Fees (whether self funded or through the Tuition Fee Loan).

All students with a household income less than £39,333 will be awarded a bursary of £350. New students with a household income between £39,334 and £60,032 will be awarded a bursary of £129.

Bolton Scholarship

If a student has completed a preparatory course at a partner institution of the university and has progressed onto a full-time degree programme, they will receive a bursary of £750 per year regardless of household income.

Excellence Scholarship

The Excellence Scholarship will be awarded to all full-time U.K. undergraduate students, irrespective of their financial means, who progress to a University undergraduate Higher Education course having successfully accumulated a minimum of 300 UCAS points at A2 level or equivalent. The award is valued at £500 per annum. The Excellence Scholarship will be payable to students in attendance on or after 1 December for September starters and an equivalent date for January starters. Payments will be made in two instalments in January and May.

Care-Leavers Scholarship

The Care-Leavers Scholarship will be awarded to full-time U.K. undergraduate students leaving a Care background, irrespective of their financial means, who progress to a University undergraduate Higher Education course. The award is worth £1,000 per annum. Payments will be made to students in eight monthly instalments from November subject to confirmation of attendance.

Vice-Chancellor's Award

The Vice Chancellor's Award will be awarded to the most outstanding academically-gifted full-time UK undergraduate students, irrespective of their financial means, who progress to a university undergraduate higher education course. There will be a maximum of three awards each year. One-off payments of £15,000 will be paid over the duration of the course, i.e. for a three year degree course a payment of £5,000 per academic year would be made. Payments will be paid in eight monthly instalments from November subject to confirmation of attendance.

Students in receipt of the Vice Chancellor's Award will not be eligible to receive the Bolton, Excellence or Care Leavers Scholarships.

INFORMATION AND APPROXIMATE FEES FOR NON-EU STUDENTS

Sixty-five countries are represented in the student body. **English language entry requirement:** IELTS 6.0 (or equivalent). Pre-sessional and in-session English tuition is available. **Fees:** £7,800 per annum in 2008/9. **Living costs:** Approximately £6,500 per annum.

University of Bolton, Deane Road, Bolton BL3 5AB; tel: 01204 900600; www.bolton.ac.uk.

BOURNEMOUTH UNIVERSITY

The Bournemouth University main campus site is two miles from the town centre. A popular seaside resort, Bournemouth offers good facilities, especially for sailing and water sports. Courses tend to have a vocational emphasis and there is a student population of 7,000.

DEGREE SUBJECTS OFFERED

Accounting; Advertising and Marketing Communications; Applied Computing; Applied Geography; Applied Psychology; Architecture; Art and Design; Business Decision Management; Business Information Systems; Business Law; Business Studies; Communication; Computing; Countryside Management; Creative and Digital Arts; Design Engineering; Electronics; Environment and Coastal Management; Fashion and Textiles; Financial Services; Food Production; Health Science; Heritage Conservation; Hospitality Business Development; International Business; International Culinary Arts; International Hospitality Management; International Marketing, Leisure and Countryside Management; Leisure Marketing; Medical Electronics Design; Midwifery; Multimedia Journalism; New Media; Nursing; Photo Media; Product Design; Public Relations; Retail Management; Scriptwriting; Social Work; Software Engineering Management; Sports Development and Coaching Sciences; Taxation and Law; Tourism.

TUITION FEES (2009/10)

£3,225.

BURSARIES AND OTHER AWARDS

The Bournemouth University Bursary of £319 will be offered to students from households with a family income below £25,000. EU students may also be entitled to the Bournemouth University Bursary and Partner College Bursaries.

Partner College Bursaries

Students enrolling at partner colleges will automatically receive a non-repayable bursary of £500. (This does not apply to Bridgwater College.)

Social Work Bursary

Social Work students will receive a Department of Health bursary of £4,000 per year and will also be entitled to the Bournemouth University Bursary of £305.

Academic Achievement Scholarship

This scholarship worth £1,000 is open to students who can demonstrate an outstanding academic profile eg Grades AAA at A-level or an average of three distinctions at BTEC National Diploma or equivalent.

Citizenship Scholarship

This £1,000 award is offered to students who can demonstrate that they have contributed significantly to community-related projects outside any formal education or work.

Music Scholarships

Talented instrumentalists or vocalists can apply for one of the 15 music scholarships each worth £100.

Excel Sports Scholarship Programme

Fifteen Sports Scholarships are offered, valued at £1,000. Athletes showing national or international promise can access facilities for sports therapy, sports injury management, fitness testing and membership of sports facilities. In some cases financial subsidies are awarded for training and competition costs. For details contact the Department of Sport and Recreation.

Bournemouth Media School
Some funds are available for students with additional learning needs through the Max and Louise Clifford Fund, which is administered through the university.

AWARDS FOR NON-EU STUDENTS
EU Student Bursary
This is open to EU students not resident in the UK and is valued of £319.

Subject Awards
Awards of up to £1,000 are made on a competitive basis to international students accepting places on courses in the following subject areas: the Bournemouth Media School, Conservation Sciences, Design, Engineering and Computing, and the School of Services Management.

POSTGRADUATE AWARDS
Awards are offered to Taiwan students accepting a place on certain master's courses.

Baroness Cox Scholarship
An award covering the tuition fees plus £1,000 is made to students from Russia or Nigeria studying a taught master's programme.

Reham-al-Farra Scholarship
This award up to the value of £3,000 is open to international students applying to the Bournemouth Media School.

INFORMATION AND APPROXIMATE FEES FOR NON-EU STUDENTS
There is a large number of international students taking courses at the university. **English language entry requirement:** IELTS 6.0 (or equivalent). A preparatory English programme is offered, starting in January, April or July depending on the applicant's level of English (entry IELTS 4.5/5.0/5.5 or equivalent). There are several language schools in the town (see www.arels.co.uk or www.baselt.org.uk). A pre-sessional study skills programme is also offered. **Fees:** £8,000–£13,000. **Living costs:** £7,500–£8,500.

Bournemouth University, Fern Barrow, Poole, Dorset BH12 5BB; tel: 01202 524111; www.bournemouth.ac.uk.

BRADFORD UNIVERSITY

The University of Bradford is located at the edge of the city of Bradford and was founded in 1966. The main focus lies in scientific and technological degree courses, with over half the 10,000 students on sandwich placements.

DEGREE SUBJECTS OFFERED
Accounting and Finance; Applied Ecology; Applied Social Studies; Archaeological Sciences; Bioarchaeology; Biochemistry; Biomedical Sciences; Business Computing; Business Management; Cellular Pathology; Chemical Processing; Chemistry; Computer Science; Cybernetics; Economics; Electronic Imaging; Engineering (Chemical; Civil; Computing Networks and Performance; Electrical and Electronic; Industrial; Manufacturing; Mechanical; Medical; Petroleum Products; Software;

Telecommunications); Environmental Pollution Management; Environmental Science; European Studies; Forensic Science; French; Geoarchaeology; Geography; German; Health and Safety Management; History; Information Technology Management; Integrated Industrial Design; Interdisciplinary Human Studies; Media Technology; Medical Microbiology; Medical Technology in Sport; Modern Languages; Networks Information Management; Optometry; Pathology; Peace Studies; Personnel in Technology; Pharmaceutical Management; Pharmacology; Pharmacy; Physiotherapy; Planning; Politics; Radiography (Diagnostic); Russian; Social Policy; Social Welfare Studies; Sociology; South Asian Area Studies; Spanish; Technology Management; Virtual Design and Innovation.

TUITION FEES (2009/10)
£3,225.

BURSARIES AND OTHER AWARDS
Students on any level of maintenance grant, or with a family income under £40,000 a year will be eligible for The University of Bradford Bursary. This is £500 in a foundation year, £500 in Year 1, £700 in Year 2 and £900 in Year 3. For incomes between £40,001–£60,005 the awards are valued between £400 and £600 over 3 years. Students who come through the Bradford Academy Compact Scheme and have attended one event at the university will be eligible for an additional Compact Award of £300 in Year 1. The bursary is available to home and EU students.

School of Social and International Studies
Peace Scholarships
Two scholarships of £1,000 per year for students on full-time courses in the Department of Peace Studies.

School of Engineering, Design and Technology
The EDT scholarship is awarded at the end of semester 1 to students following BEng, BSc or MEng courses. It is based on academic performance and is worth £500.

Benjamin Jowett Memorial Scholarships
Seven scholarships are awarded to students entering the Mechanical and Medical Engineering Department to study Mechanical, Manufacturing or Automotive Engineering. The value of the scholarship is £500.

Petroleum Products Engineering
Petroleum Products Engineering is a discipline emphasising aspects of engineering and science relevant to the processing of petroleum. It covers petroleum products from well-head crude oil and gas through to refined distillate fuels, lubricating oils, petrochemicals and polymers.

Ten industrial bursaries valued at £1,000 per year are awarded on academic merit to students with not less than 240 UCAS points (equivalent to CCC at A-level).

Technology and Management
Industrial Engineering combines concepts from several branches of engineering with management and manufacturing knowledge. The Industrial Engineering course, started in 1998, has attracted company sponsorship.

Industrial sponsorship of up to £1,000 per year, plus well-paid industrial placements and good career prospects with the sponsoring company, are available for successful students.

Accent Scholarships
Three scholarships of £1,500 per year for home and EU students on the BA or foundation degree in Community Regeneration.

Cricket

The England and Wales Cricket Board has designated Bradford University as a Centre of Cricketing Excellence. The university participates in the UCCE (Universities Centre of Cricketing Excellence) Scheme for talented and ambitious young cricketers. For further information contact The Director of Physical Education.

Social Work Awards

Awards are made by the General Social Care Council, are valued between £2,500 and £5,000 and cover travel and tuition fees.

AWARDS FOR NON-EU STUDENTS

The university offers scholarships for international students (approximately half the international student tuition fees). These include undergraduate and postgraduate candidates from Bangladesh, Pakistan, India, China, Nigeria, Kenya, Tanzania, Uganda, Ghana and Botswana.

The scholarships are awarded to self-funding international applicants holding an offer of a place on a University of Bradford full-time course (undergraduate or postgraduate) on the basis of academic achievement and/or potential. They will be available for the full duration of the course, subject to satisfactory progress.

POSTGRADUATE AWARDS

Several awards are available. See also **Awards for non-EU students** above.

INFORMATION AND APPROXIMATE FEES FOR NON-EU STUDENTS

Over 100 countries are represented. **English language entry requirement:** IELTS 6.0 (or equivalent). Some students may be admitted to Year 2, depending on qualifications. **Fees:** Management and social science courses £8,500; Engineering and science courses £11,000; Occupational Therapy, Radiography and Physiotherapy under review. Some courses have premium fees – more information can be found on the university website. **Living costs:** £5,000–£6,000.

University of Bradford, Richmond Road, Bradford BD7 1DP; tel: 0800 073 1255; www. brad.ac.uk/scholarships.

BRIGHTON UNIVERSITY

The University of Brighton attained university status in 1992 and is situated on four sites, three in the town and one at Eastbourne 25 miles to the east, where courses in Sports Science, Hotel and Catering, Teaching and Podiatry are offered. Some courses are also run in Hastings at the University Centre Hastings (UCH). Currently there are over 20,000 full- and part-time students following courses leading to BA, BSc, BEng, MEng, BEd degrees and foundation degrees.

DEGREE SUBJECTS OFFERED

Accountancy; Architectural Structures; Architecture; Art and Design; Automotive Engine Design; Biogeography; Biological Sciences; Biology; Biomedical Sciences; Building Studies; Building Surveying; Business; Civil Engineering; Communication and Media Studies; Computer Science; Construction Engineering and Management; Criminology; Cultural Studies; Design and Technology; Education (Primary/Secondary); Electrical and Electronic Engineering; Environmental Engineering; Environmental Science; Food Retail Management; French; Geography; Geology; German; Health and Social Care; History of Art and Design; Hospitality Management; Humanities; Information and Library Studies; Information and Media Studies; International Business and Finance; International

Hospitality Management/Retail Management/Tourism/Travel Management; Italian; Law and Accountancy; Leisure Studies; Manufacturing and Mechanical Engineering; Mathematics; Medicine; Nursing; Oriental Medicine; Pharmacy; Physiotherapy; Podiatry; Product Design; Psychology; Public Policy; Retail Marketing; Russian; Social Policy; Social Sciences; Software Engineering; Spanish; Sport and Exercise Science; Statistics; Tourism and Travel; Urban Conservation and Environmental Management; Visual Culture.

TUITION FEES (2009/10)
£3,225.

BURSARIES AND OTHER AWARDS
Bursaries will be awarded in line with household incomes as follows: on a sliding scale from £1,080 for incomes less than £25,000, £860 between £25,001–£27,490, £750 between £27,491–£32,340 and £540 between £32,341 and £40,330.

University of Brighton Scholarships
Two hundred merit-based University of Brighton Scholarships worth £1,000 each will be awarded to eligible students at the end of Years 1 and 2 (and Year 3 of four-year courses) and Years 1 to 4 of five years at Brighton and Sussex Medical School. These scholarships are awarded on the basis of student performance throughout that year of study, including assessments. To be eligible to receive one of these scholarships you should:

* Be a full-time undergraduate, PGCE or pre-registration MSc Nursing student.
* Be studying at the University of Brighton or the Brighton and Sussex Medical School, or be studying an HE course at one of the university's partner colleges.
* Have started your course in 2006 or later.

Holders of the University of Sussex Chancellor's Scholarship are not eligible for this award.

Sports Scholarships
The Sports Scholarships scheme is designed to help students develop their full sporting potential by giving the necessary flexibility and support required to train and compete at the highest level whilst achieving an academic qualification.

Three kinds of scholarship are available:

Elite Athletes Squad
* Bursary of up to a maximum of £1,500 per year of study
* Free access to university sport facilities
* Free sports science support by BASES accredited staff
* Access to sports medicine support at reduced rates through Sportswise
* Sports/academic mentor
* Access to University of Brighton sports coaches where available in the particular sport.

Eligibility criteria:
* You should have reached junior or senior national level of competition or performance and have the potential and dedication to reach world-class standard or performance level (or equivalent) in your sport.
* You should have been accepted on a University of Brighton undergraduate course or be a current undergraduate student of the university.

Talented Sports Performers Squad
* Access to University of Brighton sports squads and coaches where available in the particular sport
* Financial assistance up to a maximum of £300 per academic year

* A Talented Sports Performers Card allowing free use of university sports facilities
* Access to sports science and sports medicine at reduced rates.

Eligibility criteria:
* You should have represented your sport at a national or regional level or be able to demonstrate that you have the potential to compete at these levels.
* You should have been accepted on a University of Brighton course or be a current student of the university.

Disabled Athletes Scholarship
Five bursaries at £1,000 each will be available to talented disabled athletes. Further details will become available in the near future. The deadline for applications is 31 May each year.

AWARDS FOR NON-EU STUDENTS
International Scholarships
Seventy-five University of Brighton International Scholarships, worth a reduction of £2,000 off the cost of your tuition fees for each year of your course, are available to outstanding international students.

The criteria for awarding University of Brighton International Scholarships are:

* Merit – not just academic merit but could also be interpreted to include outstanding perform-ance in a variety of spheres
* Full fee-paying full-time international student status
* Demonstration of sufficient funds to pay the remainder of the fees.

In order to be eligible to apply for a scholarship you must be an international student, have applied for the course of your choice at the University of Brighton and have been offered a place.

Vietnam Scholarships
Two University of Brighton scholarships worth a reduction of 50% off the cost of your tuition fees for each year of your course are available to outstanding Vietnamese students. The criteria for this award are as for International Scholarships above.

Pestalozzi Scholarships
These scholarships, which are available for the three years of an undergraduate degree, cover the full cost of tuition fees and also provide a financial bursary which meets half the recipient's living costs. Pestalozzi students will be expected to meet the rest of their living costs from paid employment. University of Brighton Pestalozzi Scholarships are open to students at the Pestalozzi International Village, Seddlescombe, East Sussex who wish to go on to higher education and who would not be able to do so without the support of the scheme.

POSTGRADUATE AWARDS
Four research scholarships worth a 50% reduction of fees are offered to outstanding students. In addition, 500 Commonwealth Scholarships and Fellowships are offered by the UK Government.

INFORMATION AND APPROXIMATE FEES FOR OVERSEAS NON-EU STUDENTS
There are currently over 1,200 international students from over 100 countries. **English language entry requirement:** IELTS 6.0 (or equivalent); less linguistically demanding subjects IELTS 5.5 (or equivalent). The new four-year degree programme (UK4) includes a preparatory year. **Fees:** £9,000–£10,500. **Living costs:** £7,000–£8,000.

University of Brighton, Mithras House, Lewes Road, Brighton BN2 4AT; tel: 01273 644644; www.bton.ac.uk.

BRISTOL UNIVERSITY

The University of Bristol was founded in 1876 as University College, Bristol. In 1909 the University was awarded full university status and 2009 marks the University's first centenary. Today the University is a thriving, international enterprise of around 12,000 undergraduates, nearly 5,000 postgraduates and over 5,500 employees.

The majority of the University's main buildings are located within a few minutes' walk of each other in a lively part of the city centre. The halls of residence are within a 30 minute walk of the University precinct.

DEGREE SUBJECTS OFFERED

Accounting; Aeronautical Engineering; Anatomy; Ancient History; Animal Behaviour and Welfare; Anthropology; Archaeology; Astrophysics; Audiology; Biochemistry; Biological Sciences; Botany; Cancer Biology; Cellular and Molecular Medicine; Chemical Physics; Chemistry; Childhood Studies; Civil Engineering; Classical Studies; Classics; Communications Engineering; Computer Science; Czech; Deaf Studies; Dentistry; Drama; Economics; Electrical and Electronic Engineering; Engineering Design; Engineering Mathematics; English; Environmental Geoscience; European Legal Studies; Finance; French; Geography; Geology; Geoscience; German; Hispanic Studies; History; History of Art; Human Musculoskeletal Science; Immunology; Italian; Law; Management; Mathematics; Mechanical Engineering; Medicine; Medical Microbiology; Music; Neuroscience; Palaeontology; Pathology and Microbiology; Pharmacology; Philosophy; Physics; Physiology; Politics; Portuguese; Psychology; Russian; Social Policy; Sociology; Spanish; Theology and Religious Studies; Veterinary Cellular and Molecular Science; Veterinary Nursing and Bioveterinary Science; Veterinary Science; Virology; Zoology.

TUITION FEES (2009/10)

£3,225.

BURSARIES AND OTHER AWARDS

The 2010/11 University of Bristol bursary has not yet been finalised. As a guide, in 2009/10 under-graduate students whose household income is £50,000 or less and who are in receipt of a maintenance grant (or special support grant) qualify for a University of Bristol bursary.

Top-up bursaries of £1,075 per year are available to local students who qualify for a government maintenance grant and meet the income threshold. These bursaries will be available in addition to the bursary support described above.

For more details on the University of Bristol bursaries, please visit www.bristol.ac.uk/prospectus/undergraduate/2010/moneymatters.

Organ and Choral Scholarships

Organ scholarships are available at the Church of St Paul, Clifton, the Church of St Mary Redcliffe and Bristol Cathedral. Choral Scholarships are based at Bristol Cathedral and St Mary Redcliffe and are for male singers only. Students do not have to be studying for a music degree. Enquiries to Margaret Peirson, Music Department, Victoria Rooms, Queens Road, Bristol BS8 1SA; Tel 0117 954 5028 or m.e.peirson@Bristol.ac.uk.

Access to Bristol Bursaries

The Access to Bristol Bursary was introduced to supplement the Access to Bristol scheme, a programme of events designed to encourage academically motivated local students to consider applying to the University of Bristol. Only students from particular schools and colleges (as identi-fied by the Widening Participation and Undergraduates Recruitment Office) are invited to apply to the scheme and may be eligible for the Access to Bristol Bursary. Please visit the following website for more details: www.bris.ac.uk/studentfunding.

AWARDS FOR NON-EU STUDENTS
International Recruitment Office Scholarships
There are a number of scholarships available, up to a maximum of £2,000 per year of study, for high-achieving undergraduate students (overseas fee payers). Scholarships are allocated to students from a selection of countries. No more than one scholarship will be awarded per country, per year for medical students. For 2010 entry, applicants who are overseas fee payers and resident in the following regions will be considered: Hong Kong; India; Kenya; Latin America; Malaysia; Mauritius; Russia; Singapore; Sri Lanka; Thailand; USA; Vietnam.

Entrance Scholarships
Department of Anatomy
The Department offers Overseas Bursaries to the value of £2,000 per year to help pay the tuition fees of overseas students. These are awarded on the basis of academic potential and are annually renewable, subject to good progress on the degree programme.

Department of Biochemistry
As an incentive, the department may offer Merit Awards worth £2,000 per year to deserving international candidates on academic grounds.

School of Economics, Finance and Management
The School of Economics, Finance and Management is also offering three scholarships for overseas students commencing study on one of its undergraduate programmes in 2010: Scholarship for the best A-level candidate; Scholarship for the best International Baccalaureate; Scholarship for the best Indian Senior Secondary School Level XII. For single honours programmes: 50% of tuition fees for each year of undergraduate study. For joint honours programmes: 25% of tuition fees for each year of undergraduate study.

Department of Pharmacology
The department offers a limited number of scholarships worth £2,000 per year.

International Hardship Fund
The International Hardship Fund has been set up to provide emergency financial assistance to international students who find themselves in unexpected financial difficulty, as a result of a significant or unexpected event that could not have been predicted. Students seeking help must demonstrate that they had made adequate arrangements to support themselves and pay their tuition and accommodation fees before they came to university, and that these arrangements have been affected by unforeseen circumstances, or events beyond their control.

Applications meriting support might include occasions where a sponsor was suddenly unable to provide support, or where a student unexpectedly and urgently needed to return home for family reasons.

Postgraduates
There are 10 scholarships worth £2,000 each available to international taught postgraduate students (overseas fee payers) from any country. See also www.bris.ac.uk/international/fees-finances/io-pgt-scholarships.html.

INFORMATION AND APPROXIMATE FEES FOR NON-EU STUDENTS
International students currently make up 16% of the student body and come from over 100 countries. **English language entry requirement:** IELTS 6.5 (or equivalent). **Fees:** arts courses were £11,450–£14,750; science courses were £14,750; clinical courses were £26,600; engineering courses were £14,750; social sciences and law were £11,450–£14750. **Living costs:** £7,000–£9,500.

University of Bristol, Senate House, Tyndall Avenue, Bristol BS8 1TH; tel: 0117 928 9000; admissions@Bristol.ac.uk; www.bristol.ac.uk.

See Chapters 2, 4 and 6 for additional awards, applicable to all universities

BRISTOL, UNIVERSITY OF THE WEST OF ENGLAND (Bristol UWE)

(See also Hartpury College)

The university comprises four campuses: Frenchay, Bower Ashton, Glenside and St Matthias. There are also three regional centres: Hartpury College, near Gloucester; Bath Education Centre; and Swindon Education Centre. There is a total student population of over 23,000. Students follow degree, postgraduate and professional programmes.

DEGREE SUBJECTS OFFERED

Accounting; Agriculture; Analytical Science; Animal Science; Architecture; Art and Design; Biochemistry; Biology; Biomedical Science; Building; Building Surveying; Business Studies; Computer Science; Construction Management; Drama; Economics; Education (Primary); Engineering (Aeronautical; Digital Systems; Electrical; Electronic; Environmental; Manufacturing; Mechanical); English; Environmental Health; Equine Studies; European Studies; Film Studies; Finance; Forensic Science; French; Genetics; Geography; German; Health Studies; History; Housing; Immunology; Information Systems; International Business; Law; Linguistics; Marketing; Mathematics; Media Studies; Microbiology; Midwifery; Nursing; Occupational Therapy; Pharmacology; Physiology; Physiotherapy; Politics; Property; Psychology; Quantity Surveying; Radiography; Real Estate; Social Work; Sociology; Software Engineering; Spanish; Sports Conditioning and Coaching; Statistics; Tourism; Town Planning; Valuation; Veterinary Nursing.

TUITION FEES (2009/10)

£3,225.

BURSARIES AND OTHER AWARDS

An award of £1,000 is made to students from families with an income lower than £25,000 per year. Awards of £750 are made to families with incomes from £17,910 to £38,330.

Tony Papadopoullos Memorial Bursary

The bursary, which is worth £2,500, is targeted at students whose opportunities for study are limited due to financial restrictions, and is open to those who have applied for or who have been offered a place on the BSc Computer Science or the BSc Software Engineering courses.

Music Scholarships

Five bursaries valued at £1,000 are awarded each year to first-year undergraduate students of high musical ability (instrumental or vocal). Awards are tenable for three years.

Sports Scholarships

Each award may be up to £3,000 and is available to all undergraduate students of national or international standard. There is also additional financial aid for athletes attending international events.

Hartpury College Awards (See also Hartpury College)

The college is an associate faculty of the university and offers a limited number of scholarships and bursaries. Awards are made on academic merit. Further information is available from the college.

AWARDS FOR NON-EU STUDENTS
Faculty of Law
A Lord Templeman Scholarship giving a remission of fees for up to two years is available to students from Malaysia, Singapore, Hong Kong, Thailand, Indonesia, Philippines, South Africa, North America and the West Indian islands. A Bar Vocational Course Scholarship is also awarded.

Music Scholarships
See above.

Sport Scholarships
See above.

POSTGRADUATE AWARDS
Bursaries are awarded as follows: one MBA award of £3,375; two MA Economics/Human Resource Management/Marketing awards of £1,000; 10 International Management awards of £1,000.

INFORMATION AND APPROXIMATE FEES FOR NON-EU STUDENTS
There are more than 1,750 international students. **English language entry requirement:** IELTS 6.0 (or equivalent). English language preparatory and pre-sessional courses are offered. English modules can also be taken throughout the degree. **Fees:** classroom-based courses £8,250; laboratory-based courses £8,700. **Living costs:** £6,500–£8,500.

University of the West of England, Bristol, Frenchay Campus, Coldharbour Lane, Bristol BS16 1QY; tel: 0117 328 3333; www.uwe.ac.uk.

BRITISH COLLEGE OF OSTEOPATHIC MEDICINE

This internationally renowned college with teaching clinics was founded in 1936 and is the first UK osteopathic institution to gain the best-possible Recognised Qualification (RQ) 'approval without conditions' from the General Osteopathic Council. Its four-year undergraduate Masters in Osteopathy attracts public funding, including for those with previous bachelors degrees. Employment prospects are excellent with historically more than 95% of students securing employment within the first three months of graduation. A number of scholarships are available, principally to students unable to attract public funding because of ELQ status (reduction of total fees) and students from disadvantaged backgrounds in Inner London boroughs as part of a commitment to widening participation for the capital's students (reduction of top-up fee).

DEGREE SUBJECT OFFERED
Masters in Osteopathy (B312)

TUITION FEES (2009/10)
Normal top-up fees apply. For details please contact the Registry.

The British College of Osteopathic Medicine, Lief House, 122 Finchley Road, London NW3 5HR; tel: 020 7435 6464; admissions@bcom.ac.uk; www.bcom.ac.uk

See Chapters 2, 4 and 6 for additional awards, applicable to all universities

BRUNEL UNIVERSITY (UXBRIDGE)

Brunel University was founded in 1966. It is located on a campus to the west of London at Uxbridge. A large number of courses are aimed at students wishing to enter professional and vocational fields and they operate through a flexible course structure of thin and thick sandwich placements with employers. There is a total student population of nearly 14,000.

DEGREE SUBJECTS OFFERED
Anthropology; Biosciences; Business and Management; Business Mathematics; Communication and Media Studies; Computer Science; Drama; E-Commerce; Economics; Education (Secondary); Engineering (Computer Systems; Electrical/Electronic; Integrated; Internet; Mechanical; Motorsport Systems); English; Finance and Accounting; Film and TV; History; Humanities; Industrial Design; Journalism; Law; Management; Mathematics; Music; Occupational Therapy; Physical Education; Physiotherapy; Politics; Product Design; Psychology; Social Anthropology; Social Work; Sociology; Sports Sciences; Statistics.

TUITION FEES (2009/10)
£3,225.

BURSARIES AND OTHER AWARDS
The Brunel Bursary
The Brunel Bursary is a non-repayable (unless your circumstances change) sum of money awarded by the University to supplement the government's Maintenance Grant. It is designed for undergraduate students from lower-income households.

For 2009 entry, Brunel offers:

* £1,000 per year of study to all undergraduate students entitled to receive a full Maintenance Grant;
* £500 a year to undergraduate students eligible for a partial Maintenance Grant and whose annual household income is between £25,001 and £33,000.

Bursaries are paid automatically to eligible students, in termly instalments – students do not need to make a specific application, but they must indicate on their UCAS form that they consent to household financial information being shared with the University for bursary and scholarship purposes (students will be invited to opt out of data-sharing if they wish, but this will prevent an assessment of eligibility and the award of a bursary).

Music Bursaries
Many students at Brunel have skills in fields other than those they choose to study for their degrees. In recognition of this, the University makes awards from the Music Tuition Fund each year to help students from all Schools to continue their musical tuition.

Both undergraduate and postgraduate students can apply for an Award audition.

Award Holders have all or part of the cost of their individual music tuition covered by the Fund throughout their period of study at Brunel. The Awards are open to both singers and instrumentalists.

Further details and conditions can be found at: www.brunel.ac.uk/about/pubfac/artscentre/awards

Regional Partnership Scholarships

Brunel's newly-expanded Regional Partnership Scholarships are non-repayable (unless your circumstances change) cash awards of up to £3,000, paid each year to up to 25 undergraduate students on the basis of high academic achievement. The new Brunel Alumni Scholarships are non-repayable (unless your circumstances change) cash awards of £6,000, paid each year on the same basis as Regional Partnership Scholarships to the five applicants who achieve the highest number of UCAS tariff points.

Eligible students must have attended a maintained school or college (not an independent or private school) in one of the six boroughs with whom the University operates Widening Participation partnerships – Brent, Ealing, Hammersmith and Fulham, Harrow, Hillingdon and Hounslow (please refer to the website to see the full list of eligible schools).

Applicants must also fulfil one of the following under-represented criteria:

* To have a disability, including dyslexia (ie they are eligible to apply for the Disabled Student's Allowance at the time of scholarship allocation in August);
* That they are a care-leaver (ie in care for a minimum of three months and have declared this on the UCAS form);
* That they come from a low-income or low socio-economic background (ie entitled to a full Government Maintenance Grant or Special Support grant).

Students who meet the above criteria and who achieve a minimum of 360 UCAS tariff points will be considered for a Regional Partnership Scholarship of up to £3,000 per year or an Alumni Scholarship of £6,000 per year. All applicants attending a partnership school or college who choose Brunel as their firm choice will be contacted by the University in the spring and invited to complete an online application. Only those students who complete the application will be considered for a scholarship.

For more information, please refer to the Terms and Conditions on the website.

Sports Scholarships

The Sports Scholarship is designed to benefit elite performance athletes by supporting their academic study and sporting profession simultaneously. To enable a balance between these demands the scheme includes the following:

* Financial award
* Athlete-friendly accommodation on campus next to sports facilities*
* Mentoring support for general advice on balancing academic study with training requirements
* Talent workshops in strength and conditioning, plyometrics, for example
* Assistance with expenses for national and international competition
* Free use of world-class sports facilities, including High Performance Athletics Centre
* Free Brunel University Sport kit
* Sports Scholars celebration event
* Media promotion of your achievements
* Please note that the Scheme does not cover accommodation costs or tuition fees

Candidates can apply for a Sports Scholarship award once they have been given a confirmed place on a course at Brunel University. Upon receiving the application form applicants will be notified of the closing date to submit their application.

Please contact sports-scholarships@brunel.ac.uk for more information.

INFORMATION AND APPROXIMATE FEES FOR NON-EU STUDENTS

There are 2,500 international students from over 110 countries. **English language entry require-ment:** IELTS 6.5 (or equivalent); science/technology courses IELTS 6.0 (or equivalent). English language tuition is offered both during the course, and beforehand with pre-sessional courses of five to 20 weeks' duration. **Fees:** intensive foundation and pre-master's from £3,900; foundation courses £9,200; non-laboratory-based courses £9,200; laboratory-based courses £11,100. Note that this is an overview only and some courses have additional fees or special circumstances. For a full list of all UG fees see www.brunel.ac.uk/ugstudy/finance/fees09100 **Living costs:** £7,000–£8,000

Brunel University, Uxbridge, Middlesex UB8 3BH; tel 01895 265849; www.brunel.ac.uk

BUCKINGHAM UNIVERSITY

The University of Buckingham is the only independent university in the UK, founded in 1976. It is situated on two adjacent sites in the town of Buckingham. Buckingham was the first UK university to offer the academic content of a standard three-year degree in a two-year programme, running over four terms per year. Degree courses begin in July, September and January. Students are eligible for loans and maintenance awards. Buckingham has a student population of just over 1,000, with representatives from 80 different countries.

DEGREE SUBJECTS OFFERED

Accounting; Business Economics; Business Enterprise; Business and Management; Communication Studies; Computing; Economics; English Language; English Literature; Law; Marketing; Politics; Psychology.

TUITION FEES (2009/10)

£8,040 per year (Home students on a two year undergraduate course)

BURSARIES AND OTHER AWARDS

Buckingham offers the following scholarships, on an annual basis (unless otherwise stated) to students from the UK. The university is looking for academic high flyers who have something special to offer the university:

Brunner Scholarship

One scholarship of £1,700 per year awarded annually to a Law student.

Coase Scholarship

Two full fee scholarships awarded annually to undergraduate students commencing one of the following degree programmes: Economics; Economics with Law; Business Economics; Economics, Business and Law; Politics, Economics and Law; Law with Economics.

Desborough Scholarship

One £5,000 scholarship awarded bi-annually to an undergraduate Business Studies student (available for January 2010 entry).

Gregory Scholarships

Three scholarships of £2,500 each awarded annually to students, one in Business, one in Humanities and one in Sciences.

Osborn Scholarship

One scholarship of £1,000 per year awarded annually to a Law student.

Aylesbury Vale District Council Business Enterprise Scholarship
One full fee scholarship (based on undergraduate home student fee levels) awarded to an Aylesbury Vale resident. Candidates must write a business plan and submit it to the Buckingham Business School. Selected candidates will then be asked to present their ideas to the Buckingham Angels venture capital panel.

Weston Scholarships
One £3,600 scholarship awarded annually to an undergraduate Law student. In the absence of one exceptional candidate, a number of smaller awards may be made.

Buckingham offers the following open scholarships to undergraduate and postgraduate students anywhere in the world:

Anthony de Rothschild Bursary
One scholarship of £1,000 per year awarded annually to a student in the Business School.

Headley Scholarship
One scholarship of £750 per year awarded annually to a student in the Law School.

University Scholarships
Four scholarships of £1,000 per year awarded annually to international students, one in each School of Study.

Sir Ray Tindle Scholarships
Six partial-fee scholarships awarded annually to students of Journalism in the School of Humanities.

POSTGRADUATE AWARDS
Ondaatje Scholarships
Two annual postgraduate scholarships covering 50% of fees and accommodation awarded to Buckingham graduates or overseas graduates undertaking postgraduate studies at Buckingham.

INFORMATION AND APPROXIMATE FEES FOR NON-EU STUDENTS
Eighty nationalities are represented at this small university. **English language entry requirement:** IELTS 6.0 (or equivalent); Law 6.5 (or equivalent). English language courses are available for students with IELTS from 4.5. **Fees:** current (2009) undergraduate fees for 2-year programmes: £13,500. **Living costs:** £7,500–£8,000.

University of Buckingham, Hunter Street, Buckingham MK18 1EG; tel: 01280 814080; www.buckingham.ac.uk/study/fees/.

BUCKS NEW UNIVERSITY

The university is 40 minutes from London, is situated on three campuses, one being located centrally in High Wycombe, the second at Wellesbourne outside the town and the third in parkland at Chalfont. Single honours, joint honours, major/minor and modular courses are offered.

DEGREE SUBJECTS OFFERED
Air Transport and Pilot Training; Air Travel Management; Art and Design; Business Management; Computer Science; Creative Writing; Criminology; Drama; English Studies; Exercise and Health Science; Film Studies; Furniture Conservation and Design; Human Resources Management; International Football Management; Journalism; Law; Marketing; Media Studies; Music Industry

See Chapters 2, 4 and 6 for additional awards, applicable to all universities

Studies; Nursing; Policing; Psychology; Public Relations; Sociology; Sport; Three-Dimensional Design; Travel and Tourism; Video Production.

TUITION FEES (2009/10)
£3,225.

BURSARIES AND OTHER AWARDS
Students enrolling for undergraduate courses at the university from households with an income of less than £25,000 will receive a non-means-tested bursary of £2,835 each year for the duration of their course. Partial grants are available for students with a household income of up to £60,005.

Faculty Scholarships
A number of Faculty Scholarships are available, worth £300 per year. The framework of these scholarships and the specific criteria for eligibility vary between each faculty.

University Scholarships
Scholarships worth £300 are also available to students undertaking courses at one of the University's Compact schools or colleges.

INFORMATION AND APPROXIMATE FEES FOR NON-EU STUDENTS
English language entry requirement: IELTS 5.0 (or equivalent). **Fees:** £7,500–£8,000. **Living costs:** £6,000–£7,000.

Buckinghamshire Chilterns University College, Queen Alexandra Road, High Wycombe, Buckinghamshire HP11 2JZ; tel: 0800 0565 660; www.bucks.ac.uk.

CAMBRIDGE UNIVERSITY

The University of Cambridge was founded in the 13th century. It is a collegiate university with 29 undergraduate colleges situated in and around the city. There are over 17,000 undergraduate students. Application is made via UCAS, each college is responsible for organising the interview and selection procedure.

DEGREE SUBJECTS OFFERED
Aerospace and Aerothermal Engineering; Akkadian; Anatomy; Ancient Near East; Anglo-Saxon, Norse and Celtic; Arabic; Archaeology and Anthropology; Architecture; Asian and Middle Eastern Studies; Assyriology; Astrophysics; Biochemistry; Biological and Biomedical Sciences; Biology; Biomedical Engineering; Chemical Engineering; Chemistry; Chinese Studies; Civil, Structural and Environmental Engineering; Classics; Computer Science; Coptic; Dutch; Economics; Education; Egyptology; Electrical and Electronic Engineering; Electrical and Information Sciences; Energy and the Environment; Engineering; English; Environment; French; Genetics; Geography; Geological Sciences; German; Greek, Classical; Greek, Modern; Hebrew Studies; History; History and Philosophy of Science; History of Art; Information and Computer Engineering; Instrumentation and Control; Irish, Medieval; Islamic Studies; Italian; Japanese Studies; Land Economy; Latin, Classical; Latin, Insular; Law; Linguistics; Management Studies; Manufacturing Engineering; Materials Science; Mathematics; Mechanical Engineering; Medicine; Mesopotamia; Middle Eastern and Islamic Studies; Modern and Medieval Languages; Music; Natural Sciences; Neuroscience; Norse, Old; Palaeography; Pathology; Persian; Pharmacology; Philosophy; Physical Sciences; Physics; Physiology; Plant Sciences; Politics, Psychology and Sociology (PPS); Portuguese; Psychology;

Religious Studies; Russian; Sanskrit; Sociology; Spanish; Theology and Religious Studies; Veterinary Medicine; Welsh, Medieval; Zoology.

TUITION FEES (2009/10)
£3,225.

BURSARIES AND OTHER AWARDS
Cambridge Bursary Scheme
The University of Cambridge has a generous bursary scheme for UK undergraduates to ensure that students can meet the cost of their education, regardless of background. Bursaries of up to £9,750 over three years or £13,000 over four years will be available. The value of each bursary will be based on parental income, and calculated on a sliding scale up to £3,250. Those students in receipt of the full £2,906 government maintenance will receive a £3,250 bursary. Bursaries of smaller amounts will be awarded on a sliding scale to all those students who qualify for a lower level of maintenance grant. A higher level of bursary (£5,400 per year) is available for some mature students who have to remain in Cambridge throughout the year. Students will be given an application form when they arrive in Cambridge. Further details are available on the University's website, www.cam.ac.uk/admissions/undergraduate/ and from the Cambridge Admissions Office.

Organ Scholarships
Organ scholars provide the music for regular chapel services, and contribute regular hours of practice. They also perform in college concerts, where a much wider range of music can be presented, and some undertake summer tours in this country or abroad. The specific duties of the organ scholar are dependent upon the college at which the scholarship is held. The nature of the awards varies from college to college, but they all include a small financial award each year (usually £250 or £300). In most colleges the organ scholar is also given a subsidy towards organ lessons, and a piano in his/her room. Other perks, including subsidised meals and choir tours, are determined by the individual colleges. The following colleges currently offer Organ Scholarships through the intercollegiate competition (called Organ Trials): Christ's; Churchill; Clare; Corpus Christi; Downing; Emmanuel; Fitzwilliam; Girton; Gonville and Caius; Jesus; King's; Magdalene; Pembroke; Peterhouse; Queens'; Robinson; St Catharine's; St John's; Selwyn; Sidney Sussex; Trinity; Trinity Hall. If you wish to be considered for an Organ Scholarship you must submit an Organ Scholarship Application Form by 1 September. Further information can be found on www.cam.ac.uk/admissions/undergraduate/musicawards/.

Choral Awards
Choral Award-holders are required to sing in their college's Chapel Choir, attending regular rehearsals and services. Most colleges also expect Choral Award-holders to play an active role in college music-making in general. The nature of the Awards varies from college to college, but they all include a small financial award (currently £100), and some support for singing lessons. The following colleges offer Choral Awards through the intercollegiate competition (called Choral Trials): Christ's; Clare; Corpus Christi; Fitzwilliam; Girton; Gonville and Caius; Jesus; King's; Magdalene; Newnham; Peterhouse; Queens'; Robinson; St Catharine's; St John's; Selwyn; Sidney Sussex; Trinity. If you wish to be considered for one of these Choral Awards you must submit a Choral Award Application Form by 5 September. Note that Churchill, Downing, Emmanuel, Homerton, Hughes Hall, Lucy Cavendish, Murray Edwards, Pembroke, St Edmund's, Trinity Hall and Wolfson do not offer Choral Awards through the inter-collegiate competition, although some do have their own choirs and may offer Choral Awards to students once they begin their studies at Cambridge. Further information can be found on www.cam.ac.uk/admissions/undergraduate/musicawards/.

Instrumental Awards Scheme for the promotion of chamber music
The purpose of the Instrumental Awards Scheme is to enable gifted players to reach a high standard of performance in chamber music. Instrumental Award-holders receive a small financial award (called an exhibition), professional coaching of their ensemble and usually a subsidy for

their instrumental lessons. Players of violin, viola, cello, flute, oboe, clarinet, bassoon, French horn or piano are eligible to apply. Grade 8 of the Associated Board or similar is required. All colleges participate in the Instrumental Awards Scheme. Applicants receiving an offer of a place will be invited to request further information and an application form. The application form should be returned by the February deadline, and auditions will be held just before the start of the academic year.

Support for students with a disability
The University of Cambridge has a number of funds specifically for students with a disability and more information is available from the Disability Resource Centre (DRC): www.cam.ac.uk/cambuniv/disability.

Sports Grants and Bursaries
A small amount of financial support is available to outstanding sportspeople studying at the university. See www.sport.cam.ac.uk/bursaries for details.

College awards
There are additional sources of funding available at college level which students can apply for, such as book and equipment grants to help with specific study-related costs. Colleges also award scholarships and prizes for academic achievement. In addition, grants and loans are available from colleges to deal with unforeseen difficulties. Information on all these funds is available from each college. Contact details for all the colleges can be found in the Undergraduate Prospectus and on the university website.

AWARDS FOR NON-EU STUDENTS
The financial support available for overseas students is limited. Few full scholarships are available at undergraduate level; most support is a partial contribution to overall costs and is means-tested.

Cambridge Commonwealth and Overseas Trusts
The Cambridge Commonwealth Trust and the Cambridge Overseas Trust offer awards (mostly part cost) to overseas students, including affiliated students, who have been accepted for admission by a Cambridge college. Applications for funding through the trusts cannot be made until you have been offered a place at one of the colleges. At this point the college will send you full details of the trust awards and an application form. All awards are means-tested.

Prince Philip Scholarships for applicants from Hong Kong
Permanent residents of the Hong Kong Special Administrative Region applying for a first degree at Cambridge are eligible to apply for a Prince Philip Scholarship. The scholarships offer cash awards and means-tested support for tuition fees and maintenance. Applicants need to send the application for the scholarship at the same time as they submit their application to Cambridge. Further details and an application form are available from the Administrative Secretary, Friends of Cambridge University in Hong Kong, c/o Bank of East Asia Limited, 10 Des Voeux Road, Central, Hong Kong.

POSTGRADUATE AWARDS
See www.admin.cam.ac.uk/univ/gsprospectus/funding for information.

INFORMATION AND FEES FOR NON-EU STUDENTS
Undergraduate
Nine per cent of the student body is from overseas. **English language entry requirement:** IELTS 7.0 (or equivalent). **Fees:** classroom-based courses £9,747; Architecture, Geography, Music and laboratory-based courses £12,768; Medicine and Veterinary Medicine: pre-clinical £12,768, clinical £23,631. College fees: £4,000–£5,000. **Living costs:** £6,000–£7,500.

Admissions Office, University of Cambridge, Fitzwilliam House, 32 Trumpington Street, Cambridge CB2 1QY; tel: 01223 333308; admissions@cam.ac.uk; www.cam.ac.uk/admissions/undergraduate.

Postgraduate
Board of Graduate Studies, University of Cambridge, 4 Mill Lane, Cambridge CB2 1RZ; tel: 01223 760606; admissions@gradstudies.cam.ac.uk; www.admin.cam.ac.uk/univ/gsprospectus/funding.

CANTERBURY CHRIST CHURCH UNIVERSITY

The university has a student population of over 15,000 following courses at undergraduate, post-graduate and professional levels. The main campus is close to the city centre with others situated in Broadstairs, Medway and Tunbridge Wells.

DEGREE SUBJECTS OFFERED
American Studies; Applied Social Sciences; Art; Business Studies; Computing; Criminology; Education; English; Geography; Health Studies; History; Leisure; Life Sciences; Media Studies; Midwifery; Music; Nursing; Occupational Therapy; Radiography; Religious Studies; Social Care; Sport Science; Teacher Training; Tourism.

TUITION FEES (2009/10)
£3,225.

BURSARIES AND OTHER AWARDS
Bursaries are offered as follows: £860 for students on full state support; £535 for students with household incomes between £25,000 and £49,000 approx.

Music Scholarships
There are several prizes for student achievement, and scholarships are available for organ, chapel music, string and double reed players. Significant annual prizes are offered through the Alan Parnell Prize for voice and piano accompaniment, the Larissa Lovelock Memorial Scholarship, the Metropole Scholarship and the Canterbury Festival Composition Prize.

Sport Scholarships
The University offers seven scholarships to sportsmen/women in any sport. Students awarded a Sports Scholarship will be expected, as far as reasonable, to represent the University throughout the duration of their studies as a three year undergraduate student.

POSTGRADUATE AWARDS
Postgraduate scholarships are also available for students taking MPhil and PhD degrees.

INFORMATION AND APPROXIMATE FEES FOR NON-EU STUDENTS
There is an international community from 80 countries. **English language entry requirement:** IELTS 6.0 (or equivalent). **Fees:** from £7,800. **Living costs:** £9,600.

Canterbury Christ Church University, Canterbury, Kent CT1 1QU; tel: 01227 782900; www.cant.ac.uk.

See Chapters 2, 4 and 6 for additional awards, applicable to all universities

CARDIFF UNIVERSITY

The university campus is situated a few minutes' walk from the city centre. Founded in 1883 the university has a student population of over 15,500. Degree courses are largely based on a modular system. This allows considerable flexibility and choice and many students delay the final choice of their degree subject until the end of the first year. Cardiff University merged with the University of Wales College of Medicine in 2004.

DEGREE SUBJECTS OFFERED

Accounting; Anatomical Science; Ancient History; Applied Biology; Applied Psychology; Archaeology; Architectural Studies; Astrophysics; Banking and Finance; Biochemistry; Biology; Bio-technology; Business Administration; Chemistry; City and Regional Planning; Communication; Computer Science; Criminology; Dentistry; Earth Sciences; Ecology; Economics; Education; Engineering (Architectural; Civil; Computer Systems; Electrical/Electronic; Environmental; Integrated; Manufacturing; Mechanical; Medical); English; Environmental Science; European Union Studies; French; Genetics; Geography (Human; Marine); Geology; German; History; International Transport; Italian; Journalism, Film and Broadcasting; Language and Communication; Law; Marine Geography; Maritime Studies; Mathematics; Medical Molecular Biology; Medicine; Medieval Studies; Microbiology; Music; Neuroscience; Nursing; Occupational Therapy; Operating Department Practice; Optometry; Pharmacology; Pharmacy; Philosophy; Physics; Physiology; Physiotherapy; Politics; Psychology; Radiography; Religious Studies; Social Policy; Sociology; Spanish; Theology; Welsh; Zoology.

TUITION FEES (2009/10)

See www.studentfinancewales.co.uk and **Chapter 1, 'Financing your course'.**

BURSARIES AND OTHER AWARDS

Bursaries, which will be paid in each year of the degree course, will be valued at either £1,050 or £500. These figures include the Welsh National Bursary Scheme Award of £310, which the university is obliged to provide. Bursaries are in addition to the means-tested maximum £2,835 Assembly Learning Grant (Wales) or maintenance grant (England) entitlement and do not affect these awards.

Cardiff University Scholarships

Students commencing their studies in 2009 may apply for awards worth £3,000 in the following subjects: Biological and Bio-molecular Sciences; Chemistry; Computer Science; Earth and Ocean Sciences; Engineering Mathematics; Physics; Archaeology; German; Italian; Music; Welsh. (Closing date 31 July 2009.) Students are required to achieve between 340 and 360 UCAS tariff points on entry.

Sports Bursary Awards

Awards are offered in golf and rugby. Those who qualify for the Cardiff RFC Bursary will receive a minimum award of £500 per year; golf bursars will receive a minimum of £1,000, depending on handicap. Awards are renewable annually subject to satisfactory overall progress. All bursars will be entitled to the comprehensive support programme that includes planning and development programmes, fitness and nutritional guidance, psychology workshops and sports medicine services.

Architecture

A £300 scholarship is awarded to the best second-year student. Four £1,500 travelling scholarships are also awarded.

Music Scholarships

The School of Music is endowed with several valuable scholarships and prizes available to both undergraduate and postgraduate students. Many scholarships and prizes are awarded to outstanding students either during or at the end of their period of study but the following award programmes are available to prospective students as Entrance Scholarships.

Morfydd Owen Scholarship for Wind Players

One Entrance Scholarship of £500, tenable for one year, is available to a wind player of promising standard entering the school.

Morfydd Owen Scholarships for String Players

Three annual scholarships of £500 each are awarded to string players reading for a degree in Music.

David Lloyd Vocal Scholarship

One Entrance Scholarship of £250, tenable for one year, is available to a singer of promising standard entering the school.

Choral Scholarships

Llandaff Cathedral offers three Choral Scholarships of approximately £1,200 per year (male alto, tenor and bass). For further details contact Richard Morehouse, 1 St Mary's, The Cathedral Green, Llandaff, Cardiff CF5 2EB, tel: 029 2057 5218.

The Metropolitan Cathedral of St David offers Choral Scholarships of approximately £350 per year. For further details contact Dr David Neville, St John's College, College Green, Newport Road, St Mellons, Cardiff CF3 9YX.

Organ Scholarship

The Metropolitan Cathedral of St David offers an Organ Scholarship of approximately £500 per year, in association with the School of Music. For further details contact Dr David Neville, St John's College, College Green, Newport Road, St Mellons, Cardiff CF3 9YX.

Welsh Applicants Scholarships

A number of scholarships are awarded to Welsh applicants on the basis of a two-hour examination.

Undergraduate Scholarships

A limited number of scholarships are available, currently worth £300 per year and payable for three years. These are either academic scholarships or based on the student's performance in Year 1 in the School of Architecture; four travelling £1,500 scholarships are awarded at first-degree level.

University Bursaries

These are worth £500 and are awarded for one year to disabled students, dyslexic students and those with children.

Cricket

The England and Wales Cricket Board has designated Cardiff University as a Centre of Cricketing Excellence. The university participates in the UCCE Scheme for talented and ambitious young cricketers. Contact the head of sport and recreation services.

Travel Scholarships

These are the Charles Cole Travelling Scholarship and the Edward Loveluck Travelling Scholarship (for students following courses in Architecture and City and Regional Planning). The following schools/departments offer a range of scholarships, prizes and travel awards: Architecture; Biosciences; Business; Chemistry; City and Regional Planning; Computer Science; Earth Sciences; Engineering; English; European Studies; History and Archeology; Journalism; Law; Mathematics; Media and Cultural Studies; Music; Pharmacy; Welsh.

AWARDS FOR NON-EU STUDENTS
Law Scholarships
These are offered to international students on the basis of academic merit (grades AAA–AAB at A-level or equivalent). They are worth £1,000 in the reduction of fees.

INFORMATION AND APPROXIMATE FEES FOR NON-EU STUDENTS
There are 3,500 international students from 100 countries. **English language entry requirement:** IELTS 6.5 (or equivalent). There is a comprehensive selection of pre-sessional language courses from three weeks to nine months. **Fees:** arts-based courses £9,500; science-based courses (including Archaeology, Music and Marine Geography) £12,000. **Living costs:** £6,500–£7,500.

Cardiff University, 46 Park Place, Cardiff CF10 3AT; tel: 029 208 79999; www.cardiff.ac.uk.

CARDIFF (UWIC)

The University of Wales Institute, Cardiff, was founded in 1996, originally being known as the South Glamorgan Institute. It offers degree and higher diploma courses, with over 4,000 students taking BA and BSc courses. The institute is based on four campuses, each providing teaching bases for different subject groups. Transport is provided between campuses, which are convenient from the city centre.

DEGREE SUBJECTS OFFERED
Architectural Design and Construction; Art and Design; Biomedical Science; Business and Management (available with languages); Education and Teacher Training; Engineering Design Systems; Environmental Sciences; Food and Consumer Sciences; Health; Hospitality (available with languages); Humanities; IT and Computer Studies; Product Design; Social Sciences; Sport and Leisure; Tourism (available with languages).

TUITION FEES (2009/10)
See www.studentfinancewales.co.uk and **Chapter 1, 'Financing your course'.**

BURSARIES AND OTHER AWARDS
Sports Scholarships
These are valued at £1,000 per year for the agreed duration of your course. In some cases, the scholarship may be supplemented by additional sponsorship. You will receive Gold Card membership of the Sport and Leisure Club, specialist coaching, advice on planning your academic and competitive programme, liaison with national governing bodies and private healthcare insurance. Other services available are fitness training and monitoring, performance analysis, sports psychology, nutritional advice, physiotherapy and podiatry.

Entry Scholarships
These are awarded to high achievers on the basis of tariff point scores. Each scholarship is worth £1,000.

Food Industry Bursary
This award is open to those studying for the HNB/BSc in Food Science and Technology. Payments are made from £250 to £750.

Care Leavers Bursaries
Students who from the age of 14 have been in local authority or foster care can apply for this bursary worth £1,000.

POSTGRADUATE AWARDS
Awards of £1,000 are offered to students embarking on Taught Masters courses.

INFORMATION AND APPROXIMATE FEES FOR NON-EU STUDENTS
There are just over 300 international students. **English language entry requirement:** IELTS 6.0 (or equivalent). **Fees:** £7,500–£8,500. **Living costs:** £6,500–£7,500.

University of Wales Institute, Cardiff, PO Box 377, Llandaff Campus, Western Avenue, Cardiff CF5 2SG; tel: 029 2041 6070; www.uwic.ac.uk.

CENTRAL LANCASHIRE UNIVERSITY (UCLan)

The University of Central Lancashire is located close to Preston city centre. All degree courses come in a series of modules allowing maximum flexibility in the choice of subjects. The student population of over 30,000 includes postgraduate and part-time students.

DEGREE SUBJECTS OFFERED
Accounting; Advertising; American Studies; Art and Design; Asia Pacific Studies; Astronomy; Audio-visual Media; Biochemistry; Biological Sciences; Biomedical Science; Business; Business Information Systems; Complementary Medicine; Computing; Conservation; Contemporary Performing Arts; Counselling Studies; Criminology; Deaf Studies; Design Studies; Drama; Economics; Ecotourism; Education; Engineering (Building Services; Electronic); English; Environment; Fashion; Film and Media; Fire Safety; Forensic Science; Forestry; Geography; Graphic Design; Health; Heritage; History; Hospitality; Human Resource Management; Illustration; International Business; Journalism; Languages; Law; Linguistics; Management; Marketing; Mathematics; Media; Microbiology; Midwifery; Motor Sports; Nursing; Philosophy; Photography; Physics; Politics; Psychology; Public Relations; Race and Ethnic Studies; Retail Management; Social Work Policy; Sociology; Space Science; Sport Studies; Sports Science; Statistics; Surveying; Tourism and Leisure; Visual Culture.

TUITION FEES (2009/10)
£3,225.

BURSARIES AND OTHER AWARDS
Ones to Watch Scholarship
In addition to possible government support, the Ones to Watch Scholarship, worth £1,000 per year, will be available to all UK, full-time undergraduate students starting out at UCLan in 2007 who come from homes where the principal earner's gross salary is less than £60,000 per year.

Excellence Scholarships
The university offers 100 Excellence Scholarships, each worth £2,000, for students who put UCLan as their first choice.

The scholarships focus on subjects with national skills shortages, eg Engineering and sciences. Other courses targeted for the awards include a number of health-related programmes as well as Design and Technology, Law and Business. Students excelling in sport also qualify for the scheme.

The scholarships are awarded to students with predicted grades amounting to at least 300 points and on the basis of their UCAS applications. In the case of the Excellence Scholarships for Sports, applicants must demonstrate outstanding sporting achievement.

Harris Bursary Fund
Additional financial support may be available for local students.

Institute of Physics Bursary
Scholarships worth £1,000 are offered by the Institute to eligible students taking courses in Physics and Astrophysics.

POSTGRADUATE AWARDS
Bursaries are also offered to all of the university's graduates to continue at the university with post-graduate study. They are a bursary equivalent to 20% of their postgraduate fees.

INFORMATION AND APPROXIMATE FEES FOR NON-EU STUDENTS
There is a large international student population from many countries. **English language entry requirement:** IELTS 6.0 (or equivalent). Competence in written and spoken English is required on application. **Fees:** undergraduate courses £9,000; **Living costs:** £6,000–£7,000.

University of Central Lancashire, Preston PR1 2HE; tel: 01772 201201; www.uclan.ac.uk.

CENTRAL SCHOOL OF SPEECH AND DRAMA (CSSD) (LONDON)

The Central School is located on two sites, one in North London at Swiss Cottage and a second at Kennington Oval, both within easy reach of central London. The school does not usually permit students to work part time without advance notice. Students are assisted in finding suitable lodgings since there is no accommodation in the school.

DEGREE SUBJECTS OFFERED
Acting; Costume Construction; Design for the Stage; Drama and Education; Puppetry; Theatre Practice.

TUITION FEES (2009/10)
£3,225. Fees may vary depending on the length of the course: contact the school.

BURSARIES AND OTHER AWARDS
Bursaries
Depending on parental income the maximum bursary is £2,835 for household incomes below £25,000. Partial bursaries are also available. Students who qualify for the full maintenance grant will also receive a Central Bursary of £305 per year.

Milner Bursaries
These are awarded to students taking courses in Drama, Applied Theatre and Education and for PGCE students taking Media Studies and Drama.

Diana Wade Memorial Awards
These bursaries worth £1,000 are offered to students taking Acting course options.

POSTGRADUATE AWARDS

Some awards are made to students taking MA degrees in Drama and Movement Therapy, Applied Theatre and Voice Studies.

INFORMATION AND APPROXIMATE FEES FOR NON-EU STUDENTS

Fees: vary depending on the course. **Living costs:** £10,000.

Central School of Speech and Drama, Embassy Theatre, 9 Eton Avenue, London NW3 3HY; tel: 020 7722 8183; www.cssd.ac.uk.

CHESTER UNIVERSITY

The University of Chester, originally a Church of England college, was founded in 1839 and became a university in 2005. It has two campuses, one close to the city centre and a second some distance away in Warrington. There is a student population of 8,000.

DEGREE SUBJECTS OFFERED

Advertising; Animal Sciences; Art and Design; Biology; Biomedical Science; Business Studies; Communication Studies; Community Studies; Computer Science; Criminology; Dance; Drama; English; French; Geography; German; Health Science; History; History of Art; Human Nutrition; International Studies; Journalism; Law; Marketing; Mathematics; Media Studies; Nutrition and Dietetics; PE/Sport Science; Photography; Popular Music; Psychology; Publishing; Religious Studies; Social Studies; Spanish; Sport Sciences; Teacher Training; Tourism; Urban Studies.

TUITION FEES (2009/10)

£3,225.

BURSARIES AND OTHER AWARDS

The means-tested bursary scheme is based on household income. Students from households earning £25,000 or less will receive the full maintenance grant of £2,906 or more and will also receive a Chester Bursary of £1,000.

Music Scholarships

An Organ Scholarship, currently worth £750, is available to a suitable candidate. The role involves taking an active part in playing and supporting music in the university, especially through the Chapel. Details are available from the Director of Music, Vicki Bulgin.

Other Music Scholarships are available to suitable candidates: two based around the choir, currently worth £800 each, and two based around the orchestra, currently worth £150 each. The roles involve playing lead parts in the choral and instrumental activities of the university and the Chapel. Details are available from the Director of Music, Vicki Bulgin.

Choral Scholarships at Chester Cathedral

Alto, tenor and bass Choral Scholarships in Chester Cathedral Choir are available, by audition, to students at Chester. Scholarships are currently worth £1,750 per year and tenable for one year in the first instance. Further details are available from the Cathedral Organist, 12 Abbey Square, Chester CH1 2HU.

See Chapters 2, 4 and 6 for additional awards, applicable to all universities

Sports Scholarship Scheme

The scholarship geared to elite athletes in worth up to £1,000. University of Chester Sports Scholars are selected on the basis of their sporting prowess and places are offered on a selective basis to suitably qualified applicants, by a panel appointed by the Deputy Director of Sport. Applicants must be willing and able to represent the university at the highest level through playing and/or coaching. The scholarships are offered to students who have gained admission to a course on the basis of their academic qualifications. For further information about Sports Scholarships, contact Dr Stewart Bruce-Low, Director of Fitness and Training; tel: 01244 511000.

AWARDS FOR NON-EU STUDENTS

All international students applying for a place on a course will automatically become eligible to apply for an award worth £1,000.

POSTGRADUATE AWARDS

Four bursaries are awarded each year to PhD students to cover the cost of fees.

INFORMATION AND APPROXIMATE FEES FOR NON-EU STUDENTS

English language entry requirement: IELTS 6.0 (or equivalent). **Fees:** classroom-based courses £7,100–£8,500. **Living costs:** £6,000–£7,000.

All applicants for taught or research programmes will be eligible for an award worth £1,000.

University of Chester, Parkgate Road, Chester CH1 4BJ; tel: 01244 511000; www. chester.ac.uk.

CHICHESTER UNIVERSITY

The University of Chichester's reputation for teaching excellence dates back to 1839. Bishop Otter College (1839) and Bognor Regis College (1946) merged in 1977 to become the University of Chichester in 2005. There are over 4,300 students. BA and BSc courses are offered. There are single honours courses and over 60 joint honours options. In addition there are over 80 major/minor subject combinations.

DEGREE SUBJECTS OFFERED

Adventure Education; Business, IT and Tourism; Business Studies; Business Studies and IT; Childhood Studies; Childhood, Youth and Society; Commercial Music; Counselling; Dance; English; English and Creative Writing; Exercise and Health Science; Fine Art; History; Instrumental or Vocal Teaching; IT; Maths Enhancement; Media Production and Media Studies; Music; Music Technology; Performing Arts; Social Care; Social Work; Sport and Exercise Psychology; Sport and Exercise Science; Sport and Fitness Management; Sport Coaching Science; Sports Studies (Sports Development); Sports Therapy; Teacher Education (Primary, 5–11 years) – Citizenship, English, ICT, Maths, Natural Science and Advanced Study of Early Years (3–7 years). Secondary – Mathematics and Physical Education; Theology; Tourism Management and Youth and Community Work.

TUITION FEES (2009/10)

£3,225.

BURSARIES AND OTHER AWARDS
Chichester Bursaries
Bursaries are available to 'home' students who are eligible for a maintenance grant. Bursaries are awarded on a sliding scale dependent on the residual income. Thus when the income is £25,000 or below the Chichester bursary award is £1,077 plus the local authority maintenance grant of £2,906. At the other end of the scale a residual income of up to £49,999 will attract a bursary of £256.

Talented Sports Performer Bursary Scheme
Bursaries of up to £500 per year are offered to outstanding sports persons to assist their endeavours whilst studying at the University of Chichester.

INFORMATION AND APPROXIMATE FEES FOR NON-EU STUDENTS
English language entry requirement: IELTS 6.0 (or equivalent). Pre-sessional English courses are available for students with IELTS scores between 5.0 and 5.5 (or equivalent). **Fees:** £7,400–£8,200; **Living costs:** £7,000–£8,000.

University of Chichester, Bishop Otter Campus, College Lane, Chichester, West Sussex PO19 6PE; tel: 01243 816002; www.chi.ac.uk.

CITY UNIVERSITY (LONDON)

City University was founded in 1895 and is located in the London Metropolitan Borough of Islington. The Business School is based in the Barbican Centre; the School of Nursing being part of St Bartholomew's Hospital. There is a student population of over 10,000.

DEGREE SUBJECTS OFFERED
Accountancy; Actuarial Science; Banking; Business Computing Systems; Business Studies; Computing; Design and Management; Economics; Engineering (Aeronautical; Air Transport; Automotive and Motorsport; Biomedical; Civil; Computer Systems; Electronic/Electrical; Mechanical; Software; Systems and Control); Journalism; Law; Management and Systems; Mathematics; Media Communication Systems; Midwifery; Music; Nursing; Optometry; Psychology; Radiography; Social Science; Sociology.

TUITION FEES (2009/10)
£3,225.

BURSARIES AND OTHER AWARDS
There are bursaries of £770 per year for students in receipt of the full grant, some partial bursaries and pro rata bursaries for students in receipt of partial support.

Department Scholarships
Most academic departments offer various scholarships. Please check: www.city.ac.uk/studentcentre/support/scholarships/School.html for more details.

Academic Prizes
Monetary prizes are awarded each year following high academic achievement in the first or second year of the course.

See Chapters 2, 4 and 6 for additional awards, applicable to all universities

Worshipful Company of Needlemakers Awards
One scholarship of £1,000 per year.

Worshipful Company of Saddlers
Two awards of £1,000 paid each year of the course open for applications from students who completed their post-16 education in Islington.

Shirley Robson Memorial Scholarship
An award is offered worth £1,000 for one year to an undergraduate student of Music.

For more information on funding, please visit: www.city.ac.uk/studentcentre

INFORMATION AND APPROXIMATE FEES FOR NON-EU STUDENTS
English Language entry requirement: IELTS 6.0 (or equivalent). **Fees:** £8,000–£10,000. **Living costs:** £9,000.

City University London, Northampton Square, London EC1V OHB; tel 020 7040 5060; www.city.ac.uk

---

CLEVELAND COLLEGE OF ART AND DESIGN

Courses are offered in a variety of art and design fields, courses being validated by the University of Teesside. There are 600 students based on campuses in Middlesbrough and Hartlepool.

DEGREE SUBJECTS OFFERED
Antiques and Design: Theory and Practice; Applied Arts; Commercial Photography; Contemporary Textile Practice; Costume Construction for Entertainment Design Crafts; Fashion Enterprise; Fashion Design and Production; Graphic Design; Innovative Surfaces; Jewellery Design and Accessories; Photography; Stage and Screen; Textiles and Surface Design; TV and Film Production.

TUITION FEES (2009/10)
£3,225.

BURSARIES AND OTHER AWARDS
A variable bursary is paid depending on personal circumstances. Maximum of £1,350; minimum of £305. A £250 Welcome Grant is also paid to all students during their first year of study.

Excellence Scholarships
Students whose entry qualifications equate to 300 or more UCAS points (including two grade Bs at A-level, or three Bs in the Scottish Advanced Highers or DDD or DDM in National Diplomas) will receive a £1,000 scholarship.

INFORMATION AND APPROXIMATE FEES FOR NON-EU STUDENTS
Contact the College

Cleveland College of Art and Design, Green Lane, Linthorpe, Middlesbrough TS5 7RJ; tel: 01642 288000; website: www.ccad.ac.uk.

COURTAULD INSTITUTE OF ART (LONDON)

The Courtauld Institute of Art, founded in 1932, is the major centre in Britain for the study of the history and conservation of Western art, and one of the premier art history institutes in the world. The institute has approximately 400 students and all the advantages of being a small institution in terms of contact with teachers and other students, both undergraduate and postgraduate. It is also a college of the University of London, and its students enjoy access to a broad range of facilities throughout the university.

DEGREE SUBJECTS OFFERED
BA and MA History of Art; MA Painting Conservation (Wall Painting); MA Curating the Art Museum; PG Diploma Conservation of Easel Paintings.

TUITION FEES (2009/10)
£3,225.

BURSARIES AND OTHER AWARDS
Four bursaries of £4,000 per year have been established to encourage undergraduate students to study at the Courtauld Institute. These awards will be granted to students who are in receipt of the full Higher Education Maintenance Grant and come from a group previously under-represented at Courtauld. These major bursaries will be in the form of fee waivers or maintenance grants. All students in receipt of a full government maintenance grant are guaranteed an Institute bursary of £319 per year for each of the three years of the programme. There are also a range of travel grants for students.

POSTGRADUATE AWARDS
Thanks to the generosity of many individuals, trusts, foundations and organisations the Institute can provide scholarships to approximately 40 students each year, which may cover or contribute towards fees and/or maintenance costs.

INFORMATION AND APPROXIMATE FEES FOR NON-EU STUDENTS
Approximately 25–30% of students come from overseas. **English language entry requirement:** IELTS 7.0 (or equivalent) for undergraduates and 7.5 (or equivalent) for postgraduates. There is English language support. **Fees:** undergraduate courses £11,804; postgraduate art history courses £11,804; postgraduate conservation courses £14,437. **Living costs:** £12,000.

Courtauld Institute of Art, Somerset House, Strand, London WC2R 0RN; tel: 020 7848 2645; Ugadmissions@courtauld.ac.uk, or Pgadmissions@courtauld.ac.uk; www.courtauld.ac.uk.

COVENTRY UNIVERSITY

Coventry University (a purpose-built university) was founded in 1970 and is situated on a 33-acre site in Coventry city centre. All degree courses are based on a modular structure giving maximum flexibility for a choice of course and options. Higher National Diploma courses are also offered in several subject areas in full-time and sandwich options. There is a student population of over 17,000.

DEGREE SUBJECTS OFFERED

Accounting; Aerospace Technology; Applied Chemistry; Applied Ecology; Architectural Design Technology; Art and Craft; Art and Design; Automotive Technology; Autotronics; Biochemistry; Biological Sciences; Biomedical Sciences; Building Engineering; Building Surveying; Business (Administration; Computing; Economics; Enterprise; Information Technology; Studies); Chemistry; Communications and Media; Computer Science; Computer Systems; Computing; Construction Management; Dance; Dietetics; E-Commerce; Economics; Emergency and Disaster Management; Engineering (Aerospace Systems; Automotive; Avionics; Business and Technology; Civil; Communications Systems; Computer; Countryside Change and Management; Electrical/Electronic; Information Systems; International Disaster; Manufacturing; Mechanical; Software; Systems); Environmental (Biology; Chemistry; Monitoring and Assessment; Science); E-Technology; European (Business; Law; Studies); Exercise Physiology; Exercise Science; French; Geography; German; Health Science; History; Human Nutrition; Industrial Product Design; International Economics; International Relations; Italian; Law; Leisure Management; Manufacturing Management; Mathematics; Mechanical Technology; Medical Instrumentation; Multimedia Computing; Multimedia Design and Technology; Occupational Therapy; People Management; Performing Arts and Event Technology; Pharmaceutical (Chemistry; Sciences); Physiotherapy; Politics; Polymer Science; Product Design and Manufacture; Property Management; Psychology; Recreation and the Countryside; Risk and Emergency Management; Russian; Social (Policy; Public Health and Health Promotion; Welfare; Work); Sociology; Spanish; Sport and Exercise Science; Sport Management; Statistics; Telecommunications Systems; Third World Development; Tourism and Marketing; Tourism Management; Transport Design; Women's Studies.

TUITION FEES (2009/10)

£3,225.

BURSARIES AND OTHER AWARDS

There will be a bursary of £320 for eligible undergraduate students from households with an income of up to £50,020 per year and who qualify for an award of the full or partial maintenance grant from the UK government. For further information on undergraduate bursaries and UK/EU scholarships contact: The Student Funding Office, tel: 024 7615 2040 or 2050; fundingsupport @coventry.ac.uk; www.coventry.ac.uk/cu/student funding.

Academic Scholarship

Value: £2,000 per annum. **Number available:** Unlimited. **Qualifications:** 320 UCAS Tariff points from three full A-levels (General Studies and VCE Advanced Awards included) or equivalent qualifications (such as BTEC National Diploma or an Access Course) or an International Baccalaureate Diploma with at least 31 points. **Duration:** Whole of course subject to renewal criteria (normally 3 years maximum). **Application:** Students must apply by downloading an application form from the Student Funding website.

Science, Technology, Engineering and Mathematics (STEM)

Value: £3,225 for 2009. (Linked to tuition fees.) Eligible students will be entitled to have the full cost of their tuition fees paid. **Number available:** Unlimited. **Qualifications:** Students must be studying on an eligible course which can be identified by the atomic symbol in our Prospectus and achieve 320 UCAS Tariff points from three full A-levels or equivalent qualifications (see Academic Scholarship criteria). **Duration:** Whole of course subject to renewal criteria (normally 3 years maximum). **Application:** Students must apply by downloading an application form from the Student Funding website.

Achievement Scholarship

Value: £1,000 per annum. **Number available:** Unlimited. **Qualifications:** Students must gain at least 70% or more average mark across all modules in your first year at Coventry (please note that those students already eligible for a scholarship cannot be considered). **Duration:** Second and subsequent years subject to academic performance in the previous year and renewal criteria. **Application:** Students do not have to apply as eligible students will be identified from records.

SCHOLARSHIPS LINKED TO PRACTICAL PERFORMANCE ACHIEVEMENT
Creative or Performing Arts Scholarship
Value: £2,000 per annum. **Number available:** Limited to 60 (reserve list kept). **Qualifications:** Linked to prior performance where student must demonstrate a high level of originality and/or artistic ability. Students will be expected to continue to develop their creative interest whilst at the University. **Duration:** Whole of course subject to renewal criteria (normally 3 years maximum). **Application:** Students must apply by downloading an application form from the Student Funding website.

Sports Scholarship
Value: Up to £4,000 per annum (combination of cash and support services). **Number available:** Limited to 50 (reserve list kept). **Qualifications:** Linked to prior performance where student must demonstrate excellence in a sporting activity recognised by the Central Council for Physical Recreation. This must include representation at regional and national level whilst also representing the University. **Duration:** Whole of course subject to renewal criteria (normally 3 years maximum). **Application:** Students must apply by downloading an application form from the Student Funding website.

Enterprise Scholarship
Value: £2,000 per annum. **Number available:** Limited to 50 (reserve list kept). **Qualifications:** Linked to prior performance where student must demonstrate a high level of creativity, enterprise and innovation. Students will be expected to continue high achievement in their enterprise activity whilst at the University. **Duration:** Whole of course subject to renewal criteria (normally 3 years maximum). **Application:** Students must apply by downloading an application form from the Student Funding website.

EU DIRECT ENTRY SCHOLARSHIPS
EU Partnership Scholarship
Value: £300 per annum. **Number available:** Unlimited. **Qualifications:** Available to students who come to Coventry University for years two, three or four of their academic year study from a partner institution. **Duration:** Only available for first year of study. **Application:** Applications will be available from course tutors once students have enrolled.

EU Achievement Scholarship
Value: Two levels – £600 and £1,000. **Number available:** Unlimited. **Qualifications:** Available to students who come to Coventry University for years two, three or four of their academic year study. Students must have a good previous academic achievement record. **Duration:** Only available for first year of study but students can transfer to the Achievement Scholarship for the following academic year subject to criteria. **Application:** Applications will be available from course tutors once students have enrolled.

AWARDS FOR NON-EU STUDENTS
The university offers partial scholarships each year to new international students to reward outstanding academic merit and personal achievement. Undergraduate Scholarships of £6,900 are available for a three-year full-time programme, encompassing £2,000 for the first year, £2,000 for the second and £2,900 for the third year of study. Contact Halima Iqbal in the International Office for updated information.

See Chapters 2, 4 and 6 for additional awards, applicable to all universities

POSTGRADUATE AWARDS

Postgraduate scholarships of £2,000 are offered to students irrespective of subject. The Overseas Research Award Scheme is available for PhD programmes and is offered on a competitive basis for postgraduate students of outstanding merit and research potential. Contact Jayne Roberts in the Post Graduate Centre for updated information.

INFORMATION AND APPROXIMATE FEES FOR NON-EU STUDENTS

There are 2,500 international students. **English language entry requirement:** IELTS 6.0 (or equivalent). **Fees:** £7,200; foundation courses £4,500. **Living costs:** £6,700.

Coventry University, Student Funding Office, The Student Centre, Priory Street, Coventry CV1 5FB; tel: 024 7615 2040; studentfinance@cov.ac.uk; www.coventry.ac.uk/cu/studentfunding.

CRICHTON UNIVERSITY CAMPUS (Glasgow/West of Scotland Universities)

The campus caters for students at the Dumfries and Galloway College and for those willing to take some degree courses through the universities of Glasgow and the West of Scotland (formerly Paisley). There are some 1,000 students on campus.

DEGREE SUBJECTS OFFERED

Accounting; Business Administration (with European Studies/Human Resource Management/ Information Management or Marketing/Tourism); Childhood Studies; Computing; Health and Social Studies; Liberal Arts; Scottish Studies.

TUITION FEES (2009/10)

Students domiciled in Scotland receive free tuition. See www.saas.gov.uk and **Chapter 1 'Financing Your Course'**.

BURSARIES AND OTHER AWARDS
Crichton University Scholarship Agreement (CUSA)

The Crichton University Scholarship Agreement is a new scheme designed to encourage local students to take up degree courses and to study locally in Dumfries and Galloway on the Crichton University Campus.

At present CUSA is a joint scheme between Dumfries and Galloway College, and the universities of Glasgow and the West of Scotland. It is principally targeted at two groups of students:

* Those who need further encouragement and assistance to realise their potential
* Those who for personal or family reasons wish to continue their education locally.

CUSA is therefore both socially inclusive and designed to help reduce rural depopulation, as well as developing the Crichton University Campus.

Local school pupils will sign on as CUSA students and will gain the following:

* A bursary of £200 per year for up to four years
* A guaranteed place on a degree course with alternate routes should they not gain suitable grades at Higher

* A package of benefits including use of university facilities
* Help and support in attaining targets.

INFORMATION AND APPROXIMATE FEES FOR NON-EU STUDENTS
Contact the college.

Maxwell House, Crichton University Campus, Dumfries DG1 4UQ; tel: 01387 702075; www.crichtoncampus.co.uk.

CUMBRIA UNIVERSITY

The University of Cumbria has campuses in Carlisle, Newton Rigg, Penrith, Ambleside and Lancaster, and a specialist teacher-education centre in London. A wide range of courses is offered which are specific to various campuses.

DEGREE SUBJECTS OFFERED
Accountancy, Animal Science, Applied Science, Art and Design, Biology, Business Studies, Community Studies, Creative Writing, Criminology, Dance, Drama, Education, English, Environment, Film Studies, Fine Art, Forestry, Geography, Health Studies, Information Technology, Journalism, Law, Logistics, Mathematics, Media Studies, Multimedia, Musical Theatre, Nursing, Occupational Therapy, Outdoor Studies, Performing Arts, Photography, Physiotherapy, Psychology, Policing, Radiography, Religious Studies, Social Sciences, Sport, Teacher Training, Youth Studies.

TUITION FEES (2009/10)
£3,225.

BURSARIES AND OTHER AWARDS
Cumbria Bursary
The Cumbria Bursary will be awarded to full-time home and EU undergraduate students who are paying variable tuition fees. The level of bursary awarded will depend upon the student's family residual income (see list below). These bursaries are non-repayable and are paid in three termly instalments.

* Band 1: income of £25,000 or less; bursary awarded is £1,290
* Band 2: income of £25,001–£35,000; bursary awarded is £1,070
* Band 3: income of £35,001–£50,020; bursary awarded is £430
* Band 4: income of £50,021 or more; bursary awarded is £215.

Please note that these figures are correct at the time of going to print but will be subject to change following the government's pending announcement about 2009/10 funding.

Cumbria Scholarships
A Cumbria Scholarship is an award worth £1,000 per year which students may apply for if they are a first year undergraduate home student, are being charged the new variable fee, and can demonstrate significant achievement or potential in sport, community, creative arts, the environment or business enterprise and entrepreneurship. There are 35 scholarships available, seven in each specialist area.

The scholarship is conditional upon students meeting both the general criteria and the specialist criteria outlined on both the application form and the accompanying terms and conditions document. Any scholarships awarded are in addition to any bursary support provided.

See Chapters 2, 4 and 6 for additional awards, applicable to all universities

Successful students will receive the £1,000 scholarship for each year of their course, providing that they continue to meet the conditions of the scholarship and meet course requirements in relation to attendance and achievement.

INFORMATION AND APPROXIMATE FEES FOR NON-EU STUDENTS
English language entry requirement: IELTS 6.0 (or equivalent). **Fees:** £7,550. **Living costs:** £8,000.

University of Cumbria, Fusehill Street, Carlisle CA1 2HH, tel: 01228 616234; www. cumbria.ac.uk.

DE MONTFORT UNIVERSITY

At De Montfort University (DMU) many courses are professionally accredited or linked to employers. Most of the 19,000 students are based at the modern City Campus, in the heart of Leicester. The Nursing and Midwifery students are based at the Charles Frears Campus, with industry-standard clinical skills facilities.

DEGREE SUBJECTS OFFERED
Accounting; Advertising; Applied Criminology; Architecture; Art and Design (Foundation Studies); Artificial Intelligence; Arts and Festivals Management; Audiology; Audio and Recording Technology; Biomedical Sciences; Business; Business Information Systems; Clinical Physiology; Clothing; Computer Science; Computing; Contour Fashion; Creative Writing; Dance; Design and Technology; Drama; Education Studies; Engineering (Electronic/Mechanical/Software); English; Fashion Design; Finance; Fine Art; Footwear; Forensic Science; Furniture Design; Game Art Design; Graphic Design; Health Studies; History; Human Communication; Human Resource Management; Interactive Design; International Business; Journalism; Law; Marketing; Media and Communication; Media Production/Technology; Midwifery; Multimedia Computing; Music Technology; Nursing; Performing Arts; Pharmaceutical and Cosmetic Science; Pharmacy; Photography and Video; Politics; Product Design; Psychology; Public Administration; Public Policy; Radio Production; Social Work; Textiles Design; Video and Animation Production; Youth and Community Development.

TUITION FEES (2009/10)
£3,225.

BURSARIES AND OTHER AWARDS
There are bursaries of £600 for eligible students in receipt of a maintenance grant and with household incomes of £40,000 or less; and £300 for eligible students in receipt of a maintenance grant and household income of between £40,001–£50,020.

Academic Scholarships
This scholarship is worth £1,700 per year (excluding paid placement years) and is available to eligible students achieving 300 or more UCAS points in one academic sitting from three A-levels or equivalent A2 level qualifications.

Access Scholarships
£1,000 per year (excluding paid placement years) for students with an Access to Higher Education qualification (where this is an entry requirement for the course).

Looked-After/Estranged Children Bursary

This bursary is worth £1,000 per year (excluding paid placement years) and is available to eligible students entering the University from care and includes all children being looked after by a local authority at the time of application.

AWARDS FOR NON-EU STUDENTS
The Vice-Chancellor's International Scholarship

Full-time overseas students may apply for the Vice-Chancellor's International Scholarship worth £500. Full details of this scholarship are available on the website at dmu.ac.uk/international.

POSTGRADUATE AWARDS
Alumni Scholarships

All DMU Alumni are offered a £500 scholarship towards the full tuition fees of certain post-graduate courses. To qualify, students must have previously studied and successfully completed a course, of nine months or more in duration (full-time, part-time or distance learning), at any De Montfort University UK campus. Full details of this scholarship are available at www.dmu.ac.uk/grow.

INFORMATION AND APPROXIMATE FEES FOR NON-EU STUDENTS

There are approximately 2,000 international students from over 100 countries. **English language entry requirement:** usually IELTS 6.5 (or equivalent). Free pre-sessional English courses and continuing support are available from the British Council-accredited English Language Learning Centre, along with an International Welcome Week in September for all students. **Fees:** £8,500–£9,500. **Living costs:** £7,500-£8,500.

De Montfort University, The Gateway, Leicester LE1 9BH; tel: 0116 255 1551; www.dmu.ac.uk.

DERBY UNIVERSITY

Derby University has two campuses in the heart of the UK, Derby and Buxton, 30 miles apart. Derby is a bustling city about 30 minutes from Nottingham and an hour from Birmingham. Buxton is a picturesque small town in the middle of beautiful Peak District countryside, about an hour from Derby and Manchester.

DEGREE SUBJECTS OFFERED

Accounting and Finance; Advanced Computer Systems; Adventure Tourism; American Studies; Biology; Broadcast Media; Business; Children's and Young People's Services; Computing; Control and Instrumentation; Counselling; Countryside Management; Criminology; Culinary Arts; Early Childhood Studies; Education Studies; English; Electrical and Electronic Engineering; Enterprise Computing; Enterprise Management; Environmental Hazards; Environmental Health; Environmental Management; Events Management; Fashion Studies; Film and Television Studies; Financial Services; Fine Art; Forensic Science/Studies; Geography; Geology; Hairdressing and Salon Management; Hand Therapy; Healing Arts; History; Hospitality; Human Resource Management; Humanities; International Business Management; International Spa Management; International Trade; Law; Marketing; Martial Arts Theory and Practice; Mathematics; Mechanical and Manufacturing Engineering; Media Production; Media Studies; Media Writing; Occupational Therapy; Outdoor Activities; Outdoor Recreation; Photography; Physical Activity and Health; Popular Culture and Media; Psychology; Public Relations; Public Services; Social and Cultural Studies; Social Studies;

Sociology; Spa Management; Spa Therapies; Sports Coaching; Sports Development; Sports Massage and Exercise Therapy; Sports Studies/Science; Strategic Financial Management; Strategic Management; Textile Design; Third World Development; Travel and Tourism; Visual Communication (Graphic Design, Animation or Illustration); Web Based Systems; Zoology.

TUITION FEES (2009/10)
£3,225.

BURSARIES AND OTHER AWARDS
Bursaries are payable against household incomes as follows:

* £0–£25,625 – a bursary of £830 per year
* £25,626–£35,875 – a bursary of £520 per year
* £35,876–£51,520 – a bursary of £210 per year.

Local Bursaries
Students could qualify for a local bursary if they are paying tuition fees of £3,225 or £2,055 (for Foundation or HND courses).

* Students living in postal code areas: DE, NG, LE, B, ST, S, SK, DN, PE, CV or WS receive £300.
* Students from local Partner schools or colleges will receive £400.

EU Bursaries
EU students paying £3,225 in tuition fees may receive an EU Bursary if their household income is less than £12,500. The EU Bursary is £1,000.

AWARDS FOR NON-EU STUDENTS
Derby University has a limited number of partial scholarships available to non-EU students in their first year of study. They are awarded on the basis of academic merit, and take the form of a tuition fee discount, up to a maximum of £1,000 per student. In order to apply for a scholarship students must first have firmly accepted an unconditional offer to study at the University of Derby, and have also paid the required deposit.

POSTGRADUATE AWARDS
Check out: www.derby.ac.uk/postgraduate.

INFORMATION AND APPROXIMATE FEES FOR NON-EU STUDENTS
English language entry requirement: IELTS 6.0 (or equivalent). **Fees:** £7,800. **Living costs:** £7,200.

University of Derby, Kedleston Road, Derby DE22 1GB; tel: 01332 591130; international@ derby.ac.uk; www.derby.ac.uk.

DUMFRIES AND GALLOWAY COLLEGE OF TECHNOLOGY

(See also Crichton University Campus)

The college is located on five campus sites, the central campus being sited at Heathhall in Dumfries, which includes Moat Hall, the college's hall of residence providing 68 single study bedrooms. Other campuses are located at George Street, Dumfries, catering for Art, Design, Media and Drama, at Maxwell House on the Crichton University Campus, and at Stranraer and Newton Stewart for students in outlying areas.

DEGREE SUBJECTS OFFERED

Accounting; Business Administration; Child Care Studies; Computing; Construction; Electronics; European Studies; Information Management; Marketing.

TUITION FEES (2009/10)

Students domiciled in Scotland receive free tuition. See www.saas.gov.uk and **Chapter 1 'Financing your course'**.

BURSARIES AND OTHER AWARDS
Dumfriesshire Education Trust

This is for students either born or mainly educated within the former county of Dumfries. Applications are considered at the December meeting of the governors. Application forms and further information are available from the Education Offices, 30 Edinburgh Road, Dumfries DG1 3JQ; tel: 01387 261234.

Wigtown Educational Trust

This is for students residing in the former county of Wigtown. Assistance will be given to persons assessed for student grants and FE bursaries only in exceptional circumstances. Application forms and leaflets can be requested from the Department for Corporate Business, Council Offices, Sun Street, Stranraer DG9 7JJ.

Dumfries and Galloway College, Herries Avenue, Heathhall, Dumfries DG1 8LE; tel: 01387 261261; www.dumgal.ac.uk.

DUNDEE UNIVERSITY

The University of Dundee is located on a campus within 5 minutes walk of the city centre, on the east coast of Scotland. An established university, it has a progressive and dynamic outlook, constantly striving to build on its achievements: investing in excellent facilities, pushing the boundaries of research, and developing new ways of e-learning. Duncan of Jordanstone College of Art and Design is located within the University.

DEGREE SUBJECTS OFFERED

Accounting; American Studies; Anatomical Sciences; Animation, Applied Computing; Applied Physics; Architecture; Art and Design; Art, Philosophy, Contemporary Practices; Biochemistry;

Biological Chemistry and Drug Discovery; Biology; Biomedical Sciences; Biomolecular Drug Discovery; Business Economics with Marketing; Business Management; Civil Engineering; Community Education; Dentistry; Drug Design and Mechanisms; E-Commerce Computing; Economic Studies; Electronic Engineering; English; Environmental Science; Environmental Sustainability; European Philosophy; European Politics; European Studies; Finance; Financial Economics; Fine Art; Forensic Anthropology; French; Geography; German; Graphic Design; History; Illustration; Innovative Product Design; Interactive Media Design; Interior and Environmental Design; International Business; International Relations; Jewellery and Metal Design; Law; Mathematical Biology; Mathematics; Mechanical Engineering; Medicine; Microbiology; Midwifery; Molecular Biology; Molecular Genetics; Neuroscience; Nursing; Oral Health Sciences; Pharmacology; Philosophy; Physics; Planning; Politics; Primary Education; Psychology; Renewable Energy; Scots Law; Scottish Historical Studies; Social Work; Spanish; Spatial Economics; Sports Biomedicine; Textile Design; Time Based Art and Digital Film; Town and Regional Planning; Transatlantic Studies; Zoology.

TUITION FEES (2009/10)
Students domiciled in Scotland receive free tuition; see www.saas.gov.uk and **Chapter 1 'Financing Your Course'**.

BURSARIES AND OTHER AWARDS
Academic School Bursaries
Several academic schools offer scholarships and bursaries to incoming students, these include:

* Centre for Energy, Petroleum and Mineral Law and Policy
* School of Accounting and Finance
* School of Computing
* School of Engineering, Physics and Mathematics
* School of Humanities
* School of Law

City of Dundee Educational Trust
The trust offers financial support of up to £300 per year to students who are from, or have a strong connection with, Dundee. Contact the trust: tel: 01382 200000.

Golf Bursaries
In a scheme funded by the Royal and Ancient Golf Club, St Andrews, two bursaries are available each year to new undergraduates. Each bursary is intended to cover approved expenditure on equipment, green fees, tuition, competition fees and expenses and travel connected with golf. The bursary is renewable annually for up to four years, subject to satisfactory progress in both the student's academic work and golfing activity. Applicants must hold a single-figure golf handicap and have received from UCAS an unconditional or conditional offer of admission.

Excel Sports Scholarships
The Excel Sports Scholarship Programme is dedicated to supporting elite student athletes as they combine academic study with training and high levels of competition. It is the university's purpose to offer each athlete an individually tailored programme that will enable them to develop to the highest level of performance and excellence. In meeting the needs of elite student athletes the Excel Sports Scholarship Programme guarantees financial assistance with coaching, training and competition costs, a yearly education programme and options for extending the degree by one year.

Medicine and Dentistry
The Dow Memorial Trust awards a number of scholarships up to £2,000 per year for each of the five years of study, subject to a satisfactory academic record. All students awarded a place can apply.

Organ and Saxophone Bursaries

Five bursaries are available, one for organ and four for saxophone. Bursary holders will receive approximately 20 hours' free tuition in return for participating in university musical events. The Organ Bursary also carries a prize of £300 per year. Further information on these bursaries is available from the university musical adviser.

Please visit the website www.dundee.ac.uk/admissions/ for up to date information.

AWARDS FOR NON-EU STUDENTS
University of Dundee Overseas Student Scholarships

University of Dundee Overseas Student Scholarships are available to students on many undergraduate and postgraduate courses, these offer a £2,000 reduction on the tuition fee.

Visit www.dundee.ac.uk/admissions/international/fees_funding/ for full details.

INFORMATION AND APPROXIMATE FEES FOR NON-EU STUDENTS

English language entry requirement: IELTS 6.0 (or equivalent) for most courses.

Up to date tuition fees are available on the website, but are around £8,500–£11,000 for most courses.

Visit our website www.dundee.ac.uk/admissions/international/ for full details.

Admissions and Student Recruitment, University of Dundee, Dundee DD1 4HN; tel: 01382 383838. srs@dundee.ac.uk; www. dundee.ac.uk.

DURHAM UNIVERSITY

Durham University was founded in 1832. It is a collegiate university located in Durham City, with 14 colleges (one of which is for postgraduates only), the oldest of the colleges (University College) is housed in Durham Castle, which is part of a World Heritage Site with the stunning Cathedral. There are also two additional colleges on a modern purpose-built campus 25 miles away at Stockton.

DEGREE SUBJECTS OFFERED

Ancient History; Anthropology; Applied Psychology; Arabic; Archaeology; Biological Sciences; Biology; Biomedical Sciences; Business; Business Economics; Cell Biology; Chemistry; Chinese; Classical Past; Classics; Combined Studies; Computer Science; Earth Sciences; Ecology; Economics; Education Studies; Engineering (Civil; Electrical; Electronic; Information Systems; Manufacturing; Mechanical); English; Environmental Management; European Studies; French; Geography; Geology; Geosciences; German; History; Human Sciences; Italian; Japanese; Latin; Law; Management Studies; Mathematics; Medicine; Medieval Studies; Molecular Biology; Music; Natural Sciences; Philosophy; Plant Science; Politics; Psychology; Russian; Sociology; Software Engineering; Spanish; Sport; Theology; Zoology.

TUITION FEES (2009/10)
£3,225.

BURSARIES AND OTHER AWARDS
Durham Grant Scheme
The scheme offers non-repayable support over and above any grants or loans from the government. £1,300 per year guaranteed to full-time undergraduate students in receipt of the maximum Maintenance Grant or Special Support Grant from Student Finance England (or equivalent) – that's over and above all the support from Student Finance England (or equivalent). Students don't have to make a separate application for the Durham Grant – they just need to apply for statutory support from Student Finance England (or equivalent)

Vice-Chancellor's Scholarships for Sport, Music and the Performing Arts
One of the most important ways for students to further their personal development is by taking part in the extra-curricular activities on offer. Students at Durham are amongst the most active in the country in the fields of sport, music and the arts. 25 Vice-Chancellor's Scholarships for Sport, Music and the Performing Arts worth £3,000 will be awarded each per year for students starting their course in 2010/11 (or 2011/12 if deferring their place).

Vice-Chancellor's Scholarships for Academic Excellence
The University is proud of its commitment to academic excellence. This forms the corner stone of Durham's reputation and its popularity with students and employers alike. To support and promote academic excellence, the University will offer 30 scholarships for outstanding undergraduate academic performance.

Personal Development Award Funding
There are a number of funds which students can apply for once they have commenced their studies to help make the most of their time at Durham:

* Durham University Arts Management Group
* Durham University Expeditions Fund
* Durham University Funds for Student Travelling Abroad
* Personal Development Award Fund.

For further information see www.durham.ac.uk/undergraduate/finance.

Choral Scholarships
Choral Scholarships are open to incoming UK undergraduates and are awarded annually by the Dean and Chapter of Durham Cathedral. They are normally worth in the region of £1,430 – £2,000 per year. Details about the Choral Scholarships are usually available in August for entry in October the following year, with auditions taking place in late February/early March. The Chapter of Durham Cathedral offers an Organ Scholarship at the Cathedral which is normally held by an undergraduate or postgraduate student.

For more information contact the Student Financial Support Office on 0191 334 6145 or email student.support@durham.ac.uk.

AWARDS FOR NON-EU STUDENTS
Ustinov Scholarships
Scholarships are worth £2,000 per year (to be deducted from the tuition fees). All scholarships are for the duration of the course. Applicants must have IELTS 6.5 or equivalent at the time of application. Scholarships worth £2,000 per year (to be deducted from the tuition fees) are also available to nationals of and residents in Brunei, Hong Kong, Indonesia, Japan, Malaysia, Singapore, South Korea or Thailand. Applicants must be liable to pay the overseas fee rate and will be judged on academic merit. They must have already applied via UCAS for a course at Durham and have indicated a firm acceptance of an offer. Applicants must be able to demonstrate their ability to pay all other tuition and living costs while in the UK. Details are available from the International Office.

POSTGRADUATE AWARDS

Postgraduate studentship awards are offered for some courses. Students should contact Chris Harrop in the Student Financial Support Office chris.harrop@dur.ac.uk or 0191 334 6485.

Students should consult Durham's Postgraduate Funding Database which shows which scholarships are available and how to apply for them: http://www.dur.ac.uk/postgraduate/finance/search/.

INFORMATION AND APPROXIMATE FEES FOR NON-EU STUDENTS

There are 1,600 international students from over 120 countries. **English language entry requirement:** IELTS 6.5 (or equivalent). There is a three-day induction programme before the start of the academic year, and an intensive English language course if the standard of English does not meet the required level. **Fees:** Engineering, science and technology courses £13,770; all other (non-Durham Business School) courses £8,500. **Living costs:** £10,500.

Durham University, Old Shire Hall, Old Elvet, Durham DH1 3HP; tel: 0191 334 6102; www.dur.ac.uk.

EAST ANGLIA UNIVERSITY

The University of East Anglia was founded in 1963 and is located on a rural campus site two miles from Norwich, with a student population of over 14,000. Degree programmes are modular, taught on a two-semester year basis. There are now 23 academic schools of study, many of them interdisciplinary, allowing students to combine specialist courses with complementary subjects.

DEGREE SUBJECTS OFFERED

Accounting and Finance; Actuarial Science; American Studies; Archaeology and Anthropology; Art History; Biochemistry; Biological and Medicinal Chemistry; Biology; Biomedicine; Business and Management; Business Information Systems; Chemistry; Computing; Development Studies; Drama; Ecology; Economics; Education; English Literature and Creative Writing; English Studies; Environmental Chemistry; Environmental Earth Sciences; Environmental Sciences; European Studies; Film and Television Studies; French; Geography; Geophysical Sciences; History; International Studies; Law; Mathematics; Media and Culture; Medicine; Meteorology and Oceanography; Music; Natural Sciences; Nursing and Midwifery; Occupational Therapy and Physiotherapy; Pharmacy; Philosophy; Politics; Science with a foundation year; Social Work and Psychosocial Sciences; Spanish; Speech and Language Therapy; Translation and Interpreting.

TUITION FEES (2009/10)

£3,225.

BURSARIES AND OTHER AWARDS

Depending on the level of the maintenance grant, amounts payable range from £300 to £600.

Pathway Scholarships

These awards of £4,500 are open to students from households with an annual income of less than £60,000 and who achieve AAA grades at A-level.

American Studies Scholarship

The Arthur Miller Centre Scholarship is awarded as a travel grant worth £600 and is open to students spending a year abroad.

See Chapters 2, 4 and 6 for additional awards, applicable to all universities

Chemistry Scholarship
Awards worth up to £1,500 are made to all applicants to the School of Chemical Sciences and Pharmacy naming UEA as their first choice and who achieve ABB at A-level including Grade A in chemistry. Applicants achieving Grades BBB (excluding General Studies) are offered £1,000.

Pharmacy Scholarships
An award of £1,000 is offered to applicants choosing UEA as their firm choice who register on the MPharm degree course and who achieve A-level grades of AAA including chemistry and one other science.

Open Scholarship and Vice-Chancellor's Prizes
Awards worth £500 are offered to applicants achieving A-level grades of AAA.

Organ and Choral Scholarships
Students applying for the BA(Hons) Music degree may apply for the Organ Scholarship. Some Choral Awards are also made, in conjunction with Norwich Cathedral. There are many named scholarships available. Apply to the Admissions Officer, School of Music, East Anglia University, Norwich NR4 7TJ.

Sport
Awards are made up to a maximum of £1,000 to top performers to assist with training, equipment and competition costs.

Travel and Expeditions Awards
Grants are available to all students whilst special travel awards are also made to individuals.

EU Scholarship
An award of £500 is open to non-UK EU students subject to conditions.

AWARDS FOR NON-EU STUDENTS
Each year the university allocates £500,000 in scholarship funds for overseas students. Competition is considerable for these awards, which are based on academic merit. There are special awards for applicants from the following countries: Australia; Brazil; China; Hong Kong; India; Indonesia; Japan; Kenya; Malaysia; Mexico; Norway; Singapore; South Korea; Sri Lanka; Thailand; USA; Vietnam. Sponsorships and scholarships are also available to applicants in Computing Science.

POSTGRADUATE AWARDS
Awards for postgraduate study are also made in certain subjects.

INFORMATION AND APPROXIMATE FEES FOR NON-EU STUDENTS
There are 2,000 international students from 120 countries. **English language entry requirement:** IELTS 6.0 (or equivalent); some courses higher. There are four-, eight- and 12-week pre-sessional courses in English and tuition during degree courses. **Fees:** classroom-based courses £9,300; laboratory-based courses £11,500; Medicine £18,000. **Living costs:** £6,000–7,000.

University of East Anglia, Norwich NR4 7TJ; tel: 01603 456161; www.uea.ac.uk.

EAST LONDON UNIVERSITY

The University of East London was founded in 1970 and is based on two campuses in Barking and Stratford. Single honours, combined honours (two or three subject combinations), and HND courses are offered for a student population of over 12,500.

DEGREE SUBJECTS OFFERED

Accounting and Finance; Acting; Animal Biology; Anthropology; Applied Biology; Applied Language Studies; Archaeological Sciences; Architecture; Art and Design; Biochemistry; Biology; Biomedical Sciences; Biotechnology; Business Studies; Cinematics; Communications Studies; Computer Technology; Computing; Criminology and Criminal Justice; Cultural Studies; Development Studies; Distributed Information Systems; E-Commerce; Economics; Engineering (Civil; Electrical/Electronic; Extended; Manufacturing Systems; Telecommunications); Environmental Studies; European Studies; Fine Art; Fitness and Health; French; Gender and Sexualities; Geography; Global Media; Health Services Management; Health Studies; History; History of Art; Human Biology; Immunology; Infectious Diseases; Information Systems; Information Technology; International Business; International Social Work; Journalism and Print Media; Law; Linguistics; Literature; Manufacturing Systems Management; Mathematics; Media Studies; Nursing; Performing Arts in the Community; Pharmacology; Physiology; Physiotherapy; Playwork and Youth Studies; Politics; Product Design; Professional Nature Conservation; Property and Planning Information; Psychology; Psychosocial Studies; Social Policy; Social Sciences; Sociology; Software Engineering; Spanish; Spatial Business Information; Sports Development; Statistics; Surveying; Technology and Education; Third World Development; Virtual Theories; Wildlife Conservation; Wildlife Management; Women's Studies; World Cultures.

TUITION FEES (2009/10)

£3,225.

BURSARIES AND OTHER AWARDS

Students receiving the full local authority maintenance grant based on a household income of less than £25,000 will receive a bursary of £319.

UEL Progress Bursaries

Students who successfully complete the first semester of their course and proceed onto the second semester will receive up to £500 in the first year and £300 in the second and third years.

INFORMATION AND APPROXIMATE FEES FOR NON-EU STUDENTS

There are 3,300 international students from 120 countries. **English language entry requirement:** IELTS 6.0 (or equivalent). A one-year full-time preparatory English course is available. **Fees:** £9,000–12,500. **Living costs:** £9,000–10,000.

University of East London, Docklands Campus, 4–6 University Way, London E16 2RD; tel: 020 8223 2835; www.uel.ac.uk.

EDGE HILL UNIVERSITY (ORMSKIRK)

Edge Hill University's main campus is a 160-acre site located in West Lancashire, near Liverpool. The institution has been delivering higher education for over 125 years, since it became the first non-denominational teacher training college for women in 1885. There are over 23,000 students, with a good mix of young and mature students and full and part-time students.

DEGREE SUBJECTS OFFERED

Accountancy; Animation; Biogeography; Biology; Business and Management; Childhood and Youth Studies; Chinese Studies and Business; Coach Education; Coach Education and Participation Development; Computing; Computing (Business Information Technology Management); Computing

(Information Systems); Computing (Software and Systems); Creative Writing; Criminology and Criminal Justice; Criminology with Law; Dance; Design for Performance; Drama; Drama, Music and Sound; Drama, Physical Theatre and Dance; Drama, Physical and Visual Theatre; Early Childhood Studies; Early Years Education; Educational Psychology; English; English Language; English Literature; English and Chinese Studies; Environmental Science; Film Studies; Film Studies with Film Production; Film and Television Production; Geography; GeoTourism; Health and Social Wellbeing; Health Psychology; History; Human Geography; Journalism; Key Stage 2/3 Education; Law; Law with Criminology; Law with Management; Marketing; Media; Media (Advertising); Media (Film and Television); Media, Music and Sound; Midwifery; Nursing; Nursing Studies: Operating Department Practice; Physical Education and School Sport; Physical Geography; Physical Geography and Geology; Primary Education; Psychology; Public Relations; Secondary Education; Social Work; Sociology; Sport Development; Sport and Exercise Psychology; Sport and Exercise Science; Sports Studies; Sports Therapy; Television Production Management; Women's Health.

TUITION FEES (2009/10)
£3,225.

BURSARIES AND OTHER AWARDS
Bursaries of £500 per year are awarded to students in receipt of full state support. In addition, a fee remission of £1,000 is offered to new students with brothers or sisters who are students at the university, or who have graduated in the last five years.

Excellence Scholarships
Scholarships worth up to £2,000 a year are offered to full-time students pre- and post-entry to the university in recognition of determination, commitment, and achievement in sport, performing arts, creative arts, volunteering and online activities. Students can apply regardless of the subject of their course in recognition of achievements in their spare time.

In addition, £2,000 Preparation for HE Scholarships are awarded to students who have studied on the university's Fastrack and Fastforward programmes prior to commencing their degree in recognition of special achievement on the course.

Academic Achievement Scholarships are also awarded to first year students once they have enrolled at the university in recognition of performance in end-of-year examinations.

Learning Support Package
Students being charged £3,225 tuition fees are issued with a £200 voucher every year to spend on books and other learning materials.

INFORMATION AND APPROXIMATE FEES FOR NON-EU STUDENTS
English language entry requirement: IELTS 6.5 (or equivalent). **Fees:** £8,200 per academic year for undergraduate, or £8,700 for postgraduate and £9,250 if students wish to study an MBA. **Living costs:** £5,250.

Edge Hill University, Ormskirk, Lancashire L39 4QP; tel: 0800 195 5063; www.edgehill.ac.uk.

EDINBURGH UNIVERSITY

The University of Edinburgh was founded in 1583 and is one of Scotland's ancient universities. It has a student population of more than 20,000 and offers more than 350 degree programmes. The university has a central location since many of the university's buildings are to be found throughout the city.

DEGREE SUBJECTS OFFERED

Accounting, Archaeology, Architecture, Artificial Intelligence, Astronomy, Biology, Biomedical Sciences, Business Studies, Celtic, Chemistry, Chinese, Classics, Computer Science, Dentistry, Divinity, Earth Sciences, Economic and Social History, Economics, Education, Engineering and Electronics, English Language, English Literature, Environmental and Ecological Sciences, European Studies, Film Studies, Fine Art, Geography, Geology and Geophysics, History, History of Art, Informatics, Islamic Studies, Japanese, Law, Linguistics, Mathematics, Medicine, Modern European Languages, Music, Nursing, Outdoor Education, Philosophy, Physics, Politics, Psychology, Religious Studies, Sanskrit, Scottish Ethnology, Scottish History, Scottish Literature, Social Anthropology, Social Policy, Social Work, Sociology, Sport and Recreation Management, Sport Science, Veterinary Medicine.

TUITION FEES (2009/10)

Students domiciled in Scotland receive free tuition. See www.saas.gov.uk and **Chapter 1 'Financing your course'**.

BURSARIES AND OTHER AWARDS

Undergraduate Access Bursaries

Over 180 bursaries are awarded each year for undergraduate study to students from schools or colleges in the UK whose financial or personal circumstances may prevent them from entering higher education. The value of the award is a minimum of £1,000 per year of study, tenable for the duration of the undergraduate programme of study. Further information is available at www.scholarships.ed.ac.uk/bursaries.

Accommodation Bursaries

90 bursaries are awarded to first year undergraduate UK students who will be living in University accommodation. Each bursary, tenable for one academic session, is worth £1,000 and is paid directly to Accommodation Services towards the costs of accommodation. Further information is available at www.scholarships.ed.ac.uk/bursaries.

Chemistry Scholarships

A number of scholarships are available for outstanding students taking a chemistry based degree. Each scholarship is worth £1,000 per year of study and also offers the opportunity for a vacation or a 12 month placement in industry. The scholarships are sponsored by major contributions from the chemical industry including AstraZeneca, GlaxoSmithKline and Proctor and Gamble. Further information can be obtained from the School of Chemistry.

Engineering and Electronics Scholarships

A number of scholarships are available for outstanding students taking an Electronics and Electrical Engineering based degree. Each award is worth £1,000 per year of study, up to and including the third year of study. At the end of the third year students will be selected to undertake projects for one of the industrial partners supporting the scholarship scheme. Current industrial sponsors include Analog Devices; Barco AVIS; CSR; Cummins Inc; Delta Electronics Europe Ltd; Dialog Semiconductor, Gigle Semiconductor Ltd; Her Majesty's Government Communications Centre; Selex Sensors and Airborne Systems; ST Microelectronics and Wolfson Microelectronics plc. Further details can be obtained by emailing ug-admissions@see.ed.ac.uk.

Informatics Scholarships

A number of scholarships are available for undergraduate study in the School of Informatics. Three for first year students and two for third year students. A scholar will receive around £1,000 (some

See Chapters 2, 4 and 6 for additional awards, applicable to all universities

companies offer more, some slightly less) per year and will undertake a paid work placement over the summer between the third and fourth years of study. Scholarships are currently sponsored by Barclays Capital, IBM and MISYS Charitable Foundation.

Margaret Campbell Scott Scholarships for Maths and Physics
Up to 10 awards worth £1,000 are available for new students with the best entry qualifications.

Sports Bursary Scheme
The Centre for Sport and Exercise offers a substantial programme of education, support services and funding for outstanding student athletes who are selected on to the Sports Bursary programme. Details can be obtained from the Centre for Sport and Exercise, 46 Pleasance, Edinburgh EH8 9TJ; tel: 0131 650 2585.

Student Travel Fund
The fund enables selected undergraduates to make visits abroad that are considered desirable or beneficial to their programmes of study. Preference is given to honours undergraduate students in their third or fourth year. Awards are not made in respect of travel or residence abroad that is a required part of a degree programme. Visiting students are not eligible to apply. Further information is available at: www.scholarships.ed.ac.uk.financial/travel.htm.

Stevenson Exchange Scholarships
Open to undergraduates and graduates or not more than 25 years of age, these scholarships are tenable at any French, Spanish or German university. Further information is available at www.scholarships.ed.ac.uk/studyabroad.

AWARDS FOR NON-EU STUDENTS
University of Edinburgh International Undergraduate Scholarships
Ten scholarships are available to students from Canada, Japan, Hong Kong, Malaysia, Singapore, South Africa and Thailand for undergraduate study in any subject offered by the university. The scholarship has a value of £1,000 per year and will be tenable for the duration of the programme of study. Further information is available at www.scholarships.ed.ac.uk/undergraduate.

University of Edinburgh Undergraduate USA Scholarships
A minimum of three scholarships are available to students from the USA. The scholarship has a value of £1,000 per year and will be tenable for the duration of the programme of study. Further information is available at www.scholarships.ed.ac.uk/undergraduate.

University of Edinburgh Undergraduate India Scholarships
Two scholarships are available to students from India. The scholarship has a value of £3,000 per year and will be tenable for the duration of the programme of study. Further information is available at www.scholarships.ed.ac.uk/undergraduate.

POSTGRADUATE AWARDS
University of Edinburgh International Master's Scholarships
A number of scholarships worth between £3,000 and £5,000 each will be awarded to students from a number of countries and regions across the world including: Africa; Canada; China; Hong Kong; India; Japan; Korea; Malaysia; Mexico; Middle East; Norway; Russia; Singapore; Taiwan; Thailand and the USA. These scholarships are valid for any subject area at Master's level.

Further details on student funding available to prospective postgraduate students, including the scholarships mentioned above, can be found on the University of Edinburgh Scholarships and Student Finance Office website at: www.scholarships.ed.ac.uk.

INFORMATION AND APPROXIMATE FEES FOR NON-EU STUDENTS

There are approximately 4,000 international students from over 130 countries. **English language entry requirement:** IELTS: 6.5 minimum requirement (or equivalent), English language support available. **Fees (full-time):** £11,050–£26,605 per year depending on programme. **Living costs:** £7000–£8000.

Full details on current tuition fee levels can be found at www.registry.ed.ac.uk/fees.

The University of Edinburgh, Old College, South Bridge, Edinburgh EH8 9YL, tel: 0131 651 4067; www.ed.ac.uk.

EDINBURGH NAPIER UNIVERSITY

In just four decades, Edinburgh Napier University has evolved from a technical college to become a leading Scottish university. It is now one of the largest higher education institutions in Scotland, with more than 14,000 students, including more than 3,000 international students. It is a multi-campus university with all campuses situated within easy reach of the city centre. By offering creatively designed courses, flexible study methods and accessible routes to higher education graduates are equipped for success in a competitive job market.

DEGREE SUBJECTS OFFERED

Accounting, Animal Biology, Architectural Technology, Biological Science, Biomedical Science, Building Surveying, Business Information Systems, Business Management, Civil Engineering, Civil and Transportation Engineering, Civil and Timber Engineering, Communication, Advertising and Public Relations, Communication Engineering, Computer courses, Computer Engineering, Construction and Project Engineering, Creative Studies, Culture Media and Society, Economics, Ecotourism, Electrical Engineering, Electronic Engineering, Electronic and Electrical Engineering, Energy and Environmental Engineering, Engineering with Management, English, Environmental Biology, Festival and Event Management, Financial Services Management, Forensic Biology, Graphic Design, Herbal Medicine, Hospitality Management, Immunology and Toxicology, Information Technology, Interior Architecture, International Business, Journalism, Languages, Law, Marine and Freshwater Biology, Marketing Management, Mechanical Engineering, Mechatronic Engineering, Microbiology and Biotechnology, Midwifery, Music, Nursing, Photography, Polymer Engineering, Popular Music, Product Design, Product Design Engineering, Property Development and Valuation, Psychology, Psychology and Sociology, Social Sciences, Publishing, Quantity Surveying, Software Engineering, Sport and Exercise Science, Sports Technology, Tourism Management, Transport Management, Veterinary Nursing.

TUITION FEES (2009/10)

Students domiciled in Scotland receive free tuition. See www.saas.gov.uk and **Chapter 1 'Financing your course'.**

BURSARIES AND OTHER AWARDS

RUK (Rest of UK) Bursary

This RUK Bursary is for students normally residing in England, Wales or Northern Ireland, studying at a Scottish University, who would have otherwise been eligible for a £300 institutional bursary had they studied at a university in the rest of the UK. To be eligible to apply for this, students must satisfy all the following conditions:

* Be a currently matriculated student of Edinburgh Napier University
* Normally live in England, Wales or Northern Ireland

See Chapters 2, 4 and 6 for additional awards, applicable to all universities

* Be in the first or second year of a full time undergraduate course
* Receive the full Maintenance Grant (Assembly Learning Grant for Welsh students)

NOTE: This bursary is not available to nursing students.

Moving On Bursary

This bursary is funded by donations from a number of past and present Napier staff. Its aim is to help students who wish to study for their first undergraduate degree with Edinburgh Napier University, but who face significant financial barriers to doing so. It is particularly intended to help with the cost of fees for self-financing students, eg those who have previously studied to HND level and now wish to progress to degree level but, due to previously funded study, will be required to pay their own fees for one or more years.

Criteria:

* This must be the student's first undergraduate degree
* Applicants must be able to demonstrate financial hardship
* Applicants must be Direct Entry students from a Scottish Further Education College.

Applications must be submitted by the end of October each year.

Ede and Ravenscroft Bursary

This bursary is funded by Ede and Ravenscroft Ltd. Its aim is to help students of Edinburgh Napier University whose course progress may be affected by significant financial difficulties. It is intended to help undergraduate students, in their first or second year of study, with the cost of books and course materials.

Criteria:

* Applicants must be studying for their first undergraduate degree (first or second year only)
* Applicants must be able to demonstrate financial hardship
* Applicants must be Direct Entry students, or Access Course students, from a Scottish Further Education College.

Applications must be submitted by the end of October each year.
More information about the above: www.napier.ac.uk/napierlife/money.

POSTGRADUATE AWARDS

Some postgraduate awards are offered.

INFORMATION AND APPROXIMATE FEES FOR NON-EU STUDENTS

At present, there are over 3,000 students from over 100 countries on campus. **English language entry requirement:** IELTS 6.0 (or equivalent). The UK government is making major changes to the immigration system. The changes will apply to students from outside the European Economic Area wishing to study in the UK from April 2009.

It is policy for the University to request a £3,000 deposit from each international student paying over £6,500. (For September 2009 entry onwards.) This is due on, or prior to, matriculation. **Fees:** £8,600–£9,990. **Living costs:** £7,000–8,000. For more information please contact www.napier.ac.uk/prospectivestudents/undergraduate/fees/Pages/default.aspx.

Edinburgh-Napier University, Craiglockhart Campus, Edinburgh EH14 1DJ; tel: 08452 606040; www.napier.ac.uk.

ESSEX UNIVERSITY

The University of Essex was founded in 1964 and is situated on a 200-acre parkland campus two miles from Colchester. There are 6,000 students, over half in university accommodation, much of it on campus. The university offers a broad range of first-year courses with the opportunity to try new subjects and to change the degree course choice at the end of the first year.

DEGREE SUBJECTS OFFERED

Accounting; American Studies; Artificial Intelligence; Biochemistry; Biological Sciences; Biomedical Sciences; Business Management; Cell and Molecular Biology; Computer Science; Computing; Contemporary Ethics; Criminology; Data Management; Drama; Ecology; Economics; Electronics and Computers; Engineering (Audio; Computer; Electronic; Information Systems and Networks; Internet; Optoelectronics and Communications Systems; Software; Telecommunications); English; Environmental Biology; European Studies; Film Studies; Finance; French; German; Health and Social Care; History; History of Art; Human Rights; Humanities; Information Management Systems; International Relations; Internet Computing; Language Studies; Latin American Studies; Law; Linguistics; Literature; Management; Marine Biology; Mathematics; Molecular Medicine; Music; Operational Research; Philosophy; Politics; Portuguese; Psychology; Russian; Social Sciences; Sociology; Spanish; Sports Science; Statistics; Teaching English as a Foreign Language; United States Studies.

TUITION FEES (2009/10)

£3,225.

BURSARIES AND OTHER AWARDS

The university will top-up maintenance grants in line with government support for households with low incomes. For example, for students with household incomes below £25,000 the university will provide a cash maintenance bursary equivalent to £3,216, when combined with government support, eg government grant £2,906, Essex bursary £310. Similar arrangements will be made for students receiving partial government grants.

For those students who are on a foundation or preliminary year, the university intends to offer a fee waiver, charging the standard £1,225 standard fee. Subsequent years will be set at the same level as other students.

Biomedical Sciences and Clinical Physiology (Cardiology) NHS Bursaries

Students enrolling on the four-year course in Biomedical Sciences will be entitled to financial support from the NHS during the first, second and final years. Funding may also be available for students enrolling on the new Clinical Physiology course. Contact Dr Paul Dobbin in the Department of Biological Sciences.

Mathematics Entrance Scholarships

Minor Scholarships

The Department of Mathematics offers bursaries of £1,000 over two years to those students on single-subject degrees (Mathematics, Mathematics and Statistics, and Mathematics and Operational Research), and £250 to those on joint honours degrees. These bursaries are currently awarded to first-year students who firmly accepted the (pre-Clearing) offer for admission to one of the degree schemes and who have obtained at least grades ABB or AAC including an A in Mathematics. The 320 tariff points are to be counted over any three subjects. Candidates taking two A-levels and two AS-levels may be considered.

See Chapters 2, 4 and 6 for additional awards, applicable to all universities

Major Scholarships
These are worth £2,000 over two years to those who obtain grades AAA including A in Maths.

The bursaries are renewable for a second year provided that the holders obtain a mark of 65% in Mathematics and an overall average of 65% at the end of the first year.

BSc/BEng Scholarships
A number of scholarships are offered to students admitted through the UCAS system in to year 1 of these courses.

Sports Academy Bursaries
These are offered to students competing in sport at national or international levels to meet the extra costs of this participation. Up to £1,000 a year, plus other benefits, is given to undergraduates or postgraduates studying within any department. Athletes in school years 11,12 and 13 are eligible to apply.

Blomfield Memorial Travel Grant
This award is for undergraduate and postgraduate students and is to the value of £525. It is awarded to students to assist travel in pursuit of research or studies.

Mary Helen Luen Charitable Trust Fund Award
This award is open to all University of Essex students in exceptional financial difficulties.

University of Essex Foundation Bursary for Refugees and the Children of Refugees
This Foundation Bursary is open to all undergraduate students in exceptional financial difficulties who have refugee status.

Vera Carmen Lord Fund
This fund is for prospective and existing students who have resided in (or are connected with) the Worthing area, or who are nationals of, or were born in, Jamaica.

East 15 Acting School
The Howard Lloyd Lewis Scholarship (£500–1,000) and the Stanley Picker Foundation Bursary (£500–1,500) are awarded to students at the school. Both awards are for one year only. The school may also submit third-year or postgraduate students for the Laurence Olivier Award, worth £7,500. This is open to students from all drama schools.

Other financial assistance
This is available for students with adult dependants, students with children and students with disabilities. There is also an Access to Learning Fund for students facing financial difficulties. Contact Student Support at the university on sso@essex.ac.uk.

AWARDS FOR NON-EU STUDENTS
International Fund
The International Fund is open to all international students in exceptional and unforeseen financial difficulties.

POSTGRADUATE AWARDS
University of Essex Studentships
The university has established a fund to provide University of Essex Scholarships to support students starting a new postgraduate degree, particularly a PhD. This fund will increase annually, and will be distributed to individual departments and centres of the university and will be allocated by them. Awards will be in the form of an annual sum of money to be used as the student chooses, rather than as specific fee-waivers or bursaries, and can be held (in the case of PhD

students) for up to three years. They are designed for students who would be unable to take up a university place without them. Only students who have applied for admission as a postgraduate to a department or centre of the university will be eligible to be considered and the scholarships will be tenable only at the University of Essex.

University of Essex Foundation Scholarships
The University of Essex Foundation offers six scholarships of £1,500 to assist local students undertaking a full-time master's programme. Three bursaries will be allocated to University of Essex students and three to candidates from the local Essex/Suffolk area. Awards will be made on academic merit and are conditional upon achieving a first or high 2(i) in their undergraduate degree.

Fuller Fund
The Fuller Fund covers fees, plus £3,000 living expenses. There are two studentships available for Sociology postgraduates each year.

Giulia Mereu Scholarship
This covers tuition fees and a modest allowance for a student on the LLM International Human Rights Law course, meaning they can undertake an internship with a human rights organisation.

School of English Research Scholarships and Bursaries
These cover fees and a maintenance grant for three years' full-time PhD study in an English-related area, with the scholarship offered in the first instance within the area of Renaissance.

In addition, Open Field Bursaries worth £3,000 per year will be offered to a small number of students who are unsuccessful in other applications.

Poulter Studentship
The value of each Poulter Studentship will be related as far as possible to the amounts awarded by the research councils to their studentship holders. Each studentship will be awarded to a full-time undergraduate science student of the University of Essex on the result of their final degree examination.

Computer Science Awards
Bowden Studentships for Computer Science. Apply to the head of department.

Oscar Arias Scholarship
The object of this scholarship is to enable a graduate student of Costa Rican nationality to undertake full-time study for a master's degree or doctorate in any department of the university.

INFORMATION AND APPROXIMATE FEES FOR NON-EU STUDENTS
The university has international students from 125 countries. **English language entry requirement:** IELTS 6.0–6.5 (or equivalent). English language courses are available before entry to the degree course. **Fees:** non-science courses £9,250; laboratory-based courses £11,990. **Living costs:** £6,000–£7,500.

University of Essex, Wivenhoe Park, Colchester CO4 3SQ; tel: 01206 873666; www.essex.ac.uk.

EUROPEAN BUSINESS SCHOOL (LONDON)

The European Business School London (EBSL) was established in 1979 and was the first independent business school to be validated in the UK. We are now the UK's largest business school with more than 1,100 students. The student body is diverse and multicultural, with more than

See Chapters 2, 4 and 6 for additional awards, applicable to all universities

90 different nationalities currently represented. All undergraduate students study at least one foreign language, spend a one year study period abroad and undertake a minimum of 36 weeks of work experience. Nine foreign languages from beginner through to advanced level are offered.

DEGREE SUBJECTS OFFERED

BA (Hons) International Business with either one or two languages. BA (Hons) International Events Management with one language. Languages available are: Arabic, French, German, Italian, Japanese, Mandarin Chinese, Portuguese, Russian and Spanish.

TUITION FEES (2009/10)

The tuition fees are £12,300 per year. All students pay the same regardless of nationality.

BURSARIES AND OTHER AWARDS
EBS London International Scholarship

To celebrate the international spirit of EBS London, scholarship prizes are offered for BA (Hons) International Business and BA (Hons) International Events Management degree courses. Application is by way of submitting an 8 page research-based essay in response to one of a selection of business questions published annually. Judges are looking for thought-provoking and original responses. Short-listed applicants are invited to the campus to present on their chosen topic; the final awards are based upon both the written submission and the candidate's performance at the assessment day.

First prize is worth 100% of all tuition fees for the duration of the 3.5 year degree, and is worth more than £43,000. Two runners-up prizes are worth 50% of all tuition fees.

For details about the competition, please download EBSL Scholarships 2009/10 Entry information (pdf), or contact the Admissions Office at the address below.

European Business School London, Regent's College, Regent's Park, Inner Circle, London NW1 4NS; tel: 020 7487 7730, ebsl@regents.ac.uk.

EXETER UNIVERSITY

The University College of Exeter was founded in 1922 and granted a university charter in 1955. It occupies three main sites: the Streatham Campus, a 15-minute walk from the city centre; St Luke's Campus, a mile from the city centre; and the Cornwall Campus near Falmouth (including the Camborne School of Mines). This is a particularly popular university with a student population of around 15,000 students.

DEGREE SUBJECTS OFFERED

Accounting and Finance; Ancient History; Animal Behaviour; Arabic; Arabic and Islamic Studies; Arabic and Middle East Studies; Arabic and Persian; Archaeology; Archaeology with Forensic Science; Biological and Medicinal Chemistry; Biological Sciences; Biology; Business and Management; Business Economics; Civil Engineering; Civil and Environmental Engineering; Classical Studies; Classics; Clinical Sciences; Conservation Biology; Cornish Studies and Humanities; Dentistry; Drama; Economics; Electronic Engineering and Computer Science; Engineering Engineering and Management; Engineering Geology and Geotechnics; English; Evolutionary Biology; Exercise and Sport Sciences; Film Studies (Cinema and Practice); Flexible Combined Honours; French; Geography; Geology, Applied; German; History EUR; History; Human Biosciences; IT Management for Business; International Relations; Islamic Studies; Italian; Leadership and Politics; Latin; Law;

Law and Society; Law (European); Management with Leadership; Marketing; Materials Engineering; Mathematics; Mechanical Engineering; Medical Imaging (Diagnostic Radiography); Medicine; Middle East Studies; Mining Engineering; Modern Celtic Studies and Humanities; Modern Languages with TESOL; Molecular Biology; Philosophy; Physics; Physics with Astrophysics; Physics with Medical Applications; Physics with Medical Physics; Physics with Quantum and Laser Technology; Politics; Psychology; Psychology with Sport and Exercise Science; Quantum Science and Lasers; Radiography see Medical Imaging (Diagnostic Radiography); Renewable Energy; Russian; Sociology; Spanish; Sport Sciences see Exercise and Sport Sciences; Theology; Zoology.

TUITION FEES (2009/10)
£3,225.

BURSARIES AND OTHER AWARDS
Full information on all funding opportunities offered by the University of Exeter can be found at: http://admin.exeter.ac.uk/academic/scholarships/index.shtml.

Access to Exeter Bursaries
The UK Access to Exeter Bursary scheme is a guaranteed, non-competitive bursary of up to £1,500 per year; available to students from anywhere in the UK with a low household income. **All** students who qualify to receive the full Government Maintenance Grant will receive the minimum standard bursary of £319. Additional support is also allocated if you are from a household with an income of less than £35,000 per year.

South West Access to Exeter Bursary
The South West Bursary Scheme allows students resident in the region to apply for additional 'top-up' awards where they can show they are likely to incur additional and unavoidable costs that cannot be met from other sources of funding. Awards of up to £1,500 will be made to applicants who demonstrate the most need. These awards are competitive, decisions will be made by a panel in September prior to entry, based on the information and evidence provided by the applicant.

Vice Chancellor's Excellence Scholarships
Ten awards of £5,000 per year are available for students applying in any subject, who, in addition to academic excellence (normally AAA at A-level or equivalent), demonstrate achievement and potential in, and continued commitment to, at least one of the following areas: volunteering, leadership, entrepreneurship, exceptional talent in music, the arts or community sport activity outside their chosen field of study. Students from partner schools will also be considered for these awards.

Peninsula Medical School Bursaries
A bursary of £5,000 is offered depending on personal circumstances. This is paid in instalments over the five-year degree programme. Priority is given to students who are the first from their family to undertake higher education and who are financially disadvantaged. Contact the Undergraduate Admissions Team for further information.

Entrance Scholarships
The University invites applications for the Scholarships listed below from candidates who reside in Devon and the South West region of Great Britain and who are offered an undergraduate place at the University (Exeter and Cornwall campuses) through UCAS.

Special Scholarships
Offered to new students who meet the specific requirements of each scholarship scheme as follows:

* **Ballard Scholarships** – for males who have been members of the Ballard Institute, Plymouth. If funds available, also available to males from the City of Plymouth or the Borough of Saltash or the Rural District of Plympton St Mary. £50–£85 annually.

* **Cedric Hall Mardon Scholarship** – for sons of officers of the RAF or RAFVR, primarily sons of officers who have died whilst on active service. Up to £70 annually.
* **Charles Read Scholarships** – offered to individuals under the age of 19 at the time of application whose parents have resided for the preceding 15 years in the Parish of Honiton or, if funds available, the Honiton Parliamentary division of Devon. Up to £100 annually.
* **George Christopher Davie Masonic Scholarship** – offered to children of a Devonshire Freemason who,
  * was resident in Devon when initially admitted to the lodge.
  * a subscribing member of the Lodge and resident in Devon for 5 consecutive years (within 2 years of an application being made). Up to £100 annually.
* **Rendell Scholarships** – offered to those born in Devon or Somerset or ordinarily resident for at least 3 years preceding an application. Up to £125 annually.

Special Devon Scholarships
There are a number of scholarships available to new students who were born in the County of Devon or ordinarily resident in the County for at least 3 years prior to an application to University being made. Amounts payable are at the discretion of the relevant selection committee but normally range between £50 and £200 annually.

Other Entrance Scholarships
Details of other scholarships offered to new students, which are administered independently, are available as follows:

* **CV Thomas Scholarship** – for pupils of Truro School: the Headmaster, Truro School.
* **Horwill Memorial Scholarship** – for applicants who have relatives in employment with, or have retired from, the Post Office. Up to £40 annually.
* **Plymouth Naval, Military and Air Force Scholarship** – for children of members of the fighting services in Plymouth: Area Education Officer, West Devon Area, Civic Centre, Plymouth PL2 2EW

Camborne School of Mines
Approximately 15+ undergraduate scholarships are offered each year, primarily on the basis of academic merit. These are largely funded by companies working within the mining, minerals, environmental and geosciences sectors and are worth £2,000 per year of study (subject to appropriate academic performance). The scholarships are awarded to students on the following courses: BSc Applied Geology/Environmental Science and Technology/Engineering Geology/Renewable Energy and BEng Mining Engineering.

Jubilee and Millhayes Science Scholarships
Available for high achieving students who make Exeter their first choice University. By offering these high value scholarships we aim to attract the very best students to study science, mathematics and engineering at the University of Exeter. Available in the following subject areas:

* Biosciences
* Computing (Combined Honours degrees)
* Engineering
* Geography (BSc programmes only)
* Geology
* Mathematics
* Mining Engineering
* Physics
* Renewable Energy

The Scholarships are renewable annually depending on satisfactory academic performance.

Music Scholarships
Up to 30 University Music Scholarships are offered to the new intake of Freshers and a further 60 scholarships are available to existing students. The awards are allocated on the basis of a competitive audition and interview, and will be up to the value of £500. It is expected that the majority of scholarships will be used to encourage instrumentalists from any tradition, singers, jazz or band musicians or composers to have lessons and take a practical role in student music at the university. Some awards are available for students interested in acquiring expertise in sound recording. These are mostly aimed at students reading other subjects. These scholarships are in addition to the Choral and Organ scholarships listed below.

Choral and Organ Scholarships
Exeter Cathedral Choir
Choral Scholarships in the Cathedral Choir are available for Counter-tenors, Tenors and Basses. There are 6–8 choral scholars in the choir, singing with a similar number of Lay Vicars and 20 boy or girl choristers. Choral Scholarships are normally held in conjunction with degree courses at Exeter University (any subject), provided that lecture times do not clash seriously with choir commitments. The Scholarships are normally tenable for three years, though this may be extended for an extra year in certain circumstances. Scholarships are also open to postgraduates for one year or more. Each Scholarship, payable by the Dean and Chapter, is currently worth about £1,610 per annum and will be paid in monthly instalments. Cathedral accommodation may be available for Choral Scholars at a modest rent. Contact the Director of Music, Exeter Cathedral, 1 The Cloisters, Exeter EX1 1HS, music@exeter-cathedral.org.uk.

Exeter University Chapel Choir
There are 20–25 members of the Mary Harris Memorial Chapel of the Holy Trinity Church. Scholars are appointed on merit and receive £400 per year. A junior organ scholarship of £300 per year may be awarded to a person who is a competent player.

University of Exeter Sports Scholarship Scheme
Over 30 scholarships offered each year consist of a cash payment and provision of university accommodation. The value of the cash payment is currently £1,000. Students are expected to use the money to assist with sports expenses such as travel, medical provision, coaching and training. There are also Elite Sports Awards valued at up to £2,000. Eligible athletes must hold an offer of a place from the university or be already studying. Evidence of sporting achievement or potential at national level will be sought. Emphasis is placed on cricket, golf, hockey, rugby, sailing and tennis. Sports in which current scholars are active are basketball, rowing, sports acrobatics, athletics, football and lacrosse. There are also sport-specific bursaries in golf and men's rugby. All university subject areas and academic programmes are open to potential scholars, who are expected to meet the normal entry requirements and to graduate with their cohort.

Scholarships are awarded on a one-year renewable basis subject to satisfactory progress. Scholars are expected to participate fully in the activities of the appropriate university club including representing the university in competitions. Further details and application form can be obtained from the Sports Performance Administrator, Sports Park, Stocker Road, Exeter EX4 4QN; tel: 01392 263759

In addition, a number of awards are also offered to existing registered undergraduate students.

Mrs Bessie Rook Memorial Travel Scholarship
Awarded to the value of approximately £500 per successful applicant and is available to students travelling to German and/or French speaking countries.

British Chamber of Commerce in Germany Scholarship
The Scholarship Foundation of the British Chamber of Commerce in Germany was created by popular request of the members of the BCCG in 1983 to promote intercultural integration by awarding scholarships and supplementary financial support to young Britons and Germans undertaking study or research in the other country.

See Chapters 2, 4 and 6 for additional awards, applicable to all universities

Carolyn and Andrew Trevorrow Memorial Fund Travel Bursaries (Cornwall Campus)

A number of travel bursaries are available to students of all degree programmes at the Cornwall Campus to help with the costs of field trips and project work. Further information can be found on the Cornwall Campus website.

Geography Undergraduate Dissertation Travel Award (Exeter and Cornwall Campuses)

Geography students based in both campuses may apply for this award in connection with travel abroad for an individual study project or dissertation. For further information please see www.exeter.ac.uk/geography.

Glanely Vacation Scholarship

Offers financial assistance to students working broadly within a field of agricultural economics or farm management, including the environmental and economic aspects of agriculture, food and rural resource systems.

Hiles Scholarship

Available to final year students in the School of Business and Economics who are at least 25 years of age at the commencement of their final year of study. Selection is based on good academic record and the submission of a 500 word supporting statement.

Institute of Arab and Islamic Studies HRH Prince Alwaleed Al Saud Awards (Exeter – Streatham Campus)

Available to undergraduate students undertaking programmes in Middle East Studies, Middle East Studies with Arabic, Islamic Studies who are residents from the UK, EU or North America. Awards of up to £1,000 can be awarded to enable eligible candidates to spend an academic vacation in an Arab country, attached to an approved Arab educational institution.

Languages for World Peace and Understanding Scholarship

Awarded to the value of approximately £500 and is available for a student travelling to Spanish and/or French speaking countries.

Year Abroad (USA/Canada/Australia) Funding (as part of degree programme)

Students studying abroad in the USA, Canada or Australia (as part of their degree programme) may be eligible for financial assistance from their School. Please contact your School direct for more specific information.

Year Abroad Travel Bursaries for Modern Languages students

Available to students taking a third year abroad as part of a 4-year Modern Languages programme who are not eligible for funding under the Erasmus exchange scheme. Further information can be obtained from the Department of Modern Languages. Email: sml-uga@exeter.ac.uk

POSTGRADUATE AWARDS

visit the university's scholarships website and search the funding database for the latest awards: http://admin.exeter.ac.uk/academic/scholarships/postgraduate/index.shtml

INFORMATION AND APPROXIMATE FEES FOR NON-EU STUDENTS

There are over 2,000 international students from 100 countries. **English language entry requirement:** IELTS 6.5 (or equivalent) with some exceptions – see www.exeter.ac.uk/undergraduate/applications/english_requirements.php for further information. For information on English language support: www.into.uk.com/exeter/home. **Fees:** non-science courses £10,000 pa, Engineering and science courses (including Psychology and Sport sciences) £12,250 pa, courses combining science and non-science subjects: £11,125 pa – for further information see www.exeter.ac.uk/undergraduate/international/livingcosts.php. **Living costs:** estimate £650 per month. Further information: International Office tel: +44 (0) 1392 263405, fax: +44 (0) 1392 263039; intoff@exeter.ac.uk.

University of Exeter, Northcote House, The Queen's Avenue, Exeter, Devon EX4 4QJ; tel: 01392 661000; www.exeter.ac.uk.

FALMOUTH UNIVERSITY COLLEGE
(Incorporating Dartington College of Arts)

University College Falmouth is located in West Cornwall, with campuses at Woodlane in Falmouth, Tremough in Penryn and Dartington near Totnes in Devon. There are over 3,000 students following foundation diploma, undergraduate and postgraduate full-time and part-time courses.

DEGREE SUBJECTS OFFERED
A range of BA (Hons) and MA courses are offered across the Schools of Art, Design, Media and Performance. A Foundation Diploma in Art, Design and Media is also available (one year, full time). See www.falmouth.ac.uk/courses for a full list.

TUITION FEES (2009/10)
£3,225.

BURSARIES AND OTHER AWARDS
Means-tested Bursaries
The following bursaries are available to full-time UK undergraduate students: £850 per year for students with an annual household income of £25,000 or below; £500 per year for students with an annual household income of between £25,001 and £30,000; £325 per year for students with an annual household income of between £30,001 and £40,000. An additional £250 per year is available for students with children or adult dependants (you must be claiming the Childcare Grant or Adult Dependants' Grant to be eligible for this extra £250). To be eligible for these bursaries students must apply for means-tested student financial support (tuition fee and maintenance loans and grants) via their local authority, and make sure when completing the form that they and their sponsors all give their 'consent to share' their household income information for bursary purposes. A number of smaller bursaries and scholarships are available once students have enrolled, for example to assist with study trips. Contact the Bursary Advisor for further details.

INFORMATION AND APPROXIMATE FEES FOR NON-EU STUDENTS
English language entry requirement: Foundation Studies IELTS level 5.5 (or equivalent). Undergraduate degrees 6.0 (or equivalent). Postgraduate degrees 6.5 (or equivalent) **Fees:** to be confirmed for 2009 entry; Please see www.falmouth.ac.uk/international. **Living costs:** £6,000–£7,000.

University College Falmouth, Woodlane, Falmouth, Cornwall TR11 4RH; tel: 01326 213 730; www.falmouth.ac.uk

GLAMORGAN UNIVERSITY

The University of Glamorgan has campuses in Cardiff – and nearby Pontypridd. A wide range of courses and subjects are offered. There is a population of over 21,000 students studying a wide range of qualifications, from foundation degrees to postgraduate study.

DEGREE SUBJECTS OFFERED

Accounting; Architectural and Building Conservation; Art and Design; Astronomy; Biology; Biotechnology; Building Surveying; Business; Chemistry; Chiropractic; Civil Engineering; Community Development; Computer Science; Construction Management; Criminal Justice; Criminology; Digital Communications; Earth Sciences; Economics; Electronic Commerce; Electronics; Energy and Environmental Technology; Engineering (Architectural; Computer Aided; Computer Systems; Electrical/Electronic; Electromechanical; Mechanical; Mechatronic); English; Environmental Sciences; Estate Management; Finance; Forensic Science; Geography; Geological Sciences; Government; History; Human Resource Management; Humanities; Information Technology; International Accounting; Law; Leisure and Tourism Management; Marketing; Mathematics; Media Studies; Microbiology; Minerals Surveying; Music Technology; Network Management and Administration; Nursing; Philosophy; Planning; Politics; Product Design; Property Management and Valuation; Psychology; Public and Social Policy; Purchasing and Supply Chain Management; Quantity Surveying; Religious Studies; Science; Social Work; Sociology; Sports Science; Statistics; Surveying; System Security; Theatre and Media Drama; Welsh.

TUITION FEES (2009/10)

See www.studentfinancewales.co.uk and **Chapter 1 'Financing your course'**.

BURSARIES AND OTHER AWARDS

The university offers a wide variety of awards and bursaries. This includes non-means-tested scholarships for undergraduate students starting full-time undergraduate courses in 2008 and 2009, and postgraduate students starting in 2008 and 2009.

Entry Scholarships

A non-means tested scholarship worth £3,000 is available for students who achieve 300 A-level points or more on entry to the university. £1,000 will be paid each year providing that students successfully complete their Year 1 and 2 exams at the first attempt. Students in receipt of public funds will not be eligible for this scholarship. Students must be studying on a full-time undergraduate degree course. Terms and conditions apply – go to www.glam.ac.uk/money for more details.

Residential Allowance

A non-means tested scholarship worth £1,500 is available to students who have to move away from home to study at the university. The home address must be more than 45 miles away by road from the main university campus at Treforest. Students must be studying on a full-time undergraduate degree course. Terms and conditions apply.

Network75

Students who enrol on one of the five-year part-time degree courses in Mechanical, Electrical, Civil Engineering, Electrical Engineering, Aerospace Engineering, Business or Technology may be eligible for this scheme. Network75 offers students the opportunity to earn a salary and gain valuable work experience whilst studying. Students work with the host company for three days and at the university for two days each week. The starting bursary is £5,000 a year and students' academic fees will be paid in full.

Sports Scholarships

Glamorgan students can apply for a scholarship which could involve a cash award of £500 per year or a one-off kit grant of £150 or an annual grant of £150 towards membership fees, use of facilities, physiotherapy and sports massage.

Cricket

The MCC has designated Glamorgan University as a Centre of Cricketing Excellence. The university participates in the UCCE scheme for talented and ambitious young cricketers.

AWARDS FOR NON-EU STUDENTS

International students may be considered for awards of up to £1,500 for undergraduate and £2,000 for postgraduate. No application is necessary. All students will be considered.

International Development Scholarship

This is offered to students from Sri Lanka, Bangladesh, Brazil, Kazakhstan, Thailand, Vietnam, Kenya, Mexico, Mongolia, Uganda, Russia, Tanzania, Ukraine, Zambia or Zimbabwe. Applicants must be studying full time on an undergraduate degree course. This scholarship is not available to students who are sponsored. Candidates will automatically be considered for a scholarship once their application has been received by the international office.

POSTGRADUATE AWARDS

A non-means tested scholarship of up to £2,000 (£2,000 for University Glamorgan graduates, £1,500 for students who graduated elsewhere) is available for students studying for a full-time taught master's course at the university. Students must have a First or Upper Second Class undergraduate degree. Scholarships are cash limited and terms and conditions apply.

INFORMATION AND APPROXIMATE FEES FOR NON-EU STUDENTS

There are 3,200 international students from 60 countries. **English language entry requirement:** IELTS 6.5 PG and 6.0 UG (or equivalent); international foundation course IELTS 5.0 (or equivalent). Pre-sessional courses in English are available. **Fees:** Postgraduate £10,250 Undergraduate £9,250; foundation course £5,700; **Living costs:** £6,295.

University of Glamorgan, Pontypridd CF37 1DL; tel: 01443 482080; www.glam.ac.uk.

GLASGOW UNIVERSITY

(See also Crichton University Campus)

The University of Glasgow is located in the west end of the city on the Gilmore Hill Campus with a new campus in Dumfries offering a Liberal Arts degree. It was founded in 1451 and has over 21,500 students.

DEGREE SUBJECTS OFFERED

Accountancy and Finance, Aeronautical Engineering, Anatomy, Archaeology, Arts and Media Informatics, Astronomy, Audio and Video Engineering, Aerospace Systems, Biochemistry, Biomedical Sciences, Biotechnology, Business and Management, Business Economics, Celtic Civilisation, Celtic Studies, Central and East European Studies, Chemical Physics, Chemistry with Forensic Studies, Chemistry with Medicinal Chemistry, Chemistry, Civil Engineering with

Architecture, Civil Engineering, Classics, Community Development, Comparative Literature, Computing Science and Physiology (Neuroinformatics), Computing Science, Czech, Dentistry, Earth Science, Economic and Social History, Economics, Electronic and Software Engineering, Electronics and Electrical Engineering, Electronics with Music, English Language, English Literature, Environmental Biogeochemistry, Environmental Chemistry and Geography, Environmental Chemistry, Film and Television Studies, French, Gaelic, Genetics, Geography, German, Greek, Hispanic Studies, History of Art, History, Immunology, Italian, Latin, Law, Marine and Freshwater Biology, Mathematical Sciences, Mathematics/Applied Mathematics, Mechanical Design Engineering, Mechanical Engineering (European Curriculum), Mechanical Engineering with Aeronautics, Mechanical Engineering, Medical Biochemistry, Medicine, Microbiology, Microcomputer Systems Engineering, Modern Languages, Molecular and Cellular Biology, Neuroscience, Nursing, Parasitology, Pharmacology, Philosophy, Physics with Astrophysics, Physics, Physiology and Sports Science, Physiology, Sports Science and Nutrition, Plant Science, Polish, Politics, Primary Education, Product Design Engineering, Psychology, Public Policy, Religious and Philosophical Education, Russian, Scottish History, Scottish Literature, Slavonic and East European Studies, Slavonic Studies, Social Work, Sociology and Anthropology, Software Engineering, Spanish, Sports Medicine, Statistics, Technological Education, Technology and Management, Theatre Studies, Theology and Religious Studies, Veterinary Biosciences, Veterinary Medicine and Surgery, Virology, Zoology.

TUITION FEES (2009/10)
Students domiciled in Scotland receive free tuition. See www.saas.gov.uk and **Chapter 1, 'Financing Your Course'.**

BURSARIES AND OTHER AWARDS
Sports Bursaries
The Sports Bursary Programme aims to support high-level sports men and women while they are at the university. Support worth up to £1,500 includes financial assistance and access to sports science, medicine and physiotherapy back-up. Further information can be obtained from the Sport and Recreation Service.

Organ and Choral Scholarships
The university offers nine Choral Scholarships of the value of £300 per year and one Organ Scholarship of the value of £850 per year. For further information, contact the university organist, tel: 0141 330 2540.

Bursaries for second undergraduate degrees
A number of small bursaries are available in each of the faculties of the university for eligible students who are either intending to embark on or are already studying a second undergraduate degree course. While faculties may vary the value of awards, a bursary will only cover a part of your total costs. Application should be made to the relevant faculty office by 31 August.

Beaton Scholarship
The award is worth £500 and is available to students taking widening access courses.

Club 21 Business Partnership Scheme
Club 21 is a fast-growing work experience programme based within the Careers Service. Each year, students from a variety of degree disciplines benefit from quality, structured work experience opportunities with well-known local and national companies. Club 21 work experience opportunities take place for a period of eight to 10 weeks over the summer months and are paid. Some placements also attract a scholarship of £1,000. To qualify for Club 21, students must be full-time undergraduates registered at the University of Glasgow. Placement opportunities are advertised during the first semester and successful applicants are notified in the New Year.

Maintenance Bursaries

The University awards annual bursaries of £315 to students from England, Wales and Northern Ireland who receive the maximum maintenance grant awards available in each of these counties.

POSTGRADUATE AWARDS

Awards are offered in Accountancy and Finance, Arts, Biomedical and Life Sciences, Economics, Humanities, Law and Social Sciences. There are also Career Development Loans.

INFORMATION AND APPROXIMATE FEES FOR NON-EU STUDENTS

There are over 2500 international degree students. **English language entry requirement:** IELTS 6.0 (or equivalent); some courses higher. The English as a Foreign Language Unit offers intensive five week pre-sessional language courses in the foundation programme covering English language and study skills. **Fees:** Arts/Law, Business and Social Science/Education/Dumfries courses £9,800; Dentistry £23,400; Engineering/Nursing/Science/Veterinary Bioscience £12,950; Medicine £22,600; Veterinary Medicine £18,750. **Living costs:** £8,000.

University of Glasgow, Glasgow G12 8QQ; tel: 0141 330 4575; www.gla.ac.uk.

GLASGOW CALEDONIAN UNIVERSITY

Glagow Caledonian University has a student population of over 14,500. It is situated on two campuses, one in the heart of Glasgow and the other in the west end next to Kelvingrove Park. There are eight academic schools in the areas of business, health, and science and technology.

DEGREE SUBJECTS OFFERED

Accountancy; Applied Biosciences; Applied Graphics; Applied Science; Applied Statistics; Architectural Technology; Biomedical Sciences; Biotechnology; Building; Business; Chemistry; Communication; Computing; Construction; Consumer and Trading Studies; E-Business; Economics; Engineering (Business and Manufacturing Systems; Computer; Computer Aided; Electrical/Electronic; Environment; Fire Risk; Industrial; Manufacturing Systems; Mechanical Electronic Systems; Telecommunication); European Languages; Fashion; Financial Services; Food Product Design; Food Technology; History; Hospitality Management; Human Biology; Human Nutrition; Human Resource Management; Information Systems; Informations Technology; Instrumentation; Interior Design; International Travel; Journalism; Knowledge Management; Management Science; Law; Leisure Management; Marketing; Mathematics; Medical Illustration; Medical Imaging Science; Medical Technology; Midwifery; Multimedia; Music Technology; Networking and Computer Support; Nursing; Occupational Therapy; Ophthalmic Dispensing; Optometry; Physiotherapy; Podiatry; Politics; Product Design; Property Management; Psychology; Public Administration; Quantity Surveying; Radiography; Social Science; Social Work; Tourism.

TUITION FEES (2009/10)

Students domiciled in Scotland receive free tuition. see www.saas.gov.uk and **Chapter 1, 'Financing your course'**.

BURSARIES AND OTHER AWARDS

Mature Students Bursary

This is a non-repayable means-tested bursary for mature students undertaking a full-time higher education programme for the first time. The award is primarily aimed at students with childcare costs.

The Helen Kennedy Foundation Badged Award
These bursaries are aimed at attracting students from disadvantaged backgrounds into specific degree courses.

The Daiwa Scholarship
This award provides funding for a 19 month programme of language study in Japan.

Sports Bursary Programme
The Sports Bursary Programme is run jointly by Glasgow Caledonian University, Glasgow City Council, Glasgow University and Strathclyde University. It has been designed to assist the university's most talented/promising athletes in developing their sporting potential whilst studying at Glasgow Caledonian University.

Recipients must be fully matriculated students registered on a course provided by Glasgow Caledonian University. This might include students on jointly operated courses. Applicants must have reached or demonstrated a particular level/standard in their chosen sport to be considered for the programme. The Sports Bursary Programme is not wholly concerned with offering financial assistance to selected students, although this may form an integral part of the programme. Its intention is to develop a balanced programme offering the following:

* Free access to Glasgow Caledonian University, Glasgow University, Strathclyde University and Glasgow City Council-operated facilities
* Opportunity to meet others who are in similar circumstances, ie competing at a high level in sport whilst attending further education
* Exercise, health and nutrition support
* Financial assistance for the costs involved in sports training and competition
* Opportunity to use knowledge and expertise to encourage paticipation in sport by other students
* Access to high-level sports coaching and monitoring.

For further information call 0141 331 3116.

Moffat Centre for Travel and Tourism Business Development Scholarship
The Moffat Centre offers scholarship funding for UK and EU students studying on undergraduate-level courses in Travel and Tourism at Glasgow Caledonian University. These scholarships are awarded on the basis of academic ability, motivation to undertake a career in the travel and tourism industry and economic need. Each scholarship is worth £3,600 per year and successful students may reapply on an annual basis.

The Moffat Centre for Travel and Tourism Business Development is the primary university agent for the supply of contract research and consultancy in the international travel and tourism sector. Further information and application forms are available by contacting the Moffat Centre on 0141 331 8400 or via email at info@moffatcentre.com.

Masterton Bursaries
These awards are open to undergraduates in the School of the Built and Natural Environment.

Magnus Magnusson Scholarships
Awards of up to £5,000 are open to second year students.

AWARDS FOR NON-EU STUDENTS
Scholarships of £1,000 per annum are available to students taking degree courses in the Caledonian Business School. All other Schools offer similar awards. Contact the Heads of Schools.

INFORMATION AND APPROXIMATE FEES FOR NON-EU STUDENTS

There are students from 70 countries. **English language entry requirement:** IELTS 6.0 (or equivalent). English language programmes are available. **Fees:** £9,000. **Living costs:** £8,000.

Glasgow Caledonian University, Cowcaddens Road, Glasgow G4 0BA; tel: 0141 331 3449; www.caledonian.ac.uk.

GLOUCESTERSHIRE UNIVERSITY

The University of Gloucestershire has a student population of 10,000 and is situated on three campuses (The Park, Pittville and Francis Close Hall) in Cheltenham, the Oxstalls campus in Gloucester and the Urban Learning Foundation in London. The university offers a wide range of single and joint honours courses. Work placements and study placements abroad are a feature of a number of courses.

DEGREE SUBJECTS OFFERED

Accounting; Art and Design; Biology; Broadcast Journalism; Business Studies; Community Studies; Computing; Criminology; Early Childhood Studies; Environmental Studies; Geography; Health Studies; History; Hospitality Management; Human Resource Management; Information Technology; International Business; Landscape Architecture; Law; Marketing; Media Studies; Music; Nursing; Philosophy and Ethics; Photography; Primary Education; Psychology; Public Relations; Publishing; Religion; Social Work; Sociology; Sport Studies; Teacher Training; Theology.

TUITION FEES (2009/10)

£3,225.

BURSARIES AND OTHER AWARDS

For students living in Gloucestershire and bordering counties, a bursary of an additional 35% of their assessed student maintenance grant will be awarded eg maintenance grant £2,765: top-up bursary £968. Students living outside Gloucestershire and bordering counties who obtain the full maintenance grant will receive £310.

Academic Scholarships

These awards worth £500 are offered to students achieving 360 or more UCAS tariff points prior to entry.

Compact Students Bursary

£1,000 awards are open to applicants who attended schools within the compact partnership.

Music Scholarships

These awards covering organ, choral, or instrumental interests are open to prospective and current students.

An annual rebate of 10% of fees will be made to all home/EU full-time undergraduate students who successfully complete each year of study.

A number of sports scholarships and specific bursary funds are also administered by the university including the Prize and Memorial Funds and the Janet Trotter Trust Fund.

INFORMATION AND APPROXIMATE FEES FOR NON-EU STUDENTS
English language entry requirement: IELTS 5.5 (or equivalent). English language support and a mentor scheme are offered. **Fees:** £8,200. **Living costs:** £6,000–£7,000.

University of Gloucestershire, The Park, Cheltenham, Gloucestershire GL50 2RH; tel: 01242 714501; www.glos.ac.uk.

GLYNDŴR UNIVERSITY

The university was, until recently, the North East Wales Institute of Higher Education and received its university status in 2008. It is located in the centre of Wrexham with two sites, the main centre being Plas Coch, with the Regent St. base nearby housing the Art and Design faculty.

DEGREE SUBJECTS OFFERED
Accountancy, Aeronautical Engineering, Animal Studies, Art and Design, Architectural Technology, Broadcasting, Building, Business Management, Chinese Medicine, Community Studies, Computer Studies, Creative Writing, Criminal Justice, Early Childhood Studies, Education Studies, Electrical and Electronic Engineering, Environmental Science, Estate Management, Events Management, Forensic Science, Health Studies, History, Housing, Human Resources Management, Journalism, Law and Business, Library and Information Studies, marketing, Mechanical Technology, media Studies, Motorsport Design, Music Technology, Nursing, Occupational Health, Occupational Therapy, Primary Education, Psychology, Public and Social Policy, Radio Production, Renewable Energy, Sound and Broadcasting Engineering, Sport Studies, TV, Theatre Performance, Welsh Translation, Youth Studies

TUITION FEES (2009/10)
See www.studentfinancewales.co.uk and **Chapter 1, 'Financing Your Course'.**

BURSARIES AND OTHER AWARDS
Glyndŵr University Bursary
Bursaries are offered to eligible students which include the Wales National Bursary of £319. A bursary of £1,000 is awarded against a household income below £18,370 and bursaries of £750 and £500 for incomes between £18,371 and £22,000 and from £22,001 and £95,000 respectively.

Excellence Scholarships
These merit-based awards of £1,000 are open to applicants achieving 300 UCAS points or higher.

Gifted Athlete Scholarship
Awards of over £1,800 are offered to outstanding athletes in their chosen sports.

Care Leavers Scholarships
These awards of £1,000 are open to students who have been in care.

AWARDS FOR NON-EU STUDENTS
International student packages awards will be announced later in the year.

INFORMATION AND APPROXIMATE FEES FOR NON-EU STUDENTS
English Language entry requirement: IELTS 6.0 (or equivalent). **Fees:** £6,900. **Living costs:** £6,000–£7,000.

Glyndŵr University, Plas Coch Campus, Mold Road, Wrexham LL11 2AW; tel 01978 290666; www.glyndwr.ac.uk

GOLDSMITHS (University of London)

The College was originally founded in 1891 and has been part of the University of London since 1904. Its main site is situated in South-East London. There is a student population of over 8,000, with two thirds being women.

DEGREE SUBJECTS OFFERED

Anthropology; Art; Community and Youth Work; Computing; Cultural Studies; Design; Drama and Theatre Arts; Education; English and Comparative Literature; History; History of Art; Media and Communications; Music; Politics; Psychology; Social Work; Sociology.

TUITION FEES (2009/10)

£3,225.

BURSARIES AND OTHER AWARDS

Note *Information about Goldsmiths Bursaries and Scholarships for 2010 entry has not yet been finalised. However, as a guide, please find below details of scholarships that were offered to 2009 entry students. Please visit the website www.goldsmiths.ac.uk/ug/costs for possible updates and changes to the information set out below.*

Goldsmiths Bursary (home students only)

A Goldsmiths Bursary worth up to £1,000 per annum may be available to students from low household income backgrounds (below £40,000 in 2009/10), and who are in receipt of a full or partial maintenance/special support grant from the government.

The bursary is available to help you with your course-related costs including books, travel, equipment and help with childcare.

The Mayor's New Cross Award

This award was created to commemorate the 14 young people who died in the New Cross Fire in 1981. There are two awards of circa £11,000 available – one for a male student and one for a female. They will be awarded to eligible students who have strong academic ability and potential to study on an undergraduate degree at Goldsmiths. Only candidates who live in or have studied at a secondary school or further education college in the London Borough of Lewisham are eligible for these awards.

Student Residential Hardship Bursary

This scheme offers students from low income families help with accommodation fees. If your family has a low household income and you are applying for a place in one of Goldsmiths' halls of residence, you can apply for this bursary to help with your accommodation fees. If successful, you will receive a bursary reducing the cost of hall fees by 5%, 10% or 20% depending on individual need.

The Warden's Scholarships

There are two scholarships of £5,000 each, awarded to the two highest qualified scholarship applicants. To be eligible, you will need to have achieved a minimum of three As or equivalent at A-level. The final selection will be made on behalf of the Warden of Goldsmiths, on the basis of entry qualification and the potential to contribute to the academic life of the College.

The Excellence Scholarships

These are available for students with excellent A-level scores or equivalent entry qualifications. An Excellence Scholarship is an annual award of £500 paid over the duration of a degree. Each academic department makes an award on the basis of the highest A-level or equivalent score. The Department may also consider the likely academic contribution the student could make to the College.

London Student Access to Goldsmiths Scholarship Scheme

The London Student Access to Goldsmiths Scholarship Scheme is open to applicants who have attended a school or college in a London borough. There are up to 32 scholarships, each worth £500 per year over the duration of a degree. Applicants will need to demonstrate evidence of high achievement or potential despite difficult personal circumstances, a household income of less than £60,005, limited family experience of higher education, or lack of support from parents or family. Previous participation in aspiration-raising activities (such as Aimhigher, or a mentoring programme) will also be considered.

Departmental Awards

Individual academic departments may offer subject-specific funding for both undergraduates and postgraduates. For example, string players on the BMus in Music are eligible for the Rostropovich Scholarships, endorsed by the late Russian cellist Mstislav Rostropovich. Five students are chosen to receive £500 each for each of the three years of their programme. Students are advised to check with their admitting departments for further funding opportunities.

POSTGRADUATE AWARDS

Goldsmiths Postgraduate Scholarship Scheme

The Goldsmiths Postgraduate Scholarship Scheme is open on a competitive basis to students under-taking a taught or research led postgraduate programme in 2009.

There are 30 scholarships of up to £1,000 available, which will act as a partial fee waiver for the first year of study for students with a Home or EU fee liability. Each of the 16 academic depart-ments at Goldsmiths has the opportunity to award a scholarship of £1,000 to one of their full-time students (or two scholarships of £500 for part-time students).

The remaining 14 scholarships of £1,000 will be open on a competitive basis across the whole college.

Goldsmiths Research Council Grant Scheme

Home or EU postgraduate students in receipt of a fee grant from an eligible awarding body will have the difference between the amount of the fee grant and the tuition fee charged for their course paid by Goldsmiths. Eligible awarding bodies are the Arts and Humanities Research Council (AHRC), the Economic and Social Research Council (ESRC), the Engineering and Physical Sciences Research Council (EPSRC), and the General Social Care Council (GSCC).

INFORMATION AND APPROXIMATE FEES FOR NON-EU STUDENTS

Goldsmiths does not currently offer any scholarships for international undergraduate students, although there may be the possibility of assistance in the future. Please regularly check the website www.goldsmiths.ac.uk/ug/costs/ for the latest information on funding for international students. **English language entry requirement:** IELTS 6.5 (or equivalent). One year Foundation course IELTS 5.0 (or equivalent). **Fees:** range £9,870 – £13,690. **Living costs:** £8,000.

Goldsmiths, University of London, London SE14 6NW; tel: 020 7919 7171; www.goldsmiths. ac.uk.

GREENWICH UNIVERSITY

The University of Greenwich is situated on five campuses: Avery Hill in South-East London; Dartford; Maritime Greenwich on the World Heritage site; Medway (close to Chatham and Rochester); and the Woolwich campus.

DEGREE SUBJECTS OFFERED

Accounting; Architecture; Arts Management; Automotive Component Design; Biochemistry; Biological Sciences; Biopharmaceutical Science; Building; Business; Chemistry; Childhood Studies; Community Arts and Design; Complementary Therapies; Computer Systems; Computing Science; Creative Industries; Design Studies; Design/Technology Education; Digital Design; Economics; Education; Engineering (Automotive; Building; Civil; Computer Aided; Computer Networking; Computer Systems; Electrical/Electronic; Industrial Automation; Mechanical); English; Entrepreneurial Science; Environmental Science; Estate Management; Exercise Physiology and Nutrition; Facilities Management; Finance; Fitness and Health; Garden Design; Geography; Geology; Health; Heritage Management; History; Horticulture; Housing; Human Nutrition; Human Physiology; Humanities; Information Systems; International Business; Internet Technologies; Landscape Architecture/Management; Law; Learning Disabilities; Legal Practice; Leisure and Property Development; Management Science; Marketing; Mathematics; Mechatronics; Media and Communications; Mental Health Work; Midwifery; Multimedia Technology; Nursing; Operations Management; Personnel Management; Pharmaceutical Sciences; Philosophy; Physical Education and Sport; Politics; Primary Education; Product Development; Property Valuation and Management; Psychology; Public Health; Social Care/Social Work; Sociology; Sport Science; Statistics; Surveying; Theology; Tourism Management; Youth and Community Studies.

TUITION FEES (2009/10)

£2,900; Medway School of Pharmacy £3,225; partner colleges £2,320.

BURSARIES AND OTHER AWARDS

Access to Higher Education Bursary

Students from partner colleges achieving a high academic standard and progressing to an undergraduate degree at Greenwich University may apply for a scholarship of £525.

Care Leavers Bursaries

Students from local authority care can apply for a £1,000 bursary.

Greenwich Partnership Bursaries

Students qualify for those bursaries if they are on a maintenance or special support grant.

Medway School of Pharmacy Bursary

Home Students on means-tested or special support grants taking pharmacy degrees can claim £310.

UCAS Scholarships

Awards worth £525 are offered to students paying variable fees, achieving 300 UCAS points or equivalent.

John McWilliam Bursaries

School of Architecture and Construction bursaries are offered for one year only.

THUS Undergraduate Sponsorship Programme

These are open to students taking Information Technology, Business and Management courses.

See Chapters 2, 4 and 6 for additional awards, applicable to all universities

Sir William Boreman's Foundation
Awards between £500 and £1,500 are open to students from households with an annual income less than £25,000.

Gravesend Rugby Foundation
Awards are open to rugby players who have reached county level standard.

David Fussey Choral Exhibition
The bursaries are open to any new student at the university who becomes a member of the University of Greenwich Choir.

There are three bursaries worth £1,000 each per year (payable in two £500 instalments) for a maximum of three years. The bursaries are awarded in memory of Dr David Fussey, the late vice-chancellor of Greenwich, who gained great enjoyment from singing in choirs.

Mature Students Bursaries
Cash bursaries of £500 per year for a maximum of three years, dependent on satisfactory progress are available to students over the age of 25 who qualify for a means-tested local government grant.

Greenwich Hospital Bursary
Bursaries of £3,000 per academic year are available to the sons and daughters of naval ratings or former naval ratings with more than three years service in the Royal Navy or Royal Marines. Contact the Student Support Office at the university.

AWARDS FOR NON-EU STUDENTS
Scholarships valued at £1,000 are available to applicants from: Bangladesh; Botswana; China (including Hong Kong and Macau); Egypt; Ghana; India; Indonesia; Japan; Kenya; Korea (North and South); Malaysia; Mauritius; Nigeria; Pakistan; Philippines; Russia; South Africa; Sri Lanka; Taiwan; Tanzania; Thailand; Turkey; Uganda; Uzbekistan; Zimbabwe.

POSTGRADUATE AWARDS
A Merit Scholarship of £750, when the tuition fees are paid in full, is available for postgraduate students in the Business School for students who have either (a) IELTS of 6.5 or TOEFL of 600 or (b) a final-year average score of at least:

* 80% in a four-year (or longer) Chinese university degree programme
* 65% in a three-year (or longer) Indian university degree programme
* 65% in a four-year (or longer) Japanese university degree programme
* 65% in a four-year (or longer) Pakistani university honours degree programme
* GPA 3.5 (out of 4.5) in a four-year (or longer) Korean university degree programme
* GPA 3.5 (out of 4) in a four-year (or longer) Thai university degree programme

where both the university and degree are recognised and approved by the University of Greenwich.

INFORMATION AND APPROXIMATE FEES FOR NON-EU STUDENTS
There are 4,500 international students (including those from European countries). **English language entry requirement:** IELTS 6.0 (or equivalent). Pre-sessional English courses, Access and international foundation courses are offered. **Fees:** classroom-based courses £8,650; laboratory-based courses £11,000. **Living costs:** £7,000–£8,000.

University of Greenwich, Old Royal Naval College, Park Row, Greenwich, London SE10 9LS; tel: 0800 005006; www.gre.ac.uk.

GSA CONSERVATOIRE (GUILDFORD)

The GSA Conservatoire was founded in 1935 and is presently located in the centre of Guildford in a series of studios. The conservatoire is dedicated to producing professional theatre practitioners as well as focusing on stage management, production, design and general drama studies.

DEGREE AND DIPLOMA SUBJECTS OFFERED

There is a three-year BA degree course in Theatre with Acting, Musical Theatre and Production/Design pathways. A one-year diploma course is offered in Acting, Musical Theatre or a two-year diploma course in Stage Management for graduates and mature students.

TUITION FEES (FOR ALL STUDENTS) (2009/10)

BA Theatre and Professional Acting Diploma £11,210; Musical Theatre £12,270.

BURSARIES AND OTHER AWARDS

Students from households with an income of less than £30,000 will be eligible for a maintenance grant. However, students may also be liable for additional private fees which are normally payable in advance.

Sir Michael Redgrave/Sean McGrath Scholarships

The Sir Michael Redgrave and Sean McGrath Scholarships are awarded to students already at the conservatoire on the three-year performance courses to assist in their second and third years. Students are invited to apply in the spring term of each year and are selected by audition and interview.

GSA Student Support Fund

Assistance is given, generally in the form of interest-free loans towards living costs, to students already at the conservatoire who face unforeseen financial problems during their courses. Applications for assistance are made in writing through the Bursar.

Michael Gaunt/Ian Ricketts Bursaries

Through the Michael Gaunt and Ian Ricketts Bursaries, the conservatoire can offer assistance to students already at the conservatoire who suffer unforeseen financial problems. Applications for assistance are made in writing through the Bursar.

South Square Trust Bursaries

These are awarded to students on courses who are facing financial difficulties.

GSA Conservatoire, Millmead Terrace, Guildford, Surrey GU2 5AT; tel: 01483 560701; www.conservatoire.org.

HARPER ADAMS UNIVERSITY COLLEGE (SHROPSHIRE)

Harper Adams is a specialist university college offering a range of postgraduate, bachelor's and Higher National Diploma courses for careers in food and the land-based industries. It is based on a single campus with its own 230-hectare farm, in Shropshire. The current registration of students is over 1850.

See Chapters 2, 4 and 6 for additional awards, applicable to all universities

DEGREE SUBJECTS OFFERED

Agricultural Engineering; Agriculture (with specialisms); Agri-Food Marketing; Agri-Food Production; Animal Behaviour; Animal Science and Animal Health; Business Enterprise; Business Management and Marketing; Countryside and Environmental Management; Engineering Design and Development; Equine Studies; Food and Consumer Studies; Food Retail Management; Food Technology; Off-road Vehicle Design; Rural Enterprise and Land Management; Rural Leisure Management.

TUITION FEES (2009/10)

£3,225.

BURSARIES AND OTHER AWARDS

Students receiving a maintenance grant of £2,835 will receive a top-up fee of £1,000. Those receiving partial grants will receive bursaries of £500–750.

Harper Guarantee

The Harper Guarantee will provide non-repayable scholarships to benefit as many students as possible. The scholarships are in the form of Means-tested and Merit Scholarships.

Means-tested Scholarships

This type of scholarship is designed to help those students in need of financial assistance. The local authority will provide the college with information on students' household incomes and non-repayable scholarships will be awarded as appropriate.

The Claas Scholarship

One award is made worth £3000 to a second and final year Agricultural Engineering student.

Jill Williams Scholarship

An award of £1,000 is open to second year students.

Syngenta Scholarship

Three scholarships are offered to first and second year students linked to a future career with the Syngenta organisation.

Alice Ellen Cooper Dean Scholarship

The award worth £1,000 per year is open to students from Dorset or West Hampshire.

Bruce Wilson-North Scholarship

The award of £2,000 is open to students following degree courses in Rural Enterprise or Land Management.

The Longcliffe Scholarship

The scholarship is available to second and Final year students taking Countryside or Environmental Management courses.

The McConnel Scholarship

This award is open to Engineering students.

The Mercer Scholarship

All students taking Agriculture in years 1 and 2 can apply for this award of £1,000 over two years.

The Shropshire Group Scholarship

This award is open to second year students aiming for a career with the Shropshire Group.

The Vital Earth Scholarship
This award of £2,000 is open to second and final year students.

The Worshipful Company of Poulters Scholarship
An award of £1,000 is offered to students aiming for a career in the poultry industry.

Merit Scholarships
Harper Adams also believes in rewarding students with potential and/or excellence, whether it is, for example, to do with academic or sporting ability, or to reward those students who can further enrich the community at the college. Merit Scholarships are non-repayable. The eligibility for Merit Scholarships is assessed on a case-by-case basis and only one type of scholarship (Means-tested or Merit Scholarship) can be awarded to each student each year from the university college.

Subject scholarships
There are six scholarships for Engineering students valued at £500 to £2,000.

Two scholarships are offered to students following courses in Land Management or Rural Environmental Management. One award of £1,000 is available to a student aiming for a career in the Poultry industry and a further award is available for students aiming for careers in sales or marketing and there is one Rugby Scholarship open to a student from Ireland.

AWARDS FOR NON-EU STUDENTS
Students who are classed as overseas students for tuition fee purposes may apply to Harper Adams for a scholarship.

INFORMATION AND APPROXIMATE FEES FOR NON-EU STUDENTS
English language entry requirement: IELTS 6.0 (or equivalent). **Fees:** £8,000. **Living costs:** £6,000–£7,000.

Harper Adams University College, Edgmond, Near Newport, Shropshire TF10 8NB; tel: 01952 820280; www.harper-adams.ac.uk.

HARTPURY COLLEGE (Associate Faculty of the University of the West of England)

Located within 800 acres of beautiful Gloucestershire countryside, Hartpury College, Associate Faculty of the University of the West of England, has created an outstanding academic environment to enable students of all ages and abilities to gain Further and Higher education qualifications and develop important vocational skills to help them achieve their ambitions within the sport, equine, animal, veterinary nursing and agriculture related industries. The College is home to a vibrant community of 3,200 full-time students – 900 of which are residential (campus-based) students.

DEGREE COURSES OFFERED
Agricultural Business Management; Amenity Horticulture Management; Conservation and Countryside Management; Dairy Herd Management; Animal Behaviour and Welfare; Animal Science; Bioveterinary Science; Equine Veterinary Nursing Science; Veterinary Nursing Science; Veterinary Practice Management; Equine Business Management; Equine Science; Equine Performance; Equine Sports Science; Sports Performance; Sports Coaching; Sport and Exercise Management; Sports Business Management; Golf Management; Outdoor Adventure Management; Food and Drink Manufacturing

TUITION FEES (2009/10)
£3,225.

BURSARIES AND OTHER AWARDS

Hartpury College Bursary
In 2009/10, Hartpury College will offer a bursary to eligible new students paying £3,225 in tuition fees. Students who have a household income of £25,000 or below are entitled to a bursary of £1,000.

Care Leavers Bursaries
A Care Leaver Bursary of £1,000 is available to full time UK undergraduate students who have been in Local Authority Care.

Farmers Trust Bursaries
In addition, five bursaries of £1,000 funded by the Gloucestershire NFU Farmer's Trust are available to contribute towards the cost of residential accommodation at Hartpury College. The award is means tested and available to students from local farming families with an annual household income of less than £20,000.

Sports Academy Scholarships
The Hartpury Academy of Sport was created in 2000 to develop students with the potential to become elite athletes in rugby, football, golf, equine sports, netball or the modern pentathlon, whilst enabling them to continue their academic education.

Players with exceptional talent in these sports may be offered a Sports Academy Scholarship, providing assistance towards accommodation and/or tuition fees. Some players may also be offered a bursary to provide financial assistance towards expenses. To apply, send a letter with your CV and references to the appropriate sports academy director.

Gloucestershire Rugby Academy Scholarships
The Gloucestershire Rugby Academy is a joint venture between Hartpury College and Gloucester Rugby Football Club. The academy offers up to five Rugby Scholarships and Gloucester RFC Bursaries in any academic year. Successful candidates will be required to study one of Hartpury College's full-time courses at further or higher education, and take full part in the academy development programmes run by the rugby academy director. The scholar will also be expected to fulfil all of the requirements of the chosen academic course of study to the satisfaction of the course tutor and be directly responsible to the academy director.

The scholarships offer:

* Full or part assistance with college tuition fees
* Full or part assistance with accommodation fees
* Expert coaching and guidance from academy and Gloucester RFC personnel
* Sports science support services
* A chance to play for academy and Gloucester RFC teams.

Specific Gloucester Rugby Football Club bursaries will be offered in addition to scholarships to those players who have been identified as having exceptional talent and future potential and these offer:

* Financial assistance towards expenses
* Training, playing and coaching with Gloucester RFC
* Gloucester RFC special privileges.

In order to qualify applicants must possess:

* A proven track record in rugby

* A desire to develop themselves as individuals and players as part of Hartpury College and the rugby academy
* A commitment to achieve relevant educational qualifications.

AWARDS FOR NON-EU STUDENTS

Bursaries valued at £2,000 (for degree courses) and £1,000 (for BTEC Courses) represent a reduction in tuition fees. These awards are open to students from Angola, Botswana, Lesotho, Malawi, Mozambique, South Africa, Swaziland, Zambia and Zimbabwe.

INFORMATION AND APPROXIMATE FEES FOR NON-EU STUDENTS

Please contact the International Office for the current tuition fees and further information on applying on 01452 702344; enquire@hartpury.ac.uk or visit the website at www.hartpury.ac.uk.

Hartpury College, Gloucestershire GL19 3BE; tel: 01452 702133; www.hartpury.ac.uk.

HERIOT-WATT UNIVERSITY

Heriot-watt is the eighth oldest higher education institution in the UK and is a university for business and industry, with campuses in Edinburgh, the Scottish Borders and Dubai. Edinburgh Campus, the largest site, is set in an extensive woodland location to the west of Edinburgh with good connections to the city centre and to the airport. The Scottish Borders Campus in Galashiels is 38 miles south of Edinburgh, right at the very heart of the Borders. The Campus is home to the School of Textiles and Design and also runs a number of courses from the School of Management and Languages. Heriot-Watt University's Dubai Campus is a purpose-built modern campus in Dubai Academic City which formally opened in March 2006. The Campus offers a range of undergraduate and postgraduate courses which reflect the University's Scottish Schools and Institutes as well as student exchange and campus transfers.

DEGREE SUBJECTS OFFERED

Accountancy and Finance, Actuarial Mathematics and Statistics, Applied Psychology, Architectural Engineering, Biology, Chemical Engineering, Chemistry, Civil Engineering, Structural Engineering, Clothing, Computer Science Construction Management and Surveying, Design and Management, Economics, Electrical, Electronic and Computer Engineering, Fashion Design and Management, Language and Intercultural Studies (French, German, Spanish), Management, Mathematics, Mechanical Engineering, Physics, Sport and Exercise Science, Textiles, Urban Studies.

TUITION FEES (2009/10)

Scottish students domiciled in Scotland receive free tuition, see www.saas.gov.uk and **Chapter 1, 'Financing your course'.**

BURSARIES AND OTHER AWARDS
Scholarships for UK domiciled students

Several schools offer a number of scholarships worth £500 per annum for the duration of the degree course.

Access Bursaries

These awards are for a total £2,000. £1,000 is paid in the first year of study and £1,000 in the final, Honours year. Applicant must be studying an HNC, HND, Access programme or Highers at a Scottish College, or be at school and in receipt of the Education Maintenance Allowance.

See Chapters 2, 4 and 6 for additional awards, applicable to all universities

Schlumberger Scholarships

These awards are for £1,500 per annum. Some are reserved for students in the third and fourth year of courses and there are other awards specifically for women in the fields of Science, Technology and Engineering.

Sports Scholarships

Various scholarships and bursaries are available for athletes competing at a national standard. There are also special awards for golf and football.

AWARDS FOR NON-EU STUDENTS

Several Schools offer awards in the form of fee reduction to non-EU applicants.

POSTGRADUATE AWARDS

The university offers an impressive range of scholarships for taught and research postgraduate students, details of which can be obtained from the relevant Schools.

Full details of all Heriot-Watt Scholarships can be found at www.scholarships.hw.ac.uk.

INFORMATION AND APPROXIMATE FEES FOR NON-EU STUDENTS

English language entry requirement: IELTS 6.5 or equivalent but this may depend on the course applied for. Several English Language courses are offered at the Edinburgh Campus. **Fees** £9,000–£11,350 (undergraduate) and £9,250–£11,800 (postgraduate). Fees for the Institute of Petroleum Engineering may be up to £16,870. **Living costs:** in Edinburgh including accommodation and personal expenditure are estimated at around £9,000. (All figures are for 2008/09)

Heriot-Watt University, Riccarton, Edinburgh EH14 4AS; tel: 0131 449 5111, www.hw.ac.uk.

HERTFORDSHIRE UNIVERSITY

The University of Hertfordshire is situated on three campuses (Hatfield, de Havilland and St Albans) and is 30 minutes' travelling time from central London. There are approximately 13,000 students taking full-time courses in a range of vocational and non-vocational subjects. The students union provides an employment agency offering students part-time and casual work.

DEGREE SUBJECTS OFFERED

Accounting; Advertising; Aerospace Engineering; Applied Biology; Art and Design; Astronomy; Astrophysics; Automotive Engineering; Biochemistry; Biological Sciences; Biotechnology; Building; Business Studies; Civil Engineering; Computer Science; Electrical and Electronic Engineering; English; Environmental Science; French; Geography; Geology; German; History; Journalism; Leisure Management; Manufacturing Engineering; Marketing; Mechanical Engineering; Media Studies; Microbiology; Midwifery; Music; Nursing; Performing Arts; Pharmaceutical Science; Pharmacology; Philosophy; Physics; Physiotherapy; Printing; Psychology; Radiography; Sciences; Spanish; Sport Studies; Statistics; Teacher Training; Travel and Tourism.

TUITION FEES (2009/10)

£3,225.

BURSARIES AND OTHER AWARDS

The amount paid to any individual student will be equivalent to 50% of that student's local authority grant assessment, up to a maximum of £1,350 per year for those in receipt of £2,765. (Check with the university.)

Choral Scholarships

Music students can apply for these awards worth £1,200 per year.

'Entrepreneurial' and 'Gifted and Talented' scholarships are worth £2,000 and £3,000 respectively.

Hertfordshire Sports Scholarships

Theses awards are allocated to accommodation, equipment and training costs.

Accounting Scholarships

These awards are offered to students applying for degree courses in Accounting and Finance and Accounting and Management Information Systems.

Institute of Physics Bursaries

These awards are valued at £2,000 and £3,000 respectively and are offered to applicants for bachelor degrees in Physics and for MPhys/MSci degrees.

Ian Humphries Scholarship

Applicants for the BEng course in Mechanical Engineering achieving the highest grades on entry can apply for this award worth £1,000 per year for three years.

St Albans Scholarship

This is open to applicants for the Business Information Systems degree course worth £1,000 per year for three years.

Jarvis Scholarship

This award worth £2,000 per year for each year of study is open to any student resident in the AL5 postcode.

Hertfordshire Chamber of Commerce Scholarship

This award is open to applicants for the BSc Management Sciences degree and is worth £1,000 per year for three years.

Wilmot Dickson Scholarships

The awards are worth £1,000 per year for three years and are open to applicants for degree courses in Accounting, Human Resources Management, Computing Networks and Environmental Management.

Computer Science Scholarships

These are available to outstanding students at the end of Year 1.

Kurt Dannenberg Engineering Scholarships

Six scholarships are offered each year to 'The most improved students'. £500 Hardship scholarships are also available.

Hertfordshire Constabulary Scholarships

This is worth £650 and is awarded at the end of the first semester for Sports Science students.

Tesco Marketing Scholarship

This scholarship worth £1,000 is awarded at the end of the first semester to a student taking the Marketing degree.

See Chapters 2, 4 and 6 for additional awards, applicable to all universities

A.R. Woolf Charitable Trust
An award of £2,500 is awarded to final year Law students aiming to enter the profession.

Science and Engineering Scholarships
Awards worth up to £3,000 on certain science and engineering courses are available to students who achieve a minimum of 280 UCAS tariff points on entry.

Chancellor's Scholarships
These awards are limited to full-time students applying for any degree course who achieve at least 360 UCAS tariff points.

College Awards
Students from partner colleges may apply for a College Award of £1,500.

INFORMATION AND APPROXIMATE FEES FOR NON-EU STUDENTS
Students from over 90 countries are studying at the university. **English language entry requirement:** IELTS 6.0 (or equivalent). English language tuition is offered in the one-year international foundation course, in a course for the foundation certificate in English for Academic Purposes and in a pre-sessional intensive English course held during the summer months. **Fees:** £8,000. **Living costs:** £7,000–£8,000.

University of Hertfordshire, College Lane, Hatfield, Hertfordshire AL10 9AB; tel: 01707 284800; www.herts.ac.uk.

HEYTHROP COLLEGE (University of London)

Heythrop college is located in Central London, and specialises in the study of Philosophy and Theology. The supportive learning environment for its 650 students is enhanced by one-to-one tutorials for all students throughout their courses.

DEGREE SUBJECT OFFERED
Abrahamic Religions (Islam, Christianity and Judaism); Divinity; Philosophy; Philosophy and Theology; Psychology and Philosophy; Psychology and Theology; Religion and Ethics; Theology.

TUITION FEES (2009/10)
£3,225.

BURSARIES AND OTHER AWARDS
Heythrop Bursary
Students in receipt of a government grant will receive a minimum Heythrop Bursary Award of £300 rising to a maximum value of £1,453 equal to 50 per cent of the maximum grant.

INFORMATION AND APPROXIMATE FEES FOR NON-EU STUDENTS
English language entry requirement: IELTS 7.0 (or equivalent). **Fees:** £5,490 **Living costs:** £9,500–£10,500

Heythrop College, University of London, Kensington Square, London W8 5HQ; tel:020 7795 6600; www.heythrop.ac.uk.

HUDDERSFIELD UNIVERSITY

The University of Huddersfield had its origins in 1841 and became a university in 1992. The main campus is situated in the town centre of Huddersfield with teacher training taking place two miles away and Physiotherapy and Midwifery in Wakefield. There are over 16,000 students following three-year full-time and four-year sandwich courses.

DEGREE SUBJECTS OFFERED

Accountancy; Applied Science; Applied Social Studies; Architectural Computer Aided Technology; Architecture; Art and Design; Automotive Design and Technology; Behavioural Sciences; Biochemistry; Biology; Building Construction; Business; Catering Management; Chemistry; Communications; Computing; Earth Sciences; E-Commerce; Economics; Education; Engineering (Automotive; Computer Aided; Computer Control Systems; Electrical/Electronic; Environmental; Mechanical; Precision; Software); English; Entrepreneurship; Environmental Science; Fabric Sourcing; Food and Nutrition; Geography; Health Studies; History; Hospitality Management; Human Resource Management; Law; Logistics; Management; Marketing; Media; Microbial Sciences; Midwifery; Multimedia; Music; Nursing; Pharmaceutical Science; Physiotherapy; Podiatry; Politics; Product Development; Psychology; Social Work; Sociology; Software Development; Technology; Textile Technology; Theatre Studies; Tourism; Transport Management; Virtual Reality Systems.

TUITION FEES (2009/10)

£3,225.

BURSARIES AND OTHER AWARDS

In addition to the government maintenance grant, students with a family income of up to £25,000 will receive a bursary of £500. Bursaries worth £319 are also available to PGCE and Social Work students with a household income of less than £25,000.

Huddersfield RUFC Bursaries

Financial help is offered to students with a good rugby background, showing commitment and enthusiasm. Contact Simon Irving at Huddersfield RUFC; tel: 01484 469801.

BSc E-Commerce and Multimedia Golden Place Scheme

The Golden Place Scheme is a collaboration between Sun Microsystems and the university. Sun Microsystems have, as shapers and innovators in the field of the internet and e-commerce, agreed to support a fixed number of candidates on the BSc (Hons) E-Commerce and Multimedia course.

The objective of the scheme is to encourage high-calibre students to venture into the area of e-commerce and to confirm Sun Microsystems' continuing commitment to sponsor UK higher education. High-calibre students, towards the end of their first year, will be put forward by the university for interview by Sun Microsystems. Success at this interview will provide each candidate with the following benefits:

* Course fees refunded at the end of each successful year
* £1,000 maintenance at the end of each successful academic year
* Confirmed industry placement at Sun Microsystems.

It is likely that the resulting graduates of this scheme will be offered positions of employment at Sun Microsystems. Contact the Admissions Tutor for BSc E-Commerce and Multimedia.

ILT/Radical Bursary

For students taking the Transport or Logistics courses a bursary of £1,000 is offered towards tuition fees.

INFORMATION AND APPROXIMATE FEES FOR NON-EU STUDENTS

There are international students from over 80 countries. **English language entry requirement:** IELTS 6.0 (or equivalent). English language courses are available, as is a one-year international foundation course in English language with options in Business, Computing, Engineering, Mathematics and Music. Students are guaranteed entry to Huddersfield courses on completion. **Fees:** classroom-based courses £8,250; laboratory-based courses £9,250; foundation courses £1,285. **Living costs:** £6,000.

University of Huddersfield, Queensgate, Huddersfield HD1 3DH; tel: 01484 422288; www.hud.ac.uk.

HULL UNIVERSITY

The University of Hull is located on a spacious open campus north of Hull. It was founded in 1927 and has a student population of over 18,800. The academic year is divided into two semesters of 15 weeks, which facilitates a flexible modular system of teaching. The university operates one of the most extensive scholarship schemes in UK higher education (when compared with institutions of similar size and resources).

DEGREE SUBJECTS OFFERED

Accountancy; American Studies; Archaeology; Biology; Biomedical Science; British Politics; Business Studies; Chemistry; Computer Science; Creative Music Technology; Creative Writing; Criminology; Dance; Design; Technology; Ecology; Economics; Education; Ethics; Religion and Education; Engineering (Computer; Systems; Electronic; Mechanical; Medical; Mobile Communications; Software), English; Environmental Science; European Government; Film Studies; Financial Management; French; Geography; German; Global Health; Hispanic Studies; History; Information Technology; International Business; International Law; Italian; Jazz and Popular Music; Law; Logistics; Media; Modern Languages; Music; Nursing; Operating Department Practice; Pharmaceutical Science; Philosophy; Physics; Politics; Primary Teaching; Psychology; Religion; Social Policy; Sociology; Spanish; Sport and Leisure; Sport Science; Theatre Studies; Theology; Tourism; War and Security Studies; Web Design; Zoology.

TUITION FEES (2009/10)

£3,225.

BURSARIES AND OTHER AWARDS

Students in receipt of the full maintenance grant will receive a bursary of £1,000. Those students from households with a family income between £25,001 and £40,000 will receive £500.

University of Hull Scholarships

These scholarships are awarded for academic excellence and are valued at £1,500 per year for two years with a possible extension to three years. Contact the admissions tutor for your chosen programme.

Ferens Scholarships
These are awarded on the basis of A-Level scores with grades of ABB to BBB and are awarded for two years.

AWARDS FOR NON-EU STUDENTS
Awards of £2,500 are offered to undergraduates and postgraduates in the following subjects: Biological Sciences, Biomedical Sciences, Chemistry, Computer Science, Engineering, Geography, Physics, Psychology, Sports Science.

Financial support is also available to students from Africa, China, East Asia, Gulf and Middle East, South Asia, South East Asia.

INFORMATION AND APPROXIMATE FEES FOR NON-EU STUDENTS
English language entry requirements: IELTS 6.0 (or equivalent) **Fees:** classroom subjects £9,500, laboratory subjects £11,500. **Living costs:** £4,500–£5,000

University of Hull, Hull HU6 7RX; tel:01482 465100; www.hull.ac.uk.

HULL YORK MEDICAL SCHOOL

The Hull York Medical School was established in 2003 by the Universities of York and Hull in partnership with the NHS in York and North Yorkshire, Hull and the East Riding, and Northern Lincolnshire. There are 700 medical students at any one time, with 140 new students arriving every year. Students spend a significant amount of time in clinical settings – beginning their first placements in the third week of the course. The university aims to provide a medical curriculum designed to meet the needs of 21st-century doctors.

DEGREE SUBJECTS OFFERED
MB BS Medicine (5 years, or 6 years with an intercalated year).

TUITION FEES (2009/10)
£3,225.

BURSARIES AND OTHER AWARDS
Bursary support will be available to HYMS students from the UK who are assessed to receive the maintenance grant and who have a residual household income of £40,040 or less. The 2009/10 HYMS undergraduate bursaries will be:

* £1,026 for students with a residual household income of up to £25,000;
* £514 for students with a residual household income of £25,001–£40,040;
* no bursary for students with a residual household income above £40,041.

INFORMATION AND APPROXIMATE FEES FOR NON-EU STUDENTS
HYMS accepts around 10 international students each year. **English language entry requirement:** IELTS overall score of 7.5 with a minimum of 7.0 in every component, or GCSE/IGCSE English language (as a first language) grade A, or IB score of 6 at the Standard level in English Language (as a first language), or equivalent. **Fees:** £12,600. **Living costs:** first year, not including rent, about £4,000.

Hull York Medical School, University of Hull HU6 7RX; Hull York Medical School, University of York YO10 5DD; tel: 0870 1245500; info@hyms.ac.uk; www.hyms.ac.uk.

IMPERIAL COLLEGE LONDON

Imperial College was founded in 1907. It offers high-level courses focusing on Medicine, Science, Engineering and Technology. There are over 10,800 students with accommodation for 1,700 undergraduates either on or close to the college campus. There is also a campus at Wye in Ashford, Kent.

DEGREE SUBJECTS OFFERED
Aerospace Materials; Animal Science; Applied Natural Science; Biochemistry; Biology; Biotechnology; Chemistry; Computing; Earth Resources; Ecology; Engineering (Aeronautical; Biomedical; Chemical; Civil; Computing; Electrical/Electronic; Environmental and Mining; Information Systems; Mechanical; Mining; Petroleum; Software); Environmental Geology; Equine Science; Geology; Materials Science; Mathematics; Medicine; Microbiology; Petroleum Geology; Physics; Plant Science; Zoology.

TUITION FEES (2009/10)
£3,225.

BURSARIES AND OTHER AWARDS
Students receiving the full maintenance grant of £2,906 will be eligible for a bursary of £4,000, if in addition they accepted a place having obtained grade As in three A-levels then they will receive an additional £200. Students receiving partial grants will receive bursaries on a sliding scale down to £105.

Green Design Challenge Awards
Students accepting a firm offer of a place in the Faculty of Engineering and who express an interest in this scheme will be selected in June. The award is worth £1,000 per year for a maximum of four years.

City & Guilds Scholarships
These scholarships are offered to two home students from financially disadvantaged backgrounds studying in the Faculty of Engineering. The awards are each worth £2500 per annum for a maximum of four years.

Grocers Company Scholarship
This award, based on academic merit, is worth £2,250 per year for a period of four years in the Faculty of Engineering.

Holligrave Scholarship
Students from educationally and financially disadvantaged backgrounds may be eligible for an award worth £1,500 in the first year and £1,000 in subsequent years.

Imperial College Student Opportunities Fund Scholarship
Scholarships worth £1,000 are offered each year for a maximum of four years, to exceptional candidates who come from educationally and financially disadvantaged backgrounds. Premium Scholarships worth £5,000 per year are awarded for Engineering, Natural Sciences and for Energy Efficient Technologies.

RW Barnes Educational Fund
Two awards worth £2,500 per year for up to four years are open to candidates living within a 40-mile radius of Beckington Somerset who are from financially and educationally disadvantaged backgrounds.

Drama Scholarship
There is a scholarship to support the development of a student within the School of Medicine as an actor or director. The award is worth £300 per year for three years and is made to a student showing talent and commitment to drama.

School of Medicine Scholarships
A number of scholarships are available to home and EU applicants on the strength of their performance on entry at interview. The value of the awards ranges from £100–500.

Music Scholarships
Five scholarships are offered entitling lessons on a chosen instrument. Students with a distinction in Grade 8 or equivalent should send a letter of application and a copy of their Grade 8 mark sheet and supporting references to The Director of Music at the College's main address no later than 28 February 2008. UCAS applicants should advise the admissions tutor of their intention to apply for an award at the time of application.

Sports Scholarships
Three scholarships each worth £5,000 are offered in Rowing and a Developing Excellence Scheme for potential national and international sports persons.

Cockburn Rugby Scholarship/Most unselfish player awards
Two awards are open to first year male and female entrants to the School of Medicine worth £1,000. There is also an award of £500 for the most unselfish player of the year.

Chemistry Scholarships
The department's close contacts with the chemical industry have led to the establishment of a scheme of industrially sponsored scholarships for undergraduates. Several scholarships will be awarded to students entering Chemistry courses. These are usually worth £1,000 for each of the three years of the course, plus the possibility of paid vacation work with the sponsor.

Earth Sciences and Engineering Bursaries
Two bursaries worth £1,000 are available each year to students showing exceptional academic potential.

Citigroup Bursaries
Bursaries valued at £1,500 are offered to 20 student volunteers supporting pupils in local primary and secondary schools. They will help to teach subjects such as Science, Mathematics and IT.

Agricultural Science Scholarships
A number of scholarships worth £1,500 are offered, which are awarded to applicants with high A-level or equivalent scores.

Engineering Bursaries
A small number of accommodation bursaries are available worth £500 for students following courses in Engineering.

AWARDS FOR NON-EU STUDENTS
Burhouse Bursary
Two awards worth £1,000 per annum are offerd to undergraduates and postgraduates in the Department of Earth Science and Engineering.

See Chapters 2, 4 and 6 for additional awards, applicable to all universities

ICAAHK Scholarships
There are open to holders of a permanent Hong Kong ID card.

POSTGRADUATE AWARDS
There are several awards offered by various departments to postgraduate students (including a Polish Scholarship) and a Commonwealth Scholarship for MSc students by distance learning in a partnership with the University of Pretoria.

INFORMATION AND APPROXIMATE FEES FOR NON-EU STUDENTS
There are 2,200 international students from over 110 countries. **English language entry requirement:** IELTS 6.0–7.0 (or equivalent). **Fees:** £15,500–£19,450; Medicine: pre-clinical £23,800, clinical £35,500. **Living costs:** £9,500–£10,500.

Imperial College of Science, Technology and Medicine, London SW7 2AZ; tel: 020 7594 8001; www.ic.ac.uk.

KEELE UNIVERSITY

The university is situated on a large and attractive campus in the Potteries between Birmingham and Manchester. It was founded in 1949 and currently has a student population of 9,000. Courses are arranged on a modular structure with a very large range of subject combinations on offer.

DEGREE SUBJECTS OFFERED
American Studies; Ancient History; Applied Environmental Science; Applied Social Studies; Astrophysics; Biochemistry; Biological and Medicinal Chemistry; Biology; Biomedical Sciences; Business Administration; Chemistry; Classical Studies; Cognitive Science; Computer Science; Conductive Education; Criminology; Economics; Educational Studies; English; European Studies; Finance; French; Geography; Geology; Geoscience; German; History; Human Resource Management; Information Systems; International History; International Relations; Japanese; Latin; Law; Management Science; Mathematics; Medicine; Midwifery; Music; Music Technology; Neuroscience; Nursing; Philosophy; Physics; Physiotherapy; Politics; Russian; Sociology; Software Engineering; Spanish; Statistics; Visual Arts.

TUITION FEES (2009/10)
£3,225.

BURSARIES AND OTHER AWARDS
Keele will pay the mandatory bursary of £305 to all eligible students in receipt of a full maintenance award (grant).

In addition, prospective students can apply for a range of competitive bursaries. There are bursaries for students from rural areas, local partner schools and colleges, black and ethnic minority students and students taking Medicine and foundation courses as well as smaller bursaries for students taking Music, Physics and Mathematics. Eligible students will also be considered for two types of Academic Excellence Scholarship.

Once students enrol at Keele they can apply for bursaries to help them study abroad and to support them in mentoring school pupils (see below).

Vice Chancellor's Scholarships

These awards worth £4,000 for each year of study will be awarded to students for outstanding achievement at Key Stage 5. A small number of scholarships will be available to students demonstrating excellence regardless of their financial circumstances, but most will be dependent also on grant eligibility.

Dean's Scholarships

These are awarded for each year of study and are valued at £2,000 to students who can demonstrate excellent performance in any subject at Key Stage 5 and who are also in receipt of some level of maintenance grant.

Mathematics Scholarships

Eligible students must register for the single honours Mathematics degree course with a tariff score of 300 points in their three best A-level examinations (including a grade A in Mathematics). The words are worth £500.

Keele Link Bursaries

These awards worth £500 are available to students from Keele Link Schools and from households with a maximum income of £39,000 or less.

Institute of Physics Bursaries

These awards worth £4,000 over the duration of the course are open to students taking Physics or Astrophysics.

Rural Bursaries

Students who live in rural areas where daily transport to a university from home would be difficult can apply for these bursaries toward the cost of accommodation on campus. The awards are valued at £500 for each year of study.

Ethnic Minority Bursaries

These are worth £1,000 for each year of study.

Medical Bursaries

These awards of £500 are made for each of the first four years of the medical course.

Students who want to undertake work or other placements during their course

* Work-based Bursaries: £1,000 for Years 1 and 2
* Mentoring Bursaries: £1,000 for work in Year 2
* Study-abroad Bursaries: £500 for study overseas in Year 2.

There is also a Keele Link Bursary for students from partner schools and colleges, and a Foundation Year Bursary for students wishing to study on one of our foundation-year programmes.

Chapel Music Scholarship

Two scholarships may be awarded, one for choral conducting and one for an organist.

The normal tenure is for two years, from January to December, and the current value of each scholarship is £300 per year.

Bach Choir Scholarship

An Accompanist's Scholarship for the Keele Bach Choir may be awarded annually for an academic year. This award, with a value of £300 per year, is made to a student reading principal music.

Montford Instrumental Scholarship

Players of any orchestral instrument may apply for the Montford Instrumental Scholarship, which may be awarded annually for tenure in the first and second principal years. Montford scholars are required to play in such orchestral and chamber groups as the head of the Department of Music may determine. The value of the scholarship is £300 per year.

Other music scholarships

* Orchestral Leader Scholarship, offered by the Keele Philharmonic Society.
* Audley and District Male Voice Choir Scholarship, for first- and second-year singers (male or female).

AWARDS FOR NON-EU STUDENTS
Keele International Student Scholarships

Keele is offering scholarships to full-time international students from the following countries: Brunei; China (including Hong Kong); the Gulf States (Bahrain/Dubai/Kuwait/Oman/Saudi Arabia/UAE); India; Kenya; Malaysia; Singapore; Sri Lanka; Taiwan; Thailand; Vietnam.

The scholarships are £3,000 towards the cost of annual tuition fees, and the scholarship are given for each year of study of the course.

The scholarships are awarded to students who can demonstrate excellence in at least two of the following areas:

* Academic qualifications
* English language ability
* Understanding of the course and motivation to study at Keele
* Extracurricular or work experience.

Students should consult the website for details of how to apply for the above scholarships.

POSTGRADUATE AWARDS

See the university website for information about awards and funding opportunities for postgraduate students.

INFORMATION AND APPROXIMATE FEES FOR NON-EU STUDENTS

There is a large number of overseas students. **English language entry requirement:** IELTS 6.0–6.5 (or equivalent). An English language summer school is held before the start of the degree course. International foundation programmes (entry IELTS 4.5) are also held. **Fees:** £8,700–£11,300. **Living costs:** £8,000–9,000.

Keele University, Keele, Staffordshire ST5 5BG; tel: 01782 584005; www.keele.ac.uk.

KENT UNIVERSITY

The University of Kent was founded in 1965 and is located on a campus site two miles from Canterbury city centre. It is organised on a college basis, each student being a member of a college. All first-year students live on campus. There is a student population of 8,500.

DEGREE SUBJECTS OFFERED

Accounting and Finance; Actuarial Science; American Studies; Anthropology; Art and Film Studies; Biochemistry; Biological Chemistry; Biological Science; Biomedical Sciences; Business Administration; Chemistry; Classical Studies; Computing; Criminology; Cultural Studies; Drama; Economics; Engineering (Communications; Computer Systems; Electronic); English; European

Studies; Film Studies; Forensic Science; French; German; Health and Social Care; History; History of Art; History of Science; Industrial Relations; International Relations; Italian; Law; Linguistics; Literature; Management Science; Mathematics; Microbiology; Molecular and Cellular Biology; Multimedia Technology; Music; Pharmaceutical Chemistry; Philosophy; Physics; Politics; Psychology; Social Anthropology; Social Policy; Social Sciences; Sociology; Spanish; Sport, Health and Fitness; Statistics; Theology; Urban Regeneration; Visual and Performed Arts.

TUITION FEES (2009/10)
£3,225.

BURSARIES AND OTHER AWARDS
A minimum of £300 is available for those who qualify for the full maintenance grant. Further grants will be awarded depending on family income. Students from households with an income of £21,000 or less will receive £1,000. There is additional support between £750 and £250 for those from households with £40,000 income or less.

University Scholarships for Academic Excellence
There are 20 scholarships of £1,000 per year, one for each academic department. They are awarded for one year in the first instance and are renewable for the duration of a three- or four-year course. The continuation of the scholarship is subject to academic progress and is awarded on the basis of academic achievement, submission of an essay on a selected subject and satisfactory performance at interview. The closing date is 26 February.

Loyalty Discount
A discount of 10% of the first year's tuition fees will apply to family members registering on degree courses.

Partner Scholarships
Scholarships are offered to encourage pupils at local schools and colleges to register for courses at the university.

Anglo-Jewish Scholarship
Awards are available to Jewish students in financial need.

University Sports Scholarships
There are numerous awards between £1,000 and £5,000 for talented sportsmen and -women on full-time courses. Applicants should have represented their county in their chosen sport and preferably at national or BUSA-level. Scholarships are normally only allocated to those competing in major national sports which are well represented at the university. These include:

* £2,500 Cricket Scholarship in conjunction with Kent County Cricket Club. Applicants should have cricketing potential and have played at county level in junior or youth cricket and be prepared to register and play for Kent CCC
* £2,000 Rugby Scholarship in partnership with Canterbury Rugby Club and Barretts of Canterbury. Applicants should be prepared to represent the Canterbury Club and the university's first team
* £2,000 Hockey Sponsorship in partnership with Canterbury Ladies Hockey Club. Applicants should be prepared to play for the club and university.

University Music Scholarships
Ten awards are offered worth £1,000 and are awarded by way of auditions. They are valid for one year in the first instance and are renewable for the duration of the student's degree programme. There are also Music Lesson Scholarships worth £400 for free tuition to enable students to continue their instrumental and vocal studies.

AWARDS FOR NON-EU STUDENTS
Kent Business School Scholarships
Twelve scholarships are offered worth £1,500 of the tuition fee. This award requires an essay of 800 words on reasons for choosing the Business School.

INFORMATION AND APPROXIMATE FEES FOR NON-EU STUDENTS
English language entry requirement: IELTS 5.5 (or equivalent). There is a comprehensive English language support service. There are also foundation programmes (entry IELTS 5.0 or equivalent) to prepare students for arts, Business, science, Engineering and Law courses. Non-degree courses are also offered for one year or less. **Fees:** £9,400–£11,800. **Living costs:** £8,000–£9,000.

University of Kent, Canterbury, Kent CT2 7NZ; tel: 01227 827272; www.kent.ac.uk.

KING'S COLLEGE (University of London)

King's College was founded in London in 1829 and has campus locations in the Strand, Waterloo, London Bridge and Denmark Hill. It now has a population of over 16,600 students taking over 200 undergraduate degree programmes. Small-group teaching remains an important feature of study.

DEGREE SUBJECTS OFFERED
Afro-Portuguese; American Studies; Ancient History; Applied Computing; Applied Environmental Science; Aquatic Biology; Astrophysics; Biblical Studies; Biochemistry; Biological Sciences; Biomedical Sciences; Biomolecular Sciences; Biotechnology; Business Management; Cell Biology; Chemistry; Classical Archaeology; Classical Byzantine and Modern Greek Studies; Classical Studies; Classics; Clinical Science; Communication; Computer Science; Dentistry; Ecology; Education; Engineering (Computer Systems and Electronics; Electronic; Manufacturing Systems; Mechatronics; Telecommunications); English; Environmental Health; Environmental Sciences; European Studies; Film; French; Genetics; Geography; German; Hispanic Studies; History; Human Biology; Human Ecology; Immunology; Latin; Law; Linguistics; Management; Manufacturing Systems; Mathematics; Medical Biochemistry; Medicine; Microbiology; Midwifery; Modern Greek; Molecular Biology; Molecular Genetics; Music; Nursing; Nutrition; Parasitology; Pharmacology; Pharmacy; Philosophy; Physics; Physiology; Physiotherapy; Portuguese and Brazilian Studies; Religious Studies; Theology; United States and Latin American Studies; War Studies; Zoology.

TUITION FEES (2009/10)
£3,225.

BURSARIES AND OTHER AWARDS
myBursary
The bursary is set against the level of the maintenance grant received, in four stages. In the current year for those on the maximum grant the award is £1,350, lower awards being set at £1,050 and £350 as the level of the grant is reduced down to £100 for those on the minimum grant. The bursaries are non-repayable.

myScholarship
Forty scholarships are open to new entrants, based on academic performance. The awards are each worth £1,800.

AWARDS FOR NON-EU STUDENTS

12 country-specific scholarships (four for each country) are offered to applicants from Canada, Hong Kong, India and Taiwan. An additional four awards are also given to applicants from any other country.

Greek Scholarships

The Schillizzi Foundation awards up to three scholarships annually, to enable students of Greek nationality to read for a first degree in any subject at King's College. The scholarships, which have a value of £2,500 per year, are normally awarded for three years. Contact the International Liaison and Exchange Service, Cornwall House, London SE1 8WA; tel: 020 7872 3299; www.kcl.ac.uk.

POSTGRADUATE AWARDS

Scholarships are awarded annually to postgraduate students from Canada, Taiwan and the USA. The Schools of Biomedical Studies, Health and Life Sciences, Humanities, Pharmacy and Social Sciences also make awards.

INFORMATION AND APPROXIMATE FEES FOR NON-EU STUDENTS

There is a large number of international students. **English language entry requirement:** Engineering, Nursing and science courses IELTS 6.5 (or equivalent); Dentistry, Law, Medicine and Physiotherapy IELTS 7.0 (or equivalent); humanities and social science courses IELTS 7.5 (or equivalent). Pre-sessional summer courses and a one-year foundation course are available. **Fees:** £12,020–£15,080; clinical courses £27,980. **Living costs:** £9,500–£10,500.

King's College, University of London, Strand, London WC2R 2LS; tel: 020 7836 5454; www.kcl.ac.uk.

KINGSTON UNIVERSITY

The Kingston University campuses are situated in and around the Royal Borough of Kingston (dating back to Saxon times). There are four campuses: Penrhyn Road (the central base) with Faculties of Human Sciences, Science and some technology courses; Knights Park nearby, offering Art and Design, Architecture and Surveying; Roehampton Vale (Engineering) and Kingston Hill covering Business, Law, Music, Social Work and teacher training. There are over 16,000 students.

DEGREE SUBJECTS OFFERED

Accounting and Finance; Applied Geology; Architecture; Art and Design; Biochemistry; Biomedical Science; Biology; Building Surveying; Business; Chemistry; Community Care; Computing; Criminal Justice; Drama; Earth Sciences; Economics; Education (Primary); Engineering (Aerospace; Automotive; Biomechanical; Civil; Electronic/Electrical; Manufacturing Systems; Mechanical; Motorcycle); English; Environmental Studies; Family and Child Care; Film Studies; French; Geographical Information Systems; Geography; Geology; German; Health Systems Technology; History; Investigative Analysis; Landscape Architecture; Law; Legal Studies; Leisure Property Development; Linguistics; Mathematics; Medicinal Sciences; Music; Natural History; Nursing; Nutrition; Pharmaceutical Science; Physics; Politics; Property Planning and Development; Psychology; Quantity Surveying; Radiography; Real Estate Management; Sociology; Spanish; Sports Science; Statistics; Women's Studies.

TUITION FEES (2009/10)

£3,225.

BURSARIES AND OTHER AWARDS

All students eligible for state support will be entitled to a bursary. The levels will initially range from £310 to £1,000 per year. These amounts include the statutory £300 for students in receipt of a full grant. Bursaries of £300 are also available to PGCE and Social Work students.

Scholarships

There is an undergraduate scholarship scheme open to all home and EU entrants. The value of each scholarship is £1,000. There are also special categories for students studying at one of the university's seven associate colleges. The scholarship scheme is renewable annually, subject to meeting a quality criterion.

Diana Winstanley Bursaries

Four bursaries are awarded through the Faculties of Business and Law each worth £1,000.

Faculty of Computing, Information Systems and Mathematics

Fifteen awards are made each worth £1,500.

Technology Scholarships

Additional scholarships are available in Technology to undergraduate full-fee students. Scholarships to the value of £2,000 are available to Civil Engineering students who enter with 240 tariff points or over.

The university is offering a staged payment scheme (December to April) to assist in payment of tuition fees. It has also established a 'one-stop shop' advisory centre to provide a whole range of financial and other services.

Fee waiver

Fee waivers are available for students receiving a range of benefits or proof of income of self (and partner) below £14,200 per year.

School of Education

Students applying for Secondary shortage subjects (sciences or modern languages) may obtain awards of £5,000 (for those under 25) and £7,500 (for those 25 and over).

AWARDS FOR NON-EU STUDENTS
International Scholarships

Seventeen international scholarships are offered on the basis of academic merit and financial need.

Alumni and Family Bursaries

These awards are made to students who have studied and are returning to Kingston and to students members of whose families have studied or are studying at the university.

INFORMATION AND APPROXIMATE FEES FOR NON-EU STUDENTS

There are 2,000 international students from over 70 countries. **English language entry requirement:** IELTS 6.0 (or equivalent). **Fees:** £6,300–£10,000. **Living costs:** £5,500–£6,500.

Kingston University, Cooper House, 40–46 Surbiton Road, Kingston-on-Thames KT1 2HX; tel: 020 8547 7053; www.kingston.ac.uk.

LAMPETER (University of Wales)

The University of Wales, Lampeter was founded in 1822 and occupies a large area of a small county town. Degree courses are mainly focused on the humanities and liberal arts and are taught on a modular system. Single, joint and combined degrees are offered to 1,700 students, 80% of whom can be accommodated by the university.

DEGREE SUBJECTS OFFERED

American Studies; Ancient History; Anthropology; Arabic; Archaeology; Business Information Technology; Business Management; Chinese Studies; Church History; Classical Studies; Classics; Divinity; English; English with Creative Writing; English with TEFL; English: Modern Literatures; Film Studies; Greek (Ancient); History; Information Technology; Islamic Studies; Latin; Media Production; Media Studies; Medieval Studies; Modern Historical Studies; Philosophical Studies; Philosophy; Religious History; Religious Studies; Theology; Voluntary Sector Studies; Welsh; Welsh with Subtitling; Welsh Translation and Subtitling.

TUITION FEES (2009/10)

See www.studentfinancewales.co.uk and **Chapter 1, 'Financing Your Course'.**

BURSARIES AND OTHER AWARDS

Scholarships

There are 20 University Scholarships valued at £2,000 per year (for applicants in any subject), 18 Departmental Scholarships (two per department) valued at £1,000 per year, and an Organ Scholarship (£150) and Exhibition (£75). There are also departmental Entrance Scholarships in History, Theology and Religious Studies and Welsh awarded on A-level results.

Other open scholarships and exhibitions are available, most founded in the nineteenth century and ranging in value from £50 to £250. There are other awards (£50–1,500) with restrictions often linked to country, county or parish of birth or religious affiliation.

Academic prizes for excellence range from £25 to £200.

Entrance Scholarships

Five scholarships worth £100 and £150 are awarded each year.

Ferne Bates Scholarship

This is worth £100 and is restricted to natives of Wales.

The Pugh Jones Scholarship

This is valued at £100 and gives preference to students taking courses in Classics, Theology or Philosophy.

Organ Scholarship

This award is worth £150 and involves playing in the Chapel.

Welsh Department Scholarships

The Welsh Department offers a number of Entrance Scholarships worth £2,000 to students whose first or second language is Welsh.

Cliff Tucker Scholarship in History

The Cliff Tucker Scholarship, worth £2,000 per annum, is awarded to an undergraduate student studying history or a historically-orientated degree (including Ancient, Medieval and Modern History as well as Religious History).

Essay Prize
The Department of Theology and Religious Studies offers an essay prize of one year's free accommodation.

INFORMATION AND APPROXIMATE FEES FOR OVERSEAS NON-EU STUDENTS
English language entry requirement: IELTS 6.0 (or equivalent). English language tuition programmes are available, from pre-sessional courses of one month to year-long courses. **Fees:** £8,988. **Living costs:** £6,500.

Lampeter (University of Wales), Ceredigion; tel: 01570 422351; www.lamp.ac.uk.

LANCASTER UNIVERSITY

In July 1964 the Queen approved the charter that established Lancaster University. A site three miles south of the city of Lancaster was chosen, and the building of the university began. The university has nine campus colleges and a total student population of over 9,500.

DEGREE SUBJECTS OFFERED
Accounting; Advertising; American Studies; Applied Social Science; Art; Biochemistry; Biological Science; Biomedical Sciences; Business Studies; Chemistry; Combined Science; Computer Science; Creative Arts; Criminology; Culture, Media and Communication Systems; Ecology; Economics; Educational Studies; Engineering (Communication; Computer Systems; Electronic; Mathematics; Mechanical); English Language; Environmental Science; European Legal Studies; European Management; Finance; French Studies; Geography; Geophysical Sciences; German Studies; History; Information Technology; International Business; International Relations and Strategic Studies; Italian Studies; Law; Linguistics; Management; Marketing; Mathematics; Medieval and Renaissance Studies; Music; Natural Sciences; Operations Management; Organisation Studies; Peace Studies; Philosophy; Physics; Politics; Pollution Science; Psychology; Religious Studies; Social Work; Sociology; Spanish Studies; Statistics; Theatre Studies; Women's Studies.

TUITION FEES (2009/10)
£3,225.

BURSARIES AND OTHER AWARDS
In 2009, UK students receiving government funding to study first degree courses with assessed household incomes:

* Below £18,360 may receive £1,315 bursary.
* Between £18,360 and £27,800 may receive £500 bursary.

Estimated figures. Students must not object to data sharing on their government funding application, the University will then automatically receive and assess any bursary entitlement.

Scholarships
In 2009, all Undergraduate courses carry scholarships of £1,000 per annum, available to UK students making Lancaster their confirmed UCAS choice and achieving University specified scholarship grades. Continued payment is subject to satisfactory academic progression.

For information on awards, fees and funding please see: www.lancs.ac.uk/ugfinance.

Other awards

There are also a range of other awards available from the university, its colleges, trust funds and government funds. Some of these awards can be applied for prior to entry; others are for registered (attending) students only. Examples include:

* Alumni Opportunity Funds: To help registered students who face hardship.
* ALF Awards: To help UK students who have a shortfall between income and expenditure.
* College Awards: A whole range of awards to help overcome financial difficulties.
* Peel Studentship: To help students over 21 years of age to access higher education.

For full information on all awards, including their availability, eligibility and further details, see: www.lancs.ac.uk/funding.

POSTGRADUATE AWARDS

Faculty Research Studentships/Graduate Teaching Assistantships. Each of the university's three faculties (Arts and Social Sciences, Science and Technology and the Management School) will be offering a number of Research Studentships/Graduate Teaching Assistantships. Applicants must hold an excellent bachelor's or master's degree and have been accepted for full-time study leading to a PhD or MPhil. Faculties will advertise their studentships in the spring term and successful applicants will be notified in the summer term.

For further information on postgraduate awards see: www.lancs.ac.uk/pgfunding.

INFORMATION AND APPROXIMATE FEES FOR NON-EU STUDENTS

There are international students from over 100 countries. **English language entry requirement:** IELTS 5.5–6.0 (or equivalent). Pre-sessional and in-session English language tuition is available. On campus accommodation is usually available to international students throughout the degree course. Fees: see: www.lancs.ac.uk/depts/studreg/undergrads/ugfees.htm. (07-08 non-science courses £9,000; science and management courses £11,000.) **Living Costs:** see: www.lancs.ac.uk/studentservices/international/costsandbudgeting.htm.

Lancaster University, Lancaster LA1 4YW; tel: 01524 65201; www.lancs.ac.uk.

LEEDS UNIVERSITY

Leeds is one of the most popular universities in the UK, with an international reputation for its teaching and research. There are over 30,000 students taking some 700 undergraduate and 474 postgraduate degree programmes, including a wide range of joint honours degrees.

DEGREE SUBJECTS OFFERED

Accounting; Acting; Applied Biology; Arabic; Architectural Engineering; Art and Design; Asia-Pacific Studies; Astronomy; Atmospheric Science; Audiology; Biochemistry; Biology; Biotechnology; Broadcasting; Chemistry; Childhood Studies; Chinese; Cinema and Photography; Classical Civilisation; Classics; Cognitive Science; Colour Science; Communications Studies; Computer Science; Computing; Criminology; Dance; Dentistry; Development Studies; Ecology; Economics; Engineering (Architectural; Automotive; Chemical; Civil and Structural; Electronic/Electrical; Energy; Environmental Energy; Fire; Mechanical/Manufacturing; Mineral; Mining; Petroleum); English; Environmental Sciences; European Studies; Fashion Design; Fine Art; Food Science; French; Genetics; Geography; Geological Sciences; Geophysical Sciences; German; Graphic Design; Greek and Roman Civilisation; History; History of Art; Human Resource Management; Information Systems; International History and Politics; International

Relations; Islamic Studies; Italian; Japanese Latin; Law; Linguistics; Management; Materials Science; Mathematics; Mechatronics and Robotics; Medical Sciences; Medicine; Metallurgy; Microbiology; Midwifery; Mineral and Quarry Engineering; Music; Nanotechnology; Neuroscience; New Media; Nursing; Parliamentary Studies; Pharmacology; Philosophy; Physics; Physiology; Politics; Product Design; Psychology; Radiography; Religious Studies; Russian; Social Policy; Sociology; Spanish; Sports and Exercise Sciences; Science; Social Work; Statistics; Television Production; Textiles; Theatre and Performance; Theology; Transport Studies; Zoology.

TUITION FEES (2009/10)
£3,225.

BURSARIES AND OTHER AWARDS
Leeds Bursary
Bursaries will be offered ranging from £335 to £1,540 to full-time students with residual family income of up to £36,600 per year. Bursaries of £805 are also offered to part-time students regardless of income. There are some exceptions – for full details visit www.leeds.ac.uk/students/fees/bursaries.htm

Sport
The England and Wales Cricket Board has designated Leeds University as a Centre of Cricketing Excellence. The university participates in the UCCE Scheme for talented and ambitious young cricketers. Contact Mr WJC Butterworth on 0113 233 5096.

Leverhulme Trade Charities Trust Bursary
The bursary is worth up to £3000, dependent on financial need. Applicants should be UK resident students and be the son, daughter, spouse, widow or widower of a: commercial traveller – an agent of any firm of manufacturers or wholesale dealers selling directly to industry or commerce who has travelled for at least six months per year for five consecutive years; chemist – a member of the Royal Pharmaceutical Society dispensing medicines direct to the public; or grocer (excluding greengrocers) – a person engaged in selling household provisions excluding persons owning or employed by a business having more than 50 employees. Funds are intended to help with tuition fees, exam fees, travel costs or study costs and students must complete an application form illustrating their financial need.

Myrtle Boultwood Scholarships
Nine awards are available. Closing date: contact Access and Community Engagement. Nine awards are offered to new full-time UK students eligible to receive the full UK maintenance grant (with a family income of £25,000 per year or less). Applicants should be intending to study selected degrees at the University of Leeds, contact Access and Community Engagement for more information.

Centenary Alumni Scholarships
This scholarship is designed to help encourage and provide support to students exhibiting high academic performance but facing financial barriers. The scholarship is funded by University of Leeds alumni who wish to support new students throughout their study. Scholars receive opportunities to visit the University as well as use the advice, guidance and mentoring services we offer. Applicants should be UK students commencing full-time study for their first undergraduate degree at the University of Leeds and have a family income of below £40,000, per year. Applicants should also have, or achieve, three A-level grade As or equivalent UCAS points in comparable alternative qualifications (excluding General Studies).

Leeds Scholarship
This scholarship is designed to help encourage young people to enter university. To qualify, applicants should be part of the first generation in their family to go to university, be intending to study a full-time degree and not be in receipt of any other scholarship or bursary.

Applicants should be eligible to receive the full UK maintenance grant (a family income of £25,000 per year or below). Some consideration will be given to students who are on the Access to Leeds Scheme and other access programmes. The Access to Leeds Scheme is an alternative entry scheme offering special consideration to applicants with the potential to succeed at university. More information on the Access to Leeds Scheme is available at www.leeds.ac.uk/ace/access/leeds.htm

Robert Ogden Scholarship
These scholarships are available to UK students living in the Barnsley, Doncaster or Rotherham areas of South Yorkshire. Applicants intend to study a full-time undergraduate degree course at the University of Leeds. Applicants should be part of the first generation in the family to enter Higher Education, be eligible to receive the full UK maintenance grant (family income of £25,000 per year or below) and not be in receipt of any other scholarship or bursary.

Faculty of Engineering Undergraduate Scholarships
Variable number of awards. Closing date: Contact Faculty of Engineering for details.

The Faculty of Engineering is offering a contribution of £1,500 towards academic fees or maintenance to all qualified UK/EU students wishing to undertake undergraduate study within any of the schools within the faculty.

Access to Learning Fund
Variable number of awards. Funds are available for full-time and part-time UK students in financial hardship. Further details and application forms are available from the Student Advice Centre. Completed application forms should be returned to: Financial Aid, Student Administration, Marjorie and Arnold Ziff Building, University of Leeds, LS2 9JT.

INFORMATION AND APPROXIMATE FEES FOR NON-EU STUDENTS
English language entry requirement: IELTS 6.0 (or equivalent). **Fees:** £9,700–£12,500, Medicine and Dentistry Clinical £23,500. **Living costs:** £9,000.

University of Leeds, Leeds, LS2 9JT; tel: 0113 243 1751; www.leeds.ac.uk.

LEEDS COLLEGE OF MUSIC

The UK's contemporary conservatoire is located on a single site in Leeds city centre. It provides postgraduate, undergraduate and Further Education courses to around 1,200 full-time students. In addition there are another 1000 studying on part-time Outreach and Community Education.

DEGREE SUBJECTS OFFERED
Jazz Studies; Music Production; Music Production with Performance; Music and Sound Production for the Moving Image; Music Studies; Popular Music, Commercial Music Production and Recording.

TUITION FEES (2009/10)
£3,225.

BURSARIES AND OTHER AWARDS
Travel and Audition Bursary
Applicants who are invited for interview and/or audition may apply for assistance with the cost of travel to the college and a refund of the audition fee if they are in receipt of a full

Education Maintenance Allowance, or if their household is in receipt of certain income-related benefits.

Leeds College of Music Bursary

The College will provide an annual bursary to home students whose residual household income is below £39,333. The amount of the Bursary is according to three income bands. The payment will be either £1,055, £790 or £540, depending into which band the student falls.

Scholarships

The College offers up to six scholarships per year between the following two categories:

Endangered Species Scholarship

Home students whose principal instrument is one of the nationally recognised shortage instruments may apply for a scholarship of £1,500 per year. (The instruments are: oboe, bassoon, horn, trombone, tuba and strings.) Applications will be considered from those who reside in certain designated 'widening participation' postcode areas, and/or those who have received a full EMA, or those whose household is in receipt of an income-related benefit.

Music and Dance Scheme Scholarship

Students who have attended the Yorkshire Young Musicians, or another designated Centre of Advanced Training, and who are in receipt of means-tested fee support from the DCSF Music and Dance Scheme, may apply for a scholarship of £1,500 per year.

Alan Hawkshaw Scholarship

Applicants to the Music or Jazz degrees (home students) may apply for a scholarship of £1,500 per year if their Principal instrument is piano, tuba, trombone, bassoon, French horn, oboe or double bass. Selection for this will be based upon written application, musical and academic ability and potential.

Ruben Vincent Trombone Scholarship

Two Scholarships of £2,000 each are available to principal trombonists for the purchase of a new trombone, in memory of Ruben Vincent, who was an accomplished jazz trombonist and businessman. Note that students may only receive a scholarship from one category, although eligibility for the LCM bursary is not affected.

AWARDS FOR NON-EU STUDENTS

A small number of partial fee scholarships of up to £3,000, for one year, for new international students, are available on a competitive basis by application. A discount of £500 off the tuition fees for those paying the International rate, is available if the full fee is paid at or before enrolment.

INFORMATION AND APPROXIMATE FEES FOR NON-EU STUDENTS

Thirty students are from overseas. **English language entry requirement:** IELTS 6.0 (or equivalent). **Fees:** £10,290. **Living costs:** £9,000.

Leeds College of Music, 3 Quarry Hill, Leeds LS2 7PD; tel: 0113 222 3400; www.lcm.ac.uk.

LEEDS METROPOLITAN UNIVERSITY

The university is situated on two main campuses, one in the city centre and the other at Headingley Campus three miles north of the city. Over 30,000 students are following first-degree courses.

DEGREE SUBJECTS OFFERED

Accounting; Architecture; Art and Design; Biosciences; Building Surveying; Business Computing; Business Information Management; Business Studies; Childhood Studies; Clinical Language Sciences; Community and Youth Studies; Computer Science; Computing; Construction Management; Counselling; Dietetics; Economics; Education; Engineering; English; Environment; Events Management; Fine Art; Garden Art and Design; Geography; Graphic Arts; Health Studies; Hospitality Management; Human Biology; Human Nutrition; Humanities; Information and Communication Management; Information Systems; Interior Design; Landscape Architecture; Languages; Law; Leisure and Recreation; Media; Multimedia; Music; Nursing; Occupational Health and Safety; Photography; Physical Education; Physiotherapy; Playwork; Politics; Psychology; Public Relations; Quantity Surveying; Resort Management; Retail Management; Social Policy; Social Sciences; Sociology; Sports and Recreation; Three Dimensional Design; Tourism Management; Urban and Regional Planning.

TUITION FEES (2009/10)

£2,000.

'Leeds Met has chosen to charge all full-time students a lower fee of £2,000 because they believe that we can provide high quality education at an affordable price.' Leeds Met's approach to fees effectively means that all students receive the equivalent of a bursary of over £1,000.

BURSARIES AND OTHER AWARDS

The Leeds Met Bursary

The Leeds Met Bursary Scheme has 22 bursaries which are awarded each year to new students living in the Leeds or Harrogate postcode areas who have accepted a firm offer and whose family is in receipt of a means-tested state benefit. Each bursary is worth £1,000 in Year 1 and £500 in Years 2 and 3.

Carnegie Sports Scholarships

Applications are normally considered from those students who have reached international or national standard in their event.

Talented Athlete Scholarships

The University is involved in developing this national scheme which provides up to £3,000 per scholar to support their sporting programme.

AWARDS FOR NON-EU STUDENTS

Leeds Met offers a small number of scholarships for international students. These are awarded on merit and can be applied for once a student has accepted an unconditional offer from the university.

INFORMATION AND APPROXIMATE FEES FOR NON-EU STUDENTS

There are 2,500 international students from 110 countries. **English language entry requirement:** IELTS 6.0 (or equivalent); international foundation course IELTS 4.0–5.0. The international foundation course starts in September or February. There are also general English courses. **Fees:** £7,000–£9,600. **Living costs:** £9,000.

Leeds Metropolitan University, Civic Quarter, Leeds LS1 3HE; tel: 0113 812 3113; www. leedsmet.ac.uk.

See Chapters 2, 4 and 6 for additional awards, applicable to all universities

LEEDS TRINITY ALL SAINTS

Two catholic colleges, Trinity and All Saints, became established as one college in the 1960s and is now situated on a campus 20 minutes from Leeds city centre. Vocational, arts and humanities and teacher training courses are now offered.

DEGREE SUBJECTS OFFERED

Business, Childhood and Youth Studies, Early Years Education, Education Studies, English, Film and TV, Film Studies, Forensic Psychology, Health Promotion, Health Psychology, History, Humanities, Journalism, Media, Nutrition, Physical Education, Primary Education, Psychology, Religious Studies, Sport Studies, TV, Theology

TUTION FEES (2009/10)

£3,225.

BURSARIES AND OTHER AWARDS

Leeds Trinity Bursary.
In addition to full or partial maintenance grants, bursaries of £1,000 and £500 are offered based on household incomes either below £25,000 or between £25,001 and £50,000.

Leeds Trinity Excellence Scholarships.
Scholarships worth £1,000 are awarded on the basis of academic excellence with extramural activities also being taken into consideration.

INFORMATION AND APPROXIMATE FEES FOR NON-EU STUDENTS

English Language entry requirement: IELTS 6.0 (or equivalent). **Fees:** £7,725. **Living costs:** £8,000–£9,000.

Leeds Trinity All Saints, Brownberrie Lane, Leeds LS18 5HD; tel: 0113 283 7100; www. leedstrinity.ac.uk

LEICESTER UNIVERSITY

The University of Leicester is located close to the city centre and all the teaching buildings are within walking distance of each other. Halls of residence are located further away from the city centre to the back of the main campus. The university has a student population of 19,000 and was founded in 1921.

DEGREE SUBJECTS OFFERED

American Studies; Archaeology and Ancient History; Banking and Finance; Biological Sciences; Chemistry; Communications, Media and Society; Computer Science; Criminology; Economics; Engineering; English; English and American Studies; English and History; Film Studies and Visual Arts; Geography; Geosciences; Historical Studies; History of Art; Interdisciplinary Science; Law; Management Studies; Mathematics; Medical Biochemistry; Medical Genetics; Medical Microbiology, Medical Physiology; Medicine; Modern Languages; Physics and Astronomy; Politics and International Relations; Psychology; Sociology

TUITION FEES (2009/10)
£3,225.

BURSARIES AND OTHER AWARDS
All students with a household income of under £20,000 who are entitled to full state support will be eligible for an annual bursary of £1,319. Families with an income range of £20,001–£40,000 will be offered an annual bursary on a sliding scale. There is also a hardship fund which will go towards home graduates experiencing hardship because of family background or other adverse domestic circumstances.

Music Scholarships
There are a number of Music Scholarships in the form of free tuition to first-year students irrespective of the subject they are studying. Applicants should have reached Grade 7 in any instrument or voice. Two Choral Scholarships of £1,000 are also offered for male singers in conjunction with Leicester Cathedral.

Travel Scholarships
Each year up to 10 travelling scholarships worth up to £400 are available to second-year undergraduates. Details are posted on departmental notice boards each year. Additional awards (the Sheila Spire Travelling Scholarships) are available for travel to ancient sites. These are open to first-year and second-year students.

Entrance Scholarships
A non-repayable scholarship of £1,000 for one year only is available to new UK students who achieve at least ABB at A-level (best three A-levels) excluding General Studies, 36 points in the International Baccalaureate, DDM in the BTEC national diploma, and D2/M1 in the OCR National Extended diploma. Students are automatically entitled to a scholarship if they enter one of the following departments:

American Studies
Archaeology and Ancient History
Biological Sciences
Chemistry
Combined Studies
Communications, Media and Society
Computer Science
Criminology
Economics
Engineering
Film Studies and Visual Arts
Geography
Geosciences
Historical Studies
History of Art
Interdisciplinary Science
Management Studies
Mathematics
Medical Biochemistry
Medical Genetics
Medical Physiology
Modern Languages
Physics and Astronomy
Politics and International Relations
Sociology

East Midland Science and Technology Award
This award is worth £1,000 per year for three years and is open to students with a home address in the East Midlands who satisfy certain criteria; see www.aimhigher-eastmidlands.ac.uk/emsta. Eligible courses are Biological Sciences, Agriculture and related subjects, Physical Sciences including Chemistry, Mathematical Sciences, Computer Science, Engineering and Technology.

Engineering Scholarship
A first-year award of £1,000 or £2,000 is available on the basis of academic merit.

Sports Bursary

The Sports and Recreation Service offers a Sports Bursary to the value of £75 each term to encourage excellence and the development of coaching skills in sport. Individual applications should be made to the Permanent Secretary of the Sports Association.

Faculty Prizes and Exhibitions

In addition, a large number of awards are made to undergraduates for their academic performance during their course: Faculty of Arts (33); Faculty of Science (62); Faculty of Social Sciences (18); Faculty of Law (24); Faculty of Medicine and Biological Sciences (41); All Faculties (7). For further information contact the faculty heads of department.

Hardship Funds

The University administers various discretionary funds to assist full-time students in exceptional financial hardship. There are also some funds available to assist part-time, including distance learning, students towards fees and course-related costs. Information and applications are via the Student Welfare Service.

AWARDS FOR NON-EU STUDENTS
Open Scholarships

The university offers 17 scholarships of £3,000 per year to self-funded students from overseas enrolling on either undergraduate or postgraduate programmes, excluding foundation courses, distance learning and the MBA. The main criterion for the awards is academic excellence and only students who have been offered a place at the university are eligible to apply.

INFORMATION AND APPROXIMATE FEES FOR NON-EU STUDENTS

Fourteen per cent of full-time students are from outside the UK. **English language entry require-ment:** IELTS 6.0 (or equivalent); Law, Medicine, and arts and social science courses IELTS 6.5 (or equivalent); foundation year IELTS 5.5 (or equivalent). There are English language preparatory programmes and an ongoing support foundation programme. **Fees:** £9450–£12,650; Medicine £22,900. **Living costs:** £7,500.

University of Leicester, Leicester LE1 7RH; tel: 0116 224 2240; www.le.ac.uk.

LINCOLN UNIVERSITY

The University of Lincoln achieved university status in 1992 and was originally Humberside Polytechnic. The university has two sites in Lincoln (one near the city centre and another at Riseholme, five miles away) and one in Hull city centre. There are over 8,500 full-time and sandwich undergraduate students.

DEGREE SUBJECTS OFFERED

Lincoln site: Accountancy; Acupuncture, Advertising; American Studies; Animal Behaviour Science; Animal Management and Welfare; Animation, Architecture; Audio Technology; Biomedical Science; Bioveterinary Science; Business and Computer Information Systems; Computing; Computing and Cybernetics; Conservation and Restoration; Conservation Biology; Contemporary Decorative Crafts; Contemporary Lens Media; Creative Advertising; Criminology; Dance; Design for Exhibition and Museums; Drama; English; Equine Science; Equine Sports Science; European Business Studies; European Marketing; European Tourism; Fashion Studies; Fine Art; Film and Television; Finance; Forensic and Analytical Chemistry; Forensic Science; Furniture; Games Computing; Graphic Design; Health Studies; Herbal Medicine; History; Human Nutrition; Human Resource Management;

Illustration; Interactive Design; Interior Design; International Business Studies; International Relations; International Tourism; Internet Computing; Journalism; Languages; Law; Management; Marketing; Media, Culture and Communications; Media Production; Media Technology; Multimedia Technology; Nursing; Politics; Product Design; Psychology; Psychology with Child Studies; Public Relations; Social Policy; Social Science; Social Work; Software Engineering; Sports Business Management; Sport and Exercise Science; Sport Development and Coaching; Tourism; Web Technology.

Hull site: Digital and Interactive Television; Games Design; Graphic Design; Illustration; Interactive Multimedia; Social Work; Television and Film Design.

TUITION FEES (2009/10)
£3,225.

BURSARIES AND OTHER AWARDS
Students receiving the full state maintenance grant will also receive an annual bursary of £600. Proportionally smaller awards will be paid to those entitled to partial grants.

University Scholarships
UK domiciled home/EU students will receive a scholarship payment of £500 upon completion of each academic year.

Blackburn Scholarship
£1,500 is to be awarded to students previously in local authority care for each completed academic year. £500 is paid upon initial enrolment, the remainder of £1,000 to be paid when all assessments (all the required modules for a particular level of study) for the academic year are complete.

Science and Technology Awards
These awards are open to students embarking on sciences, technology, engineering and mathematics courses and are worth £1,000 per year.

Sports Bursary
These bursaries are paid on the basis of level of achievement; international level £1,000; National level £500.

POSTGRADUATE AWARDS
Awards are available for home and EU Students.

INFORMATION AND APPROXIMATE FEES FOR NON-EU STUDENTS
There are over 550 students from over 80 countries. **English language entry requirement:** IELTS 6.0 (or equivalent). **Fees:** 8,500–9,000. **Living costs:** £7,000–8,000.

University of Lincoln, Brayford Pool, Lincoln LN6 7TS; tel: 01522 886097; www.lincoln.ac.uk.

LIVERPOOL UNIVERSITY

The University of Liverpool was founded in 1881 and was the original 'red-brick' university as a result of its architectural style. The buildings are grouped in a precinct a few minutes' walk from the city centre. There is a student population of 18,312.

DEGREE SUBJECTS OFFERED

Accounting; American Studies; Anatomy; Archaeology; Architecture; Astrophysics; Biochemistry; Biology; Biomaterials Science; Business Studies; Catalan; Chemical Sciences; Chemistry; Classical Studies; Classics; Communication Studies; Computer Information Systems; Computer Science; Criminology; Dentistry; Earth Sciences; Ecology and Environment; Economics; Education; Engineering (Aerospace; Civil; Communication; Computer; Electrical/Electronic; Engineering and Management; Environmental; Integrated; Manufacturing; Maritime; Materials; Mechanical; Structural); English; Environment and Planning; Environmental Sciences; French; Genetics; Geography; Geology; Geophysics; German; Hispanic Studies; History; Human Evolution; Irish Studies; Italian; Latin American Studies; Law; Life Sciences; Management; Marine Biology; Materials Science; Mathematics; Medical Electronics; Medicine; Metallurgy; Microbiology; Modern European Languages; Music; Nursing; Oceanography; Oriental Studies (Egyptology); Orthoptics; Pharmacology; Philosophy; Physics; Physiology; Physiotherapy; Politics; Product Design; Psychology; Radiography; Sociology; Spanish; Theoretical Physics; Veterinary Science; Zoology.

TUITION FEES
£3,225.

Year 0 (the first year of the four-year foundation programme based at Carmel College, Birkenhead Sixth Form College and St John Rigby College, Wigan): £1,285 for Year 0 only and thereafter £3,225.

The Placement Year of four-year programmes where students spend either a full year abroad or a year on a placement in industry. The fee is currently £625 for that year only.

BURSARIES AND OTHER AWARDS
Please note that some of the Scholarships and Bursaries listed here are currently under review. For current information please see the University of Liverpool website at www.liv.ac.uk.

If your household income is £25,000 or less, you can currently apply for a Maintenance Grant of up to £2,906 per year. If your household income is between £25,001 and £50,020 you will receive a partial Maintenance Grant – how much you will get will depend on your income and that of your household. Note that students receiving a maintenance grant will have the amount of student loan they can apply for reduced by 50p for every £1 of Maintenance Grant they receive.

The Liverpool Bursary
If you are a Home student from a household whose income is less than £25,000 and you are liable to pay tuition fees you will be entitled to The Liverpool Bursary worth £1,400 a year. This amounts to a generous £4,306 a year when combined with the current Maintenance Grant from the government.

The Liverpool Opportunity and Achievement Scholarship
To be eligible for the Liverpool Opportunity and Achievement Scholarship worth £4,000 you will need to meet all of the following criteria:

* Be a Home student
* Come from a household earning less than £20,817 a year
* Be liable to pay tuition fees
* Attain AAB at A-level or equivalent on entry

This award will also be available for subsequent years of your degree programme, providing your progress is satisfactory. Please note that if you receive this Scholarship you will not be eligible for the Liverpool Bursary or an Attainment Scholarship.

Attainment Scholarships
The University of Liverpool provides Attainment Scholarships worth £1,500 for each year of study. These scholarships apply to all applicants (home/EU and overseas) attaining outstanding entry

qualifications (AAB at A-level or equivalent) for specified programmes within the following areas: Aerospace Engineering; Avionic Systems; Biomaterials Integrated Engineering; Chemistry; Civil Engineering; Computer Science; Earth and Ocean Sciences; Electrical Engineering and Electronics; Materials Science Engineering; Mechanical Engineering; Mechatronics; Medical Electronics; Physics, Geography and Modern Languages.

Departmental Scholarships

In addition, some departments offer a range of prizes awarded on the basis of a student's performance at the end of each academic year. Further details of the availability of such prizes can be obtained from the admissions contacts in the relevant department.

Other University of Liverpool scholarships and bursaries

A range of established University of Liverpool scholarships and bursaries is also available for home and EU students to apply for, as detailed below.

Sports Scholarships

The Sport Liverpool Scholarship Scheme is designed to help talented athletes combine excellence in academic study and sporting performance by offering the flexibility and support required to compete at the highest level. Scholarships of up to £2,000 per annum are available to student athletes who have already established themselves as a junior or senior international, or are playing at a national or regional representative level. Once an award has been offered, a specific package of support will be agreed between the athlete and the University's performance sports development officer.

University of Liverpool Alumni Awards

Based on academic excellence, these awards are currently worth £2,000 per annum and are available for the entire duration of the recipient's programme, subject to satisfactory progress.

John Lennon Memorial Scholarships

Based on financial need and academic merit, with priority being given to permanent residents of Merseyside with an active interest in the environment, these awards are worth £1,200 and are available for one year only, though you may apply for a further award in future years.

Hillsborough Trust Memorial Bursaries

Based on financial need, career intentions and academic merit, with priority given to permanent residents of Merseyside, these awards are worth £600 and are available for one year only, though you may apply for a further award in future years.

Access to Learning Fund

This fund provides discretionary financial help. All full-time and part-time UK students are eligible to apply on the basis of financial need. Students need to submit separate applications for each year of their course.

AWARDS FOR NON-EU STUDENTS

EU students may be eligible for some of the following awards:

* International Scholarships: Unlimited merit based awards giving 25% discount on tuition fees.
* Attainment Scholarships: Worth £1,500 for each year of study.
* International Baccalaureate Awards (for holders of the IB Diploma): unlimited scholarships offering a 25 per cent fee reduction for students achieving 36 points.
* Singapore Awards: Up to five awards valued at £2,000 are available for international students from Singapore.
* Hsiang Coppin Memorial Scholarship: The value and number of awards made from the fund varies, but it is unlikely that the total value of awards made will exceed £2,500 in any one year.

See Chapters 2, 4 and 6 for additional awards, applicable to all universities

* Hong Kong/China Awards: awarded annually, covering tuition fees and living costs.
* Faculty of Engineering Scholarships: Offered to students with excellent academic grades; worth £500.

The Law School also offers some bursaries.

POSTGRADUATE AWARDS

Postgraduate Loyalty Award: The Postgraduate Loyalty Award is intended to support high achieving first degree graduates of the University of Liverpool

To be eligible for the award, you must:

* be a University of Liverpool graduate
* be accepted for entry to either a taught Master's or research programme starting in September 2009 or a research programme that commences in the academic year 2009-2010 (registering by September 2010)
* have achieved a first class honours or 2.1 degree in your undergraduate studies at Liverpool
* have been in receipt of the Liverpool Bursary as an undergraduate
* be ordinarily resident in the UK.

Full-time students receive £1,500. Part-time students receive the award on a pro-rata basis.

* **Duncan Norman Research Scholarship:** The Scholarship covers full tuition fees and provides a maintenance stipend and other benefits, including accommodation on the University campus and a University standard laptop or desktop computer to a total value of £20,000 per year. The Scholarship is awarded for one year in the first instance, but subject to satisfactory academic programme, will be renewed for a total period of up to three years.
* **Dorothy Hodgkin Postgraduate Awards:** confirmation of the Dorothy Hodgkin Postgraduate Awards for 2009 has not yet been received. Information will appear here when available: www.liv.ac.uk/international/money-and-scholarships/dorothy-hodgkin.htm.
* **Shanghai Chevening Scholarships:** It is a one year award which covers the candidate's tuition fee and living expenses in Britain, and return airfare between China and the place of study in Britain.
* **Faculty of Engineering Scholarships:** The Faculty of Engineering has also established a number of International PGT Scholarships for international students joining the MSc or MRes postgraduate study. These are of £1,000 in value.

University of Liverpool Top-up Awards
For all successful ORSAS candidates (see **Chapter 6**) the University of Liverpool will waive the remaining tuition fees and make a donation of £1,000 towards living costs.

International Advancement Award
This new scholarship will be payable to all new full-time international students joining non-clinical subject areas in 2007/08. New students are those starting a new programme of study at the institution, and international students are those classified to pay fees at the overseas/specified rate. Students graduating from undergraduate study and joining postgraduate programmes will count as new students for the purposes of this exercise. The award consists of £1,000 which will be deducted direct from the tuition fee account of the student. The award will apply for every year that the student is in full-time registration, whether the student is self-funding or sponsored, and there are no performance criteria to either receive or retain the award. The only applicants who do not qualify are:

* Undergraduate students joining clinical programmes within the Faculty of Medicine, the School of Dentistry or the Faculty of Veterinary Science
* Students studying part-time, or for diplomas
* Students studying for awards of the Liverpool School of Tropical Medicine

* Students registering for pre-University studies at Liverpool International College
* Students whose study is already fully funded by a UK-Government Award, (eg Chevening, Dorothy Hodgkin and ORSAS), or those who are already fully funded from University sources eg Duncan Norman and Elizabeth Hodgkinson awards
* Students whose fees are being paid by an overseas funding body where a different agreement on fees is already in place. At the present time this includes:
  * Students funded by the Consejo Nacional de Ciencia Tecnologia (CONACYT)
  * Students funded by the Egyptian Government through the Egyptian Cultural Bureau in London
  * Students funded by the Omani Ministry of Manpower within the International Placement Programme agreed with the UK-Oman PG Consortium
  * Students receiving funding from the Fundacion Mexicana para la Educacion, la Tecnologia y la Ciencia (FUNED)
  * Holders of the University of Liverpool Postgraduate Taught Awards Scholarship do not qualify to simultaneously receive the International Advancement Award

The Law School and the School of Tropical Medicine also offer awards.

INFORMATION AND APPROXIMATE FEES FOR NON-EU STUDENTS
There are approximately 2,000 international students from over 100 countries. **English language entry requirement:** IELTS 6.0–6.5 (or equivalent); international foundation course IELTS 5.0–5.5 (or equivalent). **Fees:** arts and humanities courses and Law £9,400; Engineering and science courses £12,000; Dentistry and Medicine £18,600; Veterinary Science £18,000. **Living costs:** £5,500–£7,000.

University of Liverpool, Liverpool L69 3BX; tel: 0151 794 2000; www.liv.ac.uk.

LIVERPOOL HOPE UNIVERSITY

Liverpool Hope University was established as an ecumenical college over 150 years ago and has now been awarded university status. Its ethos, small size (7000) students and excellent facilities make it particularly attractive to international students. The university is committed to international outreach and is keen to encourage applications from students who would not be able to study in the UK without some form of financial assistance.

DEGREE SUBJECTS OFFERED
Business, Childhood and Youth Studies, Computing, Creative and Performing Arts, Criminology, Dance, Design, Disability, Drama and Theatre Studies, Early Childhood Studies, Education, English Language, English Literature, Environmental Management, Film Studies, Film and TV Studies, Fine Art, Geography, Health Therapy, Health Nutrition and Fitness, History, Human Biology, Inclusive Education, Information Technology, Law, Leisure, Marketing, Mathematics, Media, Music, Nutrition, Nutrition and Health promotion, Outdoor Recreation, Philosophy and Ethics, Politics, Psychology, Social Work, Sport Development, Sport Psychology, Sport Studies, Teacher Training (Primary), Theology and Religious Studies, Tourism.

TUITION FEES (2009/10)
£3,225.

BURSARIES AND OTHER AWARDS
Students from families with an income of less than £39,333 will receive a Liverpool Hope Bursary of £500. Those who are also eligible for an award from the Access to Learning Fund will receive an equivalent award from the Hardship Bursary Fund.

Excellence Scholarships

Students applying or courses who achieved 360 points at A-level will receive an award of £2,000 per year for the duration of their undergraduate course.

Foundation Scholarships

Awards of £500 are open to students in partner church schools and colleges.

Dean's List Scholarships

Awards of £500 are available to students not in receipt of an Excellence Scholarship. Students can apply at the end of their first and second year of study if they have achieved excellent results or have shown academic and leadership potential.

Performance Scholarships

Awards up to £2,000 are available to students who can demonstrate excellence in sports at regional, national or international level or excellence in the Performing Arts (Music, Dance or Drama).

AWARDS FOR NON-EU STUDENTS

Overseas Scholarships

An unlimited number of scholarships are offered worth £1,000 which are awarded on the basis of academic merit.

East Asian Scholarships

Six full tuition-fee scholarships are available for students from China, Hong Kong, Japan, Korea, Taiwan, and Malaysia. Each scholarship is worth £4,200 and is offered for one year only. Students who have completed two years of study at Liverpool Hope may also apply. New applicants must have proven levels of English (IELTS 6.5 or equivalent) and have an outstanding academic record.

Indian Sub-continent Scholarships

Five full tuition-fee scholarships worth £4,860 and three worth £2,430 are open to citizens of Bangladesh, Bhutan, India, Nepal, Pakistan and Sri Lanka.

POSTGRADUATE SCHOLARSHIPS

A number of scholarships are awarded each year to postgraduate applicants for degree courses worth 50% of their tuition fees. In addition scholarships worth £5,000 are awarded to the top 30 graduates each year to enable them to pursue postgraduate studies.

INFORMATION AND APPROXIMATE FEES FOR NON-EU STUDENTS

English Language entry requirement: IELTS 5 (or equivalent). English tuition is available. **Fees:** £8,800. **Living costs:** £8,800.

Liverpool Hope University, Hope Park, Liverpool L16 9JD; tel: 0151 291 3295; www. hope.ac.uk.

LIVERPOOL INSTITUTE OF PERFORMING ARTS (LIPA)

LIPA is based at Liverpool John Moores University and focuses its activities on the arts and the entertainment industry, with Sir Paul McCartney as the lead patron. There are world-class performance facilities in a city-centre campus with 600 students.

DEGREE SUBJECTS OFFERED
Performing Arts (Acting; Community Arts; Dance; Enterprise Management; Music; Theatre and Performance Design); Sound Technology.

TUITION FEES (2009/10)
£3,225.

BURSARIES AND OTHER AWARDS
Bursaries will be available on a sliding scale depending on the family income and the maintenance grant received.

LIPA Bursary
All students qualifying for a full maintenance grant or a Special Support Grant will receive a non repayable bursary of £500 per year. Students on partial grants may be eligible for bursaries of over £250 per year.

Beatles Experience Scholarship
The Beatles Experience is a Liverpool-based company offering visitors an interactive experience on the Albert Dock based around the lives and achievements of the Beatles. There are two awards available – one male, one female – for Merseyside applicants taking the one-year Diploma in Popular Music and Sound Technology. The award is worth £1,000.

Cavern Club Scholarship
Cavern City Tours Ltd is another Liverpool enterprise. Its business activities include running a number of famous music venues and restaurants, being tour operators for the 'Magical Mystery Tour' and organising one of the biggest Beatles festivals worldwide. The award is worth 50% of tuition fees together with the offer of part-time employment for the beneficiary to help towards living expenses. There is one award currently open to Merseyside-born applicants taking the Diploma in Popular Music and Sound Technology.

Chet Atkins Bursary
Gibson Guitars is an American Nashville-based company that produces world-famous guitars as well as keyboards, bass guitars, banjos and drums. There are two awards available (one for a new entrant, one for an existing LIPA student) with the condition that a recipient must be a guitar player. Each award is worth £1,250 and lasts for one year. Each award is currently open to British citizens taking music in the BA (Hons) Performing Arts at LIPA.

John Lennon Bursaries
Gibson Guitars also offers two John Lennon Bursaries (one for a new entrant, one for an existing LIPA student). The conditions of the award are as above.

Sennheiser Scholarship
The Sennheiser product range includes microphones, headphones, infrared communication systems and specialised sound reinforcement equipment. There is one award available each year for an entrant to the BA (Hons) in Sound Technology. Each award covers the costs of studying for three years (course fees, maintenance and travel) and is open to LIPA applicants from across the world.

Although the companies concerned want to support students studying at LIPA, there may be ways in which the recipients are required to acknowledge the gift; for instance by participating in promotional events. Students will automatically be entered for consideration when applying to LIPA.

AWARDS FOR NON-EU STUDENTS
All non-EU students completing the Diploma in Popular Music and Sound Technology and who continue their studies at LIPA will receive a bursary of £3,750.

See Chapters 2, 4 and 6 for additional awards, applicable to all universities

INFORMATION AND APPROXIMATE FEES FOR NON-EU STUDENTS
English language entry requirement: IELTS 5.0–6.0 (or equivalent). **Fees:** £9,500. **Living costs:** £7,000–8,000.

Liverpool Institute of Peforming Arts (LIPA), Mount Street, Liverpool L1 9HF; tel: 0151 330 3000; www.lipa.ac.uk.

LIVERPOOL JOHN MOORES UNIVERSITY

LJMU places work-related learning and graduate skills development at the heart of every under-graduate degree, without compromising academic quality. Senior business leaders in national and international companies are working closely with us to identify the higher 'world of work' (WoW) skills that give our students a competitive edge for rewarding careers. No other university, either in the UK or internationally, offers you the chance to develop these WoW skills. LJMU is committed to raising the bar on all aspects of teaching, assessment, academic support and skills development. We offer excellent facilities, high quality degree programmes, supportive staff and a thriving student community drawn from 100 countries worldwide. LJMU is a vibrant university located in one of the most exciting, and affordable, student cities in the UK.

DEGREE SUBJECTS OFFERED

Accounting and Finance; American Studies; Animal Behaviour; Applied Chemical and Pharmaceutical Sciences; Applied Languages (French and Spanish); French and Chinese; French and Japanese; Spanish and Chinese; Spanish and Japanese; Applied Psychology; Applied Sport Psychology; Architecture; Architectural Technology; Assisting Professional Practice (Radiography or Acute Care); Astrophysics; Audio and Music Production; Automotive Engineering; Biochemistry; Biology; Biomedical Science; Broadcast and Media Production; Building Services Engineering; Building Surveying; Business Management; Business Mathematics; Civil Engineering; Coaching Development; Community Nutrition; Computer Engineering; Computer Studies; Construction Management; Criminal Justice; Criminology; Dance Studies; Digital Broadcast and Media Systems; Drama; Early Childhood Studies; Education Studies; Electrical and Electronic Engineering; Energy Management and Sustainability; English; Environmental Sciences; Events Management; Exercise Sciences; Fashion; Fine Art; Food and Nutrition; Forensic Science; Genetics; Geography; Geology; Graphic Arts; History; History of Art and Museum Studies; Home Economics (Food Design and Technology); Human Resource Management; Media; Information Systems; Interior Design; International Business Studies and Chinese/French/Japanese/Spanish; International Journalism; Journalism; Law; Learning Development and Support; Marine Operations; Maritime Business; Maritime Studies; Marketing Mathematics, Statistics and Computing; Mechanical Engineering; Mechanical and Marine Engineering; Media and Cultural Studies; Medical Biochemistry; Midwifery; Music Journalism; Nautical Science; Nutrition; Nursing (Adult/Child/Mental Health); Outdoor Education; Paramedic Practice; Pharmacy; Physics with Astronomy; Politics; Popular Music Studies; Primary and Secondary Education; Modern Languages; Primary Education (QTS); Product Innovation and Development; Property and Facilities Management; Psychology; Public Health; Public Relations; Quantity Surveying; Real Estate Management; Retail Management; Science and Football; Secondary Physical Education; Sport and Dance (QTS); Social Work; Sociology; Software Engineering; Sport Development with Physical Education; Sports Science; Sports Technology; Sustainable Design; Telecommunications Engineering; Tourism and Leisure; Transport and Logistics; Wildlife Conservation; Working with Children and Young People; Zoology.

TUITION FEES (2009/10)
£3,225.

BURSARIES AND OTHER AWARDS

LJMU Bursary

Students with a household income less than £25,000 qualify for a bursary of £1,075 per year. If this is between £25,001 and £50,000 they will qualify for a bursary of £430 per year. Two thirds of undergraduate students are eligible for a LJMU bursary, indicating they come from lower income households, as are over 65% of LJMU scholarship recipients. 11% of undergraduate students are classified as a having a Black and Minority Ethnic background, 8% of undergraduates are recorded as having a disability.

Vice Chancellor's Award

This highly prestigious award is presented to students who are both academically gifted and who have achieved A-level of excellence in other areas that set them apart from their peers. A maximum of six awards are made each year. Successful students receive £10,000 a year for the duration of their course.

Dream Plan Achieve Scholarships

These scholarships are targeted at outstanding students who achieve a minimum of 360 UCAS points from three subjects. Students who qualify for the scholarship receive £1,000 a year for the duration of their degree.

Achievers Awards

Scholarships of £1,000 a year are available for students who can show A-level of commitment, determination and achievement in areas such as the arts, sports, citizenship or volunteering.

Sports Scholarships

These scholarships harness LJMU's internationally-respected sports science research and combine it with targeted learning support to help students who are also top-level sporting stars achieve both their sporting and academic potential.

INFORMATION AND APPROXIMATE FEES FOR NON-EU STUDENTS

There is a large number of overseas students. **English language entry requirement:** IELTS 6.0 or 6.5 (or equivalent) – dependent upon intended programme of study. **Fees:** classroom-based courses: £9,790; laboratory-based courses: £10,450; Foundation or HND courses: £8,820. **Living costs:** £5,400.

Liverpool John Moores University, 2 Rodney Street, Liverpool L3 5UX; tel: 0151 231 5090; www.livjm.ac.uk.

LONDON METROPOLITAN UNIVERSITY

The university was created in 2002 as a result of a merger between the University of North London and Guildhall University in the City with sites at Moorgate, Tower Hill and Aldgate. Courses continue to be offered at all sites. Both institutions were founded in the early 1970s and now have a student population of over 28,000.

DEGREE SUBJECTS OFFERED

Accountancy; American Studies; Applied Translation; Arabic; Architecture; Art and Design History; Arts Management; Audio Production; Aviation (Management; Pilots); Banking; Biochemistry; Biomedical Science; Business; Caribbean Studies; Chemistry; Communication Studies; Community Nursing; Computer Science; Consumer Studies; Criminology; Design; Development Studies; Early

Childhood Studies; Economics; Education; Electronic and Communications Engineering; English; European Studies; Events Management; Film Production; Film Studies; Financial Services; Fine Art; Food Consumer Studies; Forensic Science; French; Furniture Design; German; Health Studies; History; Home Economics; Human Nutrition; Human Resources Management; Information Systems; Information Technology; Insurance; Interior Design; International Hospitality Management; International Relations; Irish; Italian; Journalism; Law; Marketing; Mathematics; Microbiology; Music; Nursing; Performing Arts; Pharmaceutical Science; Pharmacology; Philosophy; Politics; Polymer Engineering; Psychology; Public Administration; Retail Management; Social Policy; Social Work; Sociology; Sound Recording; Spanish; Sport Science; Sports Management; Statistics; Textile Design; Theatre Studies; Transport; Travel and Tourism; Women's Studies.

TUITION FEES (2009/10)
£3,225.

BURSARIES AND OTHER AWARDS
The London Met Bursary is worth £305 (minimum) to £1,000 based on household incomes up to £40,000. Discretionary hardship funds and additional funds are available, as are scholarships for high achievers.

Eugene Attram Memorial Scholarship
In memory of Eugene Attram murdered in 2006, this new scholarship is open to any student resident in any of the London boroughs and in particular, students from the Ernest Bevin College.

Savoy Educational Trust
This award worth up to £9,000 is open to undergraduates or postgraduates taking the BA or MA degrees in International Tourism Management.

Sport Scholarships
These awards offer free tuition and accommodation and is linked to sporting excellence in Badminton, Basketball, Hockey, Squash, Table Tennis and Tennis.

Katrina Mihaere Scholarship
This award is open to women tennis players.

AWARDS FOR NON-EU STUDENTS
Family Member Bursary
An award valued at £1,000 is offered to applicants holding an unconditional offer when one other member of his or her immediate family is enrolled at the university.

Undergraduate Scholarship
The scholarship is for women applicants and is worth £2,000.

Overseas Bursaries
Two overseas bursaries are offered valued at £1,000 each and are restricted to applicants from Cyprus and Malaysia.

ISH/London Met Scholarships
These scholarships are open to applicants from the following countries.
Afghanistan; Algeria; Armenia; Botswana; Cameroon; Cuba; East Timor; Gambia; Iran; Jordan; Kazakhstan; Libya; Lebanon; Oman; Nepal; Tanzania; Tibet; Uganda; Uzbekistan; Vietnam; Zimbabwe.

POSTGRADUATE AWARDS
Seven postgraduate awards are offered.

INFORMATION AND APPROXIMATE FEES FOR NON-EU STUDENTS
There are over 4,000 students from 147 countries. **English language entry requirement:** IELTS 5.5 (or equivalent); one-year international foundation course IELTS 4.5. There is a range of English courses. **Fees:** £8,200. **Living costs:** £9,500–10,500.

London Metropolitan University, 31 Jewry Street, London EC3N 2EX; tel: 020 7133 4200; www.londonmet.ac.uk.

LONDON SCHOOL OF ECONOMICS (LSE)

Founded in 1895, LSE has a worldwide academic reputation in the social sciences. It is located in central London and has around 4,200 undergraduate students drawn from all over the world. Many influential developments in thinking about society, economics and politics have originated in work done at LSE, including the basis of the modern welfare state. LSE is part of the federation of the University of London's self-governing Colleges. It has been awarding its own degrees since 2008.

DEGREE SUBJECTS OFFERED
Accounting and Finance; Actuarial Science; Anthropology and Law; Social Anthropology; Business Mathematics and Statistics; Economic History; Economic History with Economics; Economics and Economic History; Economics; Economics with Economic History; Econometrics and Mathematical Economics; Human Resource Management and Employment Relations; Environmental Policy; Environmental Policy with Economics; Geography; Geography with Economics; Government; Government and Economics; Government and History; Politics and Philosophy; History; International Relations and History; International Relations; Law; Management; Management Sciences; Mathematics and Economics; Mathematics with Economics; Philosophy, Logic and Scientific Method; Philosophy and Economics; Social Policy; Social Policy and Criminology; Social Policy and Economics; Social Policy with Government; Social Policy and Sociology; Sociology.

TUITION FEES
£3,225.

BURSARIES AND OTHER AWARDS
LSE Bursary
The LSE Bursary is available for students from low-income backgrounds (from England and Wales) and is worth up to £7,500 over a three-year programme. The value of the LSE Bursary is linked to students' (or their family's) income levels, which are assessed by local authorities when calculating the maintenance grant. The maximum LSE Bursary of £2,500 per year is awarded to those students with the lowest residual income. These bursaries do not have to be repaid.

LSE Discretionary Bursary
The LSE Discretionary Bursary is available for new LSE students (from the UK and the EU) who face exceptional financial needs, including, for example, caring responsibilities, financial need related to disability or an unavoidable requirement to live at home. The value of the award may vary according to need. These bursaries do not have to be repaid.

See Chapters 2, 4 and 6 for additional awards, applicable to all universities

LSE Scholarships

Each year LSE awards a number of scholarships – funded by private or corporate donation – to UK/EU/overseas applicants to the school. The number, value, eligibility criteria and type of awards vary from year to year. Awards are made on the basis of financial need and academic merit. A large number of prizes are available and are offered by the school to students on the basis of academic performance, usually at the end of each session. Applications are not required.

POSTGRADUATE AWARDS

A large number of postgraduate awards are available, for both Taught Masters and Research programmes.

INFORMATION AND APPROXIMATE FEES FOR NON-EU STUDENTS

English language entry requirement: IELTS 7.0 (or equivalent). **Fees:** £12,840. **Living costs:** £9,000–£10,000.

London School of Economics and Political Science, Houghton Street, London WC2A 2AE; tel: 020 7955 7155; www.lse.ac.uk/financialsupportoffice.

LONDON SOUTH BANK UNIVERSITY

The university was first established as the Borough Polytechnic in 1892 and is now one of the largest universities in London with around 23,000 students. Situated close to Waterloo and London Bridge stations, the main campus at Elephant and Castle is at the hub of local transport only minutes away from the professional, social and cultural facilities of central London and the arts centres on the South Bank.

DEGREE SUBJECTS OFFERED

Accounting and Finance; Acting; Applied Science; Architecture; Arts Management; Business Information Technology; Biochemistry; Bioscience; Business Studies; Citizenship Studies; Computing; Construction Management; Creative Writing and English; Criminology; Digital Film and Video; Media Arts; and Photography; Drama and Performance Studies; E-Business; Engineering (Architectural/Building Services/Chemical/Civil/Computer/Electrical and Electronic/Mechanical/ Mechatronics/Petroleum/Telecommunications); English Studies; European Policy Studies; Film Studies; Food Studies; Forensic Science; Games Culture; Human Resource Management; Housing Studies; Human Biology; International Politics; International Social Policy; Law; Management; Marketing; Microbiology; Nursing; Nutrition; Politics; Product Design; Psychology; Quantity Surveying; Radiography (Diagnostic); Social Policy; Social Work; Sociology; Sonic Media; Sport and Exercise Science; Theatre Practice; Tourism and Hospitality; Urban and Environmental Planning; Writing and Media Arts.

TUITION FEES (2009/10)

£3,225.

BURSARIES AND OTHER AWARDS
LSBU Annual Grant

The majority of full-time home and EU undergraduate students starting after 1 September 2009 or continuing in 2009/10 having started in 2006/7, 2007/8 or 2008/9 will be entitled to an annual grant from the university to help with course costs. There is no means testing and it is non-repayable. The amount of the annual grant increases as students continue their studies to provide support when it is most needed.

Those students who themselves pay yearly course fees of £3,225 or more, or are taking out a tuition fee loan for all or part of the £3,225, will be entitled to the grant. For a standard three-year course, the scheme works out as follows: Year 1 of the course: £500; Year 2 of the course: £750; Year 3 (final year) of the course: £750 + graduation bonus of £250 (honours graduates only). The bursary scheme also applies to the full-time PGCE and full-time PgDip Architecture courses. (All other criteria, detailed above, apply.)

Lawrence Burrow Scholarships
These scholarships are for home undergraduate full-time students. Scholarships worth £1,000 are awarded to 10 Asian or West Indian students every year. Awards are made based on academic merit and other factors, thus the university is only able to invite applications once candidates have successfully enrolled onto the first year of their course. Contact Jayson Short, Personal Development Manager; tel: 020 7815 6401; jaysons@lsbu.ac.uk.

Access to Learning Fund (ALF)
The ALF is money given to higher education institutions by the government annually. Its aim is to provide financial assistance to home students with financial difficulties who have exhausted all other sources of support. Funds are available to home full-time, part-time undergraduate and post-graduate students and DipHE Nursing students. The funds are not available for EU students who do not meet the residence requirements, or international students.

Applicants need to demonstrate financial hardship set against accepted basic income levels for students. Income and expenditure will be compared; certain outstanding debts will also be taken into consideration. ALF is not a guaranteed form of financial support and therefore should not be relied upon as not all applications will be successful. Contact Student Advice and Guidance in Caxton House for further details or go to www.lsbu.ac.uk/learningsupport/alf.

Sports Scholarships
These scholarships are for home undergraduate full-time students competing to a high level in their sport. Benefits include:

* Up to £3,000 financial support
* Access to sports science support through the Human Performance Centre at the university
* Free access to LSBU's sports facilities.
  * Guaranteed student accommodation
  * A personal liaison officer (mentor)

Focus Sports include men's basketball, women's basketball, rugby and taekwondo, although appli-cations are invited in all sports. For further information visit www.lsbu.ac.uk/sports or contact the Academy of Sport on 020 7815 7811.

Charitable Fund
Any fully enrolled student can apply for the university's Charitable Fund if they are faced with a set of unforeseen circumstances, but priority is given to students who do not have other means of financial support. Only one successful application per student is allowed per academic year. For further details please contact Student Advice and Guidance in Caxton House.

POSTGRADUATE AWARDS
CLG Planning Bursaries
Limited bursaries are available to full-time MA Planning students. The ESRC administers these studentships for the Communities and Local Government. The bursaries will be allocated on the basis of merit and need. Contact Michael Leary (learym@lsbu.ac.uk) or Antonia Noussia (noussiaj@lsbu.ac.uk).

INFORMATION AND APPROXIMATE FEES FOR NON-EU STUDENTS

There are 3,000 international students from 120 different countries. **English language entry requirement:** IELTS 6.0 (or equivalent). There is a pre-study English course and a foundation course for overseas students. **Fees:** £8,360–£10,395. **Living costs:** £9,500.

London South Bank University, Southwark Campus, 103 Borough Road, London SE1 0AA; tel: 020 7815 7815; www.lsbu.ac.uk.

LOUGHBOROUGH UNIVERSITY

The university is located on its own campus near the market town of Loughborough, between Nottingham and Leicester. It has a student population of 14,000. A significant number of students in the Engineering and Science Faculties receive sponsorships.

DEGREE SUBJECTS OFFERED

Accounting and Finance; Air Transport Management; Architectural Engineering; Art and Design; Artificial Intelligence; Banking and Finance; Biology; Business; Chemistry; Communications and Media Studies; Computer Science; Construction; Drama; Economics; Engineering (Aeronautical; Automotive; Chemical; Civil; Communications; Electronic/Electrical; Energy; Manufacturing; Materials; Mathematical; Mechanical; Product Design and Manufacture; Systems); Engineering Physics; English; Ergonomics; European Studies; Forensic Analysis; French; Geography; German; Industrial Design and Technology; Information Management; Information Studies; International Business; Logistics; Mathematics; Physics; Politics; Product Design; Psychology; Publishing; Retail Management; Sociology; Spanish; Sports Leisure; Sports Science; Sports Technology; Transport Management.

TUITION FEES (2009/10)

£3,225.

BURSARIES AND OTHER AWARDS

The university has established a bursary scheme for full-time UK undergraduate students. These bursaries are cash payments towards living costs. Subject to certain conditions, they are renewed for each year of the course. Those students under 21 from households with an income less than £18,360 will be entitled to a bursary award of up to £1,390. Lower amounts from £1,180 to £220 are payable to family incomes up to £35,460. In order to be eligible, applicants will need to be: permanent residents of the UK (this excludes Isle of Man and Channel Islands residents) in accordance with the relevant regulations; liable for the tuition fee of £3,225; and undertaking one of the university's undergraduate degree courses as a full-time student.

Students over 21 from low income households (below £35,460) may also claim bursaries from £2,780 to £440 depending on the income level.

Care Leavers Bursaries

These are payable to students who have been in care up to the value of £750.

Loughborough University Merit-based Entry Scholarships

The university offers a number of merit-based scholarships worth £1,000 for certain undergraduate degree courses as a contribution to students' living costs. The scholarships apply to a number of courses offered by the following departments: Chemical Engineering; Chemistry; Computer Science; Electronic and Electrical Engineering; Human Sciences; Information Science; Mathematical

Sciences; Mechanical and Manufacturing Engineering; Physics; Polymer Technology and Materials Engineering. In order to be eligible, students will need to have made Loughborough their first (firm) choice university at the appropriate time within the rules of the UCAS process and will need to satisfy the required academic threshold for the scholarship. Depending on the subject, entry requirements are in the range of ABB–AAA at A-level or 36–40 IB points. One department will also take into account performance at the end of the first semester. More details are available from bursaries@lboro.ac.uk.

Sport Scholarships
Scholarships are offered to students involved in the following sports – athletics, badminton, cricket, football, golf, hockey (men and women), rugby, rowing, swimming, tennis and triathlon.

Music Scholarships
These awards are available for singing and instrumental activities.

Institute of Polymer Technology and Materials Engineering Scholarships
An unlimited number of awards are offered worth £500. Contact IPTME@lboro.ac.uk.

Institute of Physics Bursaries and Scholarships
Means-tested bursaries are payable up to the value of £1,360 or £2,720 for mature students. Merit-based scholarships of £1,000 are offered to students achieving A-level grades of AAB or higher (or equivalent).

AWARDS FOR NON-EU STUDENTS
International Scholarships
100 scholarships are offered worth 25% of programme tuition fees based on an academic achievement equivalent to A-level grades of AAA-AAB. Many subject departments also award scholarships.

POSTGRADUATE AWARDS
Graduate Full-Fee Scholarships
These are merit-based awards based on degree performances.

Santander Scholarships
These awards are open to applicants from Argentina, Brazil, Chile, Colombia, Mexico, Peru, Puerto Rico, Portugal, Spain, Uruguay and Venezuela.

INFORMATION AND APPROXIMATE FEES FOR NON-EU STUDENTS
There are 800 students from outside the UK. **English language entry requirement:** IELTS 6.5 (or equivalent). Special courses are offered by the English Language Study Unit. There is a one-week residential course for international students before the start of the academic year. **Fees:** Arts and Non-laboratory subjects £10,400. Science and Engineering £13,500. **Living costs:** £6,500–7,500.

Loughborough University, Loughborough LE11 3TU; tel: 01509 263171; www.lboro.ac.uk.

MANCHESTER UNIVERSITY

The University of Manchester founded 180 years ago is one of the well-established 'red brick' universities with subject areas in Engineering and Physical Science, Humanities, Medical and Human Sciences and Life Sciences. The Campus is extremely compact and is situated a mile south of the city centre.

DEGREE SUBJECTS OFFERED

Accounting; American Studies; Anatomy; Ancient History; Arabic; Archaeology; Architecture; Astrophysics; Audiology; Biochemistry; Biological Science; Built Environment; Business Studies; Chemistry; Classical Studies; Classics; Clothing Technology; Computer Science; Construction Management; Dentistry; Drama; Economic History; Economics; Engineering (Aeronautical; Building Services; Chemical; Civil; Communication and Control; Computer Systems; Electronic/Electrical; Environmental; Integrated; Manufacturing; Mechanical; Microelectronic; Software; Structural); English; Environmental Studies; European Studies; Fashion Textiles and Retailing; French; Genetics; Geography; Geology; German; Greek; Hebrew; Hispanic Studies; History; History of Art; Italian; Latin; Law; Life Sciences; Linguistics; Management; Materials Science; Mathematics; Medicine; Medieval Studies; Middle Eastern Studies; Modern History; Music; Neuroscience; Nursing; Optoelectronics; Optometry; Persian; Pharmacology; Pharmacy; Philosophy; Physics; Physiology; Physiotherapy; Plant Science; Politics; Polymer Science; Psychology; Religion and Theology; Russian; Social Anthropology; Social Science; Sociology; Spanish; Textile (Design; Marketing; Science); Town Planning; Turkish; Zoology.

TUITION FEES (2009/10)

£3,225.

BURSARIES AND OTHER AWARDS

Manchester Guarantee Bursary

This is a £1,250-a-year entitlement bursary for all UK students with an annual household income of around £27,120 or less.

These bursaries guarantee a substantial level of additional support for students from households with low income (in line with the thresholds used by the DCSF, Student Loans Company and local authorities). The £1,000 a year includes the minimum standard bursary of £300 (which all universities that are charging £3,070 must provide) for students who are receiving maximum state support (ie those who come from households with annual incomes of around £17,500 or less). These £1,000 bursaries are paid for each year of the student's programme of study.

Manchester Advantage Scholarship

This is a £3,000-a-year entitlement scholarship for all UK students who gain three A grades at A-level (or equivalent qualification; see below for details of the university's criteria for excellence) and have an annual household income of around £17,500 or less.

Manchester Success Scholarships

A £1,000-a-year scholarship for UK students who gain three A grades at A-level (or equivalent; see below for details of the university's criteria for excellence) regardless of household income, who choose one of the following discipline or programme areas (the university website and undergraduate prospectus have full details of these programmes):

Faculty of Engineering and Physical Sciences

* Aerospace Engineering (all programmes)
* Chemistry (all programmes)

* Computer Science (all programmes)
* Earth Sciences (all programmes)
* Electrical and Electronic Engineering (all programmes)
* Engineering with a foundation year
* Environmental Sciences (all programmes)
* Materials Science (all programmes)
* Mechanical Engineering (all programmes)
* Science with a foundation year
* Civil Engineering
* Physics and Astronomy.

The amount of these scholarships (£1,000 per year) includes the Faculty of Engineering and Physical Sciences award of a two-staged payment of £750 in the first year and £750 in the second year.

Faculty of Humanities
* Accounting with Business Information Systems
* Art History and Archaeology (all programmes)
* Combined Studies (all programmes except those including Literary Studies and Drama, Film Studies or Historical Studies)
* Informatics (all programmes)
* Languages (including Middle Eastern Studies, excluding French and Spanish)
* Linguistics (all programmes except English Language and English and Linguistics)
* Management and Leisure
* Planning and Landscape (all programmes).

To be eligible for a Manchester Advantage Scholarship or a Manchester Success Scholarship you will achieve one of the following:

* Three grade As at A-level
* Two grade As at A-level plus two grade As at AS-level (all must be taken in the same academic year)
* Three A grades in Scottish Advanced Highers (Scottish Highers alone do not qualify)
* A distinction profile at BTEC
* An International Baccalaureate Diploma of 40 points with at least 6 points in the subjects stated in your offer of a place.

Applicants should achieve these grades against the subjects that make up the conditions of their offer criteria. (For example, if an applicant is asked to achieve A-level grades BBB in Maths, Physics and Chemistry, and achieves grades AAA in these subjects, then they would receive an award. However, if they achieve AAA in Maths, Physics and General Studies, and a B in Chemistry, they would not be eligible for an award since General Studies does not form part of their offer.)

Access to Higher Education
This award is valued at £1,750 for each year of the course. Contact the Head of Faculty or School.

Faculty of Engineering and Physical Science
BP Undergraduate Scholarships
These are awarded to first and second year undergraduate students in the following discipline areas – Mechanical Engineering, Chemical Engineering, Electrical Engineering, Geology and Chemistry. The award is worth £2,000 and selection is based on the first year examination results and the content of the application.

Discipline–specific scholarships
These are awarded in Chemistry, Earth, Atmospheric and Environment Sciences, all Engineering subjects, Materials Science, Mathematics, Physics and Astronomy and Textiles.

See Chapters 2, 4 and 6 for additional awards, applicable to all universities

Astra-Zeneca Scholarships
Two Chemistry scholarships to cover tuition fees are awarded to students achieving three grade As at A-level (equivalent) excluding General Studies and a good performance in the first semester of the degree course.

Earth, Atmospheric and Environmental Sciences
Five scholarships are offered worth £1,000 per year. The scholarships are awarded on the basis of interview and achievements for the most promising students (home and international) who do not qualify for a Manchester Success Scholarship.

Engineering courses
Civil Engineering Entrance Scholarships

The Scholarship is worth £1,000 for UK and EU students who achieve three A grades (excluding General Studies) or the equivalent and are enrolled on any Civil Engineering courses.

Power Academy Scholarships
The award is open to applicants for Electrical Engineering and is worth £2,000 per year plus a contribution towards tuition fees.

Proctor and Gamble Product Supply Scholarships
Students taking Mechanical, Aerospace, Chemical or Electrical Engineering may apply for the award worth £2,000 per year plus a minimum of twelve weeks paid work placement per year.

Shell Technical Scholarship Scheme
This award is worth £10,000 over four years (£2,500) for students in the discipline areas of Mechanical Engineering or Chemical Engineering who are registered on 4 year MEng programmes.

Sir William Mather Engineering Entrance Scholarships
The Scholarship worth £1,000 per year is open to local students from Manchester who achieve good grades at A-level aiming to study engineering courses.

Materials Science Entrance Scholarships
Student taking relevant science and technology subjects at A-level and applying for a degree in Materials Science and achieving high grades can be awarded amounts accordingly eg AAA £1,750; AAB £1,500; ABB £1,250; BBB £1,000.

Mathematics Entrance Scholarships
Students enrolled on any mathematics degree courses achieving AAA (excluding General Studies) or equivalent will be awarded £750, or £1,500 if one of the A grades is in Further Mathematics.

Physics and Astronomy Entrance Scholarships
Home, EU and international students, enrolled on any physics-based degree courses gaining three grade As at A-level or equivalent (excluding General Studies) may apply for this award worth £1,500.

Institute of Physics Bursary Scheme
These bursaries are worth £1,000 and are open to students involved in Widening Participation schemes who are enrolled on Physics-based courses.

Textile Entrance Scholarships
Students enrolled on any Textile undergraduate courses who achieve AAA at A-level (excluding General Studies) or equivalent may apply for these awards worth £1,000.

School Prizes
In addition to scholarships and bursaries most Schools across the University offer annual prizes up to £300 for outstanding achievement. These prizes are awarded annually after the second semester examinations. No application is necessary.

President's Award
The President and Vice-Chancellor will give 10 highly prestigious awards worth around £10,000 a year to the most outstanding students from the UK. For details see www.manchester.ac.uk/studentfinance.

Manchester Achievement Scholarship
This scholarship awards £1,750 per year to students from the Manchester region who have successfully:

* Participated in the Manchester Access Programme; or
* Progressed from a Greater Manchester household to the university through an 'Access to higher education' programme.

Alumni Welcome Scholarships
The Alumni Fund complements the university scholarships by awarding Alumni Welcome Scholarships to the most deserving students during their first year.

Sports Scholarships
The Sports Scholarship Scheme provides structured support to individuals to enable them to excel in both their sporting and academic careers while raising the profile and standard of university sport. The level of support is dependent on the level of performance but ranges from £200 to £2,000. If you are interested in being considered for a Sports Scholarship, download an application form at www.manchester.ac.uk/sport/scholarships or contact the Sport Development Manager; tel: 0161 275 5305; andrea.williams@manchester.ac.uk.

Talented Athlete Scholarship Scheme
The university also participates in the national Talented Athlete Scholarship Scheme (TASS), which is a government-funded programme that provides a unique partnership between sport and higher and further education. TASS scholarships provide sporting services to the value of £3,000 for higher education students aged 18 to 25 (extended upper age limit of 35 for disabled TASS scholars). There are 47 sports that can be supported by TASS, of which 15 are disability sports. A full listing of these is given on the TASS website. Contact details for the governing bodies, eligibility criteria and further information about the scheme can be found on the TASS website at www.tass.gov.uk or contact Andrea Williams, the Sport Development Manager at the University of Manchester; tel: 0161 275 5305; andrea.williams@manchester.ac.uk.

Music Scholarships
The University of Manchester Music Scholarships cover the cost of tuition by a member of the Royal Northern College of Music (RNCM) and allow access to RNCM facilities for eight talented musicians per year. These scholarships are available to UK, EU and international students. Applicants must be studying subjects other than music, and should normally have achieved Grade 8 standard or equivalent. Scholarships continue throughout the length of the degree, providing that progress is assessed as satisfactory. Applicants interested in applying for Music Scholarships should complete an application form from www.manchester.ac.uk/studentfinance. Candidates are then selected for audition by the RNCM.

Accommodation Bursaries
The university provides 30 accommodation bursaries each year. These cover the full cost of university accommodation for the first year of undergraduate study. These bursaries are available to students according to their area of residence and financial circumstances, and the university will notify eligible students during the spring in their year of entry.

AWARDS FOR NON-EU STUDENTS
Mathematics International Excellence Scholarship
Ten Scholarships each worth £4,000 per year are open to international applicants who have demonstrated academic excellence.

See Chapters 2, 4 and 6 for additional awards, applicable to all universities

International Mathematics Scholarships

For those applicants who do not receive the above scholarships a large number of awards worth £2,000 are available, based on mathematical achievement.

POSTGRADUATE AWARDS

University funding and scholarships

The University of Manchester offers the following awards to students applying to study for a PhD.

In addition to the schemes listed, a range of funded studentships is available to postgraduate students working in specific research areas. Scholarships are awarded to students who have achieved outstanding academic results and submitted high-quality applications. Some scholarships may have additional criteria and these are detailed under the specific award information.

Dorothy Hodgkin Postgraduate Awards

The Dorothy Hodgkin Postgraduate Awards (DHPA) are for students from India, China, Hong Kong, Brazil, South Africa, Russia and the developing world who are seeking, or already hold, an offer of a PhD place. They are highly prestigious and successful candidates will, as a minimum, hold the equivalent of a UK first-class honours degree from an esteemed academic institution.

The DHPA are intended to support new PhD students and most students applying for DHPA funding are expected not to have started their PhD studies. However, it is recognised that some students may have commenced their PhD studies with the intention of applying for scholarships and funding for the start of the following year.

The DHPA scholarships are open to top quality Science, Engineering, Medicine, Social Science and Technology students. Awards have also been allocated in the Life Science area. Applicants must be intending to undertake research within a discipline area which was rated 5 or 5* in the UK Government Research Assessment Exercise (2001).

Applicants for the award must also be a national of one of the countries listed at www.ost.gov.uk/research/funding_schemes.

Subject to satisfactory progress, the scholarships are tenable for up to four years and will cover the full overseas tuition fees plus a maintenance allowance of £12,600 per year. The University of Manchester were allocated 10 awards for 2008/09 entry.

Students who have applied to the University of Manchester for an ORS Award (see **Chapter 6**) will be automatically considered for a Dorothy Hodgkin Award. Other interested students should indicate on their main application form that they wish to be considered for a DHPA.

Fulbright–University of Manchester Scholarship

The University of Manchester is providing funding for one Fulbright–Manchester Scholarship which will provide tuition and maintenance for one year.

Making an application for the Fulbright–Manchester Scholarship and making an application for a place to study at the University of Manchester are two separate processes, which should be undertaken in parallel.

The University of Manchester provides the funds for the scholarship in conjunction with the Fulbright Commission. American students enrolled at a US university must make an initial application to their Campus Fulbright Advisor.

Graduates should apply to US Student Programs, Institute of International Education, 809 United Nations Plaza, New York NY10017, USA.

Faculty of Engineering and Physical Science Scholarships
Awards of £2,000 per year are made in the following subject areas: Chemistry; Earth, Atmosphere and Environmental Science; Materials Science; Mathematics; Physics and Astronomy; Textiles.

International Mathematics Scholarship
This award is valued at £2,000 per year.

North American Foundation Awards for Postgraduate Study at the University of Manchester (NAFUM)
Three awards of £5,000 for one year are available to nationals of the USA and Canada to pursue postgraduate study at the University of Manchester in any subject area. The award can be renewed annually, but the candidate must re-apply along with any new applicants, and the award can be applied to tuition fees or can be received as a payment during the period of study.

Applicants should be nationals of the United States or Canada and should have applied for entry onto any full-time postgraduate course at the university.

Candidates will be considered on the basis of their Graduate School application form and ORS Award application (see **Chapter 6**) if appropriate. Applications for graduate study should be received by March. Individual schools will put prospective candidates forward to the selection committee for consideration for a NAFUM award. Candidates will be informed if they have been successful in obtaining a NAFUM award after late June. Preference will be given to PhD candidates.

University Research Studentships (URS)
The university annually provides significant funds to support students wishing to study for a PhD.

The awards normally provide support towards maintenance and/or payment of the UK tuition fees and are initially for one year but may be renewed for up to two succeeding years.

Applicants should normally hold, or be expecting to receive, a first- or upper-second-class honours degree, or equivalent, and must have applied for and been accepted onto a programme of study before being considered for a URS award.

If eligible, candidates must also have applied for UK Research Council funding. This application (or alternatively the PhD application form) will be used to assess the candidate for university funding.

Candidates in Science and Engineering, Biological Sciences, Medicine and related disciplines are automatically considered for Research Council funding by the relevant schools.

University of Manchester Loyalty Bursary Scheme
The university offers graduates of the Victoria University of Manchester, UMIST, or the newly merged University of Manchester a 20% reduction on tuition fees. There is no application procedure for this scheme – the 20% reduction is made automatically during the registration process.

INFORMATION AND APPROXIMATE FEES FOR NON-EU STUDENTS
There is a high proportion of international students. **English language entry requirement:** IELTS 6.0–7.5 (or equivalent); courses with high linguistic demands, eg Law, Management and Medicine, are at the higher end. There is a foundation course in Informatics, Engineering, Science and Biological Sciences. English language courses are also offered. **Fees:** £9,500–12,500; Clinical; Medicine and Dentistry: £22,100. **Living costs:** £8,500–£9,000.

University of Manchester, Manchester M13 9PL; tel: 0161 275 2077; www.man.ac.uk.

See Chapters 2, 4 and 6 for additional awards, applicable to all universities

MANCHESTER METROPOLITAN UNIVERSITY

The university has its origins in the nineteenth century and became a university in 1992. The main campuses are in Manchester with sites in Crewe and Alsager. Courses are divided into faculties with many sandwich options enabling students to gain paid industrial and commercial experience as part of their degree programmes.

DEGREE SUBJECTS OFFERED

Accounting; American Studies; Architecture; Art and Design; Biology; Business Studies; Chemistry; Childhood Studies; Computing; Criminology; Dance; Dental Technology; Design and Technology; Dietetics; Drama; Economics; Education; Engineering; English; Environmental Health; Environmental Science/Studies; Fashion Design; Film; Food and Nutrition; French; Geography; German; Health and Social Care; Health Studies; History; Hospitality Management; Human Resources Management; Information Management; Italian; Journalism; Landscape Architecture; Law; Leisure Studies; Marketing; Mathematics; Media Studies; Music; Nursing; Pharmacy; Philosophy; Photography; Politics; Psychology; Social Change; Social Sciences; Sociology; Spanish; Speech Pathology and Therapy; Sport Science; Youth and Community Work.

TUITION FEES (2009/10)

£3,225.

MMU INSTITUTIONAL BURSARY SCHEME

All students paying tution fees for full-time undergraduate degrees and receiving the maximum Maintenance Grant must be given a bursary of at least £319, however the scheme at Manchester Metropolitan is considerably more generous *(see below)*.

These are the rates for 2008/09. The rates for students entering in 2009 will be published shortly.

Students with an assessed household residual income of:

* Up to £20,460 may receive a £1,000 bursary
* £20,461–£22,550 may receive a £900 bursary
* £22,551–£25,000 may receive a £800 bursary
* £25,001–£26,730 may receive a £700 bursary
* £26,731–£28,825 may receive a £600 bursary
* £28,826–£30,935 may receive a £500 bursary
* £30,936–£33,015 may receive a £400 bursary
* £33,016–£35,105 may receive a £300 bursary
* £35,106–£37,195 may receive a £200 bursary
* £37,196–£39,290 may receive a £100 bursary

INFORMATION AND APPROXIMATE FEES FOR NON-EU STUDENTS

The university is home to 2,600 international students. **English language entry requirement:** IELTS 6.0 (or equivalent). English language courses are available in October, January, April, July and August. **Fees:** £7,785–8420; Architecture £12,150. **Living costs:** £8,500–9,000.

Manchester Metropolitan University, All Saints, Manchester M15 6BH; tel: 0161 247 2000; www.mmu.ac.uk.

MIDDLESEX UNIVERSITY

The university was founded in 1973 and is located on several campuses in North London. There are 18,000 students following undergraduate, postgraduate and four-year sandwich degree courses that include a 12-month work placement.

DEGREE SUBJECTS OFFERED

Accounting and Finance; Art and Design; Biomedical and Biosciences; Business and Management; Complementary Health; Computing and Information Technology; Criminology; Dance; Design Engineering; Economics; English; Environmental Health; Film, TV and Media Arts; Housing; Human Resource Management; Journalism; Law; Languages; Marketing; Media, Culture and Communication; Music; Nursing and Midwifery; Psychology; Social Policy; Social Work; Sociology; Sport and Exercise Science; Teaching and Education; Theatre Arts; Translation; Tourism; Veterinary Nursing.

TUITION FEES (2009/10)

£3,225 (£3,475 for some Art and Design courses)

BURSARIES AND OTHER AWARDS

All students receiving a maximum maintenance grant will receive a bursary of £319. Check with the university.

Chancellor's Awards

Up to 50 £2000 awards are given to new and continuing UK/EU and Non-EU students. Part–time students also eligible – awarded pro-rata ie. £1,000 per year. Applications may be submitted before your first year of study or for subsequent years. The criteria for selection covers academic, sporting or cultural achievement. The closing date for all applications: June (check with university). Please note that you cannot hold an Academic Excellence Scholarship and a Chancellor's Scholarship in the same year

* Academic scholarships are highly competitive and will only be awarded to applicants with outstanding results. For Postgraduate students, only those with a clear First Class Honours degree or equivalent will be considered. For new undergraduate or continuing students, applicants will be in the top 5% of the cohort, with A grade Advanced level results, or a student record of consistent first class grades.
* For Sporting Scholarships, applicants should be competing at national level in their sport and be active in coaching or other support activities.
* For Cultural Achievement, applicants should have made outstanding and nationally recognised contributions in an established cultural field, or have personally made significant national or international contributions to voluntary or charitable activity in community or development support.

Academic Excellence Scholarships

Five new UK Undergraduate students per school (20 in total) will be awarded £1000 for full time study upon year of entry. Students' suitability will be judged based upon actual or predicted exam results achieved at the highest level. Applicants will be in the top 10% of their cohort, and will normally have achieved or be predicted at least 360 UCAS points from A2 level or equivalent level 3 qualifications including BTEC. A list of UCAS point values for recognised level 3 awards may be found on the UCAS website. Closing date for applications: June (check with university). Please note that you cannot hold an Academic Excellence Scholarship and a Chancellor's Scholarship in the same year.

See Chapters 2, 4 and 6 for additional awards, applicable to all universities

Middlesex Rise Up Scholarships

Twenty scholarships are offered recognising educational disadvantage and strengthening links with feeder and target schools. £1,000 is awarded on year of entry to applicants who have fulfilled criteria on application form and received a nomination from their school/mentor etc. Closing date for applications: June (check with university).

Future Gold – our contribution to 2012

This award is available to new students with real potential to compete in the 2012 Olympics.

Sponsored Scholarships for prospective students

Conygar Opportunities Scholarship
This award is available to first-year UK/EU Middlesex University Business School undergraduate students who are the first in their family to go to University. For further info see www.mdx.ac.uk/scholarships.

Academic Alumni scholarship
20% discount on fees is awarded to high achieving progressing students as nominated by the relevant academic/programme leader. For further information see http://www.mdx.ac.uk/study/postgrad/moneymatters/scholarships.asp.

Alumni Bursary
All Middlesex Alumni and Partner Alumni are eligible for a 10% discount on fees (excluding PGCE students).

INFORMATION AND APPROXIMATE FEES FOR NON-EU STUDENTS

There are international students from 30 countries around the world. **English language entry requirement:** undergraduate IELTS 6.0 (or equivalent); postgraduate IELTS 6.5, foundation course IELTS 4.5. An extended English language course is also available from September to July, along with an international summer school. **Fees:** international foundation course £6,700; degree courses £9,400–£9,650. **Living costs:** £12,000.

Middlesex University, The Burroughs, London, NW4 4BT; tel: 020 8411 5555; email: enquiries @mdx.ac.uk www.mdx.ac.uk.

MOUNTVIEW ACADEMY OF THEATRE ARTS

Mountview Academy of Theatre Arts, founded 50 years ago, is situated in North London. There are two sites, one at Wood Green and one at Crouch End. Mountview has excellent facilities including a studio theatre, 15 rehearsal studios, music, radio and TV studios.

DEGREE SUBJECTS OFFERED

Performance; Technical Theatre.

TUITION FEES (2009/10)

Check with the academy.

BURSARIES AND OTHER AWARDS

The academy receives an allocation of Dance and Drama Awards from the DCSF. Students from the UK and EU are eligible to apply. See also **Chapter 4** under **Dance and Drama**.

Somerset Scholarships

Scholarships are available for: BA (Hons) in Performance, first-year Acting and Musical Theatre course and second-year Technical Theatre course. They are open only to those who will complete the course by the age of 25 years who are, or whose parents are, resident in the London Borough of Haringey or who have at any time attended as a pupil at a school in that borough. Scholarships cover tuition fees and a contribution towards maintenance. The number of scholarships varies annually.

Mackintosh Foundation Drama School Bursary Scheme

Mountview is invited to put forward two candidates for scholarships from the foundation, which provides bursaries for accredited Acting and Musical Theatre courses. The bursary covers (in whole or in part) payment of the tuition fees, and may also include a contribution towards maintenance.

Lady Rothermere Award

Mountview is invited to put forward one candidate for this external bursary for accredited Acting and Musical Theatre courses for tuition fees and maintenance.

Mountview Scholarships

These are available for the second and third years of the BA (Hons) in Performance and for the second year of the two-year Stage Technical Theatre course.

Singing Scholarships

Forty scholarships are awarded annually.

Alexander Technique Scholarships

Ten scholarships are awarded annually.

Laurence Olivier Bursary

The Society of West End Theatres offers this annual bursary to help second-year drama students who will have financial difficulty in their final year of training. Mountview is invited to put forward two candidates.

Lilian Baylis Award

The Royal Victoria Hall Foundation offers this annual bursary to help second-year drama students who will have financial difficulty in their final year of training. Mountview is invited to put forward one candidate.

Henry Cotton Scholarship

This annual award provides help towards tuition for a second-year student who has lived in or has strong connections with the Liverpool area. Mountview is invited to put forward one candidate.

POSTGRADUATE AWARDS

Sir John Mills and Dame Judi Dench Scholarships

Two awards are offered for one-year postgraduate performance courses.

INFORMATION AND APPROXIMATE FEES FOR NON-EU STUDENTS

Contact the academy. **Living costs:** £9,500–10,500.

Mountview Academy of Theatre Arts, Ralph Richardson Memorial Studios, Clarendon Road, Wood Green, London N22 6XF; tel: 020 8881 2201; www.mountview.ac.uk.

See Chapters 2, 4 and 6 for additional awards, applicable to all universities

NEWCASTLE UNIVERSITY

There are over 13,000 students following over 220 degree programmes at this university in the centre of Newcastle. The academic year is based on a two-semester system and the majority of degrees are fully modularised. This 'civic' university was founded in 1834.

DEGREE SUBJECTS OFFERED

Accounting and Finance; Agri-Business Management; Agriculture; Agronomy; Ancient History; Animal Production Science; Animal Science; Archaeology; Architectural Studies; Architecture; Astronomy; Astrophysics; Biological Science; Biology; Business; Chemistry; Classical Studies; Classics; Combined Studies; Computing Science; Countryside Management; Dentistry; Domesticated Animal Science; Ecological Resource Management; Economics; Engineering (Chemical; Civil; Computer Systems; Electrical/Electronic; Marine; Materials; Mechanical; Offshore; Planning; Software; Structural); English; Environment Planning; European Business Management; Farm Business Management; Finance and Business Economics; Fine Art; Food and Human Nutrition; Food Marketing; French; Genetics; Geography; German; Government; Greek; History; Latin; Latin American Studies; Law; Linguistics; Marketing; Mathematics; Medical Microbiology; Medicine; Music; Naval Architecture; Pharmacology; Physics; Physiological Science; Politics; Portuguese; Psychology; Religious Studies; Rural Resource Management; Small Craft Technology; Social Policy; Social Studies; Spanish; Speech and Language Sciences; Statistics; Surveying and Mapping Science; Town Planning; Wildlife Biology; Zoology.

TUITION FEES (2009/10)

£3,225.

BURSARIES AND OTHER AWARDS

All UK students assessed as being eligible for full financial support (annual income less than £25,000) will receive a bursary of £1,340 a year. In addition, those eligible for full rate support will receive a further £300. Those on partial grants where the income is between £25,001 and £32,284 will receive £670 a year.

Achievement Bursaries

Awards of £500 are offered to students on maintenance grants, achieving grades AAA (or equivalent). For those achieving two grade A passes the award is £200.

Newcastle Excellence Scholarships

Humanities, Arts and Social Sciences
Twenty-nine scholarships of £1,000, for the first year only, are given to the best-performing students on entry.

Medical Sciences
Twenty-nine scholarships of £1,000, for the first year only, are given to the best-performing students on entry.

Science, Agriculture and Engineering
Forty-eight scholarships of £1,000, for each year of the course, are given to the best-performing students on entry. At least 50 scholarships of £500 per year are awarded to students across particular subject groupings. Up to 38 awards of £1,000 are available to students from Stage 2 onwards, to reward those who have not received a scholarship on entry but have demonstrated outstanding academic achievement in their first year of study.

Organ and Choral Scholarships

The awards are valued at £799. For those awarded the Organ Scholarship duties consist of playing for a weekly service in the cathedral. The scholarship is tenable for three years, applicants for the Music degree being preferred. Details can be obtained from the Cathedral Church of St Nicholas, Newcastle upon Tyne.

The Abbeydale Scholarship

This is open to applicants for Mathematics.

Elsie Jeffrey Memorial Bursary

This is limited to students from the Tanfield School, Stanley, County Durham. It is available for all degree courses.

Charles Letts Memorial Scholarship

This award is offered to applicants for Materials Science.

Sports Awards

These cover Recruitment Sports Bursaries (£1,250–3,750) and Performance Sports Bursaries (£750). There are also awards for Talented Athletes.

Chemistry

The Chemistry department offers seven bursaries open to applicants for any of the Chemistry degrees for best performance at A-level or equivalent. The bursaries are valued at £750. For details contact the head of Chemistry.

Scholarships and prizes

There is a number of awards available, including scholarships and awards made on the basis of exam results achieved as part of the degree programme. You must be a registered student in order to be eligible for these awards. A number of these prizes are funded by companies such as Vaux Breweries, Alan Wilson, Ford Motor Company, *Building* magazine, Peat Marwick McLintock, Newcastle Building Society, PricewaterhouseCoopers, Andersen, GlaxoSmithKline, Marks & Spencer and ICI. These awards and prizes range from small book prizes to more valuable awards made specifically for travel or another particular purpose. For further information contact the relevant department.

School of Electrical, Electronic and Computer Engineering

Awards are made worth £1,000 per year.

Regional Scholarships

These awards are valued at £500.

AWARDS FOR NON-EU STUDENTS

Scholarship scheme for international undergraduate students

The university is able to offer a large number of partial scholarships to new international undergraduate students from all over the world. Any applicant who achieves an agreed level of performance (see website for further details) and who has accepted Newcastle as their first-choice university will be eligible to receive a scholarship, which will have a value of £1,500 for the first year of study.

In addition to these scholarships, some bursaries are offered to international students on certain degree programmes by the relevant academic school, for example Engineering. The university also offers International Family Scholarships (IFS) where more than one family member is studying at Newcastle or where a family member has already graduated from the university. For further information about any of these scholarships, see www.ncl.ac.uk/international/scholarships.

See Chapters 2, 4 and 6 for additional awards, applicable to all universities

POSTGRADUATE AWARDS

A number of awards are available in the following subject areas: Architecture; Chemical Engineering; Biology; Environmental Biochemistry; Law; Marine Technology; Mathematics; Modern Languages; Music.

INFORMATION AND APPROXIMATE FEES FOR NON-EU STUDENTS

There are 2,500 students from outside the UK. **English language entry requirement:** IELTS 6.5 (or equivalent); English, Law and Medicine IELTS 7.0 (or equivalent). English language support and foundation courses in Arts and Social Sciences, Business and Finance, Computing, Science and Engineering are available. **Fees:** 10,415–£13,600; Medicine and Dentistry: pre-clinical £13,620, clinical £25,220. **Living costs:** £7,500–£8,500.

Newcastle University, Newcastle upon Tyne NE1 7RU; tel: 0191 222 5594; www.ncl.ac.uk.

NEWMAN UNIVERSITY COLLEGE (Birmingham)

Situated on the outskirts of South West Birmingham, Newman University College's campus is based in Bartley Green, some 8 miles from the city centre and overlooks Bartley reservoir and the Worcestershire countryside beyond. Its location makes it convenient for access to both the M5 and M42 motorways. Being founded as recently as 1968, the buildings are modern and purpose-built. The campus is arranged around a series of inner quadrangles of lawns and trees. Halls of residence provide single-study bedrooms for some 220 students, conveniently adjacent to the teaching areas and well-stocked library. Newman has approximately 2700 students from a range of backgrounds and of all ages. All full-time degrees have a work placement module and an important part of the curriculum is developing transferable skills useful for further study or employment after graduation. Newman's mission is centred on the Catholic values of tolerance and inclusion. As a Catholic University College, Newman is proud to welcome staff and students of all religions and backgrounds.

DEGREE COURSES OFFERED

Art & Design; Counselling; Creative Arts; Creative Writing; Drama; Early Years Education Studies; English; English Literature; Global Citizenship; History; Information Technology; Initial Teacher Training; Local History & Heritage; Management Studies; Media and Communication; Philosophy and Theology; Philosophy; Religion & Ethics; Primary Teaching (Art; English; Humanities (Geography and History); Physical Education; Religious Education); Psychology; Religious Education; Social & Applied Psychology; Sports Studies; Theology; Theology for Education; Working with Children; Young People & Families. Newman is also able to provide supervision towards a PhD in a number of subject areas.

TUITION FEES (2009/10)

£3,225.

BURSARIES AND OTHER AWARDS

The following table shows finance information for UK and EU students starting at Newman in 2009. It does not apply to non-EU students.

Household income	Maintenance grant	Loan	Tuition fee loan	Newman Bursary	Total
£18,000 and under	£2,906	£3,453	£3,225	£1,100	£10,684
£25,000	£2,906	£3,453	£3,225	£800	£10,387
£34,459	£1,292	£3,453	£3,225	£500	£8,476
£40,000	£1,023	£3,620	£3,225	£305	£8,174
£50,000	£538	£4,207	£3,225	£305	£8,275
£60,032	£50	£4,695	£3,225	£305	£8,275
£70,000	£0	£3,781	£3,225	£305	£7,311

The figures are not confirmed and may be subject to change.

Newman offers discretionary hardship bursaries of up to £3,500 per year for students in financial difficulty. Priority groups for these bursaries include:

* Students with children (especially lone parents).
* Other mature students, especially those with existing financial commitments, including priority debts
* Students from low-income families
* Disabled students (especially where the Disabled Students Allowance (DSA) is unable to meet particular costs and the institution has no legal responsibility to do so)
* Applicants should note that a thorough application process requiring evidence of income and expenditure is required to access the means-tested hardship bursaries and that they are not guaranteed to any student, even those in the priority groups identified above.

INFORMATION AND APPROXIMATE FEES FOR NON-EU STUDENTS
English language requirement: IELTS 6.5 (or equivalent) **Fees:** £7,500 and can be paid in instalments. Fees for non-EU international students are £7,500 per year. No scholarships are available. **Living costs:** £7,500

Newman University College, Genners Lane, Bartley Green, Birmingham B32 3NT; tel: 0121 476 1181; www.newman.ac.uk.

NEWPORT (University of Wales)

This new university, which opened in 2005, is located on two campuses, one a short walk from the centre of Newport and a second at Caerleon. The university population consists of 300 full-time and 6,000 part-time students, 60% over the age of 21 as a result of its widening access policy.

DEGREE SUBJECTS OFFERED
Accounting; Archaeology; Art and Design; Business Management; Computer Science; Design Technology; Education (Primary); Electrical and Electronic Engineering; English; Environmental Management; Fashion Design; Film and Video; History; Human Resources Management; Information Technology; Legal Studies; Marketing; Mathematics; Performing Arts; Photography; Religious Studies; Sports Studies.

TUITION FEES
See also www.studentfinancewales.co.uk and **Chapter 1, 'Financing your course'.**

BURSARIES AND OTHER AWARDS
Newport Bursary Scheme
In 2008/09 bursaries of £1,000 were awarded to students from households with an income of less than £20,000, between £20,001 and £30,000 the award was £600 and up to £40,000 a payment of £300 was made. Check with the university for 2009/10.

Welsh National Bursary
An award of £310 is made to students when the family income is less than £18,370.

Academic Enhancement Bursary
This is awarded on the basis of academic excellence for extra-curricular activities.

Guaranteed Admissions Scheme Bursaries
The University of Wales, Newport offers a bursary to 30 eligible students from Guaranteed Admissions Scheme (GAS) partner schools and colleges. Prospective full-time UK students, who are under 25 and dependent on their parents, may receive £500 for the first year of their course if not in receipt of a Newport Bursary Scheme award.

Application forms are automatically sent to students who have accepted a place at Newport. Students can apply for the bursary even if the course they have applied for is not included in GAS, eg Education, Social Work and Art.

Registered Childcare Bursary
Up to £1,000 is available if you are on a course for which the Childcare Grant is not available and your household income is below £23,000 a year. Contact the Access Funds Coordinator for further details.

Art Foundation Bursary
A £500 bursary and halls of residence fees may be paid for full-time Art foundation students (for the first 30 eligible students to be approved) with an income below £8,000 a year. Contact the Access Funds Coordinator for further details.

Sports Scholarships/Bursaries
The university is able to offer scholarships and bursaries to students who have represented their county or region in their chosen sport.

Six students have the opportunity to benefit from Sports Scholarships to a value of £1,000 per year for the duration of their course, provided that the student maintains his/her level of performance and academic standards.

Each year, five Sports Bursaries of £500 each are available. Successful students use the scholarship/bursary support to finance sporting equipment, travel expenses and competition fees in pursuit of sporting excellence. Each student must play a full role in representing the university in the British University Sports Association Championships.

Silkset Screen Academy Wales Bursary
Students taking degree courses in Film and Video, Performing Arts and Animation can apply for this award.

Suits You Voucher Scheme
Students actively seeking employment in their final year may apply for a clothing voucher worth £200 for interview purposes.

Reginald Salisbury Photography Awards
Reginald Salisbury was passionate about photography and recognised the historic tradition of photographic education at the University of Wales, Newport.

The bursary was established in 2001 to fulfil his wish to support the work of a photography student studying at Newport. The two awards of 1,000 will enable students to make an innovative body of photographic work in another country.

INFORMATION AND APPROXIMATE FEES FOR NON-EU STUDENTS
There are international students from 50 countries. An induction course is recommended. **Fees:** £7,500–8,500. **Living costs:** £5,500–£6,500.

University of Wales, Newport, PO Box 101, Newport, South Wales NP18 3YH; tel: 01633 432432; www.newport.ac.uk.

NORTHAMPTON UNIVERSITY

Awarded full university title and research degree awarding powers in 2005, The University of Northampton is a dynamic, modern university situated in the heart of England. A medium-sized University with over 10,000 students and two Northampton-based campuses, just 2.5 miles apart, we offer hundreds of courses to meet all needs and interests. From foundation and undergraduate level to postgraduate, professional and doctoral qualifications, you can study traditional arts, humanities and sciences subjects, as well as more modern subjects such as Entrepreneurship, Product Design or Advertising.

We are able to offer places in Halls of Residence to almost all first year students and existing students and assist other students to find safe and affordable housing.

DEGREE SUBJECTS OFFERED INCLUDE
Accounting; Acting; Advertising and Design; American Studies; Applied Animal Studies; Architectural Technology; Art and Design; Biology; Business; Business and Management; Civil Engineering; Computing Studies; Creative Writing; Criminology; Drama; Early Childhood Studies; Early Years Education; Earth Science; Ecology; Economics; Education; Energy Management; English; Environmental Chemistry; Environmental Management; Event Management; Fashion; Film and TV Studies; Financial Services; Fine Art; French; Geography; German; Graphic Communication; Health Studies; History; Human Biology; Human Resource Management; Illustration; Interior Design; Journalism; Law; Leather Technology; Marketing; Mathematics; Media; Midwifery; Music; Nursing; Occupational Therapy; Paramedic; Performance Studies; Philosophy; Science; Podiatry; Politics; Product Design; Psychology; Social Work; Sociology; Sports Studies; Travel and Tourism; Third World Development; Wastes Management.

TUITION FEES (2009/10)
£3,225.

BURSARIES AND OTHER AWARDS
Full-time 'Home' and EU undergraduate students entering higher education in 2009/10 who are paying £3,225 in fees and have an assessed household income of up to £40,000 a year may be eligible to receive a University of Northampton Bursary worth between £500 and £1,000 a year.

For more information and exceptions visit www.northampton.ac.uk

See Chapters 2, 4 and 6 for additional awards, applicable to all universities

TD Lewis Scholarship

Three awards of £2,000 each and one small award for a resident of the Borough of Northampton of up to £200 are awarded annually. The purpose of the awards in the first instance is to foster educational excellence. The scholarship covers all subjects for **undergraduate or postgraduate** study within The University of Northampton or other approved establishment thereafter; and/or to assist a student to travel within the United Kingdom or abroad in pursuance of an approved course of study. A student travelling abroad must still be under 25.

AWARDS FOR NON-EU STUDENTS

Non-European students can apply for one of several international scholarships. Successful applicants must have a good academic track record. The scholarships are worth up to 25% of tuition fees per year.

POSTGRADUATE AWARDS

Dr Mike Daniel Research Degree Bursary

Established to sustain the memory of previous Pro Rector Dr Mike Daniel, the bursary awards £350 per year to support the work of a full-time research degree student following a programme of studies at the University of Northampton.

Sir John Lowther Bursary

Previous amounts awarded, £500-£1,000. The bursary is available to a student or students who have been offered a place at the University of Northampton to undertake **postgraduate research** within the School of the Arts.

INFORMATION AND APPROXIMATE FEES FOR NON-EU STUDENTS

There are over 700 international students following courses at the university. **English language entry requirment**: IELTS 6.0 (or equivalent). Language tuition is available. Fees: Not available at time of publication. Please see www.northampton.ac.uk for further details. **Living costs**: £6,500, approximately

University of Northampton, Park Campus, Boughton Green Road, Northampton NN1 7AL; Tel: 0800 358 2232; www.northampton.ac.uk

NORTHUMBRIA UNIVERSITY

Northumbria University has two campuses in Newcastle upon Tyne. The campuses are divided by the city motorway. City Campus is situated in the heart of the city and Coach Lane Campus is just three miles from the city centre in the leafy suburbs of Newcastle. City Campus houses most of Northumbria's 31,500 students.

The newest part of Northumbria's City Campus, City Campus east is home to the schools of Law, Design and the Newcastle Business School (NBS). NBS and Law are housed in one building while the School of Design is across a courtyard. Work is now underway to build a new state-of-the-art sports centre. To link the two halves of the City Campus, Ellison Quadrangle was opened up and re-landscaped; this attractive new area now links the new development to the existing campus and provides a glimpse of what City Campus West will look like when improvements have been completed.

DEGREE SUBJECTS OFFERED

Accountancy; Applied Biology; Architectural and Urban Conservation; Architectural Design; Art and Design; Art History; Biological and Food Sciences; Biomedical Science; Biotechnology; British and American Cultures; Building (Design Management; Surveying); Business; Business Computing; Care and Education; Chemistry; Computing; Construction Management; Criminology; Design; Design; History; Disability Studies; Drama; Economics; Education (Primary); Employment Studies; Engineering (Architectural; Building Sciences; Communications; Computer Aided; Electrical/ Electronic; Manufacturing Systems; Mechanical); English; Environmental (Management; Studies); Estate Management; European Health Science; European Studies; Film Studies; Financial Studies; Food Science; French; Geography; German; Government; Health; History; Housing; Human Organisations; Human Resource Management; Information Studies; International Hospitality; Internet Technology; Knowledge Management Technology; Landscape Ecology; Law; Logistics; Marketing; Mathematics; Midwifery; Mobile Communications; Music; Nursing; Occupational Therapy; Performance; Physiotherapy; Planning and Development Surveying; Playwork; Politics; Psychology; Quantity Surveying; Real Time Systems; Russian; Social Work Studies; Sociology; Spanish; Sports Science; Supply Chain Management; Travel and Tourism.

TUITION FEES (2009/10)

£3,225.

BURSARIES AND OTHER AWARDS

Northumbria provides an additional £310 non-repayable bursary to all students who receive the full maintenance grant of £2,906 or equivalent for Scottish, Welsh or Northern Irish students.

Northumbria Scholarships

In Year 1, this is a non-repayable, non-means-tested award of up to £1,000 depending on course studied (see below for details). From Year 2 onwards the full scholarship will be awarded to students who score more than 60%.

The list below indicates the cash sum awarded by subject area. Students can check the category to which the course belongs on the individual course details page on the university website, which should indicate a scholarship level. Search the course database for the course and then look for the Course Fees heading.

* Built Environment:	£500
* Business:	£500
* Computing:	£1,000
* Design:	£500
* Education:	£500
* Engineering and Mathematics:	£1,000
* English and History:	£500
* Geography and the Environment:	£1,000
* Health and Social Care:	£500
* ICT for Business:	£1,000
* Law:	£250
* Media and Communication:	£500
* Modern Languages:	£500
* Performing Arts:	£500
* Psychology:	£250
* Sciences:	£1,000
* Social Sciences:	£500
* Sports:	£250
* Visual Arts:	£500

'Home' students undertaking relevant health, nursing and midwifery courses will have their fees covered by the Health Authority, therefore the Northumbria Scholarships are not available. This relates to the following courses, Nursing, Midwifery, Operating Department Practice, Physiotherapy and Occupational Therapy. Top-up students, or students not paying the full fee are not entitled to the Scholarship.

Sport Bursaries/Scholarships

Northumbria University's Talented Athlete Scheme (TASS) helps talented athletes who wish to progress with a formal academic programme but maintain an involvement in performance sport.

Team Northumbria Scholarships are designed to support the needs of performance athletes during their time studying at Northumbria University. The support available is sport specific and tailored to the individual. It is aimed at providing practical solutions and services to students who have the talent and commitment to fulfil their potential within their chosen sport and their academic ventures.

Please see the website for further details
http://teamnorthumbria.com

School of Computing, Engineering and Information Sciences Dean's Awards

The Dean's Awards are available for students at level 4 and 5. Students who achieve an average of 70% or higher for the year will be awarded £1,000 in the following year. For more information please see the schools webpage at the address below:
http://www.northumbria.ac.uk/sd/academic/ceis/ir/deansawards2008/?view=Standard

School of Computing, Engineering and Information Sciences Progression Awards

Students progressing from Undergraduate to Postgraduate study within the school who gain a 2:1 in their undergraduate programme, will be eligible for a £500 scholarship. Those who gain a First Class degree will be given £1000. This is in addition to the 5% discount already offered by the University for progressing students.

For more information please see the schools webpage at the address below:
http://www.northumbria.ac.uk/sd/academic/ceis/ir/scholar/?view=Standard

AWARDS FOR NON-EU STUDENTS

General Scholarship Awards

A number of scholarships are available for Non-EU students coming to study at Northumbria. In most cases the amount of scholarship given will be in the range of £500-£1,000. If a scholarship is awarded, tuition fees in the first academic year will be reduced by the relevant amount.

Selection is based on outstanding academic achievement, although other factors may be taken into account, such as English proficiency and any professional/non academic achievements. No application is necessary, as all applications for courses at the university will be considered for scholarship automatically.

Tshering Lama Northumbria Scholarship Awards

These scholarships are available for suitably qualified students from Nepal who are commencing their studies in either undergraduate, taught postgraduate, or research level. For the 2009/10 academic year there are 9 scholarships at £2,000 each available across the schools.

Michael Sehgal Scholarships

This scholarship is available annually to students who originate from Lyallpur Khalsa College in Punjab, India, who are joining master's programmes in either business or information technology. The award is for 100% of the tuition fees and the award is made to a student nominated by the college.

For more information on general scholarships please see the webpage at the following address: http://www.northumbria.ac.uk/brochure/international/fees/?view=Standard

School of the Built Environment Continuing Scholarships

All international students who achieve an overall average of 60% or more in their whole year marks will receive a £500 Built Environment Continuing International Student Scholarship, this being applied as a discount to the academic fee for the following academic year. International students who achieve less than a 60% overall average will still receive 75% of the scholarship, ie £375 and they will also have the opportunity to receive the outstanding 25% if their marks reach the target 60% level through the next academic year.

A Scholarship will also be available to sandwich/placement years with a payment of 25% of the normal Scholarship, ie £125 on successful completion of the placement year.

For more details please see the Schools web page at: http://www.northumbria.ac.uk/sd/academic/sobe/schol/Intschol/

INFORMATION AND APPROPRIATE FEES FOR NON-EU STUDENTS

There are 3,000 international students from over 80 countries. **English language entry requirement:** IELTS 6.0–6.5 (or equivalent). English language and foundation courses are available. **Fees:** Classroom-based courses £8,600; Laboratory-based courses £9,050. **Living costs:** £6,500.

Northumbria University, Ellison Place, Newcastle upon Tyne NE1 8ST; tel: 0191 232 6002; www.northumbria.ac.uk.

NOTTINGHAM UNIVERSITY

The University of Nottingham was founded in 1881 and is an internationally recognised world-class university. It hosts over 30,000 students from more than 140 countries and is located on a green campus within easy reach of the city centre. The university has two other campuses in Nottinghamshire, as well as sites in Malaysia and China. Students benefit from modular degrees, allowing them to tailor their studies to their own interests, and strong international links which allow extensive study abroad opportunities.

DEGREE SUBJECTS OFFERED

Agriculture; American Studies; Ancient History; Animal Science; Archaeology; Architecture; Art History; Artificial Intelligence; Biochemistry; Biology; Biomedical Sciences; Biosciences; Built Environment; Business and Management; Chemical, Environmental and Mining Engineering; Chemistry; Civil Engineering; Classics; Computer Science and Information Technology; Contemporary Chinese Studies; Cultural Studies; Economics; Education; Electrical and Electronic Engineering; English Studies; Environment; Environmental (Biology; Design; Engineering; Science); European Studies; Film and Television Studies; Finance and Accounting; French; Genetics; Geography; German; Hispanic and Latin American Studies; History; Industrial Economics; Latin; Law; Mathematical Science; Mechanical, Materials and Manufacturing Engineering; Medicine; Midwifery; Modern European Studies; Modern Languages; Music; Neuroscience; Nursing; Nutrition; Pharmacy; Philosophy; Physics and Astronomy; Physiotherapy; Plant Science; Politics; Psychology; Russian Studies; Serbian and Croatian Studies; Sociology and Social Policy; Theology; Veterinary Medicine and Surgery; Viking Studies; Zoology.

See Chapters 2, 4 and 6 for additional awards, applicable to all universities

TUITION FEES
£3,225.

BURSARIES AND OTHER AWARDS

Guaranteed Core Bursaries will be provided up to £1,080 per student per year. Students with residual income levels up to £34,500 will receive £1,080 while those with residual income levels between £34,501 and £44,500 will receive between £810 and £270 with most receiving £540. In 2009, 40% are likely to be eligible for a Core Bursary. Additional bursaries are available for the following groups (students may be eligible for more than one bursary): entrants from non-traditional routes with a residual income less than £44,500; students joining through a collaborative Lincoln/Nottingham course; students with children or elderly dependants receiving the full statutory support. Current financial support schemes targeting low-participation groups will be continued.

First-in-the-Family Scholarships

In order to encourage applications from prospective students living in the East Midlands region who would otherwise be deterred from entering university for financial reasons, these scholarships are aimed at students who would be of the first generation in their family to attend university. Each scholarship is worth £1,000 a year for the whole of the student's full-time undergraduate degree.

Ethel and Kevin B Malone Scholarship

This is open to applicants who have undertaken all their secondary education at state schools or colleges in Nottingham or surrounding locality. For details of these bursaries and scholarships contact Student Services; tel: 0115 951 3710.

Sports Bursaries

Bursaries are awarded to outstanding students who have reached county standard, or above in sport. Bursaries are limited in number and are each worth £1,000 per year. Details are available from the Director of Physical Education at the Sports Centre; tel: 0115 951 6655.

Barber Organ Scholarship

This award valued at £500 may be held for one year, but is renewable subject to satisfactory progress. Selection is by audition, usually in October.

Choral and Instrumental Foundation Music Scholarships

Five Music Scholarships are available to honours Music students, valued at £500 each. The awards are held for one year but holders may apply for an additional award in a future year. Selection is by audition, usually in October. Candidates must normally have achieved a Grade 8 (Distinction) or higher with one of the recognised examination boards at the time of the audition. Further details can be obtained from the Department Secretary, Music Department, University of Nottingham, University Park, Nottingham NG7 2RD; tel: 0115 951 4755.

Food Science/Microbiology

Northern Foods offers a scholarship valued at £1,000. Contact David Gray, Admissions Tutor, Food Sciences, School of Biosciences, University of Nottingham.

Siblings, Children and Spouses

Ten per cent of the first-year fees will be paid to registered siblings, children and spouses of alumni.

Subject Scholarships

Scholarships and bursaries worth between £1,000 and £2,000 are offered in the following subjects: Organic, Inorganic and Physical Chemistry; Civil, Electronic and Electrical Engineering; Mechanical, Materials and Manufacturing Engineering; Pharmacy; Psychology; Mathematics.

AWARDS FOR NON-EU STUDENTS

The International Office offers a comprehensive and expanding range of scholarships in order to encourage academic excellence, aid diversity, develop relationships with sponsors and offer real financial assistance in cases of hardship, whether individually or by region.

Scholarships include:

* Full fee International Research Scholarships
* Full fee European Union Research Scholarships
* A range of Taught master's Tuition Fee Scholarships
* Developing Solutions Scholarships which reach out to those students who have the potential to make a real difference to the development and propriety of their home countries. These are available for students from Africa, India and developing countries of the Commonwealth studying a postgraduate taught master's or master's by research course in the areas of Environment, Food, Health and Technology
* High Achiever Scholarships for international undergraduate students.

Architectural Environmental Engineering

A scholarship of £1,000 (one payment only) is available to each international student joining the course.

Universitas 21 institutions

Awards are offered worth 10% full tuition fees.

Country-specific awards

* **Belarus:** one scholarship worth £5,000.
* **China:** three scholarships worth 50% full tuition fees and six awards worth 100% tuition fees.
* **Eastern Europe:** two scholarships worth £3,000.
* **Indonesia:** four 25% tuition-fee scholarships.
* **Jordan/Iraq/Lebanon/Palestine/Syria:** five tuition-fee scholarships.
* **Korea:** six scholarships covering tuition fees.
* **Malaysia:** five partial tuition-fee scholarships.
* **Mexico:** a large number of CONACYT scholarships.
* **Norway:** 10 £1,000 tuition-fee scholarships.
* **Turkey:** three 33% tuition-fee scholarships.
* **United Arab Emirates:** one scholarship worth 20% full tuition fees.
* **USA:** one scholarship worth $6,000.
* **Vietnam:** three scholarships each worth £3,000 plus one Chevening Scholarship covering full fees.

Country- and subject-specific awards

* **Brazil:** three scholarships worth 50% full tuition fees for courses in Arts, Engineering, Life Sciences, Environmental and Health Science.
* **Developing Commonwealth countries:** full tuition-fee scholarships for courses in Environmental Studies, Food, Health and Technology, plus a large number of partial fee scholarships.
* **Indonesia/Jordan/Syria:** eight scholarships for courses in Human Rights Law, Politics and International Relations.
* **Burma:** scholarships allowing 10% and 20% on tuition fees for courses in Business, Economics, Law, Science, Engineering, Arts and Social Sciences.
* **Taiwan:** scholarships for taught master's courses in Social Policy, International Relations, Diplomacy, Religious Conflict, Public Policy and Contemporary British Society.
* **Vietnam:** scholarships allowing 10% and 20% on tuition fees for courses in Business, Economics, Law, Science, Engineering, Arts and Social Sciences.

See Chapters 2, 4 and 6 for additional awards, applicable to all universities

Subject-specific awards

* One scholarship worth £3,000 for courses in Public Policy and Public Administration.
* Two scholarships worth £4,000 for studies in Contemporary British Society.
* Five scholarships worth £2,000 for courses in Social Policy and Social Work.
* Four scholarships worth 25% tuition fees for the MA Diplomacy.
* Twelve scholarships worth £2,000 for courses in Health Promotion, Health Psychology, Occupational Health Psychology, Occupational Psychology and Psychological Research Methods.
* One full tuition fee scholarship in each of the following subjects: Biology (stem cells); Health and Social Care; Nanoscience; Nanotechnology; Neuroscience; Photonics and Electronics; Slavery. (Also open to EU students.)
* Four scholarships worth 50% tuition fees in the School of Education.
* Ten scholarships worth £2,000 for the MSc Electronic and Communication Engineering course.
* Twenty-five 50% tuition fee awards for courses in American Studies, Archaeology, Art History, Classics, Film Studies, French, German, Hispanic and Latin American Studies, History, Music, Philosophy, Russian and Slavonic Studies, and Theology.

POSTGRADUATE AWARDS

There are automatic scholarships for all students enrolling on a second full-time course. Awards are valued at 15% full tuition fees for MA courses and 10% for PhD degrees for every year of the programme. Former students returning will receive 10% full tuition fees. There are also four-year Integrated Postgraduate Programmes Scholarships valued at 25% full tuition fees and seven full tuition-fee scholarships for admission to any faculty.

Students who have firmly accepted an offer and are eligible may apply for scholarships using the online application form. Closing dates for scholarships vary. To search for scholarships, to check eligibility and closing dates and to access application forms, visit the scholarship search database at:

* **Undergraduate:** www.nottingham.ac.uk/ugstudy/introduction/finance/estimator/estimator. php
* **Postgraduate:** www.nottingham.ac.uk/prospectuses/postgrad/introduction/funding/posts cholarship.php

EU students are also eligible to apply for Research Council funding and more, and information on this can be found on a designated EU student web page: www.nottingham.ac.uk/international/future_students/applying_to_nottingham/eu_students.php.

Students can also search for funding and check their eligibility at: www.Nottingham.ac.uk/pgstudy/funding. Students may also find information on available studentships at: jobs.nottingham.ac.uk/vacancies.aspx?cat=345

INFORMATION AND APPROXIMATE FEES FOR NON-EU STUDENTS

There are students from over 130 countries. **English language entry requirement:** IELTS 6.0–6.5 (or equivalent); Medicine IELTS 7.5 (or equivalent). **Fees:** Law, arts courses and social science courses £10,6100–13,910; Engineering and science courses £13,910–£14,660; Medicine £14,660–£25,480. **Living costs:** £7,600.

University of Nottingham, University Park, Nottingham NG7 2RD; tel: 0115 951 5151; www.nottingham.ac.uk.

NOTTINGHAM TRENT UNIVERSITY

NTU is a leading, modern university with 24,000 students. It is spread over three campuses, all within easy reach of each other and Nottingham city centre. There's student accommodation at all three and students usually live and study at the same campus. The **City** site houses the Business School, the Schools of Law, Architecture and the Built Environment, Art and Design, and Social Sciences and is situated in the heart of Nottingham with the major shops, night-time venues and amenities only 15 minutes' walk away.

Clifton campus is a self-contained student village with all the necessary student facilities. The Schools of Arts and Humanities, Science and Technology and Education are based here. Clifton is four miles from Nottingham and there's a regular Unilink bus service to the city.

Brackenhurst, which houses the School of Animal, Rural and Environmental Sciences, is an attractive 200-hectare estate, situated 14 miles from Nottingham with good transport links to the city. Organised around a country house built in 1828, the landscaped grounds include university residences, a library, dining room, café/bar, shop, a multi-purpose sports surface, high technology glasshouses and a lake. Students have access to a commercial farm, Veterinary Nursing Unit, Animal Management Centre, Equestrian Centre, resources for horticulture, and a range of familiar and exotic animals.

DEGREE SUBJECTS OFFERED

Accounting; Animal Studies; Architecture; Architectural Technology; Art and Design; Astronomy; Astrophysics; Biochemistry; Biology; Biomedical Science; Broadcast Journalism; Building Surveying; Business; Business Economics; Chemistry; Childhood Studies; Childhood Studies; Civil Engineering; Communication and Society; Computer Science courses; Computing; Computer Aided Product Design; Construction Management; Construction Property Management; Countryside Management; Creative Writing; Criminology; Decorative Arts; Design and Technology Education; Design for Film and Television; Ecology; Economics; Primary Education; Engineering; English; Environment Science; Environmental Design and Management; Equine Sports Science; European Studies; Fashion and Textile Management; Fashion Design; Fashion Marketing and Branding; Finance; Fine Art; Forensic Science; French; Furniture and Product Design; Games Technology; Garden Design; Geography; German; Graphic Design; Health and Environment; Health and Social Care; History; Horticulture; Business Management and Human Resources; Information Systems; Information and Communications Technology; International Fashion Business; International Relations; Interior Architecture and Design; Italian; Landscape; Languages; Law; Linguistics; Management; Mandarin Chinese; Marketing; Mathematics; Media; Medicinal Science; Microbiology; Modern Languages; Multimedia; Pharmaceutical and. Medicinal Chemistry; Pharmacology; Philosophy; Photography; Physical Geography; Physics; Planning and Property Development; Politics; Primary Education; Print Journalism; Property Investment and Finance; Psychology; Quantity Surveying; Real Estate Management; Safety, Health and Environmental Management; Social Work; Sociology; Software Engineering; Spanish; Design and Technology Education; Sport and Exercise Science; Coaching and Sport Science; Statistics; Surveying; Teaching; Technology; Television; Textile Design; Theatre Design; Veterinary Nursing; Wildlife; Youth Studies.

TUITION FEES (2009/10)

£3,225.

BURSARIES AND OTHER AWARDS
NTU Bursary

NTU bursaries up to £1,075 per year, depending on household income, are offered to students starting in 2009/10. To be eligible, students must be paying the full tuition fee of £3,225, be in receipt of a maintenance or special support grant and have a household income of £40,000 or below.

See Chapters 2, 4 and 6 for additional awards, applicable to all universities

NTU Nottinghamshire Bursary

Additionally, those who are in receipt of a NTU Bursary, may also be eligible for an extra NTU Nottinghamshire Bursary. To qualify, their permanent home address must be in Nottinghamshire or have an NG postcode at the time of their original application for support. This extra bursary is worth up to £265 per year.

NTU Academic Scholarships

Competitive Academic Scholarships of £2,000 per year are also offered. Eligibility for this bursary is based on academic performance during a student's first year of study. Payments are made in the second and subsequent years of study (excluding paid placements and repeat years). To be considered for this scholarship, students must also be eligible for the full NTU Bursary.

For more information please visit: www.ntu.ac.uk/financialsupport.

AWARDS FOR NON-EU STUDENTS

The International Development Office offers a wide range of scholarships to international (non-EU) students applying to Nottingham Trent University for an autumn or January start. The scholarships will be offered to international students on both undergraduate and postgraduate courses. This is a competitive scholarship scheme which will be judged partly on academic merit, partly on personal statement. Scholarships take the form of a partial fee contribution, normally to the value of £2,000.

There is a formal application procedure. Please visit www.ntu.ac.uk/scholarships for more information.

POSTGRADUATE AWARDS

NTU Graduate School Master's Bursaries

The University usually runs a scheme awarding a number of bursaries for students who have been accepted for enrolment on some full-time master's courses. This scheme is competitive, with selection criteria based upon academic quality and impact. Application details and further information about eligibility requirements are available from each School (see the website for contact details www.ntu.ac.uk/financialsupport).

Vice-Chancellor's PhD Bursaries

Each year Nottingham Trent University invites applications for fully funded PhD studentships; these are normally advertised in January for an October start date. The studentships will pay UK/EU fees, and provide a maintenance stipend of up to three years. The closing date for applications for 2009/10 academic year was the 16th February 2009.

Other Research Bursaries

In addition to this competition, some of the Schools within the University may offer their own bursaries for research students, either towards fees or with a tax free maintenance allowance.

Further information about the Vice Chancellor's PhD Bursaries and other research bursaries is available from our Graduate Schools (see the website for contact details www.ntu.ac.uk/financialsupport).

INFORMATION AND TUITION FEES FOR NON-EU STUDENTS

English language entry requirement: for most courses is IELTS 6.5 (or equivalent). Pre-sessional English language courses are available from 5-20 weeks. **Tuition fees:** £8,850–£13,950. **Living costs:** £7,600

Nottingham Trent University, Burton Street, Nottingham NG1 4BU; tel: 0115 941 8418; www.ntu.ac.uk.

OXFORD UNIVERSITY

The University of Oxford has 30 independent, self-governing colleges and seven permanent private halls which admit undergraduate students. Application is made via UCAS and the Oxford Application Form, each college operating its own interview procedure. There is a total student population of over 17,000.

DEGREE SUBJECTS OFFERED

Anthropology; Arabic; Archaeology; Biochemistry; Biological Sciences; Chemistry; Chinese; Classics; Computer Science; Czech; Earth Sciences; Economics; Egyptology; Engineering (Chemical; Civil; Computing; Electrical/Electronic; Information; Materials; Mechanical); English; Fine Art; French; Geography; Geology; German; Hebrew; History (Ancient; Modern); Human Sciences; Islamic Studies; Italian; Japanese; Jewish Studies; Law; Linguistics; Management; Materials Science; Mathematics; Medicine; Middle Eastern Languages; Modern Greek; Modern Languages; Molecular and Cellular Biology; Music; Oriental Studies; Persian; Philosophy; Physical Sciences; Physics; Physiology; Politics; Portuguese; Psychology; Russian; Sanskrit; Theology; Turkish.

TUITION FEES (2009/10)

£3,225.

BURSARIES AND OTHER AWARDS

Oxford Opportunity Bursaries

Those with a family income of less than £17,999 will receive £3,225 in Year 1 plus £875 in the first year and £3,000 thereafter. Similarly those with a family income between £18,000 and £25,000 will receive £3,225 in Year 1 and £2,600 thereafter and those with a family income of between £25,000 and £49,999 will receive between £3,225 and £200 on a sliding scale (declines by £100 per £1,000 of family income).

Abbott's Bursaries

These bursaries are awarded to children (including orphan children) of the clergy of the Church of England, in need of financial assistance.

Choral Awards

Thirteen colleges in Oxford University offer choral awards to students at the time of applying to the university. These are: Christ Church (6); Exeter (12); Keble (6); Magdalen (12); New (8); Oriel (6); St Edmund Hall (2); St John's (6); St Peter's (6); The Queen's (6); Trinity (6); University (3); Worcester (6).

Organ Awards

Most colleges elect an organ scholar to take charge of, or assist with, the music of the college chapel. Most organ scholars read for an honours degree in Music. Selection is by practical and written tests along with an interview. Scholarships are worth up to £1,000. Contact the Faculty of Music, Oxford University, St Aldates, Oxford OX1 1DB; tel: 01865 276125.

Instrumental Awards

A number of colleges offer Instrumental Awards. Further information can be obtained from these colleges: Balliol; Christ Church; Magdalen; New; St Anne's; St Catherine's; St Edmund Hall; St Hilda's; St Hugh's; St John's; St Peter's; Somerville; Trinity; University; Worcester.

Enhanced Bursaries

All Enhanced Bursaries are open to students in receipt of an Oxford Opportunity Bursary and are offered as follows:

The BP Bursary

This is worth £1,000 per annum and is open to students taking the following courses – Chemistry, Earth Science, Engineering Science, Engineering, Economics and Management, Geology, Mathematics, Mathematics and Computer Science/Philosophy, Statistics, Physics and Physics and Philosophy. Competition is based on academic ability and the student's interest in the energy sector.

Citi Foundation Bursary

Thirteen awards are made worth £1,000 and are open to first year students in any subject.

IBM Bursaries

Two awards of £1,000 are made and are open to students taking courses in either Computer Science or Computer Science and Mathematics.

Oxford-Man Group Scholarships

Fifteen awards of £1,000 are made to exceptional students taking courses in Computer Science, Economics and Management, Engineering Science, Materials Science, Materials Economics and Management, Mathematics, Mathematics and Computer Science/Philosophy/Statistics, Physics, and Physics and Philosophy.

Prendergast Bequest

The award is open to applicants born in the Republic of Ireland. It provides support of up to £2,500 by way of small sums for maintenance and for specific purposes.

Southern Trust Fund

Various awards are offered to disabled students.

University Hardship Fund

There is a University Hardship Fund (separate from the government Hardship Fund) to help students who find themselves in unforeseeable hardship due to unpredictable misfortune. There are seven awards, the size of which has varied widely, ranging from £100 to £1,500. Contact the college of preference.

Walter Gordon Bequest

Assistance in meeting costs may be obtained for members of the university facing serious health problems.

Financial assistance

In addition to these benefits, the colleges offer various financial awards and funds to their students.

These may include:

* **Scholarships and exhibitions:** awarded after the first year for excellent academic achievement in university exams.
* **Tutorial prizes and commendations:** for good, consistent work.
* **Study grants:** to cover accommodation for students staying in Oxford in the vacation for academic projects.
* **Travel grants:** to cover travel costs for a trip abroad related to academic work.
* **Book grants:** to cover the cost of purchasing books essential to the degree course.
* **Job opportunities:** some colleges can offer part-time work during terms and full-time opportunities in vacations to students, provided it does not interfere with their academic work.

The university and the colleges are very sympathetic to student hardship and are aware of the new financial pressures facing undergraduates. They are currently looking into further possible areas of help and funding to prevent this from happening, but students will always find a good deal of support available if they run into financial difficulty whilst at Oxford.

For further information about the financial aid available in individual colleges, contact the tutor for admissions at the college. For more general queries, contact the Oxford Colleges Admissions Office.

AWARDS FOR NON-EU STUDENTS

Under the Oxford Overseas Awards Scheme, a limited number of scholarships and bursaries are awarded by the university to supplement the funds of non-EU students who would otherwise not have enough money from other sources to begin their studies at Oxford. Students cannot apply until they have been conditionally or unconditionally accepted for entry to a course at Oxford, and students who have already begun their course are not eligible. The amount awarded is calculated to bring the student's total funds to what the university judges to be an adequate level; the maximum awarded will be 50% of the university fee, but most awards are made at a significantly lower level. The university will not consider applications from students who are substantially underfunded, and applicants will be expected to have already applied for student loans offered from their home countries.

Oxford Students Scholarships

A number of Oxford colleges offer scholarships to students of the highest calibre from developing countries. Financial need and social commitment are major criteria for selection.

Noon/OCSKET Scholarships

Awards funded jointly by the Noon Educational Foundation and the Oxford and Cambridge Society, Karachi, Educational Trust are available for students from Pakistan applying for or studying any subject except Medicine. Preference is given to those applying for first-year entry.

Waverley Scholarships

A small number of awards are given to outstanding students who require financial assistance. Preference is given to students from economically disadvantaged countries as judged by per capita GDP.

Dulverton Scholarships

A small number of full and partial Dulverton Scholarships will be available for students of outstanding merit and financial need from Central European and Eastern countries (namely Albania, Armenia, Azerbaijan, Belarus, Bosnia, Bulgaria, Croatia, Georgia, Macedonia, Moldova, Montenegro, Romania, Serbia and Ukraine).

Raffy Manoukian Scholarship

Scholarships will be available in 2008–9 for Armenian nationals or those of Armenian descent (one or both parents must be Armenian nationals) for study at the University of Oxford. The scholarships are tenable for study in the Humanities (Classical Languages and Literature, Ancient History, English, Modern Languages, Modern History), the Medical Sciences, the Mathematical and Physical Sciences, Biochemistry, Law, Economics or Politics. Students wishing to follow certain joint degrees such as Philosophy, Politics and Economics will also be eligible. Candidates should be under 20 years of age on 1 October 2008. The award will cover full fees and provide a maintenance grant of £7,000 per year.

POSTGRADUATE AWARDS
Hill Foundation Scholarships

Scholarships are for outstanding young citizens of the Russian Federation or first-generation Israelis of Russian descent who wish to study at the University of Oxford. Candidates with extremely high academic ability and personal and social qualities are favoured.

See Chapters 2, 4 and 6 for additional awards, applicable to all universities

There is no restriction as to the field of study or area of specialisation in which the scholarships are held. The scholarships may be held for one, two or three years (depending on the course chosen) but the grants for the second and third years are subject to satisfactory progress.

The Hill Foundation will pay all educational costs, including university and college fees, laboratory fees (where relevant), and any other necessary fees. In addition the scholars are provided with a maintenance allowance of £9,750 (2007–8 rate), which is adequate to cover college accommodation during the academic year. The Foundation will also cover the costs of necessary travel between Russia/Israel and Oxford up to a maximum of £1,000 per year. For further details, see www.hillfoundationscholarships.org.

INFORMATION AND APPROXIMATE FEES FOR NON-EU STUDENTS
English language entry requirement: IELTS 7.0 (or equivalent). **Tuition fees:** £11,750–£13,450 Medicine: clinical £24,500. **College fees:** £5,212. **Living costs:** £7,000–£8,000.

Oxford Colleges Admissions Office, Wellington Square, Oxford OX1 2ID; tel: 01865 288000; www.admissions.ox.ac.uk.

OXFORD BROOKES UNIVERSITY

The university was founded in 1864 and is now based on two campuses in Headington and Wheatley. It has a student population of 13,200. The main areas of study are business, languages and hotel management, arts and education, environment, life sciences and technology. A well-established modular programme operates giving students maximum choice and flexibility in constructing their own degree programme.

DEGREE SUBJECTS OFFERED
Accounting and Finance; Anthropology; Architecture; Biology; Biotechnology; Building; Business; Cartography; Cities and Society; Combined Studies; Community Arts and Crafts; Complementary Therapies; Computer Systems; Computing; Construction; Ecology; Economics; Education (Primary); Electronics; Engineering (Automotive; Civil; Electronic; Mechanical; Software; Telecommunications); English; Environmental (Biology; Design and Conservation; Geotechnology; Policy; Science); Equine Science; European Culture and Society; Exercise and Health; Fine Art; Food Science; French; Geography; Geology; Geotechnics; German; Health Care; History; Hospitality Management; Hotel and Restaurant Management; Information Systems; Intelligent Systems; Italian; Japanese Studies; Law; Leisure; Mapping and Cartography; Marketing; Mathematics; Media Technology; Midwifery; Modern History; Multimedia; Music; Nursing; Nutrition; Occupational Therapy; Performing Arts; Philosophy; Photography and Digital Imaging; Physiotherapy; Planning Studies; Politics; Psychology; Public Health; Publishing; Religious Studies; Retail Management; Social Studies; Sociology; Spanish; Sports and Coaching Studies; Statistics; Technology Management; Telecommunications; Tourism; Town and Country Planning; Transport and Travel; Water Resources; Youth and Community Work.

TUITION FEES (2009/10)
£3,225.

BURSARIES AND OTHER AWARDS
Oxford Brookes Bursary
This award based on a sliding scale ranges between £1,800 for students from households where the annual income is less than £4,999 to £150 for those from households where the income does not exceed £35,999.

Oxford Brookes Academic Excellence Scholarship

For Students achieving top A-level grades or equivalent the non-repayable scholarship is worth £2,000 per year.

Oxford Brookes Community Scholarship

This award worth £1,000 per year, is not based on academic achievement but is open to students showing potential to succeed who have studied at state-maintained schools in Oxfordshire, Milton Keynes, Buckinghamshire or Berkshire. Also at Brooklands College, Solihull College, Swindon College or New College Swindon.

AWARDS FOR NON-EU STUDENTS
International Scholarships

These are awarded on academic merit and are worth £2,000, deducted from course fees.

POSTGRADUATE AWARDS

In addition to Alumni Discounts of 10% of the tuition fees for students who have graduated from Oxford Brookes and are returning to take a second course, awards are offered in the following subjects: Business; Computer Science; Education; Engineering Science; Law; Planning; Publishing; Real Estate Management; Tourism. Visit www.brookes.ac.uk/studying/finance/support for more information.

INFORMATION AND APPROXIMATE FEES FOR NON-EU STUDENTS

There are a large number of international students. **English language entry requirement:** Engineering and Construction IELTS 5.5 (or equivalent); Business, Computing, humanities and social sciences IELTS 6.0 (or equivalent); Law and Psychology IELTS 6.5 (or equivalent). There is a large number of English language support courses, from two weeks to two years, offered by the Centre for English Language Studies. **Fees:** £9,000–£9,500. **Living costs:** £8,000–£9,000.

Oxford Brookes University, Headington Hill Campus, Headington, Oxford OX3 0BP; tel: 01865 483040; www.brookes.ac.uk.

PENINSULA MEDICAL SCHOOL
(Exeter and Plymouth)

The Medical School was established as a partnership between the Universities of Exeter and Plymouth and the NHS in Devon and Cornwall in 2000. It has a number of sites at locations across the region in Plymouth, Exeter and Truro. There are currently in excess of 1000 students enrolled on medical and dental programmes.

DEGREE SUBJECTS OFFERED

Clinical Science, Dentistry, Medicine.

TUITION FEES (2009/10)

£3225.

BURSARIES AND OTHER AWARDS
National bursaries
A national bursary scheme is offered which is open to all students applying for medical courses in the UK. Eligibility for national bursaries is based on household incomes up to £35,000 and is administered through the Local Authority. A bursary of £1,500 is awarded against household incomes of £25,000 or less and £750 for household incomes between £25,001 and £35,000.

Top-up bursary scheme
The Peninsula Medical School operates a locally targeted top-up bursary scheme to support students who have completed their post-16 studies at a school or college in Devon, Cornwall or Somerset. The scheme is partly based on financial circumstances with priority given to those from households where the income is below £25,000 and who in addition meet one or more of the following criteria:

* A first generation student to enter higher education especially where there is lack of or a limited support network at home.
* Difficult circumstances at home (eg large household, illness or disability at home).
* Peer pressure likely to affect motivation or other material circumstances to progress to higher education.

Applications to Peninsula bursary scheme must outline factors in addition to financial hardship which might affect progression to higher education.

INFORMATION AND APPROXIMATE FEES FOR NON-EU STUDENTS
English Language entry requirement IELTS: 7.5 with at least 7 in each of the speaking and listening sections from school leaving applicants only. **Fees:** BM and BS courses Years 1 & 2 - £13,500; Years 3 to 5 - £21,000. BDS course Years 1 to 4 £21,000. **(Please note that these fees will rise annually in line with inflation and are not fixed at the point of entry.) Living costs:** £9,000.

The Peninsula College of Medicine and Dentistry, The John Bull Building, Tamar Science Park, Research Way, Plymouth, Devon PL6 8BU tel: 01752 437444 email: admissions@pcmd.ac.uk or pmsenqs@pms.ac.uk; www.pms.ac.uk.

PLYMOUTH UNIVERSITY

The University of Plymouth is situated in the city centre with four halls of residence on campus. In addition there are three faculty campuses, in Exeter (Art), in Exmouth (Education) and in Newton Abbot (Agriculture). The university was founded in 1970 and has a student population of 20,500.

DEGREE SUBJECTS OFFERED
Accounting; Adventure Tourism; Agriculture; Animal Science; Architecture; Art and Design; Atomic and Formulation Science; Biological Sciences; Biology; Building Surveying; Business; Chemistry; Coastal Environmental Science; Community Work; Construction Science; Crop Science; Design Technology; Earth Sciences; Ecology; Economics; Education (Teacher Training); Engineering (Civil; Coastal; Communication; Computer Systems; Computing; Electrical/Electronic; Marine; Materials; Mechanical); English; Environmental Building; European Studies; Food and Hospitality Management; Food Quality; Gallery and Museum Studies; Geography; Geological Sciences; Geology; Health Studies; Heritage Management; History; Hospitality Management; Human Biosciences; International Relations; Internet Technologies; Law; Marine Biology; Marketing; Mathematics;

Media Arts; Medicine; Microbiology; Modern Languages; Multimedia; Nautical Studies; Neuroinformatics; Ocean Science; Personnel Management; Plant Sciences; Podiatry; Politics; Popular Culture; Psychology; Quantity Surveying; Robotics; Rural Resource Management; Social Policy; Social Research; Sociology; Sports Management; Sports Technology; Statistics; Surf Science and Technology; Theatre and Performance Arts; Tourism; Underwater Science; Visual Arts; Wildlife Conservation.

TUITION FEES (2009/10)
£3,225.

BURSARIES AND OTHER AWARDS
University of Plymouth Bursaries
Several Bursaries are offered based on personal circumstances. The maximum amount payable is £1,010 and awards are calculated on household incomes from below £25,000 to the maximum of £40,000. Mature students on income support may claim £550 whilst £1,000 Care Leavers Bursaries are also offered.

Subject Scholarships and Awards
The first £350 will be funded for each compulsory overseas and UK field trip for the following courses: Animal Science Behaviour and Welfare, Art and Design and General Primary, Bioscience, Architecture Design Structures, Building Surveying and the Environment, Construction Management and the Environment, Environmental Biology, Environmental Construction Surveying, Marine Biology, Physical Education and General Primary, Science and General Primary and Wildlife Conservation.

Arts Scholarship
This is open to applicants for the BA Course in Fine Art.

Mathematics and Statistics Entrance Scholarship
Home and EU entrants accepting an offer for a Mathematics/Statistics degree will automatically receive a scholarship of £500 per grade A in Mathematics, Further Mathematics or Statistics.

Sports Scholarships
Drake Sports Scholarship
These awards of £1,000 are open to students who are competing at a national or international standard in sailing, yachting, power boating, surfing or canoeing.

Gold/Silver Sports Scholarships
Annual awards are offered to students representing their county or country nationally or internationally. The Gold Scholarship is worth £1,500 per year and the Silver Scholarship £600. Contact the Head of Sport and Recreation.

AWARDS FOR NON-EU STUDENTS
Scholarships for Non-EU students are currently being reviewed. Contact the subject department for further information.

POSTGRADUATE AWARDS
These are open to Plymouth graduates embarking on courses in Faculties of Arts and Technology. Full Time PGCE courses can also attract a training salary of £6,000 or £9,000 per year providing they specialise in a recognized shortage subject.

See Chapters 2, 4 and 6 for additional awards, applicable to all universities

INFORMATION AND APPROXIMATE FEES FOR NON-EU STUDENTS
English language entry requirement: IELTS 6.5 (or equivalent); 'English for University' courses
IELTS 4.5 (or equivalent). **Fees:** £8,200–8,750. **Living costs:** £7,000–£7,500.

**University of Plymouth, Drake Circus, Plymouth PL4 8AA; tel: 01752 232137; www.
plymouth.ac.uk.**

PORTSMOUTH UNIVERSITY

The University of Portsmouth was originally founded in 1869 as a School of Science and awarded
its first degree in 1900. It is situated on three campuses in the heart of the city and has a population of over 16,400 undergraduates and part-time students.

DEGREE SUBJECTS OFFERED
Accountancy; Animal Development; Applied Languages; Architecture; Art and Design;
Biochemistry; Biology; Biomedical Science; Biotechnology; Business; Combined Modern Languages;
Communications Technology; Computer Science; Construction; Creative Technology and Simulation;
Criminology; Disaster Risk Management; Earth Sciences; Economics; Education; Engineering (Civil;
Communications; Computer; Construction; Electronic/Electrical; Geology/Geotechnics;
Management; Manufacture; Mechanical); English; Entertainment Technology; Environmental
Sciences; European Studies; Exercise and Health Science; Financial Services; French; General
Science; Geography; Geology; German; Health Sciences; Heritage Management; Hispanic Studies;
History; Hospitality Management; Human Resource Management; Humanities; International
Relations; International Trade; Internet Systems; Latin American Studies; Leisure; Marketing;
Mathematics; Media; Microbiology; Nursing; Palaeobiology and Evolution; Pharmaceutical Sciences;
Pharmacology; Pharmacy; Photography; Politics; Property Development; Psychology; Quantity
Surveying; Radiography; Restoration and Decoration Studies; Russian; Social Policy; Sociology;
Spanish; Sports Science; Statistics; Technology.

TUITION FEES (2009/10)
£3,225.

BURSARIES AND OTHER AWARDS
University of Portsmouth Bursary
Home students from households with an income of up to £25,000 receive an additional grant of
£900 and £600 for household incomes between £25,000 and 32,000.

Local Colleges Bursary
Students attending courses at local colleges in Hampshire and the Isle of Wight will receive a
bursary of £300.

Sports Scholarships
To help students who wish to combine their academic studies with their continued training and
competition, the University of Portsmouth offers the opportunity for students to apply for a Sports
Scholarship. They are offered in the form of either travel vouchers or financial support towards the
purchase of equipment and for high-level training and competition. These scholarships are for one
year but students can reapply. (Check with university.)

Care Leavers Bursary
Students who have previously been in care receive £1,500.

Art and Design Residential Bursary
A means-tested award worth £3,229 is offered to Art and Design students who meet their own accommodation costs or who are faced with exceptional travel costs, eg from the Isle of Wight (check with university).

Foyer Federation Bursary
Students who have previously been resident in Foyer Federation centres receive £1,500.

AWARDS FOR NON-EU STUDENTS
New overseas students are given the opportunity to apply on a competitive basis for a once-only scholarship in the form of a £1,000 reduction in tuition fees.

POSTGRADUATE AWARDS
Some awards are available.

INFORMATION AND APPROXIMATE FEES FOR NON-EU STUDENTS
There are students from over 100 countries. **English language entry requirement:** IELTS 6.0 (or equivalent); foundation course IELTS 5.5 (or equivalent). Induction, academic skills and language courses are available. **Fees:** £8,350–£9,350. **Living costs:** £7,500–£8,500.

Portsmouth University, University House, Winston Churchill Avenue, Portsmouth PO1 2UP; tel: 023 9284 8484; www.port.ac.uk.

QUEEN MARGARET UNIVERSITY

The University was previously founded as a college in 1875 and received university status in 2006. It is located on a new purpose-built campus at Musselburgh.

DEGREE SUBJECTS OFFERED
Audiology; Business Management; Consumer Studies; Costume Design; Dietetics; Drama; Events Management; Film and Media; Hospitality and Tourism Management; Human Biology; Marketing; Media; Nursing; Nutrition; Occupational Therapy; Pharmacology; Physiotherapy; Podiatry; Psychology; Public Relations; Radiography; Retail Management; Sociology; Speech and Language Therapy; Tourism Management.

TUITION FEES
Students domiciled in Scotland receive free tuition. See also www.saas.gov.uk. and **Chapter 1 'Financing Your Course'.**

BURSARIES AND OTHER AWARDS
Check with the university.

Apex Hotel Bursary
Students may be eligible for the Apex Hotel Bursary. This is an annual award of £1,000 for three years plus additional opportunities with Apex. This is awarded to the hospitality student with the highest first year assessment results.

AWARDS FOR NON-EU STUDENTS
QM Scholarships
Ten competitive scholarships of £1,000 are offered for self-funding international students in their first year of study. The scholarship is granted as a reduction of the tuition fee. Application forms will be sent out after students accept an offer of a place.

POSTGRADUATE AWARDS
Ten competitive scholarships are offered as above.

INFORMATION AND APPROXIMATE FEES FOR NON-EU STUDENTS
English language entry requirement: IELTS 6.5 (or equivalent); Speech and Language Therapy IELTS 7.5 (or equivalent); Audiology IELTS 7.0 (or equivalent); Drama, Nursing, Radiography IELTS 6.0 (or equivalent). **Fees:** £8,800–£9,700. **Living costs:** £6,000–£7,000.

Queen Margaret University, Queen Margaret University Drive, Musselburgh EH2I 6UU; tel: 0131 474 0000; www.qmu.ac.uk.

QUEEN MARY COLLEGE
(University of London)

Queen Mary College is situated in the East End of London with easy access to the city. There is a student population of over 12,000.

DEGREE SUBJECTS OFFERED
Astronomy; Astrophysics; Biochemistry; Biology; Business Management; Chemistry; Computer Science; Dentistry; Drama; Ecology and Conservation; Economics; Engineering (Aerospace; Avionics; Biomedical Materials; Communications; Computer; Electric/Electronic; Environmental Materials; Internet; Materials Science; Mechanical; Medical; Telecommunications); English; Film Studies; French; Genetics; Geography; German; Hispanic Studies; History; Law; Linguistics; Mathematics; Medicine; Statistics; Zoology;

TUITION FEES (2009/10)
£3,225

BURSARIES AND OTHER AWARDS
A payment of £1,078 is made to all students in receipt of the full maintenance grant. A bursary of £861 will be paid to students on a partial maintenance grant from households with an income of between £25,000 and £34,613.

Queen Mary and Westfield Alumni Student Bursaries
Two bursaries worth £3,000 (£1,000 for each year of study) are offered to students who have received their education in the London Boroughs of Tower Hamlets, Newham, Hackney or the City of London.

Barts and the London Alumni Association Student Bursary
The Geoffrey Flavell Student Bursary of £2,000 over three years is awarded (Year 1, £1,000, Years 2 and 3, £500 each year) to one eligible student studying for an MBBS qualification.

Aldgate and Allhallows Foundation Scholarships

These scholarships are open to undergraduate entrants who are permanent residents of either the City of London or Tower Hamlets.

The John Abernathy Barts Scholarships

These awards are to encourage applications from students facing financial hardship who would benefit from the MBBS programme. They are worth £3,000 for each of the five years of the course.

Access to Learning Fund

Additional money is also available (at all universities and colleges) for students in financial hardship who have taken out the maximum maintenance loan.

Other scholarships and prizes

A number of small scholarships and prizes are awarded annually in many of the clinical specialities. There are Entrance Scholarships available for candidates from the Universities of Oxford and Cambridge and to students of Victoria College, Jersey. A variety of internal scholarships are also offered and each year a number of financial prizes are awarded to undergraduates who achieve outstanding results in examinations.

AWARDS FOR NON-EU STUDENTS

Several departments offer international scholarship schemes for which overseas students are eligible. These change from year to year. Contact the International Office.

POSTGRADUATE AWARDS

Several research awards are offered in the following subject areas: Economics; Electronic Engineering; Geography; Mathematics; Modern Languages; Physics.

INFORMATION AND APPROXIMATE FEES FOR NON-EU STUDENTS

There is a large number of international students. **English language entry requirement:** IELTS 6.5 (or equivalent). There is an international foundation course covering English language tuition and specialist courses in Business, Economics, European Studies, Geography, Management, Mathematics and Spanish. The course guarantees progression to linked degree courses including Law. **Fees:** £9,000 – £10,500 Medicine: pre-clinical £14,600 clinical £22,500. **Living costs:** £9,500 – £10,500.

Queen Mary, University of London, Mile End Road, London E1 4NS; tel: 020 7882 5500 www.qmul.ac.uk.

QUEEN'S UNIVERSITY BELFAST

The University was founded in 1845 and now has a student population of over 17,500. It is located in a 'Victorian suburb' on the south side of the city. Courses are modular and the academic year is divided into two semesters with science, engineering and technology, humanities and medical courses predominating.

DEGREE SUBJECTS OFFERED

Accounting: Actuarial Studies; Aerospace Engineering; Agricultural Technology; Archaeology and Palaeoecology; Architecture; Biochemistry; Biological Sciences; Biomedical Sciences; Business

Economics; Business Information Technology, Business Management; Chemical Engineering; Chemistry; Civil Engineering; Computer Games Design and Development; Computer Science; Computing and Information Technology; Creative Multimedia; Criminology; Dentistry; Drama Studies; Economics; Education; Electrical And Electronic Engineering; Electronic and Software Engineering; English; Environmental and Civil Engineering; Environmental Biology; Environmental Planning; Ethnomusicology; Film Studies; Finance; Food Quality, Safety and Nutrition; French Studies; Genetics; Geography; German Studies, History (Ancient and Modern); Human Biology; International Business with a Modern Language; International Studies; Irish And Celtic Studies; Irish Studies; Land, Environment and Sustainability; Land Use and Environmental Management; Law; Linguistics; Management; Manufacturing Engineering; Marine Biology; Mathematical Studies; Mechanical Engineering; Medicine; Microbiology; Midwifery; Molecular Biology; Music; Music Technology; Nursing; Pharmacy; Philosophy; Physics; Politics; Politics, Philosophy and Economics; Product Design and Development; Psychology; Social Anthropology; Social Policy; Social Work; Sociology; Spanish; Spanish and Portuguese Studies; Structural Engineering with Architecture; Theology; Web Technology and e-Commerce; Zoology.

TUITION FEES (2009/10)
£3,225. See also **Chapter 1, 'Financing Your Course'.**

BURSARIES AND OTHER AWARDS
Institutional bursaries are available for full-time undergraduate students from families with a household income up to and including £33,820.

ORGAN SCHOLARSHIP
A scholarship is offered to the value of £600, which includes organ lessons. Candidates must be Music undergraduates. Application details may be obtained from the School of Music and Sonic Arts, Queen's University Belfast, tel: 028 9097 5337, or www.mu.qub.ac.uk.

Sports Scholarships
Since the University's foundation, sport has been an important and integral part in the Queen's student experience. The University's long tradition of sporting excellence has co-existed with the academic excellence for which Queen's is internationally renowned.

The University has a thriving and vibrant sporting culture with 50 different sports clubs providing students with the opportunity to compete in a range of competitions including Irish University Championships, British University Games and the World Student Games.

Sports Bursaries
The Bursaries Awards are in their 16th year. This is scheme designed to support top level athletes in achieving their sporting potential during their time at the university.

The awards are open to all fully-enrolled students, both sports men and women from any sporting background. This year the 25 recipients received free access to taining facilities, personal fitness coaching, sports clothing, sports science and medical support, educational workshops, a mentoring service and financial awards up to £1,000. The rewards are criteria set and applications are available during enrolment week.

Academy Scholarships
Further sports development opportunities are available through the network of Sporting Academies at the University; these include Rugby, Gaelic Games, Rowing and Soccer. These schemes allow athletes to enhance their performance by providing access to the high performance and lifestyle centre services as well as free access to the University's fantastic sport facilities and excellent coaching.

For information on Sports Bursaries and Sports Academies please contact the Sports Development Team on: tel: 028 9038 7688; email: k.oakes@qub.ac.uk; www.queenssport.com.

A-level Entrance Scholarships

Queen's University offers Entrance Scholarships on the basis of entrance qualifications. All students entering the University for the first time to undertake a primary degree, and who have achieved at least three 'A' grades at A-level (including vocational A-levels), are eligible to apply. Applicants must not already hold a degree from another university or equivalent institution.

Queen's Gold Medal Entrance Scholarships

To celebrate its Centenary year, the University established the Queen's Centenary Gold Medal Entrance Scholarships.

These scholarships will be awarded to the top candidate entering each of the three Faculties (Arts, Humanities and Social Sciences; Engineering and Physical Sciences and Medicine, Health and Life Sciences), who attains the highest place in the entrance scholarship competition.

All students entering the University for the first time to undertake a primary degree, and who have achieved at least three 'A' grades at A-level (including vocational A-levels), are eligible to apply. Applicants must not already hold a degree from another university or equivalent institution.

The value of the award, which is tenable for three years, is £2,500 per annum. It is tenable with other entrance scholarships, with the exception of the University Entrance Scholarships.

The recipients will be determined on the basis of their best three A-level marks, and applicants must forward completed application forms, along with documentary evidence of their uniform examination marks, at both AS and A2 level to Academic Affairs by the published deadline, normally mid-October.

Awards will be made by the Scholarships and Awards Group. Payment of Scholarship will be made at the beginning of second semester, subject to confirmation of satisfactory performance in semester one, ie January each year.

University Entrance Scholarships

A further twenty Scholarships of £1,000 for one year only will be awarded across all the Schools of the University. The recipients will be determined on the basis of their best three A-level marks, and applicants must forward completed application forms, along with documentary evidence of their uniform examination marks, at both AS and A2 level to Academic Affairs by the published deadline, normally mid-October.

Awards will be made by the Scholarships and Awards Group. Payment of the Scholarship will be made at the beginning of second semester, subject to confirmation of satisfactory performance in semester one.

Other Entrance Scholarships

* David Russell Lappin Scholarship
* Sullivan Scholarships
* John Sinclair Porter Scholarship
* Foundation Entrance Scholarships
* Drennan and Tennant Exhibitions
* Megaw Scholarship
* Reid-Harwood Scholarship
* Pakenham Scholarships

See Chapters 2, 4 and 6 for additional awards, applicable to all universities

Science, Technology, Engineering and Mathematics Awards (STEM)

Students entering the University for the first time to undertake a primary degree and who attain a minimum of three 'A' grades at A-level (or equivalent) will receive a one-off payment of £1,000, if applying to courses in the following Schools:

* Architecture, Planning and Civil Engineering (Civil Engineering courses only)
* Biological Sciences
* Chemistry and Chemical Engineering
* Electronics, Electrical Engineering and Computer Science
* Mathematics and Physics
* Medicine, Dentistry and Biomedical Sciences (Biomedical Sciences courses only)
* Mechanical and Aerospace Engineering

Students will not be required to apply, identification of those eligible for the STEM scholarships will be automatic. The awarding of all scholarships is subject to successful completion of semester 1 of first year (achieving at least a pass mark in each module studied). Eligible students will therefore receive their scholarships following the publication of semester 1 exam results.

Travel Scholarships for students from outside Northern Ireland

Students entering the University for the first time to undertake a primary degree and who achieve three 'A' grades at A-Level (or equivalent) will receive £600 (£200 per year over three years). Students from EU member states (excluding Northern Ireland) are eligible.

Students need not apply, identification of those eligible for the Travel scholarships will be automatic. The awarding of all Scholarships is subject to successful completion of semester 1 of first year (achieving at least a pass mark in each module studied). Eligible Students will therefore receive their scholarships following the publication of semester 1 exam results.

Further scholarships

In addition, there are four further Entrance Scholarships, the Dr George Alexander Baird Entrance Scholarships available to entrants with qualifications other than A-levels.

Students in financial difficulties

The funds listed below are dealt with by the Student Support Committee, which is chaired by a senior member of academic staff. For details of the applications process, for these and other support funds, please go to the Student support section of the Finance Directorate website at

www.qub.ac.uk/directorates/AcademicStudentAffairs/AcademicAffairs/ScholarshipsAwards/Schol arshipsAwardsHandbook/StudentsinFinancialDifficulties/Advice for students in financial hardship and further details about the application process can be obtained from the Student Financial Advisor in the Students' Union.

The Clifford Arbuthnot (CA) Benefaction

This benefaction is derived from funds which were first donated anonymously in 1961 during the donor's lifetime and augmented by a bequest from the donor in 1974. The fund may be used to assist, by direct money grants or otherwise, enrolled students, graduate or undergraduate, who are in straitened circumstances.

The funds may also be used to provide amenities for the student body generally or any club or society of students or to defray any expenses incurred in furthering the interests of the University which the Vice-Chancellor may consider desirable. These funds are administered through the Student Support Fund Committee details of which can be found on the Finance department website www.qub.ac.uk/bo/finser/suppfund.htm

Isabella Henderson Duncan Memorial Loan Fund

This fund, bequeathed in 1967, may provide a small loan to a student from County Tyrone who is in financial difficulties provided that one of the following conditions is fulfilled:

* the student is a graduate enrolled in the Faculty of Theology for either full-time or part-time study, or
* the student is an undergraduate in the Faculty of Medicine, who has passed the second medical examination.

These funds are administered through the Student Support Fund Committee, details of which can be found on the Finance department website. www.qub.ac.uk/bo/fin-ser/suppfund.htm

The St John Ervine Bequest

Mrs Ervine, the wife of the distinguished playwright, St John Ervine, left a legacy which came to the University in 1972 to be known as the 'St John Ervine Bequest'. The income of the fund is to be used as follows:

To assist any student of the University, who was born or one of whose parents was born within the boundaries of one of the nine counties of the historic province of Ulster (Donegal, Londonderry, Antrim, Down, Armagh, Cavan, Monaghan, Fermanagh, Tyrone) either by direct grant or by defraying, in whole or in part, the necessary expenses of his or her education at the University, or of the extension or completion of his or her education at any other university or hospital in Great Britain or abroad.

These funds are administered through the Student Support Fund Committee, details of which can be found on the Finance department website: www.qub.ac.uk/bo/fin-ser/suppfund.htm

The Harold Gray Fund

This fund was established in 1981 under a bequest in the will of Mrs Dorothy Kathleen Gray to provide grants by way of gift or loan to undergraduate and postgraduate students who after entering the University find it difficult or impossible for financial reasons to continue their studies. Preference will be given to students in the Faculty of Medicine. These funds are administered through the Student Support Fund Committee, details of which can be found on the Finance Department website: www.qub.ac.uk/bo/fin-ser/suppfund.htm

Hamilton (Students' Aid) Fund

This fund was established in 1922 by Thomas Hamilton, the first President and Vice-Chancellor of Queen's University, for the benefit of undergraduates who, after beginning their studies in the University, find themselves in financial difficulties for reasons beyond their control.

These funds are administered through the Student Support Fund Committee, details of which can be found on the Finance department website: www.qub.ac.uk/bo/fin-ser/suppfund.htm

Emily Sarah Montgomery Fund

This fund was instituted under a bequest of Emily Sarah Montgomery in 1961. The fund provides grants by way of gift or loan to students who, having entered the University, find it difficult or impossible for financial reasons to continue their studies. Preference will be given to undergraduates to enable them to complete their course of study. As the fund is restricted in its annual income the grants will normally be for limited amounts, and application for assistance for periods extending beyond the end of the academic year in which they are made will not normally be considered. These funds are administered through the Student Support Fund Committee, details: www.qub.ac.uk/bo/fin-ser/suppfund.htm

The Queen's Women Graduates' Association Scholarship

The Queen's Women Graduates' Association (QWGA) is interested in promoting education, especially for women, at local, national and international levels. This scholarship was established to assist mature women students from Northern Ireland taking courses at Queen's.

See Chapters 2, 4 and 6 for additional awards, applicable to all universities

It is open to women over 25 years of age who are on a low income or dependent on state benefits, attending or about to begin a Degree, Diploma, or Certificate award-bearing course at Queen's. Degree holders and previous recipients of the QWGA Award are not eligible to apply.

It may be helpful in assisting, for example, with the cost of fees, books, childcare or travel. It is available for one academic year only. The amount may vary, but it is likely to be not less than £200.

The awards are made after interview by a sub-committee of the Association, assisted by a representative of the University's academic staff. Application forms are obtained form the Academic Affairs Office.

Applicants who are shortlisted will be asked to attend for interview and provide relevant information about their income and circumstances and at the end of the year award holders will be expected to produce a brief report on their progress and how they used the award.

Academic Affairs is based at: Level 6, Administration Building, Queen's University Belfast BT7 1NN; tel: 028 9097 3006; email: academic-affairs@qub.ac.uk; www.qub.ac.uk/qap.

AWARDS FOR NON-EU STUDENTS
The University offers a limited number of scholarships for highly qualified international students. For further details, please see www.qub.uk/home/Prospective Students/International Students or Queen's University Belfast, University Road, Belfast, Northern Ireland BT7 1NN; tel: 028 9097 5081.

POSTGRADUATE AWARDS
For 2009/10 entry a number of Department for Employment & Learning (DEL), DEL Programme for Government (PFG), University funded studentships are available. These PhD studentships are available across all schools and subject areas at Queen's University. A limited amount of Taught Master's funding may also be available. For School closing dates, eligibility criteria, projects available and further information please go to www.qub.ac.uk.

INFORMATION AND FEES FOR NON-EU STUDENTS
There are approximately 1,200 international students from over 70 countries studying at Queen's. **English language entry requirement:** IELTS 6.0-6.5 (or equivalent). Special English language summer schools and pre-university language courses are available, as well as weekly language courses. The International Office organises a two-day orientation programme in mid-September, prior to the start of the first semester. A two-day programme is also held before the start of the second semester. **Fees:** classroom-based courses £9,418; laboratory/workshop based courses £11,539; Medicine/Dentistry: pre-clinical £12,757, clinical £24,066; Study Abroad: £4,238 per semester. **Living Costs:** £7,200 for a full calendar year.

For more information on any of these scholarships please visit

www.qub.ac.uk/scholarships or register on the prospective student portal £9,418; by following the links at www.qub.ac.uk, to receive regular updates on scholarships and other information about Queen's University.

Queen's University Belfast, University Road, Belfast, Northern Ireland BT7 1NN; tel: 028 9097 5081; www.qub.ac.uk.

READING UNIVERSITY

The University of Reading is ranked as one of the top 200 universities in the world. Its academic excellence and beautiful environment of a 130 hectare country estate make Reading consistently a popular higher education choice in the UK. It has a student population of 22,805 and a broad portfolio of full- and part-time degree programmes covers the arts, humanities, sciences and social sciences. The University specialises in areas such as agriculture, business and finance, construction management, cybernetics, horticulture, meteorology, real estate and typography, where there are few other national providers.

DEGREE SUBJECTS OFFERED

Accounting; Agriculture; Ancient History; Animal Science; Archaeology; Art and Design; Banking; Biochemistry; Biological Sciences; Building; Business Analysis/Economics; Chemistry; Classical Studies; Classics; Computer Science; Construction; Cybernetics; Economics; Educational Studies (Primary); Electronic Engineering; English; Environmental Science; European Studies; Film and Theatre; Food (Manufacturing; Marketing; Science; Technology); French; Geography; German; Habitat and Soil Management; History; Horticulture; Intelligent Systems; International Relations; International Securities; Investment; Italian; Language Pathology; Law; Linguistics; Management; Mathematics; Medieval Studies; Meteorology; Pharmacy; Philosophy; Politics; Psychology; Quantity Surveying; Rural Resources Management; Soil Science; Statistics; Theatre Arts Education; Zoology.

TUITION FEES (2009/10)

£3,225.

BURSARIES AND OTHER AWARDS

Access Bursaries

Students receive bursary awards on a sliding scale depending on their household income: income up to £25,000 – £1,385; £25,001 – £35,000 – £923; £35,001 – £45,000 – £462.

Pre-Entry Travel Bursaries

Pre-entry travel bursaries provide support for applicants from HEFCE-defined Widening Participation areas, with amounts up to £300 available to cover travel costs to interviews. There are also pre-entry bursaries for disabled students valued at £500.

VC/Alumni Bursary

We also offer a Vice-Chancellor's/Alumni Bursary worth £2,000 over three years aimed at students nominated by Aimhigher/state schools in Berkshire.

Dr NS Barron Fund for Applied Physical Science

These awards take the form of small bursaries and are open to candidates of good academic ability who need financial help to embark upon and complete a degree course (at either undergraduate or postgraduate level) as a student of Computer Science, Cybernetics and Electronic Engineering, or the School of Construction Management and Engineering.

Music Scholarships

Music Scholarships entitle students who satisfy the entry requirements of their chosen programme and demonstrate excellence in music to specialist music tuition worth up to £800 per year. There will be an audition to select music scholars.

See Chapters 2, 4 and 6 for additional awards, applicable to all universities

Sports Scholarships
These scholarships provide £500–2,000 and reduced-rate membership at selected facilities. These awards are offered to selected students who satisfy the entry requirements of their chosen programme and are of county or national standard in their chosen sport.

Entry Scholarships
Scholarships of £2,000, payable in the first year, are awarded to high-achieving students entering programmes of more than one year duration. For details of scholarship criteria, see www. reading.ac.uk/studentfinance.

GlaxoSmithKline Scholarships
Scholarships worth £1,100 will be awarded on the basis of academic ability, normally ABB at A-level or equivalent.

Travel Award
The Department of Real Estate and Planning offers the Michael Davidson Travel Award to students who have completed Part 2. The award is worth £1,000.

Ewan Page Prizes
The Ewan Page Prizes, of which there are three, will be awarded to new entrants to undergraduate courses in the university on the basis of A-level results. Each prize takes the form of book tokens.

International Baccalaureate
In association with the International Baccalaureate Organisation, the University of Reading offers three scholarships to outstanding holders of the IB. These are open only to undergraduate students who are required to pay fees at the full overseas rate. Each scholarship pays the full composition fee for the duration of the course, subject to successful progression, and candidates will be expected to finance their own living costs. Nominations should be forwarded by the applicant's school. More information is available at www.reading.ac.uk/studentfinance.

AWARDS FOR NON-EU STUDENTS
A number of different scholarships are available for students paying overseas fees. A scholarship of £5,000 is awarded at the end of the Programme to the student who has shown the highest level of academic excellence. Six scholarships of £1,750 each are also awarded at the end of the Programme to students who have shown exceptional academic ability. The £1,750 is then deducted from the first year undergraduate tuition fees at the University of Reading. Up to eight prizes of £250 are also awarded each year.

POSTGRADUATE AWARDS
A large number of awards are made. Applicants should refer to the booklet, *Funding Sources for Postgraduate Students*.

INFORMATION AND APPROXIMATE FEES FOR NON–EU STUDENTS
English Language entry requirement: IELTS 6.5–7.0 (or equivalent). The International Foundation Programme (IFP) at the University of Reading is an intensive, one-year access course with a long established reputation for academic excellence and student support. **Fees:** non-lab courses £9,630; lab courses £11,610. Living costs: £9,400.

University of Reading, Whiteknights House, Reading RG6 6AN; tel: 0118 987 5123; www. rdg.ac.uk.

REGENTS BUSINESS SCHOOL, LONDON

Regents Business School is a private foundation situated in Regents Park, London.

DEGREE COURSES OFFERED
Global Business Management / Business Design Management / Financial Management.

TUITION FEES (2009/10)
£11,250–£11,700.

BURSARIES AND OTHER AWARDS
Merit Awards
These scholarships offer students 50% remission of fees. They are based on academic achievement and potential.

Work Study Scholarships
These awards are offered to students with promising academic potential who are able and willing to work for a specified number of hours per week (from 5 to a maximum of 20) during term time for partial remission of fees.

INFORMATION FOR EU AND NON-EU STUDENTS
English Language entry requirement: IELTS 6.0. **Living costs:** £10,000.

Regents Business School, Inner Circle, Regents Park, London NW1 4NS; tel: 0207 487 7730; www.rbslondon.ac.uk.

ROBERT GORDON UNIVERSITY (ABERDEEN)

The original college was founded with monies bequeathed by the businessman Robert Gordon. Gray's School of Art was added in 1885, the School of Pharmacy in 1898 and the Scott Sutherland School of Architecture in 1957. The university is a leading centre in the areas of energy, health and social care and the creative industries, and has a student population of over 12,000. Most courses are vocational leading to a wide range of careers.

UNDERGRADUATE DEGREE SUBJECTS OFFERED
Accounting and Finance; Applied Biomedical Science; Applied Social Sciences; Architectural Technology; Architecture; Bioscience with Biomedical Science; Business Information Systems; Communication with Public Relations; Computer Network Management and Design; Computer Science; Computing for Graphics and Animation; Computing for Internet and Multimedia; Construction Design and Management; Construction Design and Management (Civil Engineering); Design for Digital Media; Diagnostic Radiography; Electronic and Electrical Engineering; Engineering; Fashion Design; Fashion Management; Forensic Science; Forensic Science with Law; Graphic Design; Information Systems Technology; Interior Architecture; International Hospitality Management; International Tourism Management; Journalism; Law and Management; Law; Management; Management with Economics; Management with Finance; Management with

Human Resource Management; Management with Marketing; Mechanical and Offshore Engineering; Mechanical Engineering; Media Studies; Midwifery; Multimedia Development; Nursing; Nutrition; Nutrition and Dietetics; Occupational Therapy; Painting; Pharmacy; Photographic and Electronic Media; Physiotherapy; Politics and Management; Printmaking; Product Design; Publishing with Journalism; Retail Management; Sculpture; Social Work; Sports and Exercise Science; Surveying; Textile and Surface Design; Three Dimensional Design (Jewellery and Ceramics); Visual Communication.

TUITION FEES
Students domiciled in Scotland receive free tuition. See www.saas.gov.uk and **Chapter 1, 'Financing your course'.**

BURSARIES AND OTHER AWARDS
Young Student Bursary
Scottish students under 25 from low-income families may be entitled to this award.

Talisman Engineering Scholarships
These are open to applicants for courses in Mechanical and Electronic and Electrical Engineering. They are worth £4,000 per year.

Talisman Management Scholarships
Students applying for management courses and Management with Economics, Finance, Human Resources Management may be eligible for scholarships worth £4,000 in Years 1 and 2 and £3000 in Year 3.

Technip Scholarships
These are open to first year students and are worth £2,000.

Wood Scholarships
Students applying for Mechanical Engineering and Electronic and Electrical Engineering may apply for these scholarships worth £10,000 over four years. They include paid summer work placements.

Hardship Fund
This fund is available to all home students in financial difficulty. EU students are not eligible to apply to this fund.

Childcare Fund
This fund is available to assist home undergraduate students with the cost of registered or formal childcare. Awards are discretionary and are based on personal and financial circumstances. EU students are not eligible to apply to this fund.

AWARDS FOR NON-EU STUDENTS
Partial scholarships of up to £1,000 per year are offered.

INFORMATION AND APPROXIMATE FEES FOR NON-EU STUDENTS
There are over 1,000 international students from over 60 countries. **English language entry requirement:** undergraduate courses IELTS 6.0 (or equivalent); pre-entry English programme IELTS 5.0 (or equivalent). **Fees:** £8,750–13,450. **Living costs:** £5,000–£6,000.

Robert Gordon University, Schoolhill, Aberdeen AB10 1FR; tel: 01224 262728; www.rgu.ac.uk.

ROEHAMPTON UNIVERSITY

Roehampton University started teaching in 1841, when Whitelands College was founded as a women's teacher training college, making it one of the oldest in Britain. In 1975 Whitelands and three other local colleges – Digby Stuart, Froebel and Southlands – merged to become Roehampton Institute. In 2004 Roehampton became a university in its own right. Based in South London (near Putney) Roehampton University has both beautiful green campuses and easy access to central London.

DEGREE SUBJECTS OFFERED
Anthropology; Art History; Biological Sciences; Biology; Biomedical Sciences; Business Computing; Business Information Management; Business Studies; Childhood and Society; Classical Civilisation; Computing; Conservation Biology; Counselling; Creative Writing; Criminology; Dance Studies; Drama and Theatre Studies; Early Childhood Studies; Education; English Language; English Literature; Exercise, Nutrition and Health; Film Studies; French; Health and Social Care; Health Studies; History; Human Resource Management; Human Rights; Journalism; Marketing; Media and Cultural Studies; Modern Languages; Music; Nutrition and Health; Philosophy; Primary Education; Psychology; Retail Management; Social Policy and Administration; Sociology; Sport and Exercise Science; TEFL; Theology and Religious Studies; Translation; Zoology.

TUITION FEES (2009/10)
£3,225.

BURSARIES AND OTHER AWARDS
Bursaries worth £1,000 (2008/09) are paid to students on full means-tested maintenance grants.

ROEHAMPTON SCHOLARSHIPS
The scholarship valued at £3,000 is open to applicants who achieved 320 UCAS Tariff points at A-Level or equivalent.

Sporting Excellence Scholarships
Four awards each worth £3,000 are open to talented applicants who have achieved national or regional status in their sport.

AWARDS FOR NON-EU STUDENTS
Country Scholarships
Several scholarships are awarded at Foundataion, undergraduate and postgraduate level as follows: China – two at £2,000; Japan – two at £2,000; Malaysia – one at £1,000; Norway – one at £1000; Singapore – one at £1000; South Korea – two at £2,000; Taiwan – two at £2,000; Thailand – one at £1,000;Turkey – one at £2,000; United States – four at £1,000; UK based international students – two at 1,000.

POSTGRADUATE AWARDS
See scholarships listed above.

INFORMATION AND APPROXIMATE FEES FOR NON-EU STUDENTS
English language entry requirment: IELTS 5.5–6.0 (or equivalent). **Fees:** £9,000. **Living costs:** £9,500.

See Chapters 2, 4 and 6 for additional awards, applicable to all universities

Roehampton University, Roehampton Lane, London SW15 5PU; tel: 020 8392 3232; www.roehampton.ac.uk.

ROSE BRUFORD COLLEGE (SIDCUP)

This specialist drama college is located in Lamorbey Park, Sidcup, Kent – 20 minutes from central London. The awarding body for degrees is Manchester University. About 900 students follow degree courses in all aspects of theatre arts. The college is a member of the Conference of Drama Schools.

DEGREE SUBJECTS OFFERED

Acting; Actor Musicianship; American Theatre Arts; Costume Production; Directing; European Theatre Arts; Lighting Design; Multimedia Design; Music Technology; Scenic Arts; Stage Management; Theatre Design.

TUITION FEES (2009/10)

£3,225.

BURSARIES AND OTHER AWARDS

The college offers a yearly bursary of £310 to all students in receipt of a full maintenance grant. These students are also eligible to apply for a further bursary of up to £1,000 per year. Check with the college.

AWARDS FOR NON-EU STUDENTS

The College is able to offer small bursaries for overeas students.

There are other college bursary schemes and trusts for home students and overseas students, for which students may be able to apply.

INFORMATION AND APPROXIMATE FEES FOR NON-EU STUDENTS

English language entry requirement: IELTS 5.5 (or equivalent). **Fees:** £11,025. **Living costs:** £9,000.

Rose Bruford College, Burnt Oak Lane, Sidcup, Kent DA15 9DF; tel: 020 8308 2600; www. bruford.ac.uk.

ROYAL AGRICULTURAL COLLEGE, CIRENCESTER

The College was founded in 1845 and is situated on a rural campus site in the Cotswolds. There is a student population of 835.

DEGREE SUBJECTS OFFERED:

Animal Management; Agricultural Business Management; Business Management; Business Management (International Food and Agribusiness); Crop Production; Food Production and Supply

Management; International Equine and Agricultural Management; Land Management; Organic Farming; Property Agency and Marketing; Rural Land and Property Management courses; Rural Land Management.

TUITION FEES (2009/10)
£3,225.

BURSARIES AND OTHER AWARDS
The College offers vouchers to the value of £65,000 per annum to students so they can participate on skills-based courses at our Rural Skills Centre and Food Training Kitchen to enhance their employability at the end of their programme. Individual vouchers are valued at up to £200 each and all new undergraduate students are entitled to one voucher each. Any remaining vouchers will be allocated on a first come first served basis later in the year.

All new undergraduate students are entitled to a £100 voucher which can be exchanged for books, a computer or a bicycle. Vouchers are allocated to students once registration has been completed at the start of term.

Variable Fee Bursaries
* Up to £25,000 income threshold: £1,615
* Up to £30,000 income threshold: £1,025
* Up to £34,450 income threshold: £515
* Up to £40,000 income threshold: £255
* Up to £50,000 income threshold: £102.

An additional £500 is available to students in the £25,000 and under income threshold who fulfil a minimum of three of the following criteria

* First generation higher education,
* Disadvantaged postcode (urban or rural),
* Member of a minority ethnic group,
* Specified school or college.

Contact: admissions@rac.ac.uk

Variable fee bursaries are administered by the Student Loan Company (SLC) via the Higher Education Bursary Scheme (HEBSS) and you need do nothing more than inform the College when you make an application for support. You will then be automatically assessed for an award and notified by the SLC. The payment is made in two instalments; two thirds at the end of February and the remainder at the end of April. This is non re-payable.

Hardship Awards
Hardship Awards for UK/EU students are provided from the Access to Learning Fund and are awarded in addition to the College's own Hardship Funds. Initial applications, with supporting case, should be received by 20 October. For further details and application forms please contact the scholarships@rac.ac.uk

The RAC Scholarship scheme
This scheme was established to provide worthy students with the support necessary to work towards achieving their full personal potential during their period of study at the College.

These awards are made at a critical time; at the very outset of a career when the course of success is being set. Many students have gone on to rewarding and satisfying employment and further attainment in their chosen fields when the prospect of achieving this seemed unlikely without help.

See Chapters 2, 4 and 6 for additional awards, applicable to all universities

In making these awards the College recognises that distinction can be attained in a variety of ways, and that all facets of individual merit deserve consideration. These Scholarships are therefore in two principal categories; Sports, and Outstanding Achievers. While these are primarily financial awards and will ensure some welcome relief from financial stress, the College also provides personal guidance, support, and recognition to all those in receipt of College scholarships.

Over the last 5 years the College has invested over £1.5 million in promising and deserving students. At present they have the welcome and valued support of more than 10 individuals, companies and organisations. Their generosity has allowed us to expand our provision to unprecedented levels.

FE (Jim) Turner Award
To perpetuate the memory of a well known and respected figure in the agricultural machinery world, his widow, Mrs Alice Turner, has provided for annual scholarships to assist needy students at The Royal Agricultural College. Individual award levels will vary but may be up to £1,500 per annum.

Fred and Marjorie Sainsbury Trust Scholarship
An award of up to £7,000 per year for a prospective student from a non-traditional and disadvantaged background.

McCain Scholarships
Full tuition fee payment for two students per year, students apply once they are studying their first year on an honours degree programme in Agriculture or Agribusiness Management. Applicants will need to demonstrate a strong interest in a career in the global potato business.

Produce World Travel Award
An award of £500 is available to students to assist with travel and living expenses whilst undertaking their placement.

CLA Charitable Trust Scholarship
An award of £6,000 per year created to help overcome personal hardship or deprivation and to assist deserving students realise their ambitions for satisfying and rewarding careers within the rural community and economy.

Emmott Foundation Scholarship
An award of £3,000 each year is provided to the College by the Foundation for academically able students whose parents or supporters have faced an unexpected family, medical or economic crisis which could prevent them from starting a course of study at the RAC.

Walter Smith Award
An award of up to £2,000 each year created by the generosity of the family to provide additional support to mature students studying within the School of Rural Economy and Land Management.

Dick Harrison Trust
The objects of the Trust are to provide education and training by awarding grants for fees or maintenance to students wanting to train in livestock auctioneering and/or rural estate management. Support by way of financial assistance takes the form of books, equipment or grants towards travel arrangements. Applications are invited from students who were born in Scotland or Cumbria or Northumberland and who are (or whose parents or grandparents are) resident in any of these places at the time of the award.

Further information, details of new awards, criteria for existing awards and application forms are available from the College website www.rac.ac.uk or on request from Admissions@rac.ac.uk.

AWARDS FOR NON-EU STUDENTS

Career Development Loans: Postgraduate students can apply for a Career Development Loan (CDL) via one of three banks in the UK: Barclays, Co-Operative Bank or The Royal Bank of Scotland. The key benefits of a CDL are:

* being able to borrow anything between £300 and £8,000 to help fund up to two years of learning (or up to three years if the course includes one year of relevant practical work experience)
* the Learning Skills Council pays the interest on the loan while you're learning and for one month after training is completed
* the loan is repaid to the bank over an agreed period at a fixed rate of interest.

Further details on the CDL can be found on www.direct.gov.uk. Alternatively details of further funding for postgraduate study are available from www.prospects.ac.uk

Hardship Awards for International Students

These are funded by the College's International Bursary Scheme and are means-tested. Application should be made after a formal offer of a place at College has been received. Hardship cases will be considered further into the academic year by application to the Admissions Registrar scholarships@rac.ac.uk.

Studley College Trust

The Trust has a priority to help those who cannot afford the costs of a course to gain their first qualification at the start of their land based career training and therefore help for second degrees or postgraduate study takes second priority. The type of career you plan is also taken into account as the Trust seeks to fund the sort of training that will be valuable to you and of use in the production and commercial side of land based activities. Support for postgraduate studies will only be considered if the Trust is satisfied that it is an essential part of your career training and where a period of 12 months has elapsed since graduation.

Further information on all scholarships, bursaries and awards can be found by visiting www.rac.ac.uk and clicking on the link at the bottom of the home page.

INFORMATION AND APPROXIMATE FEES FOR NON-EU STUDENTS

English language entry requirement: check with the College. **Fees:** £7,290; Living **costs:** £8,000.

Royal Agricultural College, Cirencester, Gloucestershire GL7 6JS; tel: 01285 889912; www. rac.ac.uk.

ROYAL COLLEGE OF MUSIC (LONDON)

The college is situated in central London close to the Royal Albert Hall. It has its own hall of residence accommodating 170 students with self-catering facilities and practice rooms. There is a strong tradition of Alexander Technique and it is possible to arrange lessons with visiting specialists on particular aspects such as singing, windplaying and string playing.

DEGREE SUBJECTS OFFERED

Music; Physics with Studies in Musical Performance.

TUITION FEES

£3,225.

Part-time courses: £1,695. Artist Diploma in Opera: £9,165.

BURSARIES AND OTHER AWARDS

Major RCM bursaries are for those undergraduate students who are to receive the maximum state support for tuition fees. They will receive a non-standard bursary of £1,000 per year.

AWARDS FOR NON-EU STUDENTS

RCM Euro Bursaries

These are valued at £350 per year and are awarded to all non-UK EU undergraduate students who fall below the threshold of household residual income as tested by the Student Loans Company.

Instruments may be loaned. Students can get interest-free loans to buy their own instruments. The Royal College of Music awards scholarships based on merit and potential. Everyone who auditions for a place in person is automatically considered for a scholarship. Around 120 new scholarships are awarded each year to both UK and overseas students. Undergraduate scholarships are awarded for the duration of the four-year undergraduate course, and the postgraduate scholarships are awarded for one year. Out of 700 students, around 300 are currently in receipt of an RCM scholarship or Study Award.

INFORMATION AND APPROXIMATE FEES FOR NON-EU STUDENTS

Fees: BMus course – £16,045; Asia Pacific Programme – £14,870. **Living costs:** £12,000.

Royal College of Music, Prince Consort Road, London SW7 2BS; tel: 020 7589 3643; www. rcm.ac.uk.

ROYAL NORTHERN COLLEGE OF MUSIC (MANCHESTER)

The college is situated in Manchester a short distance from the city centre in the heart of the University area. It offers four-year full-time undergraduate degree programmes in Music, with an emphasis on Performance or Composition and their attendant skills. A range of postgraduate and professional courses is also available.

DEGREE SUBJECT OFFERED

Music (BMus(Hons); BMus; PGDip; MMus; MPhil; PhD; International Artist Diploma).

TUITION FEES (2009/10)

Vary. Check the College's website: www.rncm.ac.uk

BURSARIES AND OTHER AWARDS

Scholarships and Entrance Awards are offered on the basis of performance at audition. Bursary support, operated through the College's own scheme, is available to: overseas undergraduate and postgraduate students, and UK/EU postgraduate students in financial need. In line with government policy, the College has an agreement with the Office for Fair Access (OFFA) to provide bursaries for UK/ EU undergraduate students of up to £1,050 according to an individual's financial circumstances.

INFORMATION AND APPROXIMATE FEES FOR NON-EU STUDENTS
Over 40 nations are represented. **English language entry requirement:** broadly IELTS 5.5 (or equivalent) for BMus; other programmes vary (see website). **Fees:** £13,895–17,695 according to programme. **Living costs:** approx £6,800.

Royal Northern College of Music, 124 Oxford Road, Manchester M13 9RD; tel: 0161 907 5200; www.rncm.ac.uk.

ROYAL HOLLOWAY COLLEGE
(University of London)

One of the largest colleges of the University of London, Royal Holloway is situated on a 120-acre campus in Egham, near Windsor, 19 miles west of London. The campus is home to a vibrant community of students from over 120 countries. Royal Holloway is the University of London's most successful sporting college, with a thriving cultural scene and a very active Students' Union.

DEGREE SUBJECTS OFFERED
Ancient History; Applied Physics; Astrophysics; Biochemistry; Biology; Biomedical Sciences; Classical Studies; Classics; Computer Science; Criminology & Sociology; Drama; Ecology & Environment; Economics; English; Environmental Geology; Environmental Geoscience; European Literature & Cultural Studies; European Studies; Film & Television Studies; French; Geography; Geology; Geoscience; German; Greek (Classical); History; Italian; Latin; Management; Mathematics; Media Arts; Multilingual Studies; Music; Physics; Politics; Psychology; Science Foundation Year; Spanish; Theatre Studies; Zoology.

TUITION FEES (2009/10)
£3,225.

BURSARIES AND OTHER AWARDS
Standard Bursaries
£750 per year for each year of undergraduate study. These bursaries will be awarded to all full-time students from England and Wales who will be in receipt of a partial or full Government Maintenance Grant with a specified household income for the year of study. In 2009 this household income level was £39,333 per year or less. Students must also be liable for Variable Tuition Fees during their degree programme. For full-time degree courses started in September 2009 this was £3,225 a year. The bursaries will be awarded automatically to all qualifying students. Other conditions apply.

Royal Holloway Excellence Scholarships
£500 per year for each year of undergraduate study. Royal Holloway Excellence Scholarships will be awarded to all full-time students from England and Wales who will be in receipt of a partial or full Government Maintenance Grant with a specified household income for the year of study. In 2009 this household income level was £39,333 per year or less. Students must also be liable for Variable Tuition Fees during their degree programme. For full-time degree courses started in September 2009 this was £3,225 a year. In addition to this, students must also achieve 320 UCAS tariff points (grades ABB at GCE A-level) or equivalent in those specific elements of their academic qualifications specified in their Royal Holloway UCAS offer as requirements for admission for their

programme of study at the College. A Royal Holloway Excellence Scholarship may not be held in conjunction with another College scholarship. It may, however, be held in conjunction with the Standard Bursary. A student repeating a year of undergraduate study is not eligible for scholarship support for the repeated year. Other conditions apply.

Founder's Scholarships

£3,500 per year for each year as undergraduate. Founder's Scholarships will be awarded on a competitive basis to full-time students from England and Wales who will be in receipt of a partial or full Government Maintenance Grant with a specified household income for the year of study. In 2009 this household income level was £39,333 per year or less. Students must also be liable for Variable Tuition Fees during their degree programme. For full-time degree courses started in September 2009 this was £3,225 a year. In addition to this, students must also achieve at least 360 UCAS tariff points (grades AAA at GCE A-level) or equivalent in those specific elements of their academic qualifications which are specified in their Royal Holloway UCAS offer as requirements for admission for their programme of study at the College. These scholarships are competitive and students must submit an application to the College's Bursaries and Scholarships Panel in order to be considered for the award. An application form is available in *Financing your studies, a guide for undergraduates* booklet and can be downloaded from our website. A Founder's Scholarship may not be held in conjunction with another College scholarship. It may, however, be held in conjunction with the Standard Bursary. A student repeating a year of undergraduate study is not eligible for scholarship support for the repeated year. Other conditions apply.

Access Entry Bursaries

£500 per year for each year of undergraduate study. Access Entry Bursaries will be awarded to full-time students from England and Wales who will be in receipt of a partial or full Government Maintenance Grant with a specified household income for the year of study. In 2009 this household income level was £39,333 per year or less. Students must also be liable for Variable Tuition Fees during their degree programme. For full-time degree courses started in September 2009 this was £3,225 a year. In addition to this, students must also have achieved a QAA-recognised Access to Higher Education Diploma which is specified in their Royal Holloway UCAS offer as a requirement for admission for their programme of study at the College. The bursaries will be awarded automatically to all qualifying students. Other conditions apply.

Bedford Scholarships

£1,000 per year for each year of undergraduate study. Bedford Scholarships will be awarded on a competitive basis to students irrespective of household income who achieve at least 360 UCAS tariff points (grades AAA at GCE A-level) or equivalent in those specific elements of their academic qualifications which are specified in their Royal Holloway UCAS offer as requirements for admission for their programme of study at the College. Students must also be liable for Variable Tuition Fees during their degree programme. For full-time degree courses started in September 2009 this was £3,225 a year. These scholarships are partly funded by funds originating from generous benefactions to Bedford College in the late 19th and early 20th centuries. Bedford Scholarships are competitive and students must submit an application to the College's Bursaries and Scholarships Panel in order to be considered for the award. An application form is available in our *Financing your studies, a guide for undergraduates* booklet and can be downloaded from our website. A Bedford Scholarship may not be held in conjunction with another College scholarship. A student repeating a year of undergraduate study is not eligible for scholarship support for the repeated year. Other conditions apply.

Choral, Organ and Instrumental Scholarships/RCM Exhibitions

£300-£1,000. The maximum award is £1,000 per annum for Organ Scholarships and £500 per annum for Choral Scholarships – normally held for three years. £300 tenable for one year (renewable) for Instrumental Scholarships and additional RCM Exhibitions of £200 per year (renewable). Students applying to any department may apply for the Choral, Organ and Instrumental Scholarships. The following conditions apply:

* Choral Scholars are expected to attend choir practices and to sing in the Chapel Choir and the Schola Cantorum.
* Organ Scholars are expected to help with Chapel services.
* Instrumental Scholars are expected to play in the Royal Holloway Symphony and Chamber Orchestras, where appropriate, and to take an active role in the musical life of the College.

Student Talented Athlete Recognition Scheme (STARS) Bursaries

Up to £1,000. Students who compete in their sport at national or international level may apply to the STARS. In addition to the financial award, other benefits include a guaranteed self-catered accommodation place throughout study periods and free access to on campus sports facilities.

Bioscience Entrance Scholarships

Up to £1,000 for the first year of study payable against tuition and accommodation fees. All outstanding candidates for undergraduate programmes taught within the School of Biological Sciences.

Lyell Bursaries in Geology

Up to £500 during the first year of study. All Earth Sciences students who have made Royal Holloway their first UCAS choice. Students must also be predicted, or have achieved, 300 UCAS tariff points in those specific elements of their academic qualifications specified in their Royal Holloway UCAS offer as requirements for admission for their programme of study at the College. Other conditions apply.

Physics Bursaries

Up to £1,000 during the first year of study. Outstanding students who obtain at least A grades at GCE A-level or equivalent in both Physics and Mathematics, and entering a Single Honours programme in the Department of Physics. Awards are made on a competitive basis.

Computer Science Scholarships

Up to £1,000 during the first year of study, renewable at the rate of £500 in years two and three. Applicants must be applying, or have applied, to study Computer Science or a related undergraduate degree programme in the Department of Computer Science to qualify. There are two schemes: Donald Davies Scholarships and Computer Science Challenge Scholarships. Candidates of high ability are invited to interview for the Donald Davies Scholarships. Please contact the admissions team for more information. Computer Science Challenge Scholarships are awarded to the best candidates, confirmed upon enrolment, entering the Computer Science Challenge.

Wentworth Golf Bursary

£15,000 membership fee plus £5,500 membership fee per year for three years undergraduate study. Two bursaries available each year for exceptional student golfers with a single figure handicap, and whose financial circumstances mean that they could not afford to pay for membership at Wentworth Golf Club, to become active members of Wentworth Golf Club while studying at Royal Holloway. If appropriate, awardees may represent the Club in competitions and matches.

AWARDS FOR NON-EU STUDENTS
International Excellence Scholarships

£4,000 during the first year of undergraduate study to go towards the first year's tuition fees. International Excellence Scholarships are available to new overseas students (full-fee paying non-EU students) who hold an offer from the College. Awards are made on the basis of outstanding academic achievement or potential. All non-native English speakers must meet the minimum English language requirements of their proposed programme of study.

See Chapters 2, 4 and 6 for additional awards, applicable to all universities

International Excellence Scholarships (India)

£4,000 during the first year of undergraduate study to go towards the first year's tuition fees. International Excellence Scholarships (India) are available to new overseas students from India (full-fee paying non-EU students) who hold an offer from the College. Awards are made on the basis of outstanding academic achievement or potential. All non-native English speakers must meet the minimum English language requirements of their proposed programme of study.

Master's Scholarships

£3,390 at proposed 2009–10 rates for taught master's degree study after undergraduate study at Royal Holloway. Master's Scholarships will be available to students as a competitive award and who are in receipt of a Standard Bursary in their final year of undergraduate study. The Master's Scholarships are designed to enable students to undertake postgraduate study in the academic year immediately after their undergraduate degree, or the following year. The value of the scholarship will be equivalent to the standard postgraduate tuition fee for full-time UK students. Master's Scholarships will be offered subject to the following conditions: satisfactory progress as undergraduates and the achievement of a 2.1 degree or above from 2010 or 2011, and gaining an offer of admission to a taught Master's degree programme of study at Royal Holloway. Students must complete an application form to be considered for the award. A Master's Scholarship may not be held in conjunction with another College scholarship. Other conditions apply.

Further details of Royal Holloway's bursaries and scholarships are published in *Financing your studies, a guide for undergraduates* booklet which is sent to all students who receive an offer of a place to study at Royal Holloway. To request a copy, please contact: UK Recruitment Office, tel: 01784 443399; email liaison-office@rhul.ac.uk; www.rhul.ac.uk/Prospective-Students.

INFORMATION AND APPROXIMATE FEES FOR NON-EU STUDENTS

Applications are received from students from over 120 countries every year, and around a quarter of the student population comes from outside the UK. **English language entry requirement:** undergraduate degrees – IELTS 6.0–6.5 overall with 7 in writing (or equivalent), depending upon the department. University Foundation Programme: a 10 month foundation course with studies in English language and introduction to specialist studies in a range of degree subjects; English language requirement: IELTS 5.5 with no sub score below 5.0 (or equivalent). **Fees:** University Foundation Programme £8,755; undergraduate classroom-based courses £11,55; undergraduate laboratory-based courses £12,780; undergraduate Management and Economics courses £13,120. **Living costs:** approx. £9,000.

Royal Holloway, University of London, Egham, Surrey TW20 0EX; tel: 01784 434455; www.rhul.ac.uk.

ROYAL SCOTTISH ACADEMY OF MUSIC AND DRAMA (RSAMD)

The Academy was founded in 1847, and is Scotland's only conservatoire and a world centre for training and excellence in the performing arts. As the busiest performing arts venue in Scotland, the Academy offers courses in music of all genres, theatre and production, film and television, musical theatre and opera. Further to this, dance will be introduced to the curriculum in 2009 with a BA in Modern Ballet, in collaboration with Scottish Ballet. The RSAMD is also home of The National Centre for Research into the Performing Arts, an arts-based research consultancy undertaking projects across a number of artistic and related areas, including educational arts policy and strategic development and training, continuing professional development of performing arts professionals, and practice-based compositional research. These programmes, together with the commitment to Scottish traditional music, new music, music for the under 18s and the training of classroom teachers, mean that the RSAMD has the widest remit of all UK conservatoires.

The RSAMD is a specially designed building equipped with an extensive range of modern facilities, including a the New Athenaeum Theatre, The Academy Concert Hall, The Chandler Studio Theatre, the Guinness Room and the Alexander Gibson Opera School.

DEGREE SUBJECTS OFFERED
School of Drama: Acting; Contemporary Performance Practice; Digital Film and Television; Modern Ballet, Musical Theatre, Technical and Production Arts.

School of Music: BMus Music, Performing Arts; Scottish Music; BEd Music

TUITION FEES (2009/10)
Students domiciled in Scotland receive free tuition. See www.saas.gov.uk and **Chapter 1, 'Financing Your Course'.**

BURSARIES AND OTHER AWARDS
A significant number of entrance scholarships are available for UK/EU and International students undertaking Undergraduate and Postgraduate study programmes across all disciplines. Scholarships vary in amount (ranging up to full fees plus a maintenance contribution) and are available to selected students on the basis of talent and financial need. Scholarships are awarded as part of the RSAMD audition/selection process.

INFORMATION AND APPROXIMATE FEES FOR NON-EU STUDENTS
English language entry requirement: IELTS 6.5–7.5 (or equivalent). **Fees:** £11,499. **Living costs:** £7,500.

Royal Scottish Academy of Music and Drama (RSAMD), 100 Renfrew Street, Glasgow G2 3DB; tel: 0141 332 4101; www.rsamd.ac.uk.

ROYAL VETERINARY COLLEGE
(University of London)

The college is the oldest and largest veterinary school in the UK. The first two years are spent at the Camden Campus in London and the third and first half of the fourth year at the Hawkshead Campus in Hertfordshire, with the remainder of the course taking place at various veterinary establishments thoughout the UK.

DEGREE SUBJECTS OFFERED
Veterinary Medicine; Veterinary Nursing; Veterinary Science.

BURSARIES AND OTHER AWARDS
Bursaries are offered to those students receiving a full maintance grant, the amout being linked to the percentage of the grant awarded. Students taking the BVetMed course receive a maximum of £1,650 and those taking the BSc Biovet Sci course, £1,750. Students taking a Foundation degree in Veterinary Nursing and who are receiving the full grant will be awarded £2,000.

See Chapters 2, 4 and 6 for additional awards, applicable to all universities

Merit Scholarships
Awards to the value of £3,000 are offered based on the BMAT score taken on application. Students applying for the Biovet Science course will need to take the BMAT test if they wish to be considered for this award.

INFORMATION AND APPROXIMATE FEES FOR NON-EU STUDENTS
English language entry requirement: IELTS 6.0–6.5 (or equivalent). **Fees:** £8,030–£18,400. **Living costs:** £9,500–£10,500.

Royal Veterinary College, Royal College Street, London NW1 0UT; tel: 0120 7468 5149; www. rvc.uk.

ROYAL WELSH COLLEGE OF MUSIC AND DRAMA (CARDIFF)

The college was founded in 1949 and is situated in an attractive location in Cathays Park, Cardiff. No college accommodation is available, students living out in privately owned houses and flats. Nearly 600 students follow a range of creative courses.

DEGREE SUBJECTS OFFERED
Acting; Music; Stage Management; Theatre Design.

TUITION FEES (2009/10)
See www.studentfinancewales.co.uk and **Chapter 1, 'Financing your course'.**

BURSARIES AND OTHER AWARDS
Laura Ashley Foundation Awards
To assist 10 music students.

Music Sound Foundation Awards
To assist four music students each academic year.

Sir Geraint Evans Singing Scholarship
To assist two or three vocal studies students each academic year.

Marsh Award
To assist two students, one award each for drama and music.

Sir Geraint Evans Open Scholarship
An endowment fund used to assist students in drama and music.

The Royal Welsh College of Music and Drama also has a number of smaller awards that are made annually at the end of each academic year in recognition of achievements made during the year.

INFORMATION AND APPROXIMATE FEES FOR NON-EU STUDENTS
English language entry requirement: IELTS 5.5–6.0 (or equivalent). **Fees:** full-time courses £11,045; part-time courses £5,685. **Living costs:** £6,500–7,500.

Royal Welsh College of Music and Drama, Castle Grounds, Cathays Park, Cardiff CF10 3ER; tel: 029 2034 2854; www.rwcmd.ac.uk.

ST ANDREWS UNIVERSITY

The University of St Andrews is the oldest university in Scotland, founded in 1410. It is divided into three main faculties: Arts, Divinity and Science. The university is closely integrated with the coastal town and has a student population of some 6,000.

DEGREE SUBJECTS OFFERED

Ancient History; Animal Biology; Applied Mathematics; Arabic; Archaeology; Art History; Astrophysics; Biblical Studies; Biochemistry; Biology; Classical Studies; Classics; Chemistry; Computer Science; Divinity; Economics; English; European Studies; French; Genetics; Geography; Geoscience; German; Greek; Hebrew; History; Integrated Information Technology; International Relations; Internet Computing; Italian; Latin; Linguistics; Logic and Philosophy of Science; Management; Mathematics; Medical Science; Medieval Studies; Microelectronics; Middle East Studies; Modern Languages; Neuroscience; New Testament; Pharmacology; Philosophy; Photonics; Physics; Physiology; Psychology; Quantitative Ecology; Russian; Scottish History; Social Anthropology; Spanish; Statistics; Theology.

TUITION FEES (2009/10)

Students domiciled in Scotland receive free tuition; see also www.saas.gov.uk and **Chapter 1, 'Financing Your Course'.**

BURSARIES AND OTHER AWARDS

Scholarships awarded on the basis of financial need. These scholarships are to provide assistance with maintenance costs while studying at St Andrews.

Wardlaw Scholarships

Open to UK or EU citizens – a number of individual scholarship awards made possible by donations from alumni, staff and friends of the University of St Andrews, charitable trusts and other organisations (subject restrictions or geographic restrictions may apply to specific awards). Awards range from £1,000 to 3,000 per annum.

Subject Awards

Additionally, specific awards of £1,000 will be available to students applying to study in the following Schools:

* Chemistry (Purdie Scholarships, please see http://chemistry.st-andrews.ac.uk/admissions/purdie.html)
* Computer Science
* Mathematics and Statistics
* Modern Languages
* Philosophy, Philosophical and Anthropological Studies and Film Studies
* Physics and Astronomy

Mature Student Scholarships

£1,000 for the first year of the course only.

Fife Scholarships

£500 for each of up to four years, available to students ordinarily resident in Fife. Further details and deadlines for current financial-need-based scholarships, and an application form, can be found on the St Andrews website.

Part-time Evening Degree Scholarships

Ten awards of up to £500 available for one year, though reapplication is possible. Scholarship application forms will be sent to applicants to the Evening Degree programme.

Adam Smith Thomson Bursaries

Two Adam Smith Thomson Bursaries of £1,000 per year may be awarded to former pupils of Forfar Academy. Tenure of one of these bursaries will be restricted to undergraduate entrants to the Faculty of Science among whom priority will be given to those who register, upon entry, for a degree in Mathematical or Physical Sciences. The other bursary will be available to an undergraduate entrant to any faculty of the university.

Music Scholarships

See the website www.st-andrews.ac.uk/music/Scholarships. Enquiries should be sent to the Director of Music, Music Centre, Younger Hall, North Street, St Andrews KY16 9YD; music@st-and.ac.uk.

University of St Andrews/Royal and Ancient Golf Club Golf Scholarship

The university receives a grant annually from the RandA to fund a golf development programme for talented golfers. The programme is administered through the Department of Sport and Exercise: www.st-andrews.ac.uk/sport/Sport/Golf/Bursaries/; sport@st-and.ac.uk. Students wishing to join the programme from the beginning of the academic year should submit their application before mid-September.

St Mary's College Bursaries

A number of bursaries are available to students in the Faculty of Divinity. Further details and application forms may be obtained from St Mary's College: www.st-and.ac.uk/divinity; divinity@st-and.ac.uk.

Exchange students and scholarships

There are a number of opportunities for St Andrews students to spend a period of study at a university in Europe or North America. Further information is available on the following webpage: www.st-andrews.ac.uk/admissions/Exchangestudents.

Travel Scholarships

A number of awards are made each year to matriculated students. Enquiries can be made to the Registry, 79 North Street, St Andrews KY16 9AJ.

Perth and Kinross Educational Trust

Under the provisions of the trust, persons belonging to the former county of Perthshire, that is those who were born and educated there, may qualify for bursaries for further education, special grants for mature students, grants for second or subsequent degrees, grants for student apprentices or travel scholarships or grants.

Further information is available from the Director of Education and Children's Services, Perth and Kinross Council, Pullar House, 35 Kinnoull Street, Perth PH1 5GD.

Duncan Trust

Grants are available from the Duncan Trust to students who are training, or who intend to train, for the Ministry of the Church of Scotland (regular or modified course). The grants may be awarded at any time during the students' courses in the Faculty of Arts or the Faculty of Divinity, but not after completion of the normal BD course. Preference is given to applicants within the Presbytery of Angus and Mearns. Application should be made to the Clerk to the Duncan Trust, Thorntons WS, Brothockbank House, Arbroath, Angus DD11 1NF.

Katherine Smith Bursary
This is open only to candidates who have been educated at St Leonards School. Further information is available from St Leonards School, St Andrews KY16 9QJ.

Maxton Bequest
Under the provision of this bequest, young persons who were born or one of whose parents was ordinarily resident within the Parish of Crieff or Burgh of Kirkcaldy at the time of birth, and having completed the period of compulsory attendance at school, may qualify for benefit to enable them to continue their education or to serve an apprenticeship. The trustees may give preference to minors and those in greater need of financial assistance. Application forms for consideration by the trustees must be lodged with the solicitors, who will advise on the closing date for application. Forms may be obtained from the Neighbourhood Manager, Perth and Kinross Council, Neighbourhood Office, Lodge Street, Crieff or from the solicitors, Messrs Gibson and Spears, Dow and Son, 9 East Fergus Place, Kirkcaldy, Fife KY1 1XU.

Menzies Bursaries
The bursaries are awarded for a period of four years to persons entering a course of study for a degree at any of the Universities of Edinburgh, Glasgow or St Andrews. The bursaries are awarded to those falling into one or several of the following categories and in the following order of preference.

1. Relatives of the Founder James Menzies
2. Those of the name Menzies
3. Those born on the Menzies Estates (in the Parishes of Dull, Weem and Fortingall)
4. Persons considered by the trustees best qualified and most deserving.

The current level of the bursary is £375 per year and application should be made to Blackadders Solicitors, 30 and 34 Reform Street, Dundee DD1 1RJ.

Institute of Physics (needs-based awards)
Six awards are available from the Institute of Physics for 2009 entrants to Physics and Astronomy degree programmes at St Andrews. Financial need will be the major determining factor. Further details can be found on www.st-and.ac.uk/physics and www.iop.org/activity/grants/Undergraduate_Bursary_Scheme/page_5602.html.

AWARDS FOR NON-EU STUDENTS
The USA and Canadian Scholarship
These entrance scholarships are for students from the United States or Canada who will be studying at St Andrews for four years. They are awarded on the basis of financial need with a maximum award of 5,000 US Dollars per year. These scholarships are only available for students who are entering in first year. Applicants must be classed as having Overseas fee status. Please see www.st-andrews.ac.uk/admissions/ug/Financialinformation/Scholarships/USACanadianAwards for more details.

McEuen Scholarship
This scholarship was established specifically to support a Canadian student who has already applied to study at St Andrews for a first degree. Applicants must be:

* Canadian citizens, of Scottish ancestry or whose parents include a St Andrews alumna/alumnus; and
* 21 years old or less on 1 January of the year of entry to St Andrews; and
* Eligible to attend a Canadian university, or in their first or second year of study at such an institution. The scholarship covers tuition fees and board and lodging in a university residence. For further details and an application form contact McEuen Scholarship Foundation Inc, Suite 1100, 100 Queen Street, Ottawa, Ontario K1P 1J9, or visit www.mceuenscholarship.com.

Ransome Scholarship

This is for students from North America who will be studying at St Andrews for four years. There is one undergraduate scholarship covering tuition fees and other costs for a four-year degree. The deadline for applications is 28th February each year. Please see www.st-andrews.ac.uk/develop-2/ransome or for further details email scholarships@st-and.ac.uk.

R Harper Brown Memorial Scholarship

The Illinois Saint Andrew Society sponsors this scholarship programme which honours the late R Harper Brown: society governor, 1996 Clansman of the Year, co-chair of the Kith and Kin Campaign and former chairman of the development committee. The purpose of the scholarship fund is to assist in defraying the cost of a college student's study at a university in Scotland. For eligibility criteria, see www.scholarships.stand.ac.uk/scholarships. Scholarship applications may be obtained by calling Gus Noble on tel: +001 708 426 7130 or by visiting the website of the Illinois Saint Andrew Society: www.chicago-scots.org/scholarship-programs.html.

POSTGRADUATE AWARDS

University Postgraduate Scholarships and Studentships

Various awards for Home students, Overseas students, or both, studying research or taught postgraduate degrees are available each year, although they may include further (eg subject) criteria. Please see www.st-andrews.ac.uk/admissions/pg/Financialinformation/NEWPhD Studentships for details of awards available. It is also recommended to check the website for the School in which you will be studying. The list of School websites can be found here: www.st-andrews.ac.uk/subjects. Any enquiries about the awards should be directed to the Postgraduate Office/Secretary within the appropriate School, or any other contact (eg course director) listed in the award details.

FCO/OSI Chevening Scholarships

Scholarships are available for study for the Masters in International Strategy & Economics, the Masters in Middle East and Central Asian Security Studies and the M.Litt in Peace and Conflict Studies.

Each scholarship provides tuition fees at the University of St Andrews, a stipend to cover living costs (for one person only), and return air travel from the scholar's home country. The scholarships are open to applicants from Indonesia, Tajikistan and Uzbekistan. The deadline for application is **6th February 2009**. Details of how to apply may be found on this webpage: www.soros.org/initiatives/scholarship/focus_areas/uk/saintandrews.

Commonwealth Shared Scholarship Scheme (DfID)

This scheme is designed for students from Commonwealth countries who are unable, for financial reasons, to come to the UK, and who fall outside the ambit of other British Government schemes. In 2009/10 two awards will be available for the MSc in Finance and the MLitt in Finance and Management.

Please see www.cscuk.org.uk/apply/sharedschol.asp for more details about the award, including eligibility criteria and conditions.

Karim Rida Said Foundation (KRSF)

The KRSF is able to provide full or partial scholarships for master's degrees at the University of St Andrews and other participating universities, depending on the level of financial need. All the foundation asks of its scholars is that they return to their own country or another country of the Arab League immediately upon completion of their studies and remain there for at least three years. For conditions and an application form, visit: www.krsf.org.

Ransome Trust Scholarship

This is for students from North America who will be studying at St Andrews for a taught postgraduate degree. There are four postgraduate scholarships covering tuition fees and other costs. The deadline for applications is 28th February each year. Please see www.st-andrews.ac.uk/develop-2/ransome/ or for further details email scholarships@st-and.ac.uk.

Saint Andrew's Society of the State of New York

This is open to students of Scottish/American descent who have graduated from an American university and have a New York address. Students will be required to study at any university in Scotland for one year. The closing date is 1 December each year. For further information, see www.standrewsny.org.

Saint Andrew's Society of Washington, DC

Several awards are available for postgraduate study. See www.saintandrewsociety.org/scholarships.htm for further information.

University Awards

The university has a limited number of discretionary awards for research students. Enquiries as to the possibility of support should be made to your intending supervisor.

INFORMATION AND APPROXIMATE FEES FOR NON-EU STUDENTS

Twenty-six per cent of students are from overseas. **English language entry requirement:** IELTS 6.5 (or equivalent). Pre-entry English and study skills programmes and foundation courses specialising in arts, science or social science subjects are available. **Fees:** Divinity, arts and sciences £11,350; Medicine £17,300. **Living costs:** £7,700.

University of St Andrews, College Gate, St Andrews KY16 9AJ; tel: 01334 462150; www.st-and.ac.uk.

ST GEORGE'S (University of London)

St George's is an independent dual faculty institution collaborating with Kingston University and Royal Holloway. It is situated in South-West London and in addition to Medicine it also offers degree programmes in Biomedical Sciences, Health and Social Sciences.

DEGREE SUBJECTS OFFERED

Adult Nursing; Biomedical Science; Diagnostic Radiography; Healthcare Science; Medicine; Nutrition Support; Pharmacy; Physiotherapy; Social Work; Therapeutic Radiography.

TUITION FEES (2009/10)

£3,225.

BURSARIES AND OTHER AWARDS

The bursary scheme extends beyond the minimum regulatory requirement. This recognises that the study of medicine, in particular, imposes unusually high costs on students in relation to the length of the programme and the travel and lodging requirements in the clinical programme. Students receiving the maximum state grant will receive £2,835 a year. Those receiving partial grants will receive awards on a sliding scale from £2,002 down to £50, on household incomes from £30,000 to £60,005.

St George's University of London Bursary

Students on the MB BS course and the BSc courses in Biomedical Science and Biomedical Informatics will, in addition to the state grant, receive SGUL Bursaries from £1,260 down to £160 per year.

Prizes

Numerous prizes are offered for students undertaking the MBBS degree programme. Most are awarded throughout the course, normally on the basis of examination performance.

INFORMATION AND APPROXIMATE FEES FOR NON-EU STUDENTS

English language entry requirement: IELTS 7.0 (or equivalent). **Fees:** Medicine: Years 1–2 £15,660, Years 3–5 £27,455. **Living costs:** £9,500–10,500.

St George's, University of London, Cranmer Terrace, Tooting, London SW17 0RE; tel: 020 8672; 9944; www.sgul.ac.uk.

ST MARY'S UNIVERSITY COLLEGE

The College is located on an attractive campus site by the River Thames in Twickenham and was founded in 1850. It has a student population of 3500 and courses are validated by the University of Surrey.

DEGREE SUBJECTS OFFERED

Business Law, Drama; Education and Employment; English; Film Studies; Geography; Health; History; Irish Studies; Management Studies; Media Arts; Nutrition; Philosophy, Physical Education (Secondary); Primary Education; Professional and Creative Writing; Psychology; Sociology; Sport Rehabilitation; Sport Coaching; Sport Science; Strength and Conditioning Science; Theology and Religious Studies; Tourism; Tourism Management.

TUITION FEES

£3,225.

BURSARIES AND OTHER AWARDS

St Mary's Bursaries

Students embarking on courses from 2009 in receipt of a maintenance grant and from households with an income less than £50,020 may be eligible for a grant of £500.

Sports Scholarships

These awards worth £1,000 are open to students who have achieved junior international level.

INFORMATION AND APPROXIMATE FEES FOR NON-EU STUDENTS

English language entry requirement: IELTS 6.0 (or equivalent) **Fees:** £7,200. **Living costs:** £9,000.

St Mary's University College, Waldegrave Road, Strawberry Hill, Twickenham, Middlesex TW1 4SX; tel: 020 8240 4000; www.smuc.ac.uk.

SALFORD UNIVERSITY

The University of Salford is located two miles from Manchester city centre, on its own compact campus that includes students' accommodation. There is a student population of 18,500 taking degree and HND courses.

DEGREE SUBJECTS OFFERED

Acoustics; Aerospace Business Systems; Applied Environmental and Resource Science; Applied Health Imaging; Applied Social Science; Arabic; Art and Design; Art Therapy; Audio Technology; Band Musicianship; Biochemistry; Biological Sciences; Biology; Broadcasting; Building; Building Surveying; Business Decision Analysis; Business Information Systems; Business Studies; Chemistry; Complementary Medicine; Computer and Video Games; Construction Management; Contemporary European Studies; Contemporary History; Counselling; Criminology; Cultural Studies; Economics; Engineering (Aeronautical; Civil; Computer Systems; Electrical/Electronic; Environmental; Manufacturing; Mechanical; Multimedia and Internet; Robotic); English; Environmental Science; Exercise and Health Sciences; Finance and Accounting; Financial Management; Food Industry Management; French; Geography; German; Health and Environment; Health Sciences; Hispanic Studies; History; Hospitality Management; Housing; Human Resource Management; Italian; Journalism; Law; Leisure Management; Linguistics; Management Science; Marketing; Mathematics; Media Technology; Midwifery; Modern Languages; Music Acoustics and Recording; Nursing; Occupational Therapy; Parliamentary Studies; Performing Arts; Physics; Physiology; Physiotherapy; Podiatry; Politics; Popular Music and Recording; Portuguese; Property Management; Prosthetics and Orthotics; Psychology; Quantitative Business Management; Quantity Surveying; Radiography; Social Policy; Social Research; Social Work; Sociology; Spanish; Sports Rehabilitation; Tourism Management; Translating and Interpreting; TV and Radio; Video Imaging.

TUITION FEES (2009/10)

£3,225.

BURSARIES AND OTHER AWARDS

Salford Bursary

The university will be offering three major bursaries: £319 per year for those students in receipt of a full HE maintenance grant and pro rata bursaries for those receiving a partial HE maintenance grant and a bursary scheme to cover a range of essential courses for certain students. There will be international student mobility bursaries for students from low income taking part in Erasmus Programmes.

Salford Community Bursaries

Bursaries of £500 are available for students living in the Salford area in the following postal codes – M/3, 5, 6, 7, 30, 44, 27, 28 and 38.

Subject Bursaries

Bursaries worth £1,000 each year are open to students embarking on selected courses. These include Physics, Engineering, Modern Languages, Media Language and Business, Computer and Video Games, Media Technology, Information and Communication Technology.

Vice Chancellor's Scholarship

This award of £1,000 is open to students achieving AAB at A-level or equivalent.

See Chapters 2, 4 and 6 for additional awards, applicable to all universities

AWARDS FOR NON-EU STUDENTS
Over £250,000 worth of scholarships is awarded to international students each year.

Regional Awards
The university offers a large number of its own awards to international students based on academic merit. They are valued in the region of £1,000 to £2,000 and are available to undergraduate students. Awards are offered for the following courses: Acoustics (Audio and Video); Aircraft Engineering with Pilot Studies; Computing; Engineering; Intelligent Systems; Mobile Computing; Software Engineering. There are also country-specific scholarships for students resident in the following regions: East Asia; Latin America; the Middle East and North Africa; South Asia; sub-Saharan Africa; the Americas.

POSTGRADUATE AWARDS
Awards are offered in the following subject areas – Acoustics; Computing; Corporate Risk Management; Design Management; Engineering; Gas Engineering; Health and Social Care; Languages; TV Production. Country-specific awards are also offered to students resident in Malaysia and Pakistan and to those regions listed above for overseas undergraduate courses.

INFORMATION AND APPROXIMATE FEES FOR NON-EU STUDENTS
There are 1,500 international students. **English language entry requirement:** IELTS 6.0 (or equivalent). English study programmes and a very comprehensive international foundation year are available. **Fees:** £8,400–£10,500. **Living costs:** £8,500–£9,000.

University of Salford, Greater Manchester M5 4WT; tel: 0161 295 5000; www.salford.ac.uk.

SCHOOL OF ORIENTAL AND AFRICAN STUDIES (SOAS) (University of London)

The school was founded in 1916 and is situated on the Bloomsbury campus in London. There are over 3,500 students taking subjects focusing on Africa, Asia and the Near and the Middle East.

DEGREE SUBJECTS OFFERED
Anthropology; Art and Archaeology; China and Inner Asia; Development Studies; Economics; History; International Studies; Japan and Korea; Languages and Cultures of Africa; Law; Music; Near and Middle East; Politics; Sociology; South Asia; South-East Asia and the Islands; Study of Religions.

TUITION FEES (2009/10)
£3,225.

BURSARIES AND OTHER AWARDS
SOAS Bursary
Students from households with an income less that £25,000 receive a bursary of £860 and for those within the income range £25,001 to £39,305 a bursary of £460 is payable.

Partner Colleges
Students from partner colleges in City & Islington, Westminster, Kensington & Chelsea, Tower Hamlets and Westminster Kingsway will recieve £800.

INFORMATION AND APPROXIMATE FEES FOR NON-EU STUDENTS
There is a large number of international students. **English language entry requirement:** IELTS 7.0 (or equivalent). A one-year foundation programme and English language courses are available, with an entry requirement of IELTS 4.0. There is a three-day International Students' Orientation programme. **Fees:** £11,460. **Living costs:** £9,500–£10,000.

School of Oriental and African Studies, Thornhaugh Street, Russell Square, London WC1H 0XG; tel: 020 7898 4034; www.soas.ac.uk.

SCHOOL OF PHARMACY (University of London)

The school was founded in 1925 and is situated on the Bloomsbury campus in London. There are 655 students taking the MPharm degree and a further 30 taking MSc degrees.

DEGREE SUBJECT OFFERED
Pharmacy.

TUITION FEES (2009/10)
£3,225.

BURSARIES AND OTHER AWARDS
A basic bursary is paid to students receiving a maintenance grant. Supplementary grants are payable to students with high A-level scores.

POSTGRADUATE AWARDS
Three full-time scholarships are offered each year through the Department of International Development Shared Scholarship Scheme, for full-time MSc courses.

INFORMATION AND APPROXIMATE FEES FOR NON-EU STUDENTS
English language entry requirement: IELTS 6.5 (or equivalent). **Fees:** £12,750. **Living costs:** £9,500–£10,500.

School of Pharmacy, 29 Brunswick Square, London WC1N 1AX. tel: 020 7753 5800; www. pharmacy.ac.uk.

SHEFFIELD UNIVERSITY

The University of Sheffield was founded in 1828 with the foundation of the Medical School. It is situated on a compact campus in the city with accommodation at Broomhill half a mile away and has a student population of over 24,000. Most of the courses offered are modular, giving maximum flexibility for students to plan their studies.

DEGREE SUBJECTS OFFERED

Accounting; Anatomy; Archaeology; Architecture; Artificial Intelligence; Astronomy; Biblical Studies; Biochemistry; Biological Sciences; Biology; Biomedical Science; Biotechnology; Business Studies; Ceramic Science; Chemical Physics; Chemistry; Chinese Studies; Cognitive Science; Computer Science; Criminology; Czech; Dentistry; Dutch; East Asian Studies; Ecology; Econometrics; Economics; Engineering (Aerospace; Biomedical; Chemical; Civil; Computer; Electrical/Electronic; Mechanical; Medical Systems; Software; Structural Systems); English; Environmental (Geology; Geoscience; Natural Environmental Science); Financial Management; French; Genetics; German; Glass Science; Health and Human Sciences; Hispanic Studies; History; Human Communication Sciences; Information Management; Japanese Studies; Journalism; Korean Studies; Landscape Design; Law; Linguistics; Management; Materials Science; Mathematics; Medical Biochemistry; Medicine; Metal Science; Microbiology; Mobile Communication Systems; Modern Languages; Music; Natural Environmental Science; Neuroscience; Orthoptics; Paramedical Studies; Pharmacology; Philosophy; Physics; Physiology; Planning; Plant Sciences; Polish; Politics; Polymer Science; Psychology; Russian; Social Policy; Social Studies; Sociology; Spanish; Speech Science; Statistics; Urban Studies; Zoology.

TUITION FEES (2009/10)

£3,225.

BURSARIES AND OTHER AWARDS

The University of Sheffield Bursary Scheme

Income Bursaries are offered to all UK tuition-fee paying undergraduate and PGCE students from households with incomes less than £35,515. There are also Prior Achievement Bursaries for high achieving students from lower-income households gaining three A grades at A-level (or equivalent) with higher awards being made to students with national shortage subjects. There are also Outreach Bursaries for applicants from the Compact scheme, also the Sheffield Outreach and Access to Medicine Scheme, Professions Partnership Programme, Access to Dental Occupations, Practice and Tutoring.

Hardship Funds

Financial support is available from the University for students with exceptional financial difficulties or higher than average costs. The majority of funding for UK students comes from the government's Access to Learning Fund. Financial support for international students is much more limited. The Access to Learning Fund is particularly targeted at:

* Students with children (especially lone parents)
* Mature students
* Students from low income families
* Disabled students
* Care leavers
* Students from Foyers or who are homeless
* Students receiving final-year loan rate.

Further information and application forms for University financial support are available from the Student Services Information Desk in the Union Building or on www.shef.ac.uk/ssid/finance/money.html.

Alumni Fund Scholarships

Around 30 scholarships will be available to UK undergraduate students. Each of these awards is worth £3,000, and they have been created thanks to generous annual donations from alumni (former students), staff, parents and friends of the university.

Alumni Fund Scholarships will be awarded primarily on the basis of financial need, although in exceptional cases other circumstances may be considered. Eligible candidates will be identified during the academic year and asked to apply. See www.shef.ac.uk/ssid/finance/alumni.html for more information.

South Yorkshire Higher Education and Development Trust Scholarships

Five SYHEDT scholarships will be available to undergraduate students from the South Yorkshire region. Awards are made primarily on financial need. Eligible candidates will be identified during the academic year and asked to apply.

Department bursaries

Many departments offer scholarships and bursaries of their own. For details, contact the department you are interested in direct.

Organ Scholarship

The scholarship is valued at £600 per year and linked to services in the cathedral and is open to applicants for the BMus degree. The award is tenable for three years. Details can be obtained from the Department of Music, University of Sheffield, Sheffield S10 2TN.

Choral Scholarships

Sheffield Cathedral offers up to six Choral Scholarships per year, to male university students to sing alto, tenor or bass. The scholarships are tenable for up to three years and have a value of £660 per year with an additional £300 per year for vocal tuition. Choral scholars are expected to be in Sheffield during choir terms, which run for approximately two weeks longer than the university semesters. Attendances outside university time are remunerated separately. For additional information contact the Master of Music, The Cathedral, Sheffield S1 1HA; tel: 0114 263 6069.

St John's Ranmoor also offers Choral Bursaries to the value of £300–400 per year to counter-tenors, tenors and basses. The choir consists of 18 boys and 14 men. There are two Sunday services with occasional concerts and cathedral visits. Good sight-singing is needed for a broad-ranging, cathedral-style repertoire. The bursaries are tenable for the duration of a student's course. Contact the Director of Music; tel: 0114 230 1199; ranmoor@freenetname.co.uk.

Sir Samuel Osborn Memorial Scholarships

If you are a past or present employee of Samuel Osborn and Co Ltd (or one of its subsidiary companies), or a spouse, dependant or descendant of such an employee, you may apply for a scholarship.

If successful, you will be awarded a sum of up to £1,000 which may contribute to your fees or living expenses whilst on a course at the university. Further details, including how you should apply, and a financial assessment form, are available from The Taught Programmes Office, Student Services Department, University of Sheffield, Sheffield S10 2TN.

Sports Bursaries

If you compete at international level, for England, Scotland, Wales or Ireland, in a sport recognised by Sport England, you could be eligible for free use of all our sports and fitness facilities. The scheme is open to all full-time undergraduates and postgraduates. University sport membership can cost up to £240 a year, so if you're serious about your sport it's worth applying for. Send your sporting CV and a supporting statement from a national coach to Tracey Baker, Goodwin Sports Centre, Northumberland Road, Sheffield S10 2TY.

AWARDS FOR NON-EU STUDENTS
International Scholarships

The following awards take the form of a reduction in tuition fees. Applicants must be nationals of or domiciled in the countries/territories listed. All the amounts shown are paid per year for three years of study.

* **Brunei** – one scholarship: £2,000
* **China** – three scholarships: £3,000 each

See Chapters 2, 4 and 6 for additional awards, applicable to all universities

* **Hong Kong** – three scholarships: £3,000 each
* **India** – three scholarships: £3,000 each
* **Kenya** – three scholarships: £3,000 each
* **Malaysia** – two scholarships: £5,000 each
* **Mauritius** – one scholarship: £4,000
* **Nigeria** – one scholarship: £4,000
* **Pakistan** – one scholarship: £4,000
* **Singapore** – two scholarships: £5,000 each
* **Sri Lanka** – one scholarship: £4,000
* **USA** – one scholarship: £4,000.

Sibling and Spouse Awards
These awards are worth £1,000 per year and are available for all spouses and siblings of current students for up to three years of study. For more details, see www.shef.ac.uk/international/money/scholarships/sibling.html.

Alumni Scholarships
These awards are worth £1,000 per year for up to three years of study for Sheffield graduates as well as their siblings or spouses.

Postgraduate Awards
The university offers scholarships to postgraduates who are 'home' students in the categories above relating to Sibling and Spouse Scholarships and Alumni Scholarships. In addition country-specific awards are made to nationals or those domiciled in Brazil, Canada, Hong Kong, India, Indonesia, Japan, Latin America, Libya, Malaysia, Mexico, Singapore, South Korea, Taiwan, Thailand and the USA.

INFORMATION AND APPROXIMATE FEES FOR NON-EU STUDENTS
There are 4,096 international students. **English language entry requirement:** IELTS 6.0 (or equivalent). Preparatory English courses (one to nine months) and an international summer school with English classes are available. **Fees:** arts and social science courses £10,420; Architecture £12,100; Law £10,420; science courses £13,700; Engineering £13,700; Medicine £13,700–24,760. **Living costs:** £6,400 per academic year (£8,200 for 12 months).

University of Sheffield, Sheffield S10 2TN; tel: 0114 222 2000; www.shef.ac.uk.

SHEFFIELD HALLAM UNIVERSITY

The university has a central campus in Sheffield city centre with two other campuses at Collegiate Crescent and Psalter Lane to the west. There are 23,000 students following a wide range of degree and diploma courses in 10 schools of studies.

DEGREE SUBJECTS OFFERED
Accounting; Applied Social Science; Architecture; Art and Design; Automotive Technology; Banking; Biological Sciences; Biomedical Science; Building Surveying; Business; Catering Systems; Chemistry; Communication Studies; Computer Studies; Computing; Construction Management; Countryside Management; Criminology; Early Childhood Studies; Education Studies; Engineering (Automotive; Civil; Communications; Computer; Control; Electrical/Electronic; Environmental; Forensic; Information; Mechanical; Medical; Telecommunications); Engineering Design; English; Environmental Studies; Film Studies; Financial Services; Fine Art; Food Studies; Geography; History; History of Art; Hotel Management; Housing; Industrial Design; International Business; Languages;

Law; Management Science; Marketing; Mathematics; Media Studies; Nursing; Nutrition; Occupational Therapy; Outdoor Leisure Management; Physics; Physiotherapy; Property Studies; Psychology; Public Policy; Quantity Surveying; Radiography; Recreation Management; Social Policy; Social Work; Society and Cities; Sociology; Sport Science; Statistics; Surveying Technology; Tourism; Town and Country Planning; Transport Planning; Urban Land Economics.

TUITION FEES (2009/10)
£3,225.

BURSARIES AND OTHER AWARDS
A Hallam grant of £700 cash will be available for students in receipt of a full HE grant. In addition, there is the Hallam Access Bursary (a cash sum of £300) for those who progress from partner schools/colleges and enrol on a full-time course.

EU Bursaries
These bursaries worth £1,000 are open to EU non-UK applicants.

AWARDS FOR NON-EU STUDENTS
Hallam Special Achievement Scholarships
These are worth from £1,000 to £2,000 and are open to Malaysian applicants.

INFORMATION AND APPROXIMATE FEES FOR NON-EU STUDENTS
There are 3,000 international students from over 80 countries. **English language entry requirement:** IELTS 6.0 (or equivalent). English language tuition is available on four-, eight- and 12-week courses (£810, £1,700 and £2,200 respectively and entry requirement IELTS 4.5). **Fees:** £8,000–£11,000. **Living costs:** £7,000–£8,000.

Sheffield Hallam University, Bromsgrove Road, Sheffield S10 2LW; tel: 0114 225 5555; www.shu.ac.uk.

SOUTHAMPTON UNIVERSITY

The University of Southampton was founded in the mid-nineteenth century and now has a student population of nearly 20,000. There are several campuses in Southampton and Winchester, including the main Highfield campus (three miles from the city centre), the Avenue campus, the National Oceanography Centre and Winchester School of Art.

DEGREE SUBJECTS OFFERED
Accounting; Acoustics; Actuarial Studies; Applied Social Science; Archaeology; Art and Design; Artificial Intelligence; Arts Management; Astronomy; Biochemistry; Biology; Biomedical Science; Chemistry; Computer Science; Contemporary Europe; Econometrics; Economics; Engineering (Acoustical; Aerospace; Civil; Computer; Electrical; Electromechanical; Electronic; Environmental; Mechanical); English; Environmental Management; Fashion Studies; Film and TV; French; Geography; Geology; German; Health and Social Care Management; History; Iberian Studies; Jewish History and Culture; Laser Sciences; Latin American Studies; Law; Management Sciences; Marine Sciences; Market Research and Social Analysis; Mathematics; Medicine; Midwifery; Music; Nursing; Nutrition; Occupational Therapy; Oceanography; Pharmacology; Philosophy; Physics; Physiology; Physiotherapy; Plant Science; Podiatry; Political Communication; Politics; Population Science;

Portuguese; Psychology; Public and Social Administration; Ship Science; Social Policy; Sociology; Space Science; Spanish; Zoology.

TUITION FEES (2009/10)
£3,225.

BURSARIES AND OTHER AWARDS
A £1,000 bursary will be offered to students from households where the income falls below £25,000, and £500 to students with household incomes between £25,001–£35,000.

Hampshire and Isle of Wight Bursaries
150 bursaries are offered an a competitive basis to students from FE colleges and school sixth forms in Hampshire and the Isle of Wight. The bursaries are open to students from households with an income less than £35,000.

Art (Fine Art Practice and Theory; Textiles, Fashion and Fibre)
Winchester School of Art offers a number of Entrance Scholarships to outstanding candidates who have either completed a foundation course, or are applying for direct entry to three-year BA honours programmes, on the basis of high grades in art-related subjects in A-level or equivalent examinations. Details of all scholarships appear on the school's website, www.wsa.soton.ac.uk.

Biological Sciences (Biochemistry; Biology; Biomedical Science; Pharmacology; Zoology)
The School of Biological Sciences offers 15 Entry Scholarships of £2,000 per year to new students based on pre-university qualifications. Successful applicants will continue to hold the scholarships for each successive year of the degree programme provided they achieve at least 60% per year. A further 12 Performance Scholarships of £2,000 each will be awarded to students with outstanding academic performance in their first and/or second year.

Chemistry
The School of Chemistry's Scholarship and Award Scheme provides all students with the first-year study texts. It also awards at least 10 scholarships of £1,000 for the first two years of the degree for prior achievement in pre-university qualifications. Progress and high standards, along with proficiency on graduation, will be recognised with up to 20 awards of £1,000 per year given during the senior years of the course and upon graduation.

Civil Engineering and the Environment (Civil Engineering; Environmental Engineering)
The School of Civil Engineering and the Environment is expanding its programme of scholarships linked to a number of companies; the SUCCESS scheme. SUCCESS provides continuing sponsorships to students selected in their first and second year of study. It includes a financial package of between £1,000 and £1,700, summer work placements and possible long-term employment opportunities on graduation. Students are selected during the first semester on the basis of an interview day including company representatives.

Education (Post-compulsory Education; Sport Management and Leadership; Sport Studies)
The School of Education offers a number of scholarships, each valued at up to £3,000 per year, to new entrants to undergraduate degree programmes in Sport (BSc Sport Science/BA Sport Management and Leadership). These will be awarded to candidates on the basis of both academic excellence and sporting achievement, either in performance or in relation to community sport development. The school will also offer a number of scholarships, each valued at up to £800 per year for entrants to the part-time BA Post-compulsory Education programme, awarded on the basis of academic excellence.

Electronics and Computer Science (Computer Engineering; Computer Science; Electrical Engineering; Electromechanical Engineering; Electronic Engineering; Information Technology in Organisations)

The School of Electronics and Computer Science (ECS) offers 25 scholarships to new students, each valued at £2,000 per year. Scholarships will be awarded on the basis of academic achievements prior to university. The scholarship will be held for each following year of the degree programme, providing the holder achieves an overall performance of at least 60% in coursework and examinations.

Engineering Sciences (Aerospace Engineering; Mechanical Engineering; Ship Science)

The School of Engineering Sciences offers 20 Entry Scholarships of £1,000 each to reward excellence. It also offers 40 annual scholarships of £1,000 for excellence in academic performance during the degree. The maximum possible award will therefore be £4,000 over the duration of all programmes.

Geography

The School of Geography offers a number of scholarships of £1,000 each. These include:

* Entry Awards, given to those in the first year, based on pre-university attainment
* Level 2 Awards, given to those entering their second year, based on Level 1 results
* Level 3 Awards given to those entering their third year, based on second-year results
* Progress Awards, given to those entering their third year, rewarding progress throughout the first two years at Southampton.

Health Professions and Rehabilitation Sciences (Health and Social Care; Occupational Therapy; Physiotherapy; Podiatry)

All courses in the School of Health Professions and Rehabilitation Sciences are fully funded by NHS Bursaries. For more information telephone the NHS Student Grants Unit on: 0845 358 6655.

Humanities (Archaeology; Contemporary Europe; English; Film Studies; French Studies; German Studies; History; Language Studies; Music; Philosophy; Spanish, Portuguese and Latin American Studies)

The School of Humanities offers up to 10 one-year Entrance Scholarships of £3,000 each, based on high performance in entry qualifications. At least one will be available in each of Archaeology, English, Film, History, Modern Languages, Music and Philosophy. Progression Scholarships will be awarded for high performance in first-year and second-year studies, to a similar number and value.

Institute of Sound and Vibration Research (Acoustical Engineering; Acoustics and Music)

The Institute of Sound and Vibration Research offers a number of scholarships, of £2,000 each, to outstanding applicants to the programmes in Acoustical Engineering and Acoustics and Music. It also awards a number of scholarships of up to £1,000 for outstanding performance in examinations during the course.

Law

The School of Law is employing considerable funds to enhance the learning experience of all the undergraduate law students and is offering a number of prizes/scholarships up to a value of £1,000 to students demonstrating outstanding achievement at the end of each year while on the course.

Management (Accounting and Finance; Entrepreneurship; Management Sciences and Management)

The School of Management invests in the quality of its undergraduate students by offering scholarships and prizes on its programmes from a school fund of up to £30,000 per year. A number of Entry Scholarships are offered in August to the highest-achieving UK/EU applicants, while financial prizes and overseas study funding are offered to recognise student achievement during the first year of study.

Mathematics
The School of Mathematics offers three types of scholarship, as follows:
* Up to 15 scholarships of £1,000 per year for the duration of the degree programme (subject to progress) for the best-qualified candidates, based on academic qualifications at entry
* Scholarships paying all tuition fees for the normal duration of the degree programme for any candidate entering with five A grades in distinct subjects at A-level
* A scholarship of £1,000 payable to each student upon entry into the final year of the MMath programme.

Medicine
The School of Medicine offers a number of scholarships, rewarding students who achieve excellence in the assessments during undergraduate BM degree programmes. About £25,000 per year will be available for scholarships. Individual students may be eligible for up to £1,000 of scholarship funding by achieving distinctions in the BM primary and intermediate examinations.

Nursing and Midwifery
Nursing and Midwifery students from the UK and EU do not pay tuition fees, as all these pre-registration courses are funded by the NHS. UK and EU students on degree programmes are eligible to apply for a means-tested NHS Bursary. Those pursuing Diploma and Advanced Diploma Studies are eligible for a full NHS Bursary. For more information telephone the NHS Student Grants Unit on 0845 358 6655.

Ocean and Earth Science (Geology; Geophysical Sciences; Oceanography)
The School of Ocean and Earth Science offers a number of scholarships of £1,000 each. These scholarships include:

* Entry Awards, given to those in the first year based on pre-university achievement
* Level 2 Awards, given to those entering their second year, based on Level 1 results
* Level 3 Awards, given to those entering their third year, based on second-year results
* Level 4 Awards, given to those entering their fourth year, based on third-year results.

Physics and Astronomy
The School of Physics and Astronomy awards a number of scholarships annually to outstanding students based on a written examination taken in November of the year preceding entry.

Scholarships are also available to students from outside the EU. These scholarships provide overseas students with £1,000 per year for every grade A achieved in A-level examinations up to a maximum of £3,000 per year. Students holding qualifications other than A-levels may be eligible as well.

The Institute of Physics offers means-tested bursaries of around £1,000 a year to undergraduates studying Physics in the UK and Ireland. For details see: http://education.iop.org/Schools/suptstu/ubs.html.

Psychology
The School of Psychology will be awarding 10 High Achievement Scholarships, worth £1,000 each, to new students, as well as a number of scholarships for continuing students.

Social Sciences (Actuarial Studies; Anthropology; Applied Social Sciences; Criminology; Criminology and Psychological Studies; Economics; Politics; Population Sciences; Social Work; Sociology and Social Policy)
The School of Social Sciences offers a number of scholarships up to a value of £1,000 to students demonstrating outstanding achievement, each year prior to graduation.

AWARDS FOR NON-EU STUDENTS
Subject-specific scholarships are offered to international students as follows.

Faculty of Engineering, Science and Mathematics:
Institute of Sound and Vibration Research: £1,000–2,000
School of Chemistry: £2,000–3,000
School of Civil Engineering and the Environment: £1,000–1,150
School of Electronics and Computer Science: £1,000
School of Engineering Sciences: £1,000–2,000
School of Geography: £1,000
School of Mathematics: all tuition fees
School of Physics and Astronomy: £3,000
School of Ocean Sciences: £1,000–1,500

Faculty of Medicine, Health and Life Sciences
School of Biological Sciences: £2,000
Schools of Health Professions and Rehabilitation Sciences
School of Nursing and Midwifery
School of Medicine
School of Psychology: £2,500

Faculty of Law, Arts and Social Sciences
Winchester School of Art: £500
School of Law: 50% of tuition fees
School of Humanities
School of Education
School of Management
School of Social Sciences: £1,000

POSTGRADUATE AWARDS
Funding is available in the following subject areas: Education; Engineering subjects; Geography; History; Humanities; Maritime Law; Physics and Astronomy; Psychology; Social Sciences and Sound Vibration Research.

INFORMATION AND APPROXIMATE FEES FOR NON-EU STUDENTS
There are 2,000 international students. **English language entry requirement:** IELTS 6.0–6.5 (or equivalent). English courses are offered along with an international foundation course covering arts, humanities, social sciences and Law. **Fees:** £9,380–£12,000; clinical: £21,800. **Living costs:** £7,500.

University of Southampton, Highfield, Southampton SO17 1BJ; tel: 023 8059 5000; www. soton.ac.uk.

SOUTHAMPTON SOLENT UNIVERSITY

The Southampton Institute of Higher Education became a university in 2005. It is situated on its own campus close to Southampton city centre. There are 16,000 students following degree and diploma courses.

DEGREE SUBJECTS OFFERED
Accountancy; Advertising; Architecture; Art and Design; Business Studies; Computer Studies; Engineering; Fashion Styling; Film and TV Studies; Health and Fitness; Human Resources

Management; International Business; Journalism; Law; Leisure Management; Maritime and Environmental Science; Maritime Studies; Marketing; Media Studies; Music; Performance; Psychology; Social Work; Sport Science and Coaching; Sports Studies; Tourism; Yacht and Boat Design.

TUITION FEES (2009/10)
£3,225.

BURSARIES AND OTHER AWARDS
Students paying the full fee and in receipt of the full maintenance grant will receive a bursary of £1,075. Bursaries are then paid on a four point scale in proportion to the household income as follows: £750 for incomes of £18,360–£23,000, £500 for £23,001–£28,000 and £250 for £28,001–£39,333.

Students paying variable fees of less than £3,225 and whose household income is less than £18,360 will receive a bursary of £319.

Lisa Wilson Scholarships
Four scholarships in memory of a former student are available to assist young people with the costs of higher education. Each scholarship is worth £1,000.

AWARDS FOR NON-EU STUDENTS
Some scholarships are available for applicants from Bangladesh, Caribbean, Ghana, India, Malaysia, Nigeria, Pakistan, Tanzania and Thailand.

INFORMATION AND APPROXIMATE FEES FOR NON-EU STUDENTS
Fifty countries are represented among the international student population. **English language entry requirement:** IELTS 6.0 or TOEFL 550. **Fees:** £7,500–£8,000. **Living costs:** £7,500–£8,500.

Southampton Solent University, East Park Terrace, Southampton, Hampshire SO14 0XU; tel: 023 8031 9039; www.solent.ac.uk.

STAFFORDSHIRE UNIVERSITY

The university consists of two main campuses at Stoke where students follow courses in arts, design, science, business and law, and at Stafford where some business studies are offered along with computing and engineering. There is a total student population of 16,000.

DEGREE SUBJECTS OFFERED
Accounting; Advice Work; American Studies; Applied Biology; Applied Microbiology; Applied Social Studies; Applied Statistics; Art and Design; Biochemistry; Biology; Broadcasting Technology; Building Surveying; Business; Ceramic Science; Chemistry; Computer Graphics, Imaging and Visualisation; Computer Science; Computing; Computing Science; Construction Management; Crime, Deviance and Society; Cultural Studies; Design Technology; Development Studies; Drama and Theatre Arts; Ecology; Economics; Electronic Commerce; Engineering (Computer Aided; Electrical/Electronic; Forensic; Manufacturing; Mechanical; Medical; Microelectronic; Software); English; Environmental Sciences; European Economics; European Media; Exercise and Health; Film, TV and Radio; Forensic Science; French; Geography; Geology; German; History; History of Art; Hospitality and Tourism Management; Human Biology; Human Resource Management; Industrial

Marketing; Information Systems; Intelligent Systems; International Finance; International Relations; Journalism; Law; Legal Studies; Marketing; Media Studies; Midwifery; Mobile Computing; Multimedia Computing; New Media; Nursing; Occupational Health; Philosophy; Physics; Physiology; Politics; Property; Psychology; Sociology; Spanish; Sport and Leisure; Sport Sciences; Transport Management; Travel and Tourism; Valuation Surveying; Web-Media Technology.

TUITION FEES (2009/10)
£3,225.

BURSARIES AND OTHER AWARDS
Students from households with an income below £20,817 will receive a bursary of £1,000, those with household incomes between £20,818 and £25,521 a bursary of £850, and those between £25,552 and £30,810 a bursary of £350. Foundation degree and HND students with household incomes as above will receive £700, £595 and £350 respectively.

Ashley Scholarships
Thirty Ashley Scholarships of £500 per year for the duration of the course are available for new applicants from Staffordshire, Cheshire or Shropshire and for those applying for franchised awards at partner colleges. Scholarships will be awarded to those who face particularly difficult circumstances relating to financial or social circumstances, illness or disability. Applicants must have firmly accepted a conditional or unconditional offer for a place at Staffordshire University. Details are available from the Admissions Office, Winton Chambers, College Road, Stoke-on-Trent ST4 2DE.

INFORMATION AND APPROXIMATE FEES FOR NON-EU STUDENTS
There are students from over 70 countries. **English language entry requirement:** IELTS 5.5–6.0 (or equivalent). English tuition is available. **Fees:** £9,385. **Living costs:** £7,500–£8,000.

Staffordshire University, College Road, Stoke-on-Trent ST4 2DE; tel: 01782 292753; www.staffs.ac.uk.

STIRLING UNIVERSITY

The University of Stirling is situated on a 300-acre campus just outside of the city of Stirling, with a student population of 9,000. The university year is divided into two semesters with modular programmes allowing considerable flexibility and choice. Assessment is based on both coursework and examination.

DEGREE SUBJECTS OFFERED
Accountancy; Animal Biology; Aquaculture; Biology; Business Law; Business Studies; Computer Science; Conservation Management; Criminology; Ecology; Economics; Education (Secondary); English; Environmental Science; European Social Policy; Film and Media Studies; Finance; French; Freshwater Science; History; Human Resource Management; Information Systems; International Management Studies; Journalism Studies; Law (LLB and BA); Management Science; Marine Biology; Marketing; Mathematics; Midwifery; Money, Banking and Finance; Nursing; Philosophy; Politics; Politics, Philosophy and Economics; Postcolonial Literature; Psychology; Public Management and Administration; Religious Studies; Scottish History; Scottish Literature; Social Policy; Social Work; Sociology; Software Engineering; Spanish; Sports Studies; Tourism Management.

TUITION FEES
Students domiciled in Scotland receive free tuition; see www.saas.gov.uk and **Chapter 1, 'Financing your course'.**

BURSARIES AND OTHER AWARDS
Sports scholarships
The University of Stirling has offered Sports Scholarships to talented student athletes since 1981. Awards help outstanding young athletes combine top-level sport with academic study. Awards are focused around four core sports: golf, swimming, tennis and triathlon. Athletes are required to be of junior national standard or beyond to be considered for an award. Where appropriate, award recipients benefit from:

* Top-level coaching
* Access to sports facilities
* Strength and conditioning
* Sports science support
* Essential clothing and equipment
* Agreed financial assistance towards competition costs up to a value of £5,000 per year
* Academic flexibility to combine sport with academic study.

In return, athletes are expected to compete for the University of Stirling in student sport and in mainstream national and international competitions. Applications are made through the Department of Sports Studies. For more information call 01786 466901.

INFORMATION AND APPROXIMATE FEES FOR NON-EU STUDENTS
Thirteen per cent of the student population are overseas students from 70 nationalities. **English language entry requirement:** IELTS 6.0 (or equivalent). English language tuition is available. **Fees:** £9,100–£11,200. **Living costs:** £5,500–£6,000.

University of Stirling, Stirling FK9 4LA; tel: 01786 467046; www.stir.ac.uk.

STRATHCLYDE UNIVERSITY (GLASGOW)

The University of Strathclyde was founded in 1964 and is located on two campuses, one in the heart of Glasgow, and the Jordanhill Campus to the west of the city. There is a student population of over 15,000 following courses largely based on a credit-based modular system programme on a two-semester year.

DEGREE SUBJECTS OFFERED
Advanced Marine Design; Architectural Studies; Art and Design; Arts and Social Sciences; Biochemistry; Biological Sciences; Biology; Bioscience; Business Information Systems; Chemistry; Community Arts; Community Education; Computer Science; Economics; Education (Primary); Educational Studies; Electronic Technology; Energy Studies; Engineering (Aero-Mechanical; Biomedical; Building Design; Chemical; Civil; Control; Electronic/Electrical; Environmental; Materials; Mechanical; Ocean; Offshore; Product Design; Small Craft); English; Environmental (Health; Planning/Protection); European Studies; Finance; French; Geography; German; History; Hotel and Hospitality Management; Human Resource Management; Immunology; Italian; Law; Management Science; Manufacturing; Marketing; Mathematical Biology; Mathematics; Modern Languages; Music; Naval Architecture; Outdoor Education; Pharmaceutical Sciences; Pharmacy; Physics; Planning; Politics; Pollution Control; Prosthetics and Orthotics; Psychology; Russian; Science Studies;

Scottish Studies; Social Work; Sociology; Spanish; Speech and Language Pathology; Sport and Exercise Science; Sport in the Community; Statistics; Sustainable Development and Regeneration; Technology; Tourism; Visual Simulation.

TUITION FEES
Students domiciled in Scotland receive free tuition; see www.saas.gov.uk and **Chapter 1, 'Financing your course'**.

BURSARIES AND OTHER AWARDS
Sports Bursaries
A number of Sports Bursaries are awarded each year to gifted athletes in conjunction with Glasgow City Council. These are valued at up to £1,000 and are intended to assist with costs incurred covering coaching, travel and equipment. In addition, eight Golf Bursaries are also awarded worth £250 for up to a maximum of four years. Details can be obtained from Drew Menzie on 0141 548 2246.

Scholarships
Scholarships are offered each year by individual departments. Contact the Student Finance Office.

POSTGRADUATE AWARDS
A limited number of postgraduate research scholarships are offered worth £7,000 per year.

INFORMATION AND APPROXIMATE FEES FOR NON-EU STUDENTS
Students are from 90 countries. **English language entry requirement:** IELTS 6.5 (or equivalent). Pre-entry and pre-sessional English tuition is available. **Fees:** £8,930–£11,465. **Living costs:** £7,500–£8,500.

University of Strathclyde, Glasgow G1 1XQ; tel: 0141 552 4400; www.strath.ac.uk.

SUNDERLAND UNIVERSITY

The University of Sunderland has four academic Faculties – Applied Sciences, Arts, Design & Media, Education and Society and Business and Law. There are two campuses – one in the city and one on the coast. The University has strong links with industry and business, and works closely with some of the world's leading companies.

DEGREE SUBJECTS OFFERED
Arts (Creative and Performing); Business and Management; Computing; Design; Education and Teacher Training; Engineering; English; Geography; History; Law; Media; Pharmacy; Chemistry and Biomedical Science; Psychology; Social Sciences and the Caring Professions; Sport and Exercise Sciences and Tourism.

TUITION FEES (2009/10)
£3,225.

BURSARIES AND OTHER AWARDS
University of Sunderland Bursary
2008/9 and 2009/10 intake – £525 to all eligible UK students with household incomes assessed at less than £39,305 per year.

University of Sunderland Success Scholarship 2009
UK/EU students will be eligible for up to £965 paid across three years subject to progress.

Foundation Degree/Level 0 Scholarship
As well as the scholarships above UK Foundation Degree students will also receive an extra scholarship of £525 per year. Students on Level 0 of a degree programme will also receive the £525 extra scholarship for that year only.

£1,500 University of Sunderland bursary for Care Experienced students
This will be paid in three instalments of £500 throughout the year, for each year of study and progress through your course. This bursary is in addition to any other university bursaries or grants, and therefore needs to be applied for separately. Eligible applicants will be sent an application form following receipt of an unconditional offer of a place.

INFORMATION AND APPROXIMATE FEES FOR NON-EU STUDENTS
English language entry requirement: IELTS 5.5–6.0 (or equivalent); **Fees:** £8,300; **Living costs:** £5,500–£6,000.

University of Sunderland, City Campus, Chester Road, Sunderland SR1 3SD; tel: 0191 515 3154 www.sunderland.ac.uk.

SURREY UNIVERSITY

The University of Surrey is situated on a purpose-built campus on the slopes of Stag Hill leading up to the cathedral and 10 minutes from the centre of Guildford. It was founded in 1966 and, through a large number of sandwich courses, rates highly in graduate employment league tables. Degree programmes are modular, many focusing on scientific and technological areas. There is a student population of 11,000.

DEGREE SUBJECTS OFFERED
Biochemistry; Business; Chemistry; Computer Modelling and Simulation; Computer Science; Computing; Dance and Culture; Dietetics; Digital Broadcasting; Economics; Electronics; Engineering (Aerospace; Biomaterials; Biomedical; Chemical; Civil; Electronic; Environment; Information Systems; Mechanical; Radio Frequency; Satellite Systems); European Studies; Finance; Food Science; French; German; Industrial Technology; Information Technology; Instrumentation and Analysis; International Hospitality and Tourism Management; Law; Linguistics and International Studies; Management; Materials Science; Mathematics; Microbiology; Midwifery; Mobile Communications; Music; Neuroscience; Nuclear Astrophysics; Nursing; Nutrition; Pharmacology; Physics; Psychology; Retail Management; Russian; Satellite Technology; Science Education; Science of Materials; Sociology; Statistics; Telecommunication Systems; Tourism; Toxicology.

TUITION FEES (2009/10)
£3,225.

BURSARIES AND OTHER AWARDS

University of Surrey Bursaries are available to students in receipt of the maintenance grant each year (except during the foundation and professional training years, when reduced fees are payable) where their/their family's residual income is below £35,000. Payments are on a sliding scale with the full bursary of £2,000 being awarded where income is below £10,000.

Enhanced-value University of Surrey Bursaries are awarded where a student is eligible for a University of Surrey Bursary and has also received a University of Surrey Scholarship. Students receive double the amount of bursary, up to £4,000 per year.

Extended-programme Bursaries are awarded to all eligible UK/EU students on extended degree programmes – such as five-year MEng courses – to cover the period of study which exceeds the standard length of a programme (ie three years full time/four years sandwich).

Types of scholarship

The university offers a range of scholarships to full-time students. These are awarded to:

* All full-time UK/EU students with grades of AAA at A-level, excluding General Studies (or equivalent) on entry
* Full-time UK students with slightly lower grades on entry, where defined widening participation school performance indicators are met
* Full-time UK/EU students on specific programmes with slightly lower grades on entry
* All full-time students who do not obtain an award on entry to the university, but who achieve a standard of first class honours at the end of Level 1 or 2.

For all of the above scholarships, the students will continue to receive a yearly scholarship of £1,000 throughout the remainder of their degree programme, except during periods of professional training and extended periods of study, subject to achieving a 2(i) or above in appropriate assessments.

The following scholarships were offered in 2008/09. Check with subject departments for up-to-date information.

Chemical and Process Engineering: UOP Scholarships

A bursary of £1,000 per year for each year of a student's programme is awarded to the student who in the first-semester shows outstanding ability.

Chemical Engineering and Chemical and Bio-systems Engineering

Student sponsorships and prizes are awarded by Atkins, KBR, Save and Prosper, The Salters Company and IChemE. Visit www.surrey.ac.uk/eng.

Chemical, Civil and Mechanical Engineering

Five undergraduate Save and Prosper Travel Scholarships are available. The scholarships of up to £750 each are awarded to second-year undergraduates to visit selected industrial establishments or universities to expand their understanding of the particular industry which they expect to join on graduation. Visit www.surrey.ac.uk/eng.

Civil Engineering

The UniS/ICE Scholarship scheme is a partnership between the university, the Institution of Civil Engineers (ICE) and an alliance of industrial companies. The scheme can provide Civil Engineering students with scholarships, professional training placements and links through to employment on graduation. Applications are considered prior to the start of the programme. Visit www.surrey.ac.uk/eng.

Biochemistry; Biomedical Sciences; Chemistry; Food Science; Microbiology and Nutrition

In some subjects, special prizes will be available for overseas fee-paying students achieving a first-class academic performance for their studies in the School of Biomedical and Molecular Sciences.

Students will not normally be eligible to hold both a school and a university award. A leaflet containing details of these awards is obtainable from the Admissions Secretary.

Combined Studies; Communication and Media Studies; Dance Studies; Law; Languages; Music; Politics and Sound Recording

Each year the School of Arts is able to offer one Annual Fund Scholarship to the most deserving applicant in one of its constituent departments. Well-defined criteria relating to entry qualifications and/or potential to contribute to university life are used to determine departmental nominations and selection of the eventual winner of the scholarship.

Sports Bursaries

An Elite Sports Programme is run by UniSPORT. Applications can be made by anyone on a university degree programme. The university is also part of a new government initiative, the Talented Athlete Scholarship Scheme (TASS), and is a lead institution in squash and short-track speed skating. Visit www.unisport.co.uk.

Choral and Organ Scholarships at Guildford Cathedral

Choral Scholarships, tenable for three years, are offered in conjunction with the dean and chapter of Guildford Cathedral; an Organ Scholarship is also offered. These scholarships are open to any undergraduate or postgraduate student. Details of these scholarships can be obtained from 5 Cathedral Close, Guildford, Surrey GU2 5TL.

Westwood Travel Bursary

A £600 bursary is awarded annually to enable a full-time undergraduate student to participate in the Surrey/USA exchange scheme. The award may be offered on a shared basis.

AWARDS FOR NON-EU STUDENTS

Aerospace, Civil, Chemical, Chemical and Bio-systems, Mechanical, Medical and Sustainable Systems Engineering

Scholarships of up to £2,500 per year of study are awarded to suitably qualified overseas fee-paying students. Visit www.surrey.ac.uk/eng.

Computing; Electronic Engineering; Mathematics and Statistics; and Physics

The School of Electronics and Physical Sciences has a scholarship scheme for those international students who achieve very high grades at A-level (or equivalent). Visit www.eps.surrey.ac.uk.

Civil Engineering International Students Scholarship Scheme

The department offers a scholarship to full overseas fee-paying students who achieve a high standard in their entry qualifications. Typically candidates attaining 300 tariff points or the equivalent, such as a Polytechnic Diploma at grade B, are considered to be eligible. The value of the award is £1,000 per year for the normal duration of the programme. (For details of requirements and conditions contact the admissions tutor, Department of Civil Engineering.)

POSTGRADUATE AWARDS

Awards are made in the fields of Biomedical and Molecular Sciences, Sociology, Sport and Electronic Engineering.

INFORMATION AND APPROXIMATE FEES FOR NON-EU STUDENTS

The university has a large international community with 43% being from the Far East. **English language entry requirement:** IELTS 6.0 (or equivalent). English language courses and summer courses are offered. **Fees:** £8,600–£11,000. **Living costs:** £7,000–£8,000.

University of Surrey, Guildford, Surrey GU2 5XH; tel: 01483 689305; www.surrey.ac.uk.

SUSSEX UNIVERSITY

The University of Sussex is a campus university located in parkland on the edge of the South Downs, north of Brighton. It was founded in 1961. The courses followed by the 10,000 students are based on the modular principle with schools of study allowing for flexibility in the choice of courses.

DEGREE SUBJECTS OFFERED

American Studies; Anthropology; Art History; Biochemistry; Biological Sciences; Biology; Business and Management Studies; Chemistry; Computer Science; Conservation; Development Studies; Drama Studies; Ecology; Economics; Engineering; English; English Language and Linguistics; Environmental Science; Film Studies; Geography; History; Human Science; Information Technology Systems; International Relations; Law; Linguistics; Mathematics; Media Studies; Medicine; Molecular Genetics; Molecular Medicine; Molecular Sciences; Music; Neuroscience; Philosophy; Physics; Politics; Product Design; Psychology; Social Work; Sociology.

TUITION FEES (2009/10)

£3,225.

BURSARIES AND OTHER AWARDS

Students from households with an income below £25,000 will receive the full grant of £2,906 and a Sussex Bursary of £1,000. Chancellor's Scholarships worth £1,000 are also open to students from households with an income of less than £30,000. All these awards are non-repayable.

High-Flyer Scholarships

These awards worth £1,000 are offered to students achieving the highest grades and applying for courses in Chemistry, Engineering, Informatics, Mathematics, Physics and Astronomy.

Mrs Emily O. Akinluyi Scholarship

This scholarship worth £5,000 over three years is open to female applicants intending to study in the School of Science and Technology. It is limited to those from households with an income of less than £30,000.

Sports Scholarships

These scholarships are offered to students who have reached national standard in their chosen sport.

AWARDS FOR NON-EU STUDENTS
International Chancellor's Scholarships

Forty International Chancellor Scholarships of £2,500 are awarded on the basis of academic ability.

Business and Management Scholarships

Fifteen scholarships worth £3,500 by way of a reduction of fees are offered on the basis of academic ability.

POSTGRADUATE AWARDS

The Geoff Lockwood Scholarship is offered to high-calibre applicants for MSc programmes.

The university offers two Sasakawa Fellowships for Master's students – one from the UK and one from Eastern Europe – with the objective of educating graduate students who have high potential for future leadership in international affairs.

See Chapters 2, 4 and 6 for additional awards, applicable to all universities

Several scholarships are offered to postgraduate students including specific awards for Imaging in Biomedical Research, History of Art, Music and Law.

INFORMATION AND APPROXIMATE FEES FOR NON-EU STUDENTS

There are 2,500 international students. **English language entry requirement:** IELTS 6.5 (or equivalent). English language and study skills courses are available. International foundation courses are offered, covering English language tuition and a choice from Humanities, Law, Media Studies, Social Sciences and Cultural Studies, and Science and Technology. **Fees:** £9,975–£12,750. **Living costs:** £8,000–£8,500.

University of Sussex, Sussex House, Falmer, Brighton BN1 9RH; tel: 01273 678416; www. sussex.ac.uk.

SWANSEA (University of Wales)

The university was founded in 1920 and is located on a spacious seafront campus overlooking the Gower Peninsula and a short distance from Swansea. There is a student population of 9,600. A modular system operates with students taking compulsory and optional modules.

DEGREE SUBJECTS OFFERED

Actuarial Studies; American Studies; Ancient History; Anthropology; Biochemistry; Biological Sciences; Biology; Business; Business Information Technology; Catalan; Chemical, Analytical and Forensic Science; Classics; Communications; Computer Simulation; Computer Studies; Computing Science; Development Studies; Ecology; E-Commerce Technology; Economics; Egyptology; Engineering (Biochemical; Chemical; Civil; Computing; Electrical/Electronic; Materials; Mechanical; Product Design and Manufacture; Process); English; Finance; French; Genetics; Geography; German; Greek; History; Humanities; International Relations; Internet Technology; Italian; Language Studies; Latin; Law; Legal Studies; Management Science; Marine Biology; Marketing; Materials Science; Mathematics; Medical Genetics; Medical Sciences; Medieval Studies; Mobile Communications; Nursing; Operational Research; Philosophy; Politics; Psychology; Recycling Technology; Russian Studies; Social Policy; Social Sciences; Sociology; Spanish; Sports Science; Statistics; Teaching English as a Foreign Language; Topographic Science; Welsh; Zoology.

TUITION FEES (2009/10)

See www.studentfinancewales.co.uk and **Chapter 1, 'Financing your course'.**

BURSARIES AND OTHER AWARDS
Excellence Scholarships

These awards worth £3,000 over the first two years are open to applicants who achieve AAA grades at A-level and are holding Swansea CF or UF. They are not available to Health Sciences or Social Work applicants who receive bursaries from their respective professional bodies.

Sporting Excellence Scholarships

These awards worth £1,000 are open to students who have achieved national status in the chosen sport.

Departmental awards
Business Management
One West Wales Chamber of Commerce Scholarship (£250) is available for the most promising first-year student.

Computer Science
The following awards last one year:

* Mertec Computer Award (£1,000) to the most promising first-year student
* JT Morgan Foundation Award (£500)
* Huw Griffiths Jones Award (£400)
* Coopers and Lybrand Award (£300)

Each of these awards is based on interview. There are also five cash prizes and five book prizes.

Engineering (Materials)
The following awards last one year:

* Departmental Scholarships (£500) to all new students with at least CCC at A-level or equivalent.
* Institute of Materials, Minerals and Mining Scholarships (£1,000 plus free institute membership and certificate) to students with at least ABB at A-level or equivalent.
* Armourers and Braziers Scholarship (£500 in addition to the Institute of Materials, Minerals and Mining Scholarship) to students with at least AAB at A-level or equivalent.
* Endowment Scholarships and departmental prizes (£100–500) available to new and current students.

Armourers and Braziers Scholarships are granted to students undertaking relevant vacation employment and a Tin Plate Workers Scholarship (£1,000) is awarded to the best second-year student seeking vacation employment with Corus (British Steel Tin Plate).

Geography
Two one-year scholarships (£500) are available to students with the highest tariff points in approved subjects.

History
There are David Jones Bursaries of up to £500 payable to students in financial difficulties, Alun Davis Travel Awards of up to £100 towards travel for academic or cultural purposes and three bursaries of £1,075 for first-year undergraduates.

Mathematics
Four one-year awards (£400) are based on A-level results or on a special interview.

Physics
Several awards lasting three or four years are based on school reports, interview, A-level grades and satisfactory progress in subsequent years. The Institute of Physics also make awards worth £1,000 per year. Contact Email physics@iop.org.

AWARDS FOR NON-EU STUDENTS
Scholarships and other awards are offered in all subject areas. Contact the Heads of Department.

INFORMATION AND APPROXIMATE FEES FOR NON-EU STUDENTS
Students come from over 100 countries. **English language entry requirement:** IELTS 6.0 (or equivalent). Pre-sessional English language courses are available with ongoing support during degree courses. **Fees:** £9,010–11,460. **Living costs:** £5,500–6,500.

University of Wales Swansea, Swansea SA2 8PP; tel: 01792 295111; www.swan.ac.uk.

SWANSEA METROPOLITAN UNIVERSITY

The university was founded in 1853 as an art school and later as a teacher training institute. It has three faculties, Applied Design and Engineering, Art and Design and Humanities. It is located on two campuses in Swansea at Mount Pleasant and Townhill.

DEGREE SUBJECTS OFFERED

Accountancy; Art and Design; Art History; Automotive Design; Building; Business; Civil Engineering; Computer courses; Counselling and Psychology; Education Studies; English; Environmental Conservation; Health and Social Care; Human Resources Management; Leisure Management; Marketing; Mechanical and Manufacturing Engineering; Marine Technology; Performing Arts; Photography; Photojournalism; Product design; Sport and Recreation Management; Tourism; Transport Management; Video.

TUITION FEES (2009/10)

See www.studentfinancewales.co.uk and **Chapter 1, 'Financing your course'**.

BURSARIES AND OTHER AWARDS

A non-means tested grant of £500 will be paid to students who live in excess of 45 miles from the Mount Pleasant campus.

INFORMATION AND APPROXIMATE FEES FOR NON-EU STUDENTS

English Language entry requirement: IELTS 6.0. **Fees:** £7,500. **Living costs:** £6,000–£7,000.

Swansea Metropolitan University, Mount Pleasant, Swansea SA1 6ED; tel: 01792 481000; www.smu.ac.uk.

TEESSIDE UNIVERSITY

The University of Teesside is located on a campus in the centre of Middlesbrough in the North-East of England. There are currently over 20,000 full-time and part-time students taking a range of degree and diploma courses, including sandwich options. Some opportunities exist for study abroad in Europe and the USA and all students have the opportunity to study a foreign language.

DEGREE SUBJECTS OFFERED

Accounting; Advertising; Art and Design; Biology; Business Studies; Chemistry; Computer Science; Criminology; Engineering; English; Food and Nutrition; Forensic Science; Health Studies; History; Human Resources Management; International Business; Law; Leisure Studies; Media Studies; Midwifery; Music; Nursing; Occupational Therapy; Photography; Physiotherapy; Psychology; Public Relations; Radiography; Social Studies; Social Work; Sociology; Sport Science; Tourism; Youth Studies.

TUITION FEES (2009/10)

£3,225.

BURSARIES AND OTHER AWARDS

All students required to pay tuition fees of £3,225 per year are eligible for some financial support. In addition to government grants, those students from households with an income of £25,000 or less will receive £1,025 for each year of undergraduate study. Lower amounts are paid depending on parental income.

Excellence and Subject Scholarships

At least 250 scholarships are available each year to students wishing to study in specific subject areas up to a maximum of £1,000. In addition, awards are also made to new applicants on the basis of achievement in examinations, eg 320 UCAS points (excluding AS-level and Key Skills), from 3 A-levels.

Elite Athletic Bursary Scheme

Financial support is offered to talented students who are competing at national level or who have the potential to do so. Bursaries of up to £2,000 may be used for coaching fees, travel expenses, competition entry, clothing, equipment etc.

AWARDS FOR NON-EU STUDENTS
International Bursary

A bursary of £1,500 is available for full-fee-paying students. Details are available from the Finance Department.

INFORMATION AND APPROXIMATE FEES FOR NON-EU STUDENTS

There are international students from over 75 countries. **English language entry requirement:** IELTS 6.0 (or equivalent); Law, English and humanities courses IELTS 6.5 (or equivalent); Engineering, Computing, and science and technology courses IELTS 5.5 (or equivalent); English tuition is available throughout the year while following a degree programme. **Fees:** £8,000–£8,500. **Living costs:** £5,500–£6,500.

University of Teesside, Middlesbrough, Tees Valley TS1 3BA; tel: 01642 218121; www. tees.ac.uk.

THAMES VALLEY UNIVERSITY

Thames Valley became a university in 1992, although it has over 130 years' experience in technical and vocational education. Founded as the Lady Byron School in 1860, from the start its focus has been on providing educational training designed to further the careers of its students. There is a student population of 25,500.

DEGREE SUBJECTS OFFERED

Accounting; Advertising; Arts and Multimedia Event Management; Ayurvedic Studies; Business Finance; Business Studies; Catering and Food Management; Culinary Arts Management; Design for Interactive Media; Digital Arts; Digital Broadcast Media; Digital Imaging; E-Business; Entrepreneurship; Film and Television Studies; Health and Community Psychology; Hospitality Management; Human Resource Management; Information Systems; Interactive Software Design; International Hotel Management; International Restaurant Management; Journalism; Languages; Law; Legal Studies; Leisure Management; Marketing; Media Arts; Media Journalism; Media Studies; Midwifery; Multimedia Computing; Music; New Media Journalism; Nursing; Photography; Psychology; Psychology with Counselling Theory; Radio Broadcasting; Sound and Music Recording; Sport, Health and Fitness Management; Tourism Management; Video Production; Web and E-Business Computing.

TUITION FEES (2009/10)
£3,225.

BURSARIES AND OTHER AWARDS
All full-time undergraduate students receiving higher education maintenance grants based on family income of between £25,000 and £40,000 will receive, in addition, a TVU annual £530 (2009/10) cash bursary. Students receiving the higher education maintenance grant with a family income of less than £25,000, will be eligible for a bursary of £1,060. Check with the university.

The university is often able to provide support for students experiencing particular financial difficulties. The student finance team administers Hardship Loans and Access Funds. These funds have been significantly increased in recent years. The university also receives Student Bursaries from a range of trusts including the Dr William Barry Trust, the Lord Molloy Fund and the Haymills Trust. Hospitality Scholarships such as the Dr William Barry Trust and the Savoy Educational Trust are only open to continuing students. Music Awards are given for specific instruments, eg double bass, horn etc. Students are strongly encouraged to discuss any financial problems they have with the student advice team – it is likely that the university will be able to help.

Subject Scholarships
These awards are offered in the 2nd year of the course to students following courses in Culinary Arts, Event Management, Hospitality and Catering and Music Composition and Performance.

INFORMATION AND APPROXIMATE FEES FOR NON-EU STUDENTS
There is a large number of international students. **English language entry requirement:** international foundation course IELTS 5.0 (or equivalent); undergraduate courses IELTS 5.5 (or equivalent). English language support is available, along with pre-sessional courses. **Fees:** £4,500–£7,800. **Living costs:** £9,500–£10,500.

Thames Valley University, St Mary's Road, London W5 5RF; tel: 0800 036 8888; www. tvu.ac.uk.

TRINITY UNIVERSITY COLLEGE (CARMARTHEN) (University of Wales)

Trinity University College is a church college founded in 1848 and is situated in Carmarthen, a small market town in West Wales.

DEGREE SUBJECTS OFFERED
Acting; Adolescent Psychology; Business Information Technology; Christianity and Community Studies; Community Development; Computing; Creative Writing; Early Years Education; Education Studies; Film; Film and Media; Fine Art; Health Studies; Health, Nutrition and Lifestyle; Information Systems Management; Multi-Agency Working; Nursery Management; Outdoor Education; Physical Education; Primary Education; Psychology; Religion and Society; Religious Education; Religious Studies; Social Inclusion; Special Education Needs; Sport Studies; Theatre Design and Production; Tourism; Welsh and Bilingual Practice in Early Years; Youth and Community Work.

TUITION FEES (2009/10)
See www.studentfinancewales.co.uk and **Chapter 1, 'Financing Your Course'.**

BURSARIES AND OTHER AWARDS
Scholarships
A number of competitive awards are offered under the following headings:

* Students applying from FE colleges – £500
* On-campus accommodation – £400
* Field courses, conferences, materials – £500
* Study through Welsh or Bilingual studies – £600 per year
* Use of facilities at the College nursery – £350.

Academic school awards
Awards worth £600 per year are offered covering studies as follows:

* Computing, Business, Tourism
* Education Studies, Social Inclusion
* Initial Teacher Training
* Theatre, Performance.
* Sport, Health, Outdoor Education.
* Theology, Religious Studies.

All awards take into consideration students from low income households.

INFORMATION AND APPROXIMATE FEES FOR NON-EU STUDENTS
English language entry requirement: IELTS 6.0 (or equivalent). **Fees:** £6,500. **Living costs:** £6,000–£7,000.

Trinity University College, College Road, Carmarthen SA31 3EP; tel: 01267 676767; www.trinity-cm.ac.uk.

ULSTER UNIVERSITY

The University of Ulster was established in 1984 and is located on four campuses. The Coleraine Campus is a short distance from the town and the nearby resorts of Portstewart and Portrush. The Jordonstown Campus is located a few miles north of Belfast. The Belfast Campus is close to the centre of the city, housing the School of Art and Design and the Magee Campus is in Londonderry.

DEGREE SUBJECTS OFFERED
Accounting; American Studies; Applied Languages; Architecture; Art and Design; Biology; Biomedical Sciences; Business Studies; Chiropractic; Combined Arts; Communication Studies; Computer Science; Construction; Consumer Studies; Dietetics; Drama; Economics; Engineering; English; Environmental Health; Environmental Studies; Food and Nutrition; French; Geography; German; Health and Social Care; History; Hospitality Management; Housing Management; Human Resource Management; International Business; International Politics; Irish; Irish History; Law; Leisure Studies; Linguistics; Marine Science; Marketing; Mathematics; Music; Nursing; Occupational Therapy; Optometry; Physiotherapy; Podiatry; Politics; Property Investment; Psychology; Quantity Surveying; Radiography; Retail Management; Social Administration; Social Policy; Social Work; Sociology; Spanish; Sport Studies; Travel and Tourism.

TUITION FEES (2009/10)
£3,225. See **Chapter 1, 'Financing Your Course'.**

See Chapters 2, 4 and 6 for additional awards, applicable to all universities

BURSARIES AND OTHER AWARDS

Means-tested grants and loans are available; the information not available at the time of publication. Check with university.

Elite Athletic Scholarships

Sports Scholarships worth £100 will be offered to world-class performers.

INFORMATION AND APPROXIMATE FEES FOR NON-EU STUDENTS

There are international students from over 40 countries presently studying at the university. **English language entry requirement:** IELTS 6.0 (or equivalent). **Fees:** £8,540. **Living costs:** £5,500–£6,500.

University of Ulster, Cromore Road, Coleraine, County Londonderry BT52 1SA; tel: 028 7032 4221; www.ulster.ac.uk.

UNIVERSITY COLLEGE LONDON (UCL)

Founded in 1826, UCL is one of the largest of the London University colleges with a student population of 21,100. It is situated close to the centre of London, in Bloomsbury near to the British Museum.

DEGREE SUBJECTS OFFERED

Anatomy; Anthropology; Archaeology; Architecture; Art and Design; Astronomy; Astrophysics; Audiology; Biochemistry; Biology; Biomedical Sciences; Biotechnology; Bulgarian; Chemical Physics; Chemistry; Classics; Construction Management; Czech; Dutch; Earth and Space Science; East European Studies; Ecology; Economics; Engineering (Biochemical; Chemical; Civil; Electrical/Electronic; Environmental; Geomatic; Marine; Mechanical; Structural); Engineering and Business Finance; English; Environmental Geosciences; European Social and Political Studies; Exploration Geophysics; Finnish; French; Genetics; Geography; Geology; Geophysics; German; Greek; Hebrew; Hispanic Studies; History; History and Philosophy of Science; Human Sciences; Hungarian; Icelandic; Immunology; Information Management for Business; Italian; Jewish Studies; Latin; Latin American Studies; Law; Linguistics; Management; Mathematics; Medicine; Natural Sciences; Naval Architecture; Neuroscience; Palaeobiology; Pharmacology; Philosophy; Physics; Physiology; Planetary Science; Polish; Psychology; Romanian; Russian; Scandinavian Studies; Science Communication and Policy; Serbian and Croatian Studies; Slovak; Spanish; Speech Sciences; Statistics; Town and Country Planning; Ukrainian; Viking Studies; Zoology.

TUITION FEES (2009/10)

£3,225.

BURSARIES AND OTHER AWARDS

UCL has a wide range of scholarships and financial support at undergraduate and graduate degree level, funded by UCL as well as by registered charities and individual donors, the UK government, international governments and agencies, and by corporate sponsors.

Listed here is a selection of central schemes. In addition, many departments offer scholarships and awards for their prospective and current students. For a full list and comprehensive information about scholarships and funding at UCL, please visit www.ucl.ac.uk/scholarships.

Students receiving the government maintenance grant will receive a UCL Bursary equal to at least half of their grant. Students with household incomes of £16,200–£14,001 will receive a bursary of £1,650; £14,000–11,901 a bursary of £2,200; less than £11,900 a bursary of £2,775. Students following a four-year MSci or MEng programme or a course involving a year abroad in the fourth year will receive an award equal to 100% of their grant or double their UCL Bursary, whichever is the greater. Check with the university.

SCHOLARSHIPS
UCL – Africa Educational Trust Undergraduate International Outreach Bursaries
Two full scholarships per year providing tuition fees, maintenance, international economy travel and further benefits for the duration of an undergraduate degree programme. Open to prospective UCL undergraduates, nationals and residents of Africa, schooled in Africa, who lack the financial means to study at UCL. Candidates must apply for admission by January.

UCL – United World Colleges Undergraduate International Outreach Bursaries
Two full scholarships per year providing tuition fees, maintenance, international economy travel and further benefits for the duration of an undergraduate degree programme. Open to final-year UWC students (except UWC KaMhlaba) liable to pay overseas tuition fees, admitted to UCL for undergraduate studies, who lack the financial means to study at UCL. Candidates must apply for admission by January.

AWARDS FOR NON-EU STUDENTS
UCL Hong Kong Alumni Scholarships
(Professor Denys Holland and Cowan Cheung Scholarship, UCL Hong Kong Alumni Scholarship, Vinson Chu Charitable Foundation Scholarship).

One scholarship is awarded each year, worth £10,000 toward fees for a maximum of four years. Open to prospective UCL undergraduates resident in Hong Kong and other regions of the People's Republic of China. Application deadline 1st April.

Denys Holland Undergraduate Scholarship
One scholarship annually worth around £9,000-10,000 (2007/08: £9,300) tenable for up to 3 years. Open to prospective UCL undergraduates from any country. The application deadline is 1st August.

Ernest Hecht UCL Undergraduate Scholarships
Two overseas and two UK scholarships at £2,000 and £500 respectively are available annually to prospective undergraduates from Latin America and to prospective undergraduates from the UK intending to pursue Spanish and Latin American Studies at UCL. The application deadline is 1st April.

UCL Global Excellence Scholarships
Sixteen scholarships of £5,000 each awarded to the best prospective undergraduate and graduate students from different regions of the world. Candidates holding an offer of admission to UCL will be considered. For deadlines, see www.ucl.ac.uk/scholarships.

POSTGRADUATE AWARDS
UCL Futures Scholarship
One scholarship of £10,000 open to former or final-year UCL undergraduates continuing into Master's study at UCL. Candidates must apply by 1st March.

Karim Rida Said Foundation/UCL Joint Scholarships
Up to six scholarships including tuition fees plus maintenance are available annually to prospective graduate students from Iraq, Jordan, Lebanon, Palestine or Syria. Candidates must apply by 31st January (1st May for UK resident applicants).

See Chapters 2, 4 and 6 for additional awards, applicable to all universities

OSI UCL Chevening Scholarships
Five scholarships annually consisting of tuition fees, maintenance and other agreed allowances including return air travel, are open to prospective students from Macedonia, Moldova, certain regions of Russia, or Serbia admitted to selected Master's Programmes at UCL's School of Slavonic and East European Studies (SSEES). Candidates must apply to local OSI offices by mid-February.

Abbey Master's Scholarship
Ten scholarships of £5,000 each are available to prospective Master's students. Candidates must apply by 1st March.

Gay Clifford Fees Awards
Four awards providing £2,500 toward fees available to female students intending to pursue Master's degree studies in the faculties of Arts and Humanities or Social and Historical Sciences. Candidates must apply by 1st March.

UCL Shell Centenary Scholarships and UCL Shell Chevening Scholarships
Eight full scholarships providing tuition fees, maintenance and other agreed allowances including return air travel, available to prospective Master's students from non-OECD countries. Candidates must apply by 1st March.

UCL Celebration 60 Scholarship
One tuition fee scholarship available to prospective Master's students from Hong Kong. Candidates must apply by end February.

UCL Marshall Scholarship
One scholarship providing full tuition fees and a maintenance stipend for up to two years is available to prospective graduate students from the USA. Details available from the Marshall Aid Commemoration Commission.

British Chevening Scholarships
Full or partial scholarships are available to prospective graduate students. Candidates must normally apply 12 months before the start of the relevant academic year.

UCL Graduate Research Scholarships
Fifteen scholarships providing standard UK/EU graduate fees plus a maintenance stipend (2008/09: £14,988) available to MPhil/PhD and EngD research students from any country. Candidates must apply by mid-February.

UCL Overseas Research Scholarships (UCL-ORS)
Ca. 40 scholarships providing fees equivalent to the difference between overseas fees and the standard graduate UK/EU fee rate are available to prospective MPhil/PhD and EngD research students liable to pay fees at the overseas rate. Candidates must apply by mid-February. A second round of applications may be held with a deadline at the start of May.

UK-China Scholarships for Excellence
Up to 10 scholarships providing full fees, plus a maintenance stipend and international travel funded by UCL, the UK Department of Innovation, Universities and Skills (DIUS) and the China Scholarships Council (CSC) are available to prospective MPhil/PhD students from China. Candidates must apply for UCL-ORS by mid-February, and to DIUS and CSC by mid-March.

Dorothy Hodgkin Postgraduate Awards
Awards, funded by the UK Research Councils and corporate sponsors, provide funding to cover full tuition fees and an annual maintenance stipend of (2008/09: £14,988) and are available to prospective M.Phil./PhD and EngD students from developing countries. Over the past years, UCL has normally secured 10-12 such awards per year. Candidates must apply by mid-February.

Frederick Bonnart-Braunthal Scholarships

Two scholarships of £12,000 each are available to prospective MPhil/PhD students seeking to explore the nature of religious, racial and cultural prejudices, and find ways of combating them. Candidates must apply by 1st March.

INFORMATION AND APPROXIMATE FEES FOR NON-EU STUDENTS

Students (34% of the total student body) are from countries outside the UK. **English language entry requirement:** engineering and science courses IELTS 6.5 (or equivalent); arts courses IELTS 7.0 (or equivalent); Speech Science and Law IELTS 7.5 (or equivalent). **Fees:** arts and social science courses £12,280; Law £12,280; science courses, Engineering, Archaeology, Fine Art, Built Environment and Architecture £16,080; Medicine £23,980. **Living costs:** £8,000.

USEFUL WEBSITES

* Information on undergraduate degree programmes and entry: www.ucl.ac.uk/prospectus
* Information on tuition fees: www.ucl.ac.uk/current-students/tuition-fees
* Information on financial support: www.ucl.ac.uk/scholarships.

University College London, Gower Street, London WC1E 6BT; tel: 020 7679 3000; www. ucl.ac.uk.

UHI MILLENNIUM INSTITUTE

UHI Millennium Institute provides diploma, degree courses and research opportunities throughout the Highlands and Islands of Scotland. There are UHI campuses located in: Dunoon Argyll, Dingwall, Inverness, Isle of Lewis, Fort William, Elgin, Orkney, Scalloway Shetland, Thurso, Perth, Isle of Skye, Dunstaffnage, Lerwick Shetland, and one associated institution: the Sustainable Development Research Centre, Forres Moray. "The Highlands and Islands of Scotland are one of the most beautiful and unspoilt regions in Europe, so no matter which UHI campus you choose, your learning will benefit from the natural environment around you."

DEGREE SUBJECTS OFFERED

UHI specialises in offering courses in diverse subject areas, relevant to the needs of business, industry and community alike offering more than 30 undergraduate degrees and 15 postgraduate degrees including: Adventure Tourism Management; Aircraft Engineering; Business Administration; Child and Youth Studies; Computing; Contemporary Textiles; Culture Studies of the Highlands and Islands; Engineering with Renewable Energy; Environmental Management; Fine Art; Golf Management; Gaelic and Traditional Music; Marine Science; Mechanical Engineering; Music; Natural and Environmental Science; Rural Health Studies; Sustainable Rural Development; Sustainable Construction; Sustainable Forest Management; Theological Studies; Tourism. Please check www.uhi.ac.uk for more details.

TUITION FEES

Students domiciled in Scotland receive free tuition. See www.saas.gov.uk and **Chapter 1 'Financing Your Course'**.

BURSARIES AND OTHER AWARDS
Gaelic Bursaries
Students entering their first year of a UHI Gaelic-medium degree are eligible to apply for one of 11 Gaelic Bursaries. Students may be based at Inverness College, Sabhal Mòr Ostaig UHI, Lews Castle College UHI or Argyll College UHI. The bursaries are jointly funded by UHI Millennium Institute, the Highland Council, Western Isles Council and Argyll and Bute Council. Each bursary is worth £1,000. Award criteria are reviewed annually.

ILA Scotland offer £200 and £500 learner account bursaries; see www.ilascotland.org.uk/ for more information.

Scottish means-tested grants are available for specific groups of students, more information from the SAAS website at www.saas.gov.uk.

INFORMATION AND APPROXIMATE FEES FOR NON-EU STUDENTS
UHI has a diverse student community and welcomes students from all over the world. **English language entry requirement:** IELTS 6.0 (or equivalent). **Fees:** £6,410–7,565.

UHI Millennium Institute, Caledonia House, 63 Academy Street, Inverness IV1 1LU; tel: 01463 279,000; www.uhi.ac.uk.

UNIVERSITY COLLEGE PLYMOUTH ST MARK AND ST JOHN (MARJON)

This Church of England College was founded in 1923 and moved to Plymouth in 1973, being located on a large site overlooking Plymouth, Plymouth Sound and Dartmoor. It is usually referred to as 'Marjon' and is a leading provider of teacher training courses in the south west. It is situated about five miles from the city centre and has a student population of 3500.

DEGREE SUBJECTS OFFERED
Art and Design; Children's Physical Education; Community Studies; Drama Studies; English; English Language; English Literary Studies; Geography; History; Information Technology; Leisure and Tourism; Management Studies; Media Production; Media Studies; Public Relations; Sociology; Sport and Recreation; Sports Media; Sports Science; Sustainable Development; Teacher Training (Primary/Secondary); Theology; Theology and Philosophy; Working with Children and Young People.

TUITION FEES (2009/10)
£3,225.

BURSARIES AND OTHER AWARDS
Until 2010 Marjon is offering all new and part-time students a free wireless-enabled laptop.

Scholarships
Sports Scholarships are available to students who are competing at national level in their sport. The award equates to £1,500 that may be used towards paying for campus accommodation. A cash equivalent may be offered to students not requiring campus accommodation. Students would then

be expected to use the money for training, equipment and travel expenses relating to their sport. Students receiving scholarships have free access to all the sports facilities on campus.

Bursaries
Sports Bursaries worth £500 are available to students who are competing below national level but who have the potential to achieve this standard. Students are expected to use the money for training, equipment and travel expenses relating to their sport. Students receiving bursaries have free access to all the sports facilities on campus.

Contracts
Students receiving either award are expected to sign a contract agreeing to represent the college in the British Universities Sports Association competitions and to promote the work of the college locally and nationally in negotiation with the Director of Sport. All awards are reviewed on an annual basis.

Teachers' Awards
Teachers from European countries enrolling for short courses may be eligible for a grant.

INFORMATION AND APPROXIMATE FEES FOR NON-EU STUDENTS
English language entry requirement: IELTS 6.5 (or equivalent). **Fees:** £8,500. **Living costs:** £7,500–£8,500.

University College Plymouth St Mark and St John, Derriford Road, Plymouth PL6 8BH; tel: 01752 636890; www.marjon.ac.uk.

UNIVERSITY OF THE ARTS LONDON

The University of the Arts consists of six internationally renowned colleges: Camberwell College of Arts; Central Saint Martins College of Art and Design; Chelsea College of Art and Design; London College of Communication; London College of Fashion; Wimbledon College of Art. It is Europe's largest university covering this field with more than 24,000 students.

DEGREE SUBJECTS OFFERED
Acting; Book Arts and Crafts; Ceramics; Computer Animation; Conservation; Cosmetic Science; Creative Writing for Film and TV; Directing; Drawing; Fashion Design; Fashion Photography; Film and Video; Fine Art; Graphic Design; Illustration; Interior Design; Jewellery Design; Journalism; Knitwear; Marketing; Media Studies; Painting; Photography; Product Design; Public Relations; Retail Management; Sculpture; Sound Arts and Design; Spatial Design; Technical Effects and Make-up; Textile Design; Theatre Design; Three-dimensional Design; Tourism and Travel Enterprise.

TUITION FEES (2009/10)
£3,225.

BURSARIES AND OTHER AWARDS
All full-time students who receive the full maintenance grant will be able to apply for an Access Bursary of £1,000. Students who receive the maintenance grant in full will also be entitled to a £319 standard bursary. If the application for an Access Bursary is not successful you will be considered for an award from the Access to Learning Fund (ALF). This award is given by the government to help students experiencing financial hardship. Check with the university.

See Chapters 2, 4 and 6 for additional awards, applicable to all universities

Foyer Accommodation Bursaries

These awards are open to homeless 10–25 year olds to help them to realise their full potential.

Some scholarships are available to support students with outstanding ability. Contact the university.

BBFC Film and Video Bursaries (London College of Communication)

Three bursaries have been established through a gift from the British Board of Film Classification. The successful applicants will receive a total of £6,000 over three years (two instalments per year of £1,000).

To be eligible, candidates must be accepted on to the BA Film and Video degree course. Applications will be judged according to financial need and academic potential.

BPIF Educational Scholarships

These awards of £2,500 are funded by the British Printing Industries Federation, the Printers' Charitable Corporation and the union Unite. In 2007, 11 scholarships were awarded. To be eligible, students must be:

* UK citizens
* Aged 16–30
* Accepted on any course at the university associated with the printing and graphic arts industries.

All applications must be countersigned by an appropriate referee, such as a course lecturer. Applications should be made by 31 March. Award decisions will be made in May and based on financial need. Contact Terry Ulrick on 01444 831918 or terryulrick@tucommunications.co.uk for further information.

INFORMATION AND APPROXIMATE FEES FOR NON-EU STUDENTS

There is a large number of international students. **English language entry requirement:** IELTS 6.0 (or equivalent); Fashion Promotion, Acting, Directing IELTS 7.5 (or equivalent). Language Centre courses in academic English run for 12, 24, 34 or 36 weeks. **Fees:** degree courses £6,800–£10,500. **Living costs:** £9,500–£10,500.

University of the Arts London, 65 Davies Street, London W1K 5DA; tel: 020 7514 6000; www.arts.ac.uk.

WARWICK UNIVERSITY

The University of Warwick is a campus university situated outside Coventry that was founded in 1965. It has become one of the most popular UK universities and excels in teaching and research quality. There is a total student population of about 16,000 with postgraduates forming a third of this total. All first-year students are guaranteed accommodation on campus. Off-campus accommodation is available in Coventry, Leamington and Warwick.

DEGREE SUBJECTS OFFERED

Accounting and Finance; Ancient History; Biochemistry; Biological Sciences; Biomedical Chemistry; Business Studies; Chemical Biology; Chemistry; Classical Archaeology; Classical Civilisation; Comparative American Studies; Computer Science; Creative Writing; Early Childhood Studies; Economics; Education (Primary); Electronics; Engineering (Civil; Communication; Computer Systems;

Electronic/Electrical; General; Manufacturing; Mechanical); English; European Law; European Literature; Film and Literature; Film with Television Studies; French; Gender Studies; German; History (Modern; Modern European; Renaissance); History of Art; Industrial Economics; International Studies; Italian; Latin Literature; Law; Management Sciences; Mathematics; Medicine; Microbiology; Operational Research; Philosophy; Physics; Politics; Psychology; Social Policy; Sociology; Statistics; Theatre Studies; Virology.

TUITION FEES (2009/10)
£3,225.

BURSARIES AND OTHER AWARDS
Warwick Undergraduate Aid Programme (WUAP)
WUAP is available only to home full-time undergraduates commencing study in 2009/10 (not part-time, MBChB or PGCE students). WUAP is a non-repayable support package for students whose family income is less than £36,000 per year. These students will also be offered a Warwick Scholarship worth £1,800 or £1,100 per annum for the length of the course (3 or 4 years).

Work/study opportunities: For students who are eligible for WUAP but do not qualify for a scholarship at Warwick there will be opportunities to earn £1,000 per year through work/study. Students will gain valuable work experience, as well as funding towards their studies, by working approximately five hours per week during term time.

Further details of the WUAP scheme can be obtained from the Student Funding office; tel: 024 7615 0096; studentfunding@warwick.ac.uk.

Music Scholarships
Awards to the value of £450 per year will be offered each year to full-time students of any degree subject entering the university. The scholarships will be awarded for ability in musical performance to be judged on the basis of trials to be held at the university.

In addition, the Warwick Choral Trust and All Saints Church, Leamington Spa both offer an Organ Scholarship to the value of £300 per year, plus travel expenses. The scholarships are tenable at the university by full-time registered students on the basis of a trial to be held at St Mary's Church, Warwick and All Saints Church, Leamington Spa respectively.

Application forms and further details of these scholarships are available from the Secretary, Music Centre; tel: 024 7652 3799.

Lord Rootes Memorial Fund Awards
The Lord Rootes Memorial Fund provides funding to support individuals and groups of students carrying out projects involving observation and intelligent use of experience in a scientific, cultural or business context or examining problems of economic, environmental, social or technological significance. Each award ranges from £100–5,000 and awards are only available for projects that do not receive credit from or fulfil requirements of a degree course. Further information is available at www2.warwick.ac.uk/insite/info/learningteaching/rootes.

Sports Bursaries
Bursaries of up to £500 are available to individuals who are competing at the top level in their chosen sport. Warwick Sport Bursaries of £500 are awarded to athletes performing at a senior national or international level, Warwick Sports Scholarships of £300 are awarded to athletes competing at a junior national or international level, and Warwick Sport Awards of £100 are awarded to athletes competing at a senior county level or who are ranked in the top three in British universities in individual sports. As part of the bursaries athletes also receive free membership to

the fitness suite, discounted physiotherapy and sports massages, performance mentoring, access to a sports science programme and nutritional advice. Warwick Sport Assistance Bursaries are also available for those athletes that are competing at a regional level to assist with entry fees and transport costs. Further details are available from the Sports Development Coordinator; tel: 024 7657 5112.

AWARDS FOR NON-EU STUDENTS
Scholarships
Twenty scholarships each worth £2,000 to overseas students from the countries and regions listed below under Postgraduate Awards. In addition there is a MORSE scholarship (Mathematics, Operational Research, Statistics and Economics) worth £3,000.

POSTGRADUATE AWARDS
Awards for Taught Masters courses are offered in several subject areas, including Business, Computer Science, Engineering, French Studies, Law, Psychology and Statistics, in addition to which there are special awards for overseas students from Argentina, Brazil, the Caribbean, Colombia, East Africa, Eastern Europe, Ghana, India, Japan, Korea, Latin America, Mexico, the Middle East, Nigeria, North Africa, North America, Pakistan, Russia, South Africa, South Asia, South-East Asia, sub-Saharan Africa, Taiwan, Thailand and Turkey.

INFORMATION AND APPROXIMATE FEES FOR NON-EU STUDENTS
There are 3,500 international students. **English language entry requirement:** science courses IELTS 6.0 (or equivalent); arts and MORSE courses IELTS 6.5 (or equivalent); Social Studies and Business courses IELTS 7.0 (or equivalent). English support is available. **Fees:** £10,250–£13,350; science courses £11,100; Medicine: pre-clinical £10,800, clinical £19,900. **Living costs:** £6,500–£7,500.

University of Warwick, Coventry CV4 7AL; tel: 024 7652 3723; www.warwick.ac.uk.

WESTMINSTER UNIVERSITY

The University of Westminster has a student population of 22,000 and is located at three West End campuses and one campus at Harrow, each campus being the dedicated base of a set of subjects. The Cavendish Campus is home to Biosciences, Complementary Therapies, Electronics and Communications Technology and Mathematics; the Marylebone base houses Architecture, the Built Environment and the Business School; and Social Sciences and English courses are based in Regent Street. The Harrow Campus houses the School of Media, and Art and Design as well as the School of Computer Science and the Harrow Business School.

DEGREE SUBJECTS OFFERED
Applied Biology; Arabic; Architecture; Art and Design; Artificial Intelligence; Biochemistry; Biological Sciences; Biomedical Sciences; Biotechnology; Building Engineering; Business Studies; Chinese; Commercial Law; Commercial Music; Computing; Construction Management; Electronic Engineering; Engineering; English Language and Literature; Environmental Science; European Legal Studies; Fashion Merchandising; Film and TV; French; Geography; German; Health Sciences; History; Housing Management; Human Nutrition; Human Physiology; Information Systems; International Business; Italian; Law; Leisure Management; Mathematics; Media Studies (Journalism; Radio; TV); Microbiology; Nutrition; Photographic Arts; Physiology; Politics; Psychology; Quantity Surveying; Social Science; Sociology; Software Engineering; Spanish; Sport and Exercise Science; Statistics; Tourism; Town Planning.

TUITION FEE (2009/10)
£3,225.

BURSARIES AND OTHER AWARDS
Students in receipt of any part of the maintenance grant up to a household income of £50,022 will receive a £319 bursary.

Applicants from Iceland, Liechtenstein, Norway, Switzerland and Turkey should contact the university concerning awards to Home and EU students.

Gold/Silver Scholarships
These awards are based on the scores achieved at A-level from AAA-BBB (or equivalent).

Progression Scholarships
These are open to students entering the second year of their course of study and are worth up to £3,000.

The university will be significantly extending its scholarship scheme to attract students who have the potential to achieve academic excellence. This will also include part-time students. Some scholarships will be available for foundation-level courses. The awards will be a mix of cash, fee waivers and accommodation credits.

AWARDS FOR NON-EU STUDENTS
Diplomatic Scholarships
These scholarships are worth a 50% fee waiver for undergraduate courses and are open to the children of diplomats based in London.

East Timor Scholarship
This is a full tuition waiver award for a student from East Timor, with accommodation, airfare to and from London and living expenses during the duration of the course.

Ken Bird Memorial Scholarship
This award gives a full tuition fee waiver plus accommodation, preference being given to female students from India or Sri Lanka wishing to study a full-time degree course in a technology-based subject.

University of Westminster Scholarships
These are awarded to applicants from the Scindia School or the Lala Lajpat Rai College Mumbai. They are awarded for academic excellence.

Gambia Biomedical Scholarship
This is open to applicants from the Gambia on the HND/BSc Biomedical Science course.

POSTGRADUATE AWARDS
Applicants are recommended to obtain a copy of the booklet *Scholarships at the University of Westminster*, in which details are published of over 60 international and postgraduate awards. These include country-specific awards relevant to students from the following countries: Balkan states; Brazil; Bulgaria; Central America; Chile; Colombia; Denmark; Ecuador; Egypt; Estonia; Finland; Greece; Guinea; Hungary; India; Indonesia; Kazakhstan; Korea; Laos; Latvia; Mexico; Norway; Peru; Poland; Portugal; Tajikistan; Turkey; Ukraine; Uruguay; the USA; Venezuela; Vietnam.

See Chapters 2, 4 and 6 for additional awards, applicable to all universities

INFORMATION AND APPROXIMATE FEES FOR NON-EU STUDENTS

Students come from 148 countries (51% Asian). **English language entry requirement:** IELTS 6.0 (or equivalent). International foundation certificate courses are available focusing on the Built Environment, Mathematics and Computing, or Social Sciences and Literature. **Fees:** £9,400–£10,000. **Living costs:** £9,500–£10,500.

University of Westminster, 111 New Cavendish Street, London W1W 6UW; tel: 020 7911 5000; www.wmin.ac.uk.

WEST OF SCOTLAND UNIVERSITY

The university offers courses to over 11,000 students with campuses in Ayr, Dumfries, Hamilton and Paisley. The university offers a wide range of sandwich courses with paid placements and has several links with universities in Europe.

DEGREE SUBJECTS OFFERED

Accounting; Biological Sciences; Biology; Business Economics; Business Information Technology; Business Studies; Chemical Engineering; Chemistry; Civil Engineering; Computer Sciences; Design; Economics; Education; English; Environmental Studies; Forensic Science; French; German; Health Studies; Human Resources Management; Law; Marketing; Media Studies; Midwifery; Music; Nursing; Pharmaceutical Science; Physics; Politics; Psychology; Social Sciences; Social Work; Sociology; Sport Studies; Tourism.

TUITION FEES (2009/10)

Students domiciled in Scotland receive free tuition. See www.saas.gov.uk and **Chapter 1 'Financing Your Course'.**

BURSARIES AND OTHER AWARDS

Young Student Bursaries of up to £2,150 are available to Scottish students from low-income families. With sponsorship from commercial companies and industrial partners, the university offers a small number of scholarships of £500 each to full-time students in their first year on undergraduate programmes.

INFORMATION AND APPROXIMATE FEES FOR NON-EU STUDENTS

There are 700 international students. **English language entry requirement:** IELTS 6.0 (or equivalent). An English language foundation course is available. **Fees:** £7,500–£8,300. **Living costs:** £6,500–£7,000.

University of the West of Scotland, Paisley PA1 2BE; tel: 0141 848 3293; www.uws.ac.uk.

WINCHESTER UNIVERSITY

The University of Winchester is a new university originally founded as a college in 1840 and given university status in 2005. It is a university on a human scale, with under 6,000 students studying a broad range of programmes at both undergraduate and postgraduate level. The King Alfred Campus is located close to the centre of Winchester.

DEGREE SUBJECTS OFFERED

American Literature; American Studies; Ancient and Medieval Archaeology and Art; Applied Theatre; Archaeological Practice; Archaeology; Arts Management; Business Management; Childhood, Youth and Community Studies; Choreography and Dance; Creative Writing; Design for Digital Media; Drama; Education Studies; English; English Literature and Language; Ethics and Spirituality; Event Management; Film and Cinema Technologies; Film Studies; Finance and Economics, Global Tourism; Health and Wellbeing; History; History and the Medieval World/Modern World; Resource Management; Information Technology; Journalism; Law; Marketing; Media Production; Media Studies; Performance Management; Performing Arts; Politics and Global Studies; Psychology; Public Service Management; Social Care Studies; Social Work; Sports Development; Sports Science; Sports Studies; Stage Management; Street Arts; Sustainable Development Management; Teaching (Primary Education); Theology and Religious Studies; Tourism and Management.

TUITION FEES (2009/10)

£3,225.

BURSARIES AND OTHER AWARDS

Winchester Bursary

All students entitled to a full maintenance grant and whose household income is £25,000 or below will receive an annual bursary of £820. Students with a household income between £25,000 and £39,333 will receive an annual bursary of £410.

Winchester Scholarship

All full-time, UK or EU, undergraduate students are eligible to receive a Winchester Scholarship which aims to assist with day-to-day living and study expenses. The award is payable in May of each year of study. The award is worth £175 in the first year, £100 in the second, £100 in the third and £100 in the fourth (if applicable).

Winchester Partner Schools Scholarships

Students applying to the university from partner schools may be eligible for an award of £105 and a further £205 if applying via the compact scheme, paid in the first year of study.

King Alfred Scholarships

These are open to students under 25 who have been looked after in care for a minimum of 13 weeks since the age of 14 and who have now left care. The awards are worth £2,050 and paid in the first year of study.

Academic Achievement Awards

These are open to UK or EU students, studying a specific course on a full time basis, who have achieved 360 UCAS points or more. The award is worth up to £4,000 across a 3 year course and is designed to reward consistent high achievers.

For full details and eligibility criteria see the university website.

Excellence Awards

These are open to UK or EU students, studying any fulltime, undergraduate course, who have excelled in Music or Sport. The award is worth up to £4,000 across a 3 year course and is to be used to support your studies and further your achievement in your field of excellence.

For full details and eligibility criteria see the university website.

AWARDS FOR NON-EU STUDENTS

On a competitive basis, the University offers a small number of Bursaries each year for non-EU students on full time undergraduate and postgraduate programmes. Bursaries constitute a yearly reduction in tuition fees of no more than £1,000 per annum normally for the duration of the course. The deadline for applications is normally the second week of June. Apply to Course.Enquiries@winchester.ac.uk

INFORMATION AND APPROXIMATE FEES FOR NON-EU STUDENTS
English language entry requirement: IELTS 6.0 (or equivalent). **Fees:** £7,890. The tuition fees shown are for a single year of study in 2009/10 for international students. Please remember that tuition fees will increase each year, although normally only at a rate equivalent to inflation. **Living costs:** £7,500–£8,000.

University of Winchester, Hampshire SO22 4NR; tel: 01962 841515; www.winchester.ac.uk.

WOLVERHAMPTON UNIVERSITY

The University of Wolverhampton is a multi-million pound infrastructure of new buildings, technology and teaching methods. There are around 24,000 students who benefit from a wide range of work-related courses and facilities. A futuristic new Technology Centre recently opened with specialist IT, engineering, design and media facilities. It includes 600 high-specification computers and is one of the leading IT facilities of its kind in Europe. The new Walsall Sports Centre opened in 2004. Supported by Sport England, it has excellent new facilities and houses a Judo Centre of Excellence. It is being used to train judo hopefuls for the 2012 Olympic Games.

DEGREE SUBJECT AREAS OFFERED
Accounting and Finance; Amenity Horticulture; American Studies; Animal Management; Architectural Property Development; Architectural Design and Technology; Art and Design; Biochemistry; Biological Sciences; Biomedical Sciences; Biotechnology; Building; Building Surveying; Business and Management; Complementary Therapies; Computer Aided Design; Computing and IT; Conductive Education; Construction; Creative and Professional Writing; Criminology and Criminal Justice; Deaf Studies; Design and Technology; Digital Media; Early Childhood Studies; Education Studies; Engineering (Automotive Systems; Electronics and Communication; Civil; Mechanical; Virtual); English; Entertainment Industries Management; Environmental Health; Environmental Science and Management; Equine Studies; Event and Venue Management; Exercise Science; Forensic Science; French; Genetics and Molecular Biology; German; Geography; Health Sciences; History; Human Resource Management; Illustration; International Hospitality Management; Interior Architectural Design; Interpreting (British Sign Language); Journalism; Law; Linguistics; Marketing; Mathematics and Statistics; Mechatronics; Media; Microbiology; Multimedia; Nursing and Midwifery; PE; Performing Arts (Dance, Drama and Music); Pharmaceutical Science; Pharmacy; Philosophy; Photography; Physiology; Policing; Politics; Product Design; Psychology; Public Health; Quantity Surveying; Rehabilitation Studies; Religious Studies; Social Policy; Social Work; Sociology; Spanish; Special Needs and Inclusion; Sport and Exercise Science; Science; Teaching (Primary, Secondary and Post-Compulsory); Tourism Management; Video and Film; Virtual Reality; War Studies.

TUITION FEES (2009/10)
£3225.

BURSARIES AND OTHER AWARDS
Students on a full time degree course receiving maximum grant (family income of £25,000 or less) receive a Start Right Bursary of £500. Students from households with incomes between £25,001 and £35,000 receive a Start Right Bursary of £300.

There is also a Sports Excellence Scholarship of up to £3,000 for those competing at national or international level.

AWARDS FOR INTERNATIONAL STUDENTS
Excellence Scholarships worth £2,000 are available to applicants based on outstanding academic achievement.

INFORMATION AND FEES FOR INTERNATIONAL STUDENTS
English language entry requirement: IELTS 6.0 (or equivalent). English courses are available over one month or up to a year. **Fees:** undergraduate courses £8,850; postgraduate £9,150. Living costs approx £7,000.

University of Wolverhampton, Wulfruna Street, Wolverhampton WV1 1LY; tel: 0800 953 3222; website www.wlv.ac.uk.

WORCESTER UNIVERSITY

The University of Worcester is a new university established from a former university college located on the outskirts of Worcester. Eight thousand students follow courses in science, the social sciences, humanities and education.

DEGREE SUBJECTS OFFERED
American Studies; Archaeology and Heritage Studies; Art and Design; Biology; Business; Computing; Early Childhood Studies; Education (Primary); Environmental Science; Film Studies; Forensic and Applied Biology; Geography; Health Studies; Information Technology; Marketing; Media; Midwifery; Outdoor Recreation Management; Physical Education; Psychology; Sociology; Sports Coaching; Sports Studies.

TUITION FEES (2008/09)
£3,225.

BURSARIES AND OTHER AWARDS
Students in receipt of the full maintenance grant will receive a university bursary of £750. £625 and £500 will go respectively to those students on a partial grant and those receiving no grant. These bursaries are non repayable.

University of Worcester Scholarships
Every year, the University of Worcester will award up to 40 scholarships of £1,000 after the first and second year of study to reward outstanding academic achievement and to assist students to pursue voluntary or cultural activities.

Sports Scholarships
Cricket Scholarship
The chosen candidate will be able to follow a three-year degree course at the university and join the county squad during the summer each year during the course. Any successful applicant for the scholarship must satisfy the academic requirements of the University of Worcester and fulfil the performance requirements of Worcestershire County Cricket Club (WCCC) at the annual trials day.

See Chapters 2, 4 and 6 for additional awards, applicable to all universities

Benefits include an annual bursary of £1,500 from the WCCC towards expenses, a guaranteed place in University of Worcester accommodation paid for by the WCCC, sports science support and monitoring by expert staff in the field, and professional winter coaching and practice with the Worcestershire playing staff.

Hockey Scholarships
An award is also available for those proficient in hockey. The University has established a partnership with The Worcester Hockey Club.

Basketball Scholarship
A £300 annual bursary is offered to applicants with an excellent track record in basketball. Successful students will have the opportunity to participate in the Worcester Basketball Player Development Programme and will have sports science support services and injury treatment in association with the Worcester Wolves basketball team. There will be full training facilities and an opportunity for British university selection.

For further information contact the Head of the School of Sport and Exercise Science.

AWARDS FOR NON-EU STUDENTS
Scholarships up to the value of £2,000 are open to applicants designated as overseas students.

POSTGRADUATE AWARDS
PGCE students
Students in receipt of a full maintenance grant will receive a £305 bursary. PGCE students are eligible to apply for a maintenance grant of £2,700, of which the first £1,200 is available to all and the remaining £1,500 is dependent on household income.

INFORMATION AND APPROXIMATE FEES FOR NON-EU STUDENTS
English language entry requirement: IELTS 5.0–6.0 (or equivalent). **Fees:** £8,000. **Living costs:** £6,000–£6,500.

University of Worcester, Henwick Grove, Worcester WR2 6AJ; tel: 01905 855111; www. worc.ac.uk.

WRITTLE COLLEGE (Chelmsford)

Located in a small village near Chelmsford, Writtle College is set in its own 220-hectare estate with conservation areas, landscaped gardens, design studios, animal, equine and stud units, working farm, science centre, sport and leisure facilities and business operations. The college has over 1,000 students, with on-site accommodation for up to 400.

DEGREE SUBJECTS OFFERED
Agriculture; Agricultural Business Management; Animal Science; Agricultural Crop Production; Animal Management; Art and Design; Business Management; Conservation and Environment (Biological Surveying); Countryside and Wildlife Management; Digital Art and Design; Equine Breeding and Stud Management; Equine Sports Therapy; Equine Science; Equine Studies; Equine Studies and Business Management; Farm Livestock Production; Fine Art and the Environment, Garden Design, Restoration and Management; Horticulture; Horticulture and Business Management; Horticultural Crop Production; Human and Equine Sports Performance; Interior Architecture; Interior Design; International Horticulture; Landscape Architecture; Landscape and Amenity

Management; Landscape and Garden Design; Green Space Management; Landscape Construction; Marketing and Supply Chain Management; Outdoor Recreation with Conservation; Professional Floristry; Rural Resource Management; Social and Therapeutic Horticulture; Spatial and 3D Design; Sports and Exercise Performance; Sports Turf and Golf Course Management; Sustainable Food Management.

TUITION FEES (2009/10)
£2,906 per annum

BURSARIES AND OTHER AWARDS
Progressive bursaries of £300, £400 and £500 are offered for full-time three-year programmes for students in receipt of full support from the local authority. Part-time students may be entitled to a £50 per module bursary if they are studying at least 50% of the Full-Time Equivalent (FTE) and are in receipt of specified means-tested benefits. There are also Alumni-based Funds awarded to students showing high vocational skills from lower-income families.

INFORMATION AND APPROXIMATE FEES FOR NON-EU STUDENTS
English language entry requirement: IELTS 5.5 (or equivalent). **Fees:** £7,700. **Living costs:** £6,000.

Writtle College, Writtle, Chelmsford, Essex CM1 3RR; tel: 01245 424200; www.writtle.ac.uk.

YORK UNIVERSITY

The University of York was founded in 1963 and is situated on a spacious 450-acre campus site on the edge of the city, of which 250 acres is set aside for the campus expansion 'Heslington East'. There is a student population of 11,800, with 8,600 full time undergraduates of whom 3,000 live on or near the main campus. Because the campus is relatively flat it is particularly popular with disabled students. A second campus in York city centre, Kings Manor, houses the Departments of Archaeology and History of Art.

DEGREE SUBJECTS OFFERED
Animal Physiology; Archaeology; Astrophysics; Biochemistry; Biology; Biostatistics; Business Management; Chemistry; Chemistry, Resources and the Environment; Computer Science; Computer Simulation; Ecology, Conservation and the Environment; Econometrics; Economics; Educational Studies; Electronic Engineering (Avionics; Communications; Computer; Electronics; Media Technology; Music Technology; Radio Frequency; Software); English; French; Genetics; German; Health Sciences; History; Languages; Life Systems and Pharmaceuticals; Linguistics; Management, Information Technology and Language; Mathematics; Medicine; Modern Languages; Molecular Cell Biology; Music; Music Technology; Philosophy; Physics; Politics; Resources and the Environment; Spanish; Social Policy; Sociology; Statistics; Writing, Directing and Performance.

TUITION FEES (2009/10)
£3,225.

BURSARIES AND OTHER AWARDS
Students whose residual household income is less than £25,000 will receive a university bursary of £1,436. Those with a household income from £25,001 to £35,910 will receive a bursary of £718 and those with a household income between £35,911 and £41,040 will receive a £360 bursary.

See Chapters 2, 4 and 6 for additional awards, applicable to all universities

Choral Scholarships
A Choral Scholarship to the value of £3,000 is awarded by the dean and chapter of York Minster and is open to any student. Choral scholars become members of the Minster Choir. They are required to attend rehearsals and services on four weekdays per week, plus an afternoon rehearsal and service on Saturdays, and morning and afternoon services on Sundays, during the three choir terms (which include Easter and Christmas). Further details are available from Mr Philip Moore (Master of the Music) or Canon Paul Ferguson (Preceptor) at Church House, Oglethorpe, York YO1 2JN, or from Dr Jonathan Wainwright (Assistant Choir Trainer) c/o Department of Music, University of York, Heslington, York YO10 5DD.

Golf Bursaries
There are eight Golf Bursaries awarded annually by the Royal and Ancient Golf Club to the value of £1,500. If you meet the university entry qualifications and have a handicap of three or better, you could apply for one of these awards.

The benefits are:

* Full membership of Fulford Golf Club
* Representing Fulford and the university in tournaments and matches
* Receiving regular coaching and training.

If you are interested and meet the requirements, contact the Director of Physical Recreation, The Sports Centre, University of York.

Mike Pinson Bursary
An annual bursary of up to £250 is awarded to a second-year student facing adversity to improve the quality of his/her university life. Precedence is given to students with a hearing impediment and students from the Computer Science Department.

Susan Joyce Bursary
An annual bursary of up to £500 is awarded to a student in financial difficulties.

Gladstone Memorial Prize
An annual prize of £300 is made available by the Gladstone Memorial Trust for outstanding work by final-year students in History, Politics or Economics.

York Settlement Trust Prizes
Four annual prizes of up to £50 are awarded, by departments in rotation, to undergraduate students.

York Townswomen's Guild Prizes
Three annual book prizes of £50 are awarded, by departments in rotation, to women students at the end of their first year.

Archaeology Awards
Charles Wellbeloved Prize
An annual cash prize is awarded by the Yorkshire Philosophical Society for the best dissertation by a third-year Archaeology student.

Biology Awards
The department awards three prizes annually, each of £200. One is for the best academic performance by a student at the end of the second year. The Head of Department's Prize is for the best all-round contribution by a student to the academic and social life of the department at the time of graduation. Finally, there is a prize awarded for the final-year project that gains the highest grade.

Chemistry Awards

The following prizes are awarded on the basis of performance in BSc and MChem degree examinations in Chemistry: Whinfield Medal and prizes; BP Chemicals Prize; Margaret Bishop Prize; ICI Prize. Each prize is worth £150.

Castrol Prize

One prize, value £300, is awarded for achievement on the research project carried out at York by a student on the MChem programme.

Glaxo-Wellcome Prize

This prize, value £200, is awarded annually for the best research project carried out at York by a student on the MChem degree programme.

John Twycross Prize

This prize, value £500, provides financial support for an MChem student spending Year 4 either at York or at a foreign university.

Procter & Gamble Prize

This prize, value £500, is awarded annually to a third-year student in recognition of academic performance and a proven record of extra-curricular achievement.

Robert Jackson Awards

One award of value £250, and one or two of £130, are made annually to second-year students who have made significant contributions to departmental and university activities. The awards are intended to assist students' plans for personal development.

Whinfield Project Awards

Funds of up to £400 are available annually to enable students to carry out scientific projects. An award of £250 is made on completion of the project and submission of a satisfactory report.

Fine Organics Sponsorship

Each year Fine Organics sponsors a student reading for an honours BSc or MChem degree in the Department of Chemistry. Candidates for all courses run by the department may apply for sponsorship. Under the terms of the sponsorship, the student receives £1,000 per year during the degree course, subject to a satisfactory performance being maintained. For courses F101, F123, F143 and F163 students will spend a year in France, Germany or Italy. The student will enter paid employment with Fine Organics for a minimum of eight weeks during the second summer vacation. The company may also be able to provide employment during another summer vacation. If the student is on one of the MChem courses F102, F124, F144 or F164, he or she may apply to spend the final year of the course in industrial training with the company. If accepted, the student will be paid a salary in place of his or her sponsorship payment for that year. Further details of the industrial training schemes will be provided at the end of the second year of the course.

Castrol Sponsorship

Each year Castrol sponsors a student reading for an honours BSc or MChem degree in the Department of Chemistry. Candidates for all courses run by the department may apply for sponsorship. Under the terms of the sponsorship, the student receives £1,000 per year from Castrol during the degree course, subject to a reasonable performance being maintained. For courses F101, F123, F143 and F163, this will include the year spent in France, Germany or Italy. The student will enter paid employment with Castrol for eight weeks during the second summer vacation.

BP Chemicals European Sponsorship

Each year BP Chemicals sponsors University of York students on the MChem course 'Chemistry with a year in Europe'. BP Chemicals normally chooses one student intending to spend a year in France (at Marseille) and one in Germany (Aachen). The sponsorship payment is for the year in Europe, and is intended to assist with expenditure on travel, accommodation, subsistence, books and, where necessary, language training in France or Germany.

See Chapters 2, 4 and 6 for additional awards, applicable to all universities

BP Chemicals Scholarship

Each year BP Chemicals sponsors a student reading for an honours BSc or MChem degree in the Department of Chemistry. Candidates for all courses run by the department may apply for the scholarship. Under the terms of the scholarship, the student receives £750 per year during the degree course, subject to a reasonable performance being maintained. A separate book allowance of up to £100 per year will also be paid. The selected student will enter paid employment at BP Chemicals' research centre at Hull for eight weeks during the second summer vacation. The company may also be able to provide employment during another summer vacation. A student on one of the MChem courses may also apply to spend the entire final year of the course in industrial training with the company; if accepted, the student will be paid a salary by BP Chemicals in place of his or her sponsorship payment for that year. Further details of the industrial training scheme will be provided at the end of the second year of the course.

Hickson Fine Chemicals Sponsorship

Each year Hickson Fine Chemicals sponsors a student reading for an honours BSc or MChem degree in the Department of Chemistry. Candidates for all courses run by the department may apply for sponsorship. Under the terms of the sponsorship, the student receives £810 per year during the degree course, subject to a reasonable performance being maintained. This will include the year spent in France, Germany or Italy. A separate book allowance of up to £100 will also be paid on production of detailed receipts. The student will enter paid employment with Hickson Fine Chemicals for eight weeks during the first and second summer vacations. A student on one of the MChem courses will spend a similar period with the company during the third summer vacation, but may alternatively apply to spend the entire final year of the course in industrial training with the company; if accepted, the student will be paid a salary in place of his or her sponsorship payment for that year. Further details of the industrial training scheme will be provided at the end of the second year of the course.

Pfizer Central Research Sponsorship

Each year Pfizer Central Research sponsors a student reading for an honours BSc or MChem degree in the Department of Chemistry. Candidates for all courses run by the department may apply for sponsorship. Under the terms of the sponsorship, the student receives £1,000 per year from Pfizer during the degree course, subject to a reasonable performance being maintained. This will include the year spent in France, Germany or Italy. The student will enter paid employment with Pfizer for eight weeks during the second summer vacation. If the student selected is on one of the MChem courses, he or she may apply to spend the final year of the course in industrial training with the company; if accepted, the student will be paid a salary in place of the sponsorship payment for that year. Further details of the industrial training scheme will be provided at the end of the second year of the course.

Group Research Centre Sponsorships

Each year the Group Research Centre sponsors a student reading for an honours BSc or MChem degree in the Department of Chemistry. Candidates for all courses run by the department are eligible to apply. Under the terms of the scholarship, and subject to a reasonable standard being maintained, the student receives £750 per year from Smith and Nephew during the degree course. This will include the year spent in France, Germany or Italy. The student will enter paid employment at the Group Research Centre for eight weeks during the second summer vacation. The company may also be able to provide employment during another summer vacation. If the student selected is on one of the MChem courses, he or she may apply to spend the final year of the course in industrial training at the Group Research Centre; if accepted, the student will be paid a salary by Smith and Nephew in place of his or her sponsorship payment for that year. Further details of the industrial training scheme will be provided at the end of the second year of the course.

'Year in Industry' Scheme

The department also operates a 'Year in Industry' Scheme through which Chemistry students on the four-year MChem course can apply to spend a year of the course in paid and assessed industrial training with any of the companies participating in the scheme. To apply for sponsorship or other awards, write to the Department of Chemistry, University of York, York YO10 5DD. You should give your full name, your address and your UCAS number. No other information is required at this stage. You may apply as early as you like, but applications must reach the university by early May.

Computer Science and Engineering Awards
Sir William Siemens Medal
The Sir William Siemens Medal and a prize of £250 is awarded by Siemens-Plessey to the best MEng (fourth-year) finalist.

Institution of Electrical Engineers (IEE)
A £50 prize is awarded together with a year's associate membership on graduation, to the best finalist on an IEE-accredited course: that is, for the best third-year CS or fourth-year CSSE performance.

Company Prizes
The following companies award prizes variously for the best overall performance in the first, second, third or fourth year, or in project work in the third or fourth year: ARM (three at £150), Logica (one at £150) and Nortel (two at £150).

Economics Awards
The Tassie Medallion is awarded to the best Economics candidate in the final examination, and the Head of Department's Prize to the best overall departmental student. The CIMA/Nestlé Prize is awarded for the best performance by a second-year Economics/Finance student.

Electronics Awards
Electronic Engineering
By special arrangement with British Telecommunications plc up to 32 students benefit from becoming a BT scholar. These awards are available in every year of the course and are applied for after arrival.

Edward Dabill Prizes
Two prizes are awarded annually to students taking the Electronic Engineering course, one of £30 and one of £50.

Texas Instrument Prizes
Students taking Electronic Engineering are eligible to apply for examination prizes worth £50, £100 and £150, whilst the best MEng project carries a prize of £500.

Farnell Project Prize
One prize of £15 is offered for the best final-year project.

Radio Communications Agency Prize
£250 is awarded for the best RFEEI (Radio Frequency Engineers Education Initiative) project.

Admissions Tutor's Prize
£50 is awarded for the highest performance given unconventional entry qualifications.

Racal Prize
£50 is awarded for high-quality avionics work.

IEE Prize
£50 is awarded for the best third-year project.

Westland Helicopters' Prize
£100 is awarded to the most improved student between the second and third years.

Varta Prize
£25 is awarded for the best battery-powered project.

English awards
Cobham-Longfellow Bequest
This is a scholarship of a little over £100 annually. The award is by competition based on the criteria of academic merit and financial need, and is open to first- and second-year students.

FR Leavis Fund
Awards may be made from this fund to students in the Department of English and Related Literature. These awards take a variety of different forms, including Travel Bursaries.

Linguistics Awards
Ursula Wadey Annual Prize
£75 is awarded for original work by students in English or Linguistics alternately.

Mathematics Awards
The Chartered Institute of Management Accountants (CIMA) offers £150 annually for the CIMA Mathematics Prize for the best performance in the second-year examination. In the final year the department offers a £50 prize for the best performance and the Institute of Mathematics and its Applications offers free membership for one year.

Music Awards
Vinson Award
This award, valued at £3,000, originating in a gift to the Department of Music, is available annually and is tenable for one year. To be considered for the award applicants must already have been offered undergraduate or postgraduate places to study music at York, and must be ineligible for any other form of grant.

Wilfrid Mellers Music Prizes
A book prize of £70 is awarded to the first-year student with the highest preliminary course mark and a travel prize of £70 is offered by competition to a second-year student. These prizes are annual and originate from a covenant by Professor Wilfrid Mellers.

Essay Prize
This prize of £100 is awarded annually for the best undergraduate essay.

Beecham Scholarship
This is a competitive entrance award for performance, worth £250 per year for three years. Preference will be given to those playing the less usual orchestral instruments (eg bassoon).

Blake Prize
This prize is awarded to a student who has made a distinguished contribution to the orchestra.

Physics Awards
Vacation Research Scholarships
This scholarship scheme enables a limited number of undergraduates to gain experience of working in a research laboratory during the long vacations. One or two scholarships are awarded annually, usually to second-year students. Each scholarship covers six to eights weeks' work on a research project. Unlike final-year projects, some of which are linked to research programmes, a vacation project will be full-time and will allow the student to become immersed in work that is at the forefront of a particular aspect of physics. A few examples of research-based projects are: sono-luminescence; molecular dynamics; measuring the characteristics of novel magnetic materials; evaluating the performance of newly developed radiation detectors; developing data analysis software and data-processing of signals from detectors used for gamma ray detection in nuclear physics research.

AWARDS FOR NON-EU STUDENTS
The university offers a number of scholarships each year for students who pay fees at the overseas rate. All scholarships are awarded on a competitive basis.

Part-scholarships provide an amount equivalent to a maximum of one-third of the appropriate tuition fees. Details of scholarships may be obtained from the international office.

INFORMATION AND APPROXIMATE FEES FOR NON-EU STUDENTS

Fifteen per cent of students are from outside the UK. **English language entry requirement:** IELTS 6.0 (or equivalent). Six-month and pre-sessional English language courses are available. There are also intensive vacation courses. **Fees:** science courses £11,500; other courses £8,900. **Living costs:** £6,500.

University of York, Heslington, York YO10 5DD; tel: 01904 433533; www.york.ac.uk.

YORK ST JOHN UNIVERSITY

York St John was founded in 1841 and became a university in 2006. The university is close to the vibrant city centre of York. There is a population of almost 6,000 students, with accommodation for over 90% of first years in university-owned accommodation.

DEGREE SUBJECTS OFFERED

American Studies; Business Management; Counselling Studies; Creative Writing; Dance; Education Studies; English Language & Linguistics; English Literature; Film & Television Production; Film Studies; Finance; Fine Arts; History; Human Resource Management; Information Technology (Web Technologies); Languages; Marketing Management; Media; Music; Occupational Therapy; Performance; Physical Education; Physiotherapy; Primary Education; Product Design; Psychology; Sport; Theatre; Theology & Religious Studies; Tourism Management.

TUITION FEES £2009/10

£3,225.

BURSARIES AND OTHER AWARDS

Students from households with a family income less than £18,360 will receive a York St John Bursary worth £1,610 in addition to their Maintenance Grant. Students from households where the income is between £18,361 and £20,970 will be offered bursaries of £1,075 in addition to their Maintenance Grant. Students from households where the income is between £20,971 and £25,000 will be offered bursaries of £540 in addition to their Maintenance Grant. Any students whose household income is above £25,001 are not eligible for any of the bursaries.

AWARDS FOR NON-EU STUDENTS

Continuation of the scheme already in operation whereby all direct overseas entrants are offered a scholarship discount of £1,000 per year from the standard fee.

INFORMATION AND APPROXIMATE FEES FOR NON-EU STUDENTS

English language entry requirement: IELTS 6 (or equivalent). **Fees:** £8,100. **Living costs:** £6,500.

York St John University, Lord Mayor's Walk, York YO31 7EX; tel: 01904 624624; www. yorksj.ac.uk.

See Chapters 2, 4 and 6 for additional awards, applicable to all universities

3 | SPECIAL AWARDS

This chapter lists awards for those students who for various reasons are disadvantaged. Some may have faced financial difficulties after joining the course and others may need assistance with housing, childcare or travel costs. There are others in local authority care, students with physical disabilities and those whose education has been undermined by severe emotional, social or health problems.

Secondly, it lists awards for students residing or studying in certain areas. Finally, other awards for particular groups are listed.

In many cases enquiries regarding these awards should be made initially through the university or college finance office as soon as possible when an offer of a place has been made, since some funds are limited and are not necessarily available to all deserving cases.

AWARDS FOR DISADVANTAGED STUDENTS

Access to Learning Fund

Additional financial help is available to assist students who have genuine financial difficulties. Certain groups are given priority, including mature students and students with childcare costs etc. Payments made from the fund will usually be in the form of non-repayable grants.

Details of financial aid and student support can be obtained from the DCSF website www.dcsf.gov.uk.

Alfred Bourne Trust

Small grants may be offered to students in financial need in their final year of study.

Apply to the British and Foreign School Society, Croudace House, Godstone Road, Caterham, Surrey CR3 6RE; tel: 01883 331177.

Anglo-Jewish Association

Scholarships are available to students intending to take a full-time course at a UK university. Applicants must demonstrate academic ability, financial need and a commitment to the Jewish community.

Apply to the Anglo-Jewish Association, Suite 4, Gloucester Place, London W1V 6BY. Application forms and selection criteria can be found on the website www.anglojewish.co.uk.

Buttle Trust

The aim of the trust's Student and Trainee Grants Scheme is to provide assistance with the acquisition of academic, trade, professional and vocational qualifications to young people facing severe social, emotional or health problems, or whose education has been undermined by problems of this kind in the past. Help is not available to young people with two fit and caring parents.

Assistance may be given to those who are looked after by adoptive parents, family members or friends, to young people who have a substantial continuing responsibility for caring for sick or disabled parents or other relations, or to young people who are orphaned or estranged.

Full details are available from the Secretary, Frank Buttle Trust, Audley House, 13 Palace Street, London SW1E 5HX; tel: 020 7828 7311; www.buttletrust.org.

Disabled Students' Allowances

These allowances will help a student towards any costs incurred in attending his or her course as a direct result of their disability. They can be applied for at any time before or during the course and are available to full- and part-time students, although the latter must be attending at least 50% of a full-time course.

The amount payable does not depend on a student's income or that of his or her family. Unlike a student loan, this assistance does not have to be repaid.

Information can be obtained from *Into Higher Education*, published by Skill, The National Bureau for Students with Disabilities; tel: 020 7450 0620; skill@skill.org.uk.

Students with disabilities need to make their choice of university or college with great care since they are likely to require special facilities, for example specialist equipment, a personal helper, special access facilities or accommodation. In each case they should contact the admissions tutor or the head of department for their chosen course, or the university or college adviser for students with disabilities, to find out exactly what facilities can be provided. Students applying for, or already at, college/university should apply through their local authority for expenses related to their disability.

Dyslexia Assessment

Undergraduate and postgraduate students may be able to recover the cost of such assessment. Contact your university or college student support office.

Fee Waivers and Remission

Fee remission may be offered by some universities and colleges to cover the cost of tuition fees for the whole of the course. This would normally apply only to home students.

Foyer Bursary

The Foyer Federation is a registered charity working with disadvantaged young people, who are homeless or in housing need, providing them with holistic support and affordable accommodation.

The charity seeks to raise aspirations among residents who have the potential to benefit from higher education and to provide additional support for those who obtain a university place. Foyer residents on full-time undergraduate courses receive a bursary of £1,000 per year.

For more information, contact the Foyer Federation, 3rd Floor, 5–9 Hatton Wall, London EC1N 8HX; tel: 020 7430 2212; inbox@foyer.net; www.giveusavoice.net/foyer-bursary-details-and-form.

Foyer–Uniaid Accommodation Bursaries

The bursary scheme gives supported and free accommodation to students who are at risk of having to leave university because of extreme hardship.

Over 90% of applications are from students already at university. 10% of applications come from students entering their first year at university. For 2007/8, bursary places are available in the following cities: Birmingham; Bristol; Cardiff; Leeds; Leicester; Liverpool; London; Manchester; Nottingham; Plymouth; Preston; Sheffield; Southampton.

The bursary is for one year's free accommodation in a student hall. The bursary-holder will have to pay a refundable security deposit of £250 when he or she arrives at the hall. All other charges levied by the hall (eg broadband, parking and other services) will be his or her responsibility.

The application deadline is around the end of March. Final selection decisions will be made in mid-April. In considering applications, the selection panel will base their assessment on students' particular needs. Decisions will be based on the content of the supporting statement, including how the award will make a difference, the student's personal and financial circumstances, his or her ability to support other costs and supporting statements from referees.

For more information, contact the Foyer Federation, 3rd Floor, 5–9 Hatton Wall, London EC1N 8HX; tel: 020 7430 2212; inbox@foyer.net; www.giveusavoice.net/foyer-uniaid-accommodation-bur or www.uniaid.org.uk/bursaries.

Gardner's Trust for the Blind
The maximum award is £300. Requests for help usually relate to the purchase of computer equipment, course fees, household equipment etc.

Applications should be made in writing to the Secretary/Treasurer, Gardner's Trust, Boundary House, 91–93 Charterhouse Street, London EC1M 6PN; tel: 020 7253 3757.

Lawrence Atwell's Charity
The charity is aimed at refugee young people (16–27) who are from low-income backgrounds and have been granted indefinite leave by the Home Office to remain in the UK. It is interested in funding vocational training, as opposed to purely educational courses, and equipment essential for work. Applications cannot be accepted from undergraduates whose tuition fees are paid by the local authority or who have access to a student loan. However, the trustees will look carefully at how far the degree may be considered 'vocational' and essential for work. They will consider students who have to pay their own fees or cannot receive a student loan and whose parents' earning threshold is less than £24,400 with an additional £2,650 for each additional dependent child.

The trustees can make awards towards the costs of tuition, enrolment, examination or registration fees, general living expenses during study or training and, in some cases, towards specific items of equipment.

Further information can be obtained from Lawrence Atwell's Charity, Skinners' Hall, 8 Dowgate Hill, London EC4R 3SP; tel: 020 7213 0561.

Leverhulme Trade Charities Trust Undergraduate Bursaries
The bursaries are intended for those in financial hardship who require funds to assist in their studies by way of maintenance, tuition, examination fees, travel costs, study materials, accommodation or childcare costs. Applicants must be the son, daughter, spouse, widow or widower of a commercial traveller, chemist or grocer. The maximum value of any bursary is £3,000. Details are available from the Financial Support Office, Leverhulme Trust, 1 Pemberton Row, London EC4A 3BG; tel: 020 7822 5227; www.leverhulme.org.uk.

Prince's Trust Action
Disadvantaged young persons between the ages of 14 and 25 may apply for assistance for a specific purpose. A member of the local committee will interview all applicants. Initial applications can be made by telephone or letter to The Prince's Trust, Mount St Michael, Craigs Road, Dumfries DG1 4UT; tel: 01387 269176.

Snowdon Award Scheme
The award scheme provides grants of up to £2,000 (£2,500 in exceptional circumstances) per year for physically and sensorily disabled students in further or higher education or training within the UK towards additional costs of studying as a result of their disabilities. These can include costs for translators, note takers, computers, carers, wheelchairs and other disability-related equipment and services. The preferred age range is 17–26 but older applicants will be considered if funds permit. Applications are accepted from January.

Details are available from the Snowdon Award Scheme, Unit 18, Oakhurst Business Park, Wilberforce Way Southwater, Horsham, West Sussex RH13 9RT; tel: 01403 732899; www.snowdonaward scheme.org.uk.

Other support from local authorities
Full-time students may be eligible for:

* Dependants' grant
* Childcare grant
* Travel, books and equipment grant
* School meals grant

* Lone parents' grant
* Learner support funds
* Housing benefit
* Council tax exemption
* Carers' awards
* Disabled students' allowance (see above)
* Care leavers' grant
* Additional course travel costs.

Contact your local authority, university or college for further information.

AWARDS FOR UK STUDENTS STUDYING OR RESIDING IN PARTICULAR AREAS

Carnegie/Caledonian Postgraduate Scholarships

Graduates of a Scottish university holding a degree with first class honours in any subject and intending to pursue three years of postgraduate research for a PhD degree can be considered for the award of a Carnegie Scholarship.

Carnegie Trust for the Universities of Scotland

The trust is prepared to consider applications for assistance with fees by students of Scottish birth, parentage or schooling for courses leading to a first degree of a Scottish university. Such assistance will not be given to supplement an award from the Scottish Awards Agency or a local authority.

Further information is available from the Secretary, Carnegie Trust for the Universities of Scotland, Cameron House, Abbey Park Place, Dunfermline KY12 7PZ; tel: 01383 622148.

Carnegie Vacation Scholarships

The scholarships are open to Scottish undergraduates who will be of at least two years' standing at the end of the current academic year, who have shown exceptional merit at the university and who would like to devote their full time during some part of the long vacation to a programme of study or research that will be of direct benefit to them in their academic work. Applications must be submitted during the spring term, on forms obtainable from college offices.

JP Morgan Fleming Bursary

This is open to all UK students but was set up specifically to help mature students who are returning to study after a number of years and normally reside in South-East Essex. See under Foyer Bursary.

Royal Caledonian Schools Trust

The Caley, as it is affectionately known, was established in 1815 to help educate the sons and daughters of Scots who were serving, or who have served, in the armed forces and the children of poor Scots in London.

Help is given with Education grants ranging from £150 for school clothing or a school trip, as well as help towards the cost of school fees and living expenses for those in higher or further education. There is no age limit.

The Caley also sponsors projects that benefit groups of qualifying students and awards scholarships to help those who decide to use a gap year to help less fortunate communities.

To apply, contact The Royal Caledonian Schools Trust, 80a High Street, Bushey, Hertfordshire WD23 3HD; tel: 020 8421 8845; rcts@caleybushey.demon.co.uk; www.royalcaledonianschools. org.uk.

Scottish Italian Scholarships
These scholarships are open to undergraduates of any faculty at any Scottish university offering a study of Italian (Edinburgh, Glasgow, St Andrews, Strathclyde). They are tenable at Italian universities.

Sir John Cass's Foundation
The foundation supports education for young people who live in inner London. Applications will only be considered from those under 25 who have been permanent residents for at least three years in the London boroughs of Camden, City of London, Greenwich, Hackney, Hammersmith and Fulham, Islington, Kensington and Chelsea, Lambeth, Lewisham, Newham, Southwark, Tower Hamlets, Wandsworth and Westminster.

Applicants should be studying on courses of further education above GCSE (NVQ level 2) and to the point of entry to degree-level courses at publicly maintained universities and colleges. Medical students wishing to study for an intercalated degree can be considered for awards and there are also some awards for postgraduate students.

The foundation has historical links with the former London Guildhall University (now merged with the University of North London as London Metropolitan University), in recognition of which art students experiencing financial difficulties may apply for help with the costs of materials or a contribution to studio fees. Grants may be made at any point in the year and there is no closing date.

Initial letters of enquiry should be sent to the Clerk to the Governors, 31 Jewry Street, London EC3N 2EY; tel: 020 7480 5884; contactus@sirjohncass.org.

Sir William Boreman's Foundation
Educational grants are made to full-time or part-time students living in either the London boroughs of Greenwich or Lewisham whose parents' joint income is below £25,000. Grants cover school and college fees, travel, tools, books, musical instruments and school excursions. Preference will be given to the children of parents who served in the armed forces, particularly those following a seafaring career.

Details can be obtained from the Clerk to the Governors, Sir William Boreman's Foundation, Drapers' Hall, London EC2N 2DQ; tel: 020 7448 1309; www.thedrapers.co.uk/Charities/boremans.

Stevenson Exchange Scholarships
The level of the award varies each year. The scholarship is open to undergraduates and postgraduates of any faculty at any Scottish university offering a study of French, Spanish and German and is tenable at any university in these countries.

Stewartry Educational Trust
This is for students residing in the former Stewartry area who require assistance for a specific purpose. Students may make an application for each year of their course. Application forms and further information are available from the Clerk to the Governing Body; tel: 01557 330291 extension 66236. You may also write to The Secretary, Stewartry Educational Trust, Council Offices, Kirkcudbright DG6 4JQ.

Tredegar Memorial Trustees Agricultural Scholarship
Value: £40 per year. This scholarship is open to a candidate who, at the time application is made, is living in the former County of Gwent and who proposes to enter the University of Wales or some other approved university or university college to take an honours degree in an agricultural subject including Agricultural Engineering. Contact the university finance office.

University of Wales Scholarships
Aberfan Children's Scholarship
Value: approximately £800 per year. The scholarship is awarded annually by the university to a young person of school age whose parents were living in Aberfan at the time of the disaster, or if

there is no suitably qualified applicant, to a person of school age living in Merthyr Tydfil. The scholarship will be tenable for three years.

In either of the above cases, the order of preference shall be:

1| Applicants who propose to enter the University of Wales, Cardiff, as first-year undergraduate students.
2| Applicants who propose to enter any other of the constituent institutions or university colleges of the University of Wales, as first-year undergraduate students.
3| Applicants who propose to enter any of the associated Institutions of the University of Wales, as first-year undergraduate students.

Forms of application for the scholarship may be obtained from The Secretary-General, University Registry, Cathays Park, Cardiff, CF10 3NS and must be returned to him/her by 1 June of the year in which the applicant proposes to enter the university.

Dr Howell Rees General Scholarship
Value: £500 per year. This scholarship is restricted to Welsh-speaking candidates who were born in Cwmaman (Carmarthenshire), Brynaman, Gwaun-cae-Gurwen or Cwmgors.

D Lloyd Thomas Memorial Scholarship
Value: approximately £400 per year. This scholarship is open to Welsh-speaking applicants, born or who have been resident in the county of Mid Glamorgan.

OTHER AWARDS

All Saints Educational Trust
The aim of the trust is to assist those students (home and EU only) who are primarily seeking to enter the teaching profession in the field of religious education, home economics and related subjects, multicultural and inter-faith education. Teachers of other subjects are eligible to apply for an award but they will be expected to show clearly in what way their course or project may be expected to benefit the Church or enhance the Church's contribution to education within the framework of the objects of the trust. The following specialisms are associated with the objectives of the trust when determining priorities:

* Religious education (Christian education)
* The multi-faith/inter-faith/multicultural dimension
* Home economics/dietetics/nutrition courses
* Development education
* Awareness of Third World issues
* Provision of suitable materials for schools
* Worship in education establishments
* Access courses leading to teacher training
* Further education (as opposed to higher education)
* Special educational needs including moral and ethical aspects
* Ethical issues from a Christian standpoint.

The trust cannot support schools, the general funds of any organisation, public appeals or the establishment of courses.

Applications for financial assistance must be submitted on the appropriate form available from the Secretary to the Trust, All Saints Educational Trust, St Catherine Cree Church, 86 Leadenhall Street, London EC3A 3DH; tel: 020 7283 4485; www.aset.org.uk.

British Federation of Women Graduates
The British Federation of Women Graduates has limited funds to make awards to women graduates undertaking postgraduate research in Great Britain (ie all of the United Kingdom except

Northern Ireland). These awards are made without reference to financial need. If you have a query about eligibility, contact the Secretary of BFWG on awards@bfwg.org.uk.

National awards are available for women research students in their final year of study towards a PhD degree. Awards are based on academic excellence and are open to any nationality. See www.bfwg.org.uk for an application form. There is an April entry deadline.

International awards are available for the academic year 2007/8 for women involved in study, research or training at the doctoral or post-doctoral level. Geographic restrictions apply – see www.bfwg.org.uk for eligible countries and further details. Email awards@bfwg.org.uk.

Job Link
Most universities and some colleges make arrangements to enable students to obtain part-time employment through 'Job Link' or 'Earn as You Learn' schemes. These are usually organised through the students' union or the university or college careers service.

Queen Elizabeth Scholarships
Scholarships are awarded to fund further study, training and practical experience for men and women who wish to improve their craft or trade skills. The amounts vary between £2,000 and £15,000. There is no age limit but applicants must be able to demonstrate a high level of skill and commitment to the craft or trade. Applications should be submitted before the end of December. Details are available from the Queen Elizabeth Scholarship Trust, 1 Buckingham Place, London SW1E 6HR; tel: 020 7828 2268; www.qest.org.uk.

Sidney Parry Foundation
The foundation aims primarily at helping first-degree students. Grants are intended to be supplementary – with a maximum payment of £700 (allocated only in exceptional circumstances). Applicants should have a university or college place confirmed before applying and students in the following categories cannot be considered:

* Students wanting to study outside the UK
* Expeditions overseas
* Medical students during elective periods and intercalated courses
* Second-degree courses where the first degree held is lower than 2(i)
* As above, unless part of a professional training, eg Medicine, Dentistry
* Courses leading to degree-level entry, for example, A-levels, GNVQs etc
* Distance-learning, correspondence and part-time courses
* Students over 35 when their courses start, except in exceptional cases.

Full details and application forms are available from the Secretary, Sidney Parry Foundation, PO Box 1689, Hindon, Wiltshire SP3 6TP.

UK 9/11 Scholarships
The United Kingdom 9/11 Scholarships Fund provides awards for study in higher or further education in the United Kingdom to children or dependants of victims of the terrorist attacks on the United States on 11 September 2001. Programmes covered are:

* Undergraduate courses lasting no more than four years and leading to a degree at recognised higher education institutions in the UK
* Master's courses at recognised higher education institutions in the UK
* Courses leading to recognised qualifications at further education institutions in the UK
* Accredited study periods of up to one year's length at recognised British higher education institutions for students whose college or university has an exchange agreement with a partner institution in the UK.

For further information, see www.britishcouncil.org/911scholarships.

Yorkshire Ladies' Council of Education Awards Funds

Variable number of awards. Applications are assessed in September, January, March and June. Applications must be received by the first day of the relevant month.

Awards are available to British women wishing to study in order to further their career prospects. Applicants should be over 21, have been offered a place at a British educational institution, be unable to finance their chosen course, be able to present a case for special need, and not qualify for local authority support. These awards are subject to confirmation of funding from the YLCE. Contact The Secretary, YLCE, Forest Hill, 11 Park Crescent, Leeds LS8 1DH; tel: 0113 269 1471.

4 | AWARDS OFFERED BY PROFESSIONAL, COMMERCIAL AND OTHER ORGANISATIONS

This chapter gives details of various career organisations offering course-related awards.

AGRICULTURE
RASE Award
The Royal Agricultural Society of England, through its Student Award Scheme set up in 2001, awards an annual prize to the best student on an agriculture-related course at each agricultural college. The prizes are free membership of the society for five years. For further details contact Chloe Foxton, Royal Agricultural Society of England, Stoneleigh Park, Warwickshire CV8 2LZ; tel: 024 7669 6969; info@rase.org.uk.

ARMED SERVICES
The Army, Royal Air Force and Royal Navy offer sponsorships and other schemes through universities. Contact the Liaison Officer attached to your school or college for further information.

ART AND DESIGN
Means-tested bursaries may be available to some foundation-course students. Contact the students services department at the university or college for further details.

Royal Commission for the Exhibition of 1851 – Industrial Design Studentship
About six Industrial Design Studentships are offered each year for outstanding potential designers with a good first degree in engineering or science who wish to develop their capabilities in industrial design and who aspire to becoming leading designers in industry. Eligibility:

* British nationals, resident in the UK
* Intending to make a career in British industry
* Good first degree in engineering or science
* Must have obtained admission to a suitable postgraduate course
* Normally aged 21–24, but older candidates may apply.

All tuition fees are paid, up to normal UK course level for UK students, plus a stipend of £10,000 per year and an allowance of £850 per year for materials. Duration is one year, although a second year will be supported if the course demands it and the first year has been satisfactorily completed.

For an application form and deadline, visit www.royalcommission1851.org.uk/ind_des.html.

BUILDING
CIOB Queen Elizabeth II Jubilee Fund Scholarships
A number of scholarships will be offered by the Chartered Institute of Building. Full details can be obtained from the Chartered Institute of Building, Englemere, Kings Ride, Ascot, Berkshire SL5 7TB; tel: 01344 630700; www.ciob.org.uk.

DENTISTRY
See **Medical and related courses** below.

The Chartered Institute of Building (CIOB) represents for the public benefit the most diverse set of professionals in the construction industry. We have over 40,000 members around the world and are considered to be the international voice of the building professional.

As a champion of the built environment, the CIOB offers a range of scholarships and awards to support students, graduates, academics and practitioners in order to promote and reward the industry's future leaders. The scholarships, prizes and bursaries on offer include awards for research, travel, course fees and projects covering the whole construction process.

The CIOB scholarships are available to bright, motivated and ambitious individuals who show the potential to succeed in the construction industry. Our current scholarships are:

For Undergraduates:

Queen Elizabeth 11 Jubilee Fund Scholarships

These awards are made to students on a construction related CIOB accredited course, who have shown potential in the early part of their studies and are intended to provide study support during the final year. www.ciob.org.uk/events/jubileefund

For Postgraduates:

University Research Scholarship

The aim of the scholarship is to produce vocationally significant and practical research which will ultimately benefit the construction industry. The scholarship provides the necessary financial support to a post-graduate student for the purpose of undertaking research which may be required for completion of a dissertation or thesis. www.ciob.org.uk/events/scholarship

Tony Gage Scholarship

The CIOB's Tony Gage Scholarship is a prestigious award worth up to £10,000 that is awarded to a candidate selected as the best future leader in construction. If you are aged between 26 and 35, employed by a UK contractor and are planning further study at post graduate level, this award may be for you. www.ciob.org.uk/events/tonygage

For Practitioners:

Sir Ian Dixon Scholarship

Established in 1998 in conjunction with the Worshipful Company of Constructors, the scholarship supports research in the general field of construction management and offers an annual scholarship award of £2,000. www.ciob.org.uk/events/dixonscholarship

The Faculty of Architecture and Surveying Scholarship

In conjunction with the Faculty of Architecture and Surveying and the Worshipful Company of Constructors, this scholarship supports research in the field of architecture and surveying and offers an annual scholarship award of £2,000. www.ciob.org.uk/events/fasscholarship

Sustainability Scholarship

Established in 1998 in conjunction with the Worshipful Company of Constructors and the Happold Trust, the scholarship supports research in sustainability and offers an annual scholarship award of £2,000. www.ciob.org.uk/events/sustainabilityscholarship

For more information on CIOB scholarships or the CIOB visit www.ciob.org.uk/events or contact Sarah Peace quoting ref: TADSP09 on 01344 630 776. To apply for a CIOB scholarship or request any further information please email research@ciob.org.uk.

DRAMA
Dance and Drama Awards
Dance and Drama Awards, made on a competitive basis, enable students to be funded for a substantial part of their courses. Funding for these courses is provided by the Higher Education Funding Council for England (HEFCE) through the new Dance and Drama Awards Scheme. The school is given a number of awards by HEFCE, which provide the full cost of tuition with the exception of the £1,025, which must be paid by all HE students. The student element of the fees is assessed and paid in the same manner as any university course, as are student loans. The drama schools are responsible for deciding who receives an HEFCE scholarship, the decision being made on the attainment at audition.

Institutions invited to offer places: Academy of Live and Recorded Arts; Arts Educational Schools; Birmingham School of Speech and Drama; Bristol Old Vic Theatre School (Schools of Acting and Musical Theatre); Central School of Ballet; College of the Royal Academy of Dancing; Doreen Bird College of Performing Arts; Elmhurst Ballet School; English National Ballet School; GSA Conservatoire; Hammond School; Italia Conti Academy; Laban Centre for Movement and Dance; Laine Theatre Arts; London Academy of Music and Dramatic Art; London Academy of Performing Arts; London Contemporary Dance School; London Studio Centre; Merseyside Dance and Drama Centre (Liverpool); Midlands Academy of Dance and Drama (Nottingham); Mountview Theatre School; Northern Ballet School; Oxford School of Drama Theatre; Performers College; Royal Academy of Dramatic Art; Stella Mann College; Studio Le Point; Urdang Academy; Webber Douglas Academy of Dramatic Art.

Applications should be made through the institution of choice.

As is the case with other courses, students with low-income support may also apply to the government's Hardship Fund for further support towards their fee.

ENGINEERING
ICE QUEST Scholarships
The Queen's Jubilee Scholarship Trust (QUEST) awards are worth up to £3,000 to undergraduate students embarking on accredited courses aiming to achieve Chartered, Incorporated or Technician Membership of the Institution of Civil Engineers. Travel awards of £1,500 are also offered.

For more information contact the Institution of Civil Engineers, 1 Great George Street, Westminster, London SW1P 3AA; tel: 020 7665 2193; www.ice.org.uk.

Institution of Engineering and Technology (IET)
A number of valuable awards are offered each year by the Institution of Engineering and Technology. Contact: Scholarships and Awards, IET, Savoy Place, London WC2R 0BL; tel: 020 7240 1871; www.theiet.org/scholarships.

Top Flight Bursary Scheme
The highest calibre entrants to Engineering are eligible for bursaries of £500 per year under a scheme funded by government and organised by the Engineering Council.

ENGINEERING (MECHANICAL)
Institute of Mechanical Engineers (IMechE)
The following awards are all offered by the Institute of Mechanical Engineers. Contact the Education Services Department, IMechE, Northgate Avenue, Bury St Edmunds, Suffolk IP32 6BN; tel: 01284 765172; www.imeche.org.uk.

Communication Skills Awards
Ten awards worth £500 are offered to students to enhance their presentation skills. These awards are only available to members of the IMechE.

Foreign Language Awards
Ten awards valued at up to £500 are offered to students undertaking language programmes. These awards are only available to members of the IMechE.

Ian Alexander Stuart Memorial Scholarships
Three awards valued at £500 per year for a maximum of four years are offered to exceptional students intending to pursue Mechanical Engineering degrees with European or Management Studies.

Overseas Study Awards
Twenty awards are available for students studying or gaining work placements overseas as part of their Mechanical Engineering degree programmes. The awards are worth up to £750 and are only available to members of the IMechE.

Overseas/Third World Engineering Project Awards
Three awards worth up to £1,000 are offered for students intending to undertake voluntary or project work to assist the developing world. These awards are only available to members of the IMechE.

Postgraduate Awards
Nineteen awards are offered to postgraduate students. These awards are only available to members of the IMechE.

Special Experience Awards
Ten awards valued at up to £500 are offered to support students to gain special industrial experience. These awards are only available to members of the IMechE.

Undergraduate Scholarships
Forty-seven scholarships valued at £500 per year are offered for a maximum of four years, and are available for exceptional students wishing to pursue Mechanical Engineering degrees.

Whitworth Scholarships for Young Engineers
Awards are normally made for the four-year study on a degree-level programme. They are valued at £3,000 for full-time study and for sandwich students will be paid on a pro rata basis.

Royal Academy of Engineering
Engineering Leadership Awards
Engineering Leadership Awards provide motivation and support for exceptional Engineering undergraduates with the potential for high-level industrial leadership. Awards worth up to £7,500 per student are made to provide second-year students, over two or three years, with carefully planned training and experience to complement their academic studies and to help prepare them for fast-track careers in industry. Each application must be endorsed by the candidate's university department.

Pre-university schemes
As part of its Engineering Education Continuum, the academy promotes four schemes at pre-university level that encourage young people to consider professional engineering as a career:

* **The Year in Industry:** This scheme selects high-calibre students to gain pre-university experience of industry backed by comprehensive 'off-the-job' training. Contact www.yini.org.uk.
* **Headstart:** This programme provides a residential week at university engineering departments to brief lower sixth-form students about engineering careers and undergraduate courses in engineering. Contact www.headstartcourses.org.uk.
* **Smallpeice Trust Engineering Courses:** These events are arranged through schools or universities. Contact www.smallpeicetrust.org.uk/homecourses.
* **The Engineering Education Scheme:** This collaborative scheme enables lower sixth-form students studying relevant subjects to work on real industrial problems for which companies

need solutions. A professional engineer from the company liaises with and advises the teams of students and their teachers in solving the problem and producing the report and presentation. Universities are actively involved in supporting the scheme and provide a residential workshop period during the course of the project. Contact www.raeng.org.uk.

Undergraduate Programme
The Undergraduate Programme is designed to encourage university students to retain an interest in pursuing a career in engineering through a series of awards and activities. These include business awareness courses, organised industrial tours, personal development training courses and foreign travel awards. The programme is open only to students who have participated in one or more of the academy's pre-university schemes.

Full details can be obtained from the Scheme Manager, Royal Academy of Engineering, 29 Great Peter Street, Westminster, London SW1P 3LW; tel: 020 7227 0054; www.raeng.org.uk.

ENGINEERING (MINING)
Awards are offered by the Mining Engineering Trust.

Full details from the Secretary, Mining Association Educational Trust (Rio Tinto plc), 6 St James's Square, London SW1Y 4LD or from admissions tutors.

FOOD SCIENCE
Institute of Food Science and Technology
The institute awards prizes for professional commitment to students taking BSc courses in Food Science and/or Technology at each university offering these courses.

Full details can be obtained from the Secretary, Institute of Food Science and Technology, 5 Cambridge Court, 210 Shepherd's Bush Road, London W6 7NJ; tel: 020 7603 6316; www.ifst.org.

HILDA MARTINDALE EDUCATIONAL TRUST
The trust fund is administered by the Council of Royal Holloway, London University and was established with the object of helping 'women of the British Isles whose intention it is to fit themselves for some profession or career likely to be of use or value to the community and for which vocational training is required'. However, because of the limited funds available the trustees will only consider applicants aged 21 years or over. Awards do not normally exceed £1,000 and are not awarded to those who are eligible for grants from local authorities, the research councils, the British Academy and other public sources. They are also not available for the following:

* Short courses, Access courses, courses attended abroad or elective studies
* Intercalated BSc years during UK medical, dental, veterinary or nursing courses
* Wholly academic courses or academic research
* Special projects in the UK and abroad
* Master's courses taken immediately after a first-degree course.

Candidates eligible for Career Development Loans (available from certain banks for training courses) are expected to have explored this option first.

Full details and application forms from the Secretary to the Hilda Martindale Trustees, c/o The Registry, Royal Holloway, University of London, Egham, Surrey TW20 0EX; tel: 01784 434455.

HORTICULTURE
The Royal Horticultural Society administers a number of bursary funds that are established and maintained through generous bequests and donations given into its charge for the improvement of horticulture and horticultural knowledge.

Scope of awards

Applications are invited, particularly from horticulturists, for financial grants for horticultural projects including study visits or working placements in gardens, plant exploration and study, taxonomy and research, attendance at conferences and distinct projects of educational or historical value.

General eligibility for RHS Bursaries

* Priority will be given to professional and student gardeners, but applications are invited from serious amateur gardeners, botanists and related professions and institutions.
* Applicants not resident in the British Isles may apply only for projects tenable in the British Isles (England, Scotland, Wales, Northern Ireland, Republic of Ireland, Channel Islands and the Isle of Man).
* Applicants need not be members of the Royal Horticultural Society.

Exclusions

* Funds are limited and may be sufficient to cover only part of the costs. They are principally provided for individuals with limited resources and are not available for large projects.
* Salary costs for projects are not funded. The underwriting, or support, of commercial enterprises is also not eligible for bursary grants.
* Tuition fees, exam fees and living costs for educational courses (college, university etc), training certificates etc, are not eligible for bursary grants. Grants may however be made to horticultural students towards certain undergraduate and postgraduate projects such as overseas travel to collect information.
* Funding for group expeditions from colleges will not normally be given more often than once every three years.
* Conservation, botanical, ecological and related projects that are not primarily horticultural are outside the remit of the Royal Horticultural Society bursaries awards, although such projects by horticulturists may be considered.
* Costs for personal equipment such as cameras, boots and clothing are not funded by RHS bursaries.
* Institutions wishing to send more than one member of staff to a conference should apply on a corporate application form.

Full details are available from the Secretary, RHS Bursaries Committee, Education Department, RHS Garden, Wisley, Woking, Surrey GU23 6QB; tel: 0845 260900; www.rhs.org.uk.

HOSPITALITY MANAGEMENT

Savoy Educational Trust

The Savoy Educational Trust has agreed to provide funds for a number of scholarships for UK students accepted on an International Hospitality Management degree programme.

Further details of these scholarships and the application procedure are available from the admissions team. See www.savoyeducationaltrust.org.uk/grants.asp.

INSURANCE

The Insurance Charities' Orphans' Fund currently considers applications from the student children of long-serving insurance employees and pensioners where those children are studying for a first degree.

Help can be considered for the duration of the course if there is significant financial hardship. If parents are not experiencing hardship, help is restricted to a maximum of 12 months.

Applications in writing, giving details of parents' insurance service and the student's degree course, should be submitted to the Insurance Charities, 20 Aldermanbury, London EC2V 7HY; tel: 020 7606 3763.

JOURNALISM
RADAR
The Royal Association for Disability and Rehabilitation offers a bursary to disabled people wishing to enter journalism. Successful applicants will receive course fees and payment for accommodation at university or college. Candidates should have applied for a place on a one-year full-time course.

Full details can be obtained from Steve Davis, RADAR, 12 City Forum, 250 City Road, London EC1V 8AF; tel: 020 7250 3222.

LEVERHULME TRADE CHARITIES TRUST
Bursaries are offered to students following first degree courses in any subject in institutions in the UK who are in financial need. The maximum value is £3,000 per year, but the sum may be adjusted according to individual circumstances. Applicants should be the son, daughter, spouse, widow or widower of commercial travellers, chemists or grocers. Contact www.leverhulme-trade.org.

MATERIALS SCIENCE
Institute of Materials, Minerals and Mining
The Institute of Materials, Minerals and Mining awards several bursaries to applicants for Materials Science degrees.

Interested applicants should contact the Institute of Materials, Minerals and Mining, 1 Carlton House Terrace, London SW1Y 5DB; tel: 020 7451 7300; www.iom3.org/awards.

MEDICAL AND RELATED COURSES
NHS Bursaries are available for pre-registration students of Medicine and Dentistry in their fifth and later years of study in any UK country. Support for the first four years of study will be on the same basis as for other higher education students, so that for students starting in 2004/5 any NHS bursary becomes payable from 2008/9. English-domiciled students on the new four-year Medical courses for graduate entrants will be eligible for NHS bursaries in Years 2, 3 and 4 of the medical course. See also **Paramedical and other healthcare courses**.

These bursaries are available to students on the following degree courses: Audiology, Dental Hygiene, Dental Therapy, Dietetics, Midwifery, Nursing, Occupational Therapy, Orthoptics, Physiotherapy, Podiatry, Prosthetics and Orthotics, Radiography, Radiotherapy, and Speech and Language Therapy. Details can be obtained from NHS Student Bursaries, Hesketh House, 200–220, Broadway, Fleetwood, FY7 8SS. Tel 0845 358 6655.

General Dental Council Awards for current students
An award of £3,300 is made each year for a UK dental student intending to take an intercalated science degree at a UK university.

An interest-free loan of up to £3,000 is available to fourth- and fifth-year dental students whose financial circumstances may prevent them from completing their course at a UK university.

Full details can be obtained from the General Dental Council, 37 Wimpole Street, London W1M 8DQ; tel: 020 7887 3800.

MUSIC
Organ and Choral Scholarships
In each case, contact the Director of Music.

Arundel Cathedral (RC) (organ); Contact the Director of Music.

Bangor Cathedral (Church in Wales) (organ; choral) (University of Wales, Bangor); Contact: the Director of Music.

Barnes: St Mary's Church (choral); Contact: the Director of Music.

Bath Abbey (CofE) (choral) (Bath Spa University); Contact: the Director of Music.

Belfast Cathedral (Church of Ireland) (organ) (Belfast, Queen's University); Contact: the Director of Music.

Beverley Minster (CofE) (organ; choral) (University of Hull); Contact: the Director of Music.

Birmingham: St Chad's Cathedral (RC) (organ; choral) (Birmingham Conservatoire); Contact: the Director of Music.

Birmingham: St Philip's Cathedral (CofE) (organ; choral) (Birmingham University or Birmingham Conservatoire).

Bishop's Stortford College (organ); Contact: the Director of Music.

Blackburn Cathedral (CofE) (organ); Contact: the Director of Music.

Bristol Cathedral (CofE) (organ; choral) (University of Bristol)

Bristol: Keynsham Parish Church See under **Keynsham Parish Church**.

Bristol: St Mary Redcliffe (CofE) (organ) (University of Bristol). Contact: the Director of Music.

Bristol: St Paul Clifton (CofE) (organ) (University of Bristol); Contact: the Director of Music.

Bristol: Tyndale Baptist Church (organ) (University of Bristol); Contact: the Director of Music.

Cambridge University (general) (organ; choral); Contact: Choral Awards: Secretary to the Choral and Organ Scholarships Competition, Selwyn College, Grange Road, Cambridge CB3 9DQ; seam100@cam.ac.uk; Organ Awards: Jesus College, Cambridge CB5 8BL.

Cambridge: Jesus College (organ; choral) (University of Cambridge); Contact: Director of College Music, Jesus College, Cambridge CB5 8BL; director-of-music@jesus.cam.ac.uk.

Cambridge: King's College (CofE) (organ; choral) (University of Cambridge); Contact: Director of Music; choir@kings.cam.ac.uk.

Cambridge: St John's College (CofE) (organ; choral) (University of Cambridge); Contact: Assistant to the Director of Music.

Cambridge: Selwyn College (CofE) (organ) (University of Cambridge); Contact: Secretary to the Choral and Organ Scholarships Competition, Selwyn College, Grange Road, Cambridge CB3 9DQ.

Canterbury Cathedral (CofE) (organ; choral) (University of Kent or Canterbury, Christ Church University); Contact: Master of the Choristers and Organist.

Canterbury: St Stephen (CofE) (organ); Contact: the Director of Music.

Cardiff: University Parish Church of SS Andrew and Teilo (Church in Wales) (organ) (University of Wales College of Cardiff); Contact: the Director of Music.

Carlisle Cathedral (CofE) (choral); Contact: Master of the Choristers, 7 The Abbey, Carlisle, Cumbria CA3 8TZ; office@carlislecathedral.org.uk.

Chelmsford Cathedral (CofE) (organ; choral); Contact: Director of Music.

Chester Cathedral (CofE) (organ) (Chester College); Contact: Cathedral Organist, 12 Abbey Square, Chester CH1 2HU.

Chichester Cathedral (CofE) (organ); Contact: The Royal Chantry, Cathedral Cloisters, Chichester, West Sussex PO19 1QA; tel: 01243 784790; organist@chichestercathedral.org.uk.

Clifton Cathedral (RC) (organ); Contact: Head of Music Service; music@cliftondiocese.com.

Datchet: St Mary the Virgin (CofE) (organ; choral); Contact: The Director of Music, The Parish Office, The Vicarage, London Road, Datchet, Berkshire SL3 9JW.

Derby Cathedral (CofE) (organ; choral); Contact: Master of the Music, Derby Cathedral, Iron Gate, Derby DE1 3GP; masterofmusic@derbycathedral.org.

Durham Cathedral (CofE) (organ; choral); Contact: Organist and Master of the Choristers, 6 The College, Durham; organist@durhamcathedral.co.uk.

Durham: College of St Hild and St Bede (CofE) (organ) (University of Durham); Contact: The College of St Hild and St Bede, Durham DH1 1SZ.

Durham: Hatfield College (organ) (University of Durham); Contact: The Chaplain, Hatfield College, Durham DH1 3RQ.

Durham: St Chad's College (CofE) (organ; choral) (University of Durham); Contact: Director of Music, St Chad's College, 18 North Bailey, Durham DH1 3RH.

Durham: St John's College (CofE) (organ) (University of Durham); Contact: The Principal, St John's College, 3 South Bailey, Durham DH1 3RJ.

Durham: St Oswald's Parish Church (CofE) (organ) (University of Durham); Contact: The Vicar, St Oswald's Vicarage, Church Street, Durham DH1 3DG.

Durham: University College (organ) (University of Durham); Contact: Organ Scholar, University College, The Castle, Palace Green, Durham DH1 3RW.

Edinburgh Episcopal Cathedral: St Mary (Scottish Episcopal Church) (organ; choral); Contact: The Bursar, St Mary's Cathedral, Palmerston Place, Edinburgh EH12 5AW; office@cathedral.net.

Edinburgh: St Giles' Cathedral (Church of Scotland) (organ); Contact: Organist and Master of the Music, St Giles' Cathedral, Edinburgh EH1 1RE.

Edinburgh University (organ); Contact: University of Edinburgh Music Office, Alison House, 12 Nicolson Square, Edinburgh EH8 9DF.

Ewell Parish Church: St Mary Virgin (CofE) (organ; choral); Contact: Director of Music, Parish Office, London Road, Ewell, Epsom KT17 2BB; directorofmusic@stmarysewell.com.

Exeter Cathedral (CofE) (choral) (University of Exeter); Contact: Director of Music, 11 The Close, Exeter EX1 1EZ; tel: 01392 285985; music@exeter-cathedral.org.uk.

Exeter: Collegiate Church of The Holy Cross, Crediton (CofE) (organ); Contact: Parish Office, The Boniface Centre, Church Street, Crediton EX17 2AH; holycross@btopenworld.com.

Exeter University Chapel (CofE) (organ; choral); Contact: Director of Music.

Exeter University School of Education (organ); Contact: On arrival at institution, through the Chaplain.

Faversham: St Mary of Charity (CofE) (organ); Contact: Kingston House, Chapel Street, Faversham, Kent ME13 8EP.

Glasgow University (organ); Contact: The University music department

Gloucester Cathedral (organ); Contact: Director of Music, 7 Miller's Green, Gloucester GL1 2BN.

Greenwich University (choral); Contact: courseinfo@greenwich.ac.uk.

Grimsby Parish Church (CofE) (organ; choral); Contact: Parish Office, St James' Square, Grimsby DN31 1EP; parishoffice@saintjames.freeserve.co.uk.

Guildford Cathedral (CofE) (organ; choral) (University of Surrey); Contact: Director of Music, Guildford Cathedral, Stag Hill, Guildford GU2 5UP.

Hampton Court See under **London: Chapel Royal**.

Harrogate: Christ Church (CofE) (organ; choral); Contact: Director of Music, Christ Church Parish Centre, The Stray, Harrogate, North Yorkshire HG1 4SW. director@cchh.org.co.uk.

Harrogate: St Peter's Church (CofE) (organ; choral); Contact: Director of Music, St Peter's Church, Cambridge Street, Harrogate HG1 1RW.

Huddersfield Parish Church (CofE) (organ) (Huddersfield University); Contact: Department of Music and Drama, University of Huddersfield, Queensgate, Huddersfield HD1 3DH.

Hull University (organ; choral) (Beverley Minster) Contact: the Director of music.

Keele University Chapel (CofE) (organ; choral); Contact: Keele University Chapel, Keele, Staffordshire ST5 5BG.

Kent University (organ; choral) (Canterbury Cathedral) Contact: Master of the Choristers and Organist.

Keynsham Parish Church of St John the Baptist (near Bristol) (CofE) (organ); Contact: Director of Music, 23 Handel Road, Keynsham, Bristol BS31 1BT.

Leamington Spa: All Saints' Parish Church (CofE) (organ) (University of Warwick); Contact: Choir Master, PO Box 163, Leamington Spa CV31 3AE.

Leeds Cathedral (RC) (organ; choral) (Universities of Bradford, Huddersfield and Leeds); Contact: Director of Music, Cathedral House, Great George Street, Leeds LS2 8BE; music@leeds-diocese.org.uk.

Leeds Parish Church (CofE) (organ) (University of Leeds); Contact: Scholarships Office, University of Leeds, Leeds LS2 9JT; scholarships@leeds.ac.uk.

Leicester Cathedral (CofE) (organ; choral); Contact: Director of Music, Leicester Cathedral, 1 St Martin's East, Leicester LE1 5FX; leicestercathedral@leccofe.org.

Leicester: St Thomas's, Wigston (CofE) (organ); Contact: the Director of Music.

Lichfield Cathedral (CofE) (choral); Contact: Organist and Master of the Choristers.

Lincoln: Bishop Grosseteste College (organ; choral) (Lincoln Cathedral); Contact: The Music Department, Bishop Grosseteste College, Lincoln LN1 3DY; info@bgc.ac.uk.

Lincoln Cathedral (CofE) (organ; choral) (Lincoln, Bishop Grosseteste College); Contact: The Music Department, Bishop Grosseteste College, Lincoln LN1 3DY; info@bgc.ac.uk.

Liverpool Cathedral (CofE) (organ); Contact: Music Director, 6 Cathedral Close, Liverpool Cathedral L1 7BR.

Liverpool Metropolitan Cathedral (RC) (organ; choral); Contact: Director of Music, Metropolitan Cathedral, Cathedral House, Mount Pleasant, Liverpool L3 5TQ; music@metcathedral.org.uk.

Llandaff Cathedral (Church in Wales) (choral) (Royal Welsh College of Music and Drama); Contact: The Organist and Master of the Choristers, c/o Administration Officer, Llandaff Cathedral, Cardiff CF5 2EB; office@llandaffcathedral.org.uk.

London: All Saints', Fulham (CofE) (organ; choral); Contact: Organist and Director of Music, Parish Office, 70a Fulham High Street, London SW6 3LG; secretary@allsaints-fulham.org.uk.

London: Chapel Royal, Hampton Court Palace (CofE – Royal Peculiar) (organ; choral); Contact: the Director of Music.

London: Chelsea Old Church (CofE) (organ); Contact: Director of Music, Parish Office, Petyt Hall, 64 Cheyne Walk, London SW3 5LT; chelsea.oldchurch@virgin.net.

London: King's College (organ; choral); Contact: Department of Music, King's College, Strand, London WC2R 2LS.

London: Old Royal Naval College Chapel (CofE) (organ; choral) (Trinity College of Music); Contact: Trinity College of Music, King Charles Court, Old Royal Naval College, Greenwich, London SE10 9JF; tel: 020 8305 4444; enquiries@tcm.ac.uk.

London: Royal Holloway College (organ; choral) (Royal Holloway, University of London); Contact: Director of Choral Music and College Organist, Royal Holloway, University of London, Egham, Surrey TW20 0EX.

London: St Mary's Church, Barnes (CofE) (organ); Contact: The Rector, The Church Office, St Mary's Church, Barnes, London SW13 9HL; rector@stmarybarnes.org.

Manchester Cathedral (CofE) (organ); Contact: Organist and Master of the Choristers.

Newcastle Cathedral (CofE) (organ; choral) (University of Newcastle); Contact: Director of Music, Cathedral Church of St Nicholas, Newcastle upon Tyne NE1 1PF; newcathorganist@tiscali.co.uk.

Northampton: All Saints' Church (CofE) (organ; choral); Contact: Director of Music, the Music Department Office, All Saints' Church, George Row, Northampton NN1 1SF; music@allsaints northampton.co.uk.

Norwich Cathedral (CofE) (organ; choral) (University of East Anglia); Contact: The Cathedral Organist, 12 The Close, Norwich NR1 4DH; organ.scholar@cathedral.org.uk.

Nottingham: St Barnabas' Cathedral (RC) (organ; choral); Contact: Organist and Director of Music, St Barnabas' Cathedral, Cathedral House, North Circus Street, Nottingham NG1 5AE.

Nottingham: St Mary the Virgin (CofE) (organ; choral); Contact: John Keys, Director of Music, St Mary's Church, High Pavement, The Lace Market, Nottingham NG1 1HN; stmarysmusic@innotts. co.uk.

Nottingham University (organ); Contact: Head of Music Department, University of Nottingham, University Park, Nottingham NG7 2RD; music-enquiries@nottingham.ac.uk.

Old Royal Naval College Chapel, London See under **London: Old Royal Naval College Chapel**.

Oxford University (general) (organ; choral); Contact: Administrator, Faculty of Music, St Aldates, Oxford OX1 1DB.

Oxford: Christ Church (CofE) (organ; choral) (University of Oxford); Contact: Christ Church, Oxford OX1 1DP.

Oxford: Exeter College (CofE) (organ; choral) (University of Oxford); Contact: Tutor for Admissions, Exeter College, Oxford OX1 3DP; admissions@exeter.ox.ac.uk.

Oxford: Hertford College (CofE) (organ) (University of Oxford); Contact: Admissions, Hertford College, Catte Street, Oxford OX1 3BW.

Oxford: Keble College (CofE) (organ; choral) (University of Oxford); Contact: Keble College, Oxford OX1 3PG; college.office@keble.ox.ac.uk.

Oxford: Lincoln College (CofE) (organ; choral) (University of Oxford); Contact: Chaplain, Lincoln College, Turl Street, Oxford OX1 3DR.

Oxford: Magdalen College (CofE) (organ; choral) (University of Oxford); Contact: Organist, Magdalen College, Oxford OX1 4AU.

Oxford: New College (CofE) (organ; choral) (University of Oxford); Contact: Faculty of Music, St Aldates, Oxford OX1 1DB; tel: 01865 276125.

Oxford: Oriel College (CofE) (organ; choral) (University of Oxford); Contact: Oriel College, Oriel Square, Oxford OX1 4EW.

Oxford: Queen's College (CofE) (organ; choral) (University of Oxford); Contact: The Queen's College, Oxford OX1 4AW.

Oxford: Worcester College (CofE) (organ; choral) (University of Oxford); Contact: Director of Chapel Music, Worcester College, Oxford, OX1 2HB.

Peartree Church (CofE) (organ); Contact: peartreechoir@hantsweb.org.uk.

Portsmouth Cathedral (CofE) (organ; choral) Portsmouth Grammar School Contact: Portsmouth Cathedral Music Office, St Thomas' Street, Old Portsmouth PO1 2HH; organist@portsmouth cathedral.org.uk.

Repton Preparatory School (organ); Contact: Director of Music, Repton Preparatory School, Foremarke Hall, Milton, Derbyshire DE56 6EJ.

Ripon Cathedral (CofE) (organ; choral) (York St John University); Contact: Director of Music, Ripon Cathedral Office, Liberty Court House, Minster Road, Ripon HG4 1QS; postmaster@ripon cathedral.co.uk.

Rochester Cathedral (CofE) (organ; choral); Contact: Director of Music, Rochester Cathedral, The Chapel Office, The Precinct, Rochester ME1 1SX.

Romsey Abbey (CofE) (organ) Contact: Organist and Master of the Choristers, 82 Winchester Road, Romsey SO51 8JE.

Royal College of Music (organ); Contact: Professor in Charge of Junior Fellows, Royal College of Music, Prince Consort Road, London SW7 2BS.

Royal Hospital, Chelsea (CofE) (organ); Contact: The Organist, Royal Hospital, Chelsea, London SW3 4SR; tel: 020 7881 5204; info@chelsea-pensioners.org.uk.

Royal Northern College of Music (organ); Contact: Admissions, Royal Northern College of Music, 124 Oxford Road, Manchester M13 9RD.

St Albans Cathedral (Abbey) (CofE) (organ); Contact: Music Department, Cathedral and Abbey Church of St Alban, St Albans AL1 1BY; music@stalbanscathedral.org.uk.

St Edmundsbury Cathedral (CofE) (choral); Contact: Director of Music, St Edmundsbury Cathedral, Angel Hill, Bury St Edmunds, Suffolk IP33 1LS; cathedral@burycathedral.fsnet.co.uk.

St Martin-in-the-Fields (CofE) (organ; choral); Contact: Director of Music, St Martin-in-the-Fields, Trafalgar Square, London WC2N 4JJ; church.music@smitf.org.

St Paul's Cathedral (CofE) (organ); Contact: Director of Music, The Chapter House, St Paul's Churchyard, London EC4M 8AD; music@stpaulscathedral.org.uk.

Salford Cathedral (RC) (organ; choral); Contact: Choirmaster, St John's Cathedral, Chapel Street, Salford M3 5LL.

Salisbury Cathedral (CofE) (organ); Contact: Head of Liturgy and Music, The Chapter Office, 6 The Close, Salisbury SP1 2EF; litmus@salcath.co.uk.

Selby Abbey (CofE) (organ); Contact: Dr Roger Tebbet, Director of Music, Selby Abbey, The Crescent, Selby YO8 0PU.

Sheffield Cathedral (CofE) (organ; choral) (University of Sheffield); Contact: Master of Music, The Cathedral Church of St Peter and St Paul, Church Street, Sheffield S1 1HA; musicians@sheffield-cathedral.org.uk.

Sheffield: St John's Church (choral); Contact: Director of Music, St John's Church, Ranmoor, Sheffield S10 3GX; dom@stjohnsranmoor.org.uk.

Sherborne Abbey (CofE) (organ) (Sherborne School); Contact: Director of Music, The Parish Office, 3 Abbey Close, Sherborne, Dorset DT9 3LQ; dirofmusic@sherborneabbey.com.

Solihull: St Alphege (organ); Contact: Director of Music, 2 St Alphege Close, Church Hill Road, Solihull, West Midlands B91 3RQ.

Solihull: St Mary, Lapworth (CofE) (organ); Contact: Organist and Choirmaster, c/o The Rectory, Church Lane, Lapworth, Solihull B94 5NX.

Southwark Cathedral (CofE) (organ); Contact: Organist and Director of Music, Southwark Cathedral, London Bridge, London SE1 9DA.

Southwark: St George's Cathedral (RC) (organ); Contact: Director of Music, St George's Cathedral, Cathedral House, Westminster Bridge Road, London SE7 7HY; info@southwark-rc-cathedral.org.uk.

Southwell Minster (CofE) (organ); Contact: Rector Chori and Organist, 4 Vicar's Court, Southwell NG25 0HP.

Sussex University (organ); Contact: Scholarship and Bursaries Office, Sussex House, University of Sussex, Falmer, Brighton BN1 9RH; scholarships@sussex.ac.uk.

Tewkesbury Abbey (CofE) (choral); Contact: Organist and Master of the Choristers, Abbey Office, Church Street, Tewkesbury GL20 5RZ; organist@tewkesburyabbey.org.uk.

Tiverton: St Peter (CofE) (choral); Contact: St Peter's Rectory, 32 The Avenue, Tiverton.

Truro Cathedral (CofE) (organ; choral); Contact: 14 St Mary's Street, Truro, Cornwall TR1 2AF; music@trurocathedral.org.uk.

Wakefield Cathedral (CofE) (organ) (Huddersfield University); Contact: Department of Music and Drama, University of Huddersfield, Queensgate, Huddersfield HD1 3DH; music@hud.ac.uk.

Warwick: St Mary's Parish Church (CofE) (organ) (University of Warwick); Contact: Director of Music, University of Warwick, Coventry CV4 7AL.

Wellington School (organ); Contact: Director of Music, South Street, Wellington, Somerset TA21 8NT; music@wellingtonschool.org.uk.

Wells Cathedral (CofE) (organ; choral); Contact: Music Secretary, Cathedral Offices, Chain Gate, Cathedral Green, Wells BA5 2UE; musicoffice@wellscathedral.uk.net.

West Byfleet: St John's (CofE) (organ); Contact: Director of Music, 5 Merrow Place, Guildford GU4 7DL.

Westminster Abbey (CofE – Royal Peculiar) (organ); Contact: Organist and Master of the Choristers, The Chapter Office, 20 Deans Yard, Westminster Abbey, London SW1P 3PA; music@westminster-abbey.org.

Westminster Cathedral (RC) (organ); Contact: Master of Music, Westminster Cathedral, 42 Francis Street, London SW1P 1QW; musicdepartment@westminstercathedral.org.uk.

Winchester Cathedral (CofE) (choral); Contact: Organist and Director of Music, The Cathedral Office, 1 The Close, Winchester SO23 9LS.

Winchester College (organ) (The Pilgrim's School, Winchester); Contact: Director of Chapel Music, Winchester College Music School, Culver Road, Winchester SO23 9JF; information@wincoll.ac.uk.

Windsor: St George's Chapel (CofE – Royal Peculiar) (organ); Contact: The Chapter Clerk, Chapter Office, St George's Chapel, Windsor Castle, Windsor, Berkshire; chapteroffice@stgeorges-windsor.org.

Woking See under **West Byfleet: St John's**.

Worcester Cathedral (CofE) (organ); Contact: Worcester Cathedral, Chapter Office, 10a College Green, Worcester WR1 2LH; info@worcestercathedral.org.uk.

York Minster (CofE) (organ; choral) (University of York); Contact: Master of the Music, York Minster, St Williams College, 4–5 College Street, York YO1 7JF.

York St John University Contact: Admissions, York St John University, Lord Mayor's Walk, York YO31 7EX; admissions@yorksj.ac.uk.

NURSING
HSA Charitable Trust Scholarships for enrolled nurse conversion courses
Annual scholarships for enrolled nurses taking conversion courses.

Closing date: 1 November. Send SAE for application form (available August until 20 October each year) to HSA Charitable Trust Scholarships for EN Conversion Courses, c/o Awards Officer, RCN, 20 Cavendish Square, London W1G 0RN.

Margaret Parkinson Scholarship, Awards for Pre-registration Graduates
These are annual scholarships offering £1,000 to £3,000 per year for graduates with a non-nursing degree who wish to take up nursing.

Application forms are available by sending an SAE to Margaret Parkinson Scholarship, Awards for Pre-registration Graduates, Room 304, RCN, 20 Cavendish Square, London W1G 0RN.

PARAMEDICAL AND OTHER HEALTHCARE COURSES
National Health Service
NHS Bursaries are available to pay full fees with means-tested maintenance grants for the following: Dental Hygiene; Dental Therapy; Dietetics; Midwifery (degrees and diplomas); Nursing (degrees and diplomas); Occupational Therapy; Orthoptics; Physiotherapy; Podiatry; Prosthetics/ Orthotics; Radiography; Speech and Language Therapy.

To be eligible for an NHS Bursary you must be accepted for an NHS-funded place. If you are eligible the NHS will pay your tuition fee liability in full. No contribution will be required from you or your family. If you are not eligible for an NHS Bursary, you may still be entitled to help from your local authority.

For Nursing and Midwifery diploma courses you will not have to satisfy any residence conditions, regardless of your country of origin, but it is for you to ensure that you have any necessary immigration clearance. You will be eligible for a maintenance grant that is not income assessed, but you will not be able to get a loan or help from Access funds.

Depending on where you plan to study, more information about the financial support available for health professional courses can be obtained from:

England
NHS Student Grants Unit
Hesketh House
200–220 Broadway
Fleetwood
Lancs FY7 8SS
Tel: 08453 586655
www.nhsstudentgrants.co.uk

Scotland
Student Awards Agency for Scotland (SAAS)
Gyleview House
3 Redheughs Rigg
Edinburgh EH12 9HH
Tel: 08451 111711
www.saas.gov.uk

Wales
NHS Wales Student Awards Unit
NLIAH North Wales
Croesnewydd Hall
Wrexham Technology Park
Wrexham LL13 7YP
Tel: 01978 727873
www.nliah.wales.nhs.uk

Northern Ireland
Department for Employment and Learning
Student Support
Adelaide House
39–49 Adelaide Street
Belfast BT2 8FD
Tel: 028 9025 7778
www.delni.gov.uk

PHYSICS
Students taking courses accredited by the Institute of Physics are eligible for £1,000 per year. For details of bursaries contact The Secretary, The Institute of Physics, 76 Portland Place, London W1B 1NT; www.iop.org.

Institute of Physics
The Institute of Physics is offering means-tested bursaries of up to £1,000 a year to undergraduates studying physics in the UK and Ireland. Only students from the UK and Ireland on courses accredited by the institute will be eligible for consideration. Full details of the scheme are available on http://learningphysics.iop.org.

SCIENCE
Nuffield Foundation
The foundation offers 1,450 funded places each year in two separate schemes:

* 1,000 places for post-16 science students in the UK to spend 4–6 weeks gaining experience of science careers in universities, industry and research
* 450 places for undergraduates to gain an insight into science research careers.

Contact the Nuffield Foundation, 28 Bedford Square, London WC1B 5JS; tel: 020 7631 0566; info@nuffieldfoundation.org.

SOCIAL WORK
The Prescription Pricing Division of the NHS Business Services Authority (NHSBSA) administers bursaries for degrees in social work.

Social Work Bursaries
These are available to students ordinarily resident in England studying on approved (full- or part-time) undergraduate courses, or approved part-time postgraduate courses.

The bursaries are non-means tested. They include a basic grant, a fixed contribution towards practice learning opportunity related expenses and tuition fees if the student is not subject to variable fees. Financial awards are dependent on individual circumstances.

Social Work Bursaries for Students on Full-time Postgraduate Courses

The Social Work Bursary for students on full-time postgraduate courses is available to students ordinarily resident in England studying on approved full-time postgraduate courses.

The bursary consists of a non-means-tested basic grant including a fixed contribution towards practice learning opportunity-related expenses and tuition-fee support.

It also includes an income-assessed maintenance grant and income-assessed allowances to assist with certain costs of living, as recipients of the postgraduate bursary will not ordinarily be entitled to local authority funding. Financial awards are dependent on individual circumstances.

See www.ppa.org.uk/ppa/swb.htm for more information on both bursaries.

TEACHING

PGCE Student Awards

Bursaries and 'Golden Hellos' are offered to students taking the Professional Graduate Certificate in Education (PGCE) in the following subject areas:

Bursary £9,000; Golden Hellos
Secondary shortage subjects (£5,000 awards for Mathematics; Science; Applied Science. £2,500 awards for Information and Communication Technology; Applied Art, Design and Technology; Modern Languages; Music; Religious Studies).

Training Bursaries
£9,000 tax free bursaries are available for the subjects above and £4,000 for the Primary phase.

Full details can be obtained from the Training and Development Agency for Schools, Portland House, Bressenden Place, London SW1E 5TT; tel: 08456 000991 (in English) or 08456 000992 (in Welsh); www.tda.gov.uk.

US Scholarship

Every year the NUT awards the Walter Hines Page Scholarship to a teacher to undertake a study project in the United States. For an application form, write to NUT, Hamilton House, Mabledon Place, London WC1H 9BD; tel: 020 7380 4704.

TOWN PLANNING

George Pepler International Award

The award is made to applicants who wish to visit Britain or who are resident in Britain and wish to visit another country to study some particular aspect of town and country planning. Candidates should note that this award is not intended to provide finance for postgraduate studies or those working for a doctorate. The value of the award is £1,500. For more information contact the Awards and Events Assistant, Royal Town Planning Institute, 41 Botolph Lane, London EC3R 8DL; tel: 020 7929 9473; awards@rtpi.org.uk.

Now check: www.scholarship-search.org.uk/scholarships.

5 | SPONSORSHIP AND SANDWICH COURSES

Sponsorships for students in higher education are offered by a range of employing organisations. These may be companies in the private sector or public sector organisations such as government departments like the Ministry of Defence, the Army and Royal Air Force. Most sponsorships are for degree-level courses in vocational subjects: Electrical, Mechanical and Production Engineering attract the greatest number of sponsorships, followed by Accountancy, Banking, Business Studies and Computer Sciences.

Financial arrangements for sponsorships vary widely. Some employers offer a bursary for each year of study; some give a bursary during term time and pay a salary during vacation periods that students work for them. Some employers sponsor final-year students only, whilst some (unusually) treat their students as employees and pay them a full salary during their course. Sponsorship can be in the form of funds to be spent on books, accommodation or a cash bursary, together with guaranteed vacation work. Sponsorship for sandwich course students also includes guaranteed work experience placements with the employer and sometimes the offer of employment after graduation. Whilst for most employers students are not obliged to accept such offers of employment, for some, such as the Armed Services, sponsored students have to give a minimum period of service. Students need to check contractual arrangements for sponsorship before making their final course decisions.

Companies generally prefer to sponsor students on courses in particular subject areas (eg engineering, business studies) or a specific course at a specific university. They also usually prefer to sponsor students on 'thick' or 'thin' sandwich courses. 'Thick' sandwich courses have two patterns:

* **1–3–1:** The student spends one year in employment, followed by three years of full-time study (often with vacations spent working with the sponsoring organisation) and then a final year in employment with the sponsor
* **2–1–1:** The first two years are spent in full-time study, followed by a year employed by the sponsor, and a final year back at university/college.

On a 'thin' sandwich course students spend part of each year in academic study and part in employment. They usually spend the whole of the final year in full-time study.

Many higher education institutions offer sandwich courses and have contacts with employers who regularly offer work placements to their students. Some of these employers offer sponsorships to students already on such sandwich courses who are doing well in work placements with them. Sponsorship for these students could mean financial support in their final year and a commitment by the company for employment after they have graduated.

Below are lists of universities and colleges offering 'thick' or 'thin' sandwich courses in specified degree subjects. These courses include work placements that students usually obtain themselves with the help of course or departmental staff. **However, students should be aware that whilst most universities have good employer contacts they do not guarantee work placements for all sandwich course students and occasionally students may have to undertake work-related projects instead.** Sponsored students, however, have guaranteed work placements, depending on their contractual arrangements. Students interested in sponsorship and/or sandwich courses should contact the university or department of their preferred subjects to obtain the latest information about the availability of sandwich courses and full details of the course arrangements prior to making their course application. They also need to find out details of possible sponsorship from relevant employers and leave plenty of time for their research. It is important to remember that sponsorships are very popular and competitive – and that sandwich courses often lead to good employment opportunities because of the work experience they give to their students.

During a period of recession, universities and colleges may have problems placing students on sandwich courses. Applicants applying for these courses are strongly advised to check with admissions tutors that courses are not subject to review.

ACCOUNTANCY AND FINANCE
Aston; Bath; Bournemouth; Bradford; Brighton; Bristol UWE; Brunel; City; Coventry; Derby; De Montfort; Glamorgan; Greenwich; Hertfordshire; Huddersfield; Lancaster; Leeds Met; London South Bank; Loughborough; Middlesex; Nottingham Trent; Plymouth; Portsmouth; Queen's Belfast; Sheffield Hallam; Staffordshire; Sunderland; Surrey; Swansea; Swansea Met; Teesside; West Scotland; Worcester; UCE Birmingham; Ulster; Westminster; Wolverhampton.

ACTUARIAL STUDIES
Queen's Belfast

AGRICULTURE (INCLUDING FORESTRY)
Aberystwyth; Bangor; Harper Adams University College; Nottingham Trent; Plymouth; Royal Agricultural College; UHI Millennium Institute; Warwickshire College.

ANATOMY/ANATOMICAL SCIENCES
Bristol; Manchester.

ANIMAL SCIENCES
Aberystwyth; East London; Edinburgh Napier; Harper Adams University College; Nottingham Trent; Royal Agricultural College; Warwickshire College.

ANTHROPOLOGY
Brunel; Liverpool John Moores; Oxford Brookes.

ARCHAEOLOGY
Bradford.

ARCHITECTURE (INCLUDING ARCHITECTURAL TECHNOLOGY)
Bath; Bristol UWE; Cardiff; De Montfort; Dundee; Huddersfield; Leeds Met; London South Bank; Northumbria; Nottingham Trent; Plymouth; Queen's Belfast; Sheffield Hallam; Ulster.

ART AND DESIGN (FASHION/TEXTILES)
Brighton; Central Lancashire; De Montfort; Glasgow Caledonian; Huddersfield; Manchester Met; Northumbria; Nottingham Trent; Southampton Solent; Westminster.

ART AND DESIGN (GRAPHIC DESIGN)
Aberystwyth; Arts London; Huddersfield; Kingston; Northumbria; Sheffield Hallam; Staffordshire; Teesside.

ART AND DESIGN (INDUSTRIAL/PRODUCT DESIGN)
Aston; Bournemouth; Bradford; Brighton; Bristol UWE; Brunel; De Montfort; East London; Glamorgan; Glasgow Caledonian; Hertfordshire; Huddersfield; Lincoln; Liverpool John Moores; London South Bank; Manchester Met; Middlesex; Nottingham Trent; Portsmouth; Robert Gordon; Sheffield Hallam; Staffordshire; Sunderland; West Scotland; Wolverhampton.

ASIA–PACIFIC STUDIES
Central Lancashire.

ASTRONOMY/ASTROPHYSICS
Hertfordshire; Kingston; Nottingham Trent.

BIOCHEMISTRY
Aston; Bangor; Bath; Bristol; Bristol UWE; Brunel; Cardiff; De Montfort; East London; Essex; Glamorgan; Hertfordshire; Huddersfield; Kent; Kingston; Leeds; Liverpool John Moores; London South Bank; Manchester; Manchester Met; Nottingham Trent; Salford; Sheffield Hallam; Sussex; Ulster; West Scotland; York.

BIOLOGICAL SCIENCES
See under **Biology**.

BIOLOGY
Aston; Bangor; Bath; Bradford; Bristol UWE; Brunel; Cardiff; Coventry; De Montfort; East London; Edinburgh Napier; Glamorgan; Harper Adams University College; Hertfordshire; Huddersfield; Kent; Kingston; Liverpool John Moores; London South Bank; Loughborough; Manchester; Manchester Met; Middlesex; Northumbria; Nottingham Trent; Plymouth; Reading; Sheffield Hallam; Surrey; Sussex; Teesside; Ulster; West Scotland; Wolverhampton; York.

BIOTECHNOLOGY
Aston; Bristol; Bristol UWE; Cardiff; Edinburgh Napier; Manchester; Northumbria; Reading; Sussex.

BUILDING
Aston; Bath; Bolton; Bristol UWE; Brunel; Cardiff; De Montfort; Edinburgh Napier; Glasgow Caledonian; Kingston; Leeds Met; London South Bank; Loughborough; Northumbria; Nottingham Trent; Oxford Brookes; Plymouth; Sheffield Hallam; Teesside; Ulster; Wolverhampton.

BUSINESS STUDIES/MANAGEMENT
Abertay Dundee; Aberystwyth; Aston; Bath; Birmingham CFTCS; Bournemouth; Bradford; Brighton; Bristol UWE; Central Lancashire; City; Coventry; De Montfort; Edinburgh Napier; Glamorgan; Glasgow Caledonian; Gloucestershire; Greenwich; Harper Adams University College; Hertfordshire; Huddersfield; Hull; Kingston; Lancaster; Leeds Metropolitan; Liverpool John Moores; Loughborough; Manchester; Manchester Metropolitan; Middlesex; Newcastle; Northumbria; Nottingham Trent; Oxford Brookes; Plymouth; Portsmouth; Queen Mary College London; Reading; Swansea Met; Sheffield Hallam; Southampton Solent; Staffordshire; Surrey; Teesside; Ulster; Westminster; West Scotland; Wolverhampton; York.

CHEMISTRY
Aston; Bangor; Bath; Bradford; Cardiff; De Montfort; Dundee; Glamorgan; Kingston; Liverpool John Moores; Loughborough; Manchester; Manchester Met; Northumbria; Nottingham Trent; Queen's Belfast; St Andews; Surrey.

COMMUNICATION STUDIES
Arts London; Birmingham City; Bournemouth; Bristol UWE; Brighton; Brunel; Central Lancashire; City; De Montfort; Edinburgh Napier; Gloucestershire; Greenwich; Hertfordshire; Huddersfield; Kingston; Leeds Met; Nottingham Trent Portsmouth; Ulster.

COMPUTER STUDIES

Aberystwyth; Aston; Bath; Birmingham City; Bournemouth; Bradford; Brighton; Bristol UWE; Brunel; Cardiff; City; Coventry; De Montfort; Derby; East London; Edinburgh Napier; Glamorgan; Glasgow Caledonian; Gloucestershire; Greenwich; Hertfordshire; Huddersfield; Kent; Kingston; Leeds Metropolitan; Lincoln; Liverpool John Moores; London South Bank; Loughborough; Manchester; Manchester Metropolitan; Northumbria; Nottingham Trent; Oxford Brookes; Plymouth; Portsmouth; Queen's Belfast; Reading; Salford; Sheffield Hallam; Southampton Solent; Staffordshire; Surrey; Teesside; Ulster; West Scotland; Westminster; Wolverhampton; York.

DIETETICS

Cardiff (UWIC); Glasgow Caledonian; Leeds Met; Surrey; Ulster.

ECONOMICS

Abertay Dundee; Aston; Bath; Brunel; City; Hertfordshire; Kingston; Lancaster; Loughborough; Middlesex; Newcastle; Oxford Brookes; Plymouth; Portsmouth; Reading; Staffordshire; Surrey; Swansea Met; Ulster; Westminster; West Scotland.

ENGINEERING (GENERAL COURSES)

Aston; Bath; Bournemouth; Bradford; Bristol UWE; Brunel; Cardiff; Coventry; De Montfort; Harper Adams UC; Leicester; London South Bank; Loughborough; Manchester Metropolitan; Northumbria; Sheffield Hallam; Ulster; Wolverhampton.

ENGINEERING (AERONAUTICAL)

Bath; Brunel; Brighton; Bristol UWE; City; Coventry; Glamorgan; Hertfordshire; Kingston; Liverpool; Loughborough; Queen's Belfast; Queen Mary College London; Salford; Staffordshire; Surrey.

ENGINEERING (CHEMICAL)

Aston; Bath; London South Bank; Loughborough; Manchester; Queen's Belfast; Surrey; Teesside; West Scotland.

ENGINEERING (CIVIL, INCLUDING ENVIRONMENTAL)

Bolton; Bradford; Brighton; Bristol UWE; Brunel; Cardiff; City; Coventry; Glamorgan; Glasgow Caledonian; Kingston; London South Bank; Loughborough; Nottingham Trent; Plymouth; Portsmouth; Queen's Belfast; Salford; Surrey; Teesside; Ulster; West Scotland.

ENGINEERING (ELECTRICAL/ELECTRONIC, INCLUDING COMPUTER, CONTROL, SOFTWARE AND SYSTEMS)

Aston; Bath; Birmingham City; Bradford; Brighton; Bristol UWE; Cardiff; Central Lancashire; City; Coventry; De Montfort; East London; Glamorgan; Glasgow Caledonian; Hertfordshire; Huddersfield; Liverpool John Moores; London Metropolitan; London South Bank; Loughborough; Manchester Metropolitan; Northumbria; Plymouth; Portsmouth; Queen's Belfast; Reading; Sheffield Hallam; Staffordshire; Surrey; Teesside; Ulster; West Scotland; York.

ENGINEERING (MANUFACTURING AND MECHANICAL, INCLUDING AGRICULTURAL)

Aston; Bath; Birmingham City; Bournemouth; Bradford; Brighton; Bristol UWE; Brunel; Cardiff; Central Lancashire; City; Coventry; De Montfort; East London; Glamorgan; Glasgow Caledonian; Greenwich; Harper Adams University College; Huddersfield; Kingston; Leicester; Liverpool John Moores; London South Bank; Loughborough; Manchester Metropolitan; Northumbria; Nottingham Trent; Oxford Brookes; Plymouth; Portsmouth; Queen's Belfast; Queen Mary College London; Salford; Sheffield Hallam; Staffordshire; Sunderland; Surrey; Teesside; Ulster; West Scotland.

ENVIRONMENTAL SCIENCE

Aston; Bangor; Bradford; Brighton; Bristol UWE; Cardiff; Cardiff (UWIC); Coventry; Edinburgh Napier; Glamorgan; Harper Adams University College; Hertfordshire; Liverpool John Moores; London South Bank; Loughborough; Manchester Metropolitan; Northumbria; Nottingham Trent; Reading; Salford; Southampton Solent; Surrey; Teesside; Ulster; West Scotland; Wolverhampton.

FILM, RADIO, VIDEO AND TELEVISION STUDIES

See under **Media Studies**.

FINANCE

Abertay Dundee; Aston; Bath; Birmingham City; Bournemouth; Brighton; Bristol UWE; Brunel; City; Coventry; De Montfort; Glamorgan; Gloucestershire; Hertfordshire; Huddersfield; Kingston; Lancaster; Leeds Met; London Met; Loughborough; Manchester Met; Middlesex; Nottingham Trent; Plymouth; Portsmouth; Sheffield Hallam; Surrey; Swansea (Met); Teesside; Westminster; Wolverhampton; Worcester.

FOOD SCIENCE AND TECHNOLOGY (INCLUDING CONSUMER STUDIES AND NUTRITION)

Birmingham U.C.; Brighton; Bournemouth; Cardiff (UWIC); Glamorgan; Harper Adams University College; Huddersfield; London South Bank; Manchester Metropolitan; Newcastle; Northumbria; Queen's Belfast; Reading; Royal Agricultural College; Sheffield Hallam; Surrey; Teesside; Ulster.

GEOGRAPHY

Aberystwyth; Bradford; Cardiff; Coventry; Glamorgan; Hertfordshire; Kingston; Loughborough; Manchester Metropolitan; Nottingham Trent; Oxford Brookes; Plymouth; Queen's Belfast; Salford; Ulster; West Scotland; Wolverhampton.

GEOLOGY

Glamorgan; Greenwich; Kingston; West Scotland.

HORTICULTURE

Greenwich; Writtle Coll.

HOSPITALITY, HOTEL AND CATERING MANAGEMENT

Birmingham UC; Bournemouth; Brighton; Cardiff (UWIC); Central Lancashire; Derby; Edinburgh Napier; Gloucestershire; Huddersfield; Leeds Metropolitan; London Metropolitan; Manchester Metropolitan; Oxford Brookes; Plymouth; Portsmouth; Sheffield Hallam; Sunderland; Surrey; Ulster; Wolverhampton.

HUMAN RESOURCES MANAGEMENT

Aston; Bath; Birmingham City; Bournemouth; Bradford; Bristol UWE; Coventry; De Montfort; East London; Edinburgh Napier; Glamorgan; Gloucestershire; Hertfordshire; Leeds Met; Lincoln; Liverpool John Moores; London Metropolitan; Northumbria; Plymouth; Portsmouth; Royal Agricultural College; Sheffield Hallam; Staffordshire; Sunderland; Swansea Met; Teesside; Ulster; Westminster; West Scotland; Wolverhampton; Worcester.

INFORMATION MANAGEMENT

Bristol UWE; Coventry; Loughborough; Northumbria; Nottingham Trent; Plymouth; Staffordshire; Teesside.

LANDSCAPE ARCHITECTURE (INCLUDING GARDEN DESIGN)
Edinburgh CA; Writtle College.

LAW
Abertay Dundee; Birmingham City; Bournemouth; Bradford; Brighton; Brunel; City; Coventry; De Montfort; Edinburgh Napier; Hertfordshire; Huddersfield; Lancaster; Nottingham Trent; Oxford Brookes; Plymouth; Portsmouth; Staffordshire; Surrey; Teesside; Westminster.

LEISURE AND RECREATION MANAGEMENT/STUDIES
Aberystwyth; Birmingham UC; Bournemouth; Brighton; Glamorgan; Gloucestershire; Harper Adams UC.; Huddersfield; Sheffield Hallam; Sunderland; Swansea Met; Teesside; Ulster.

MARINE SCIENCES
Bangor; Cardiff; Edinburgh Napier; Greenwich; Liverpool John Moores; Plymouth; Portsmouth; Southampton Solent.

MARKETING
Abertay Dundee; Aston; Birmingham City; Bournemouth; Bradford; Brighton; Bristol UWE; Brunel; Central Lancashire; Coventry; De Montfort; East London; Edinburgh Napier; Glamorgan; Glasgow Caledonian; Gloucestershire; Greenwich; Harper Adams University College; Hertfordshire; Huddersfield; Hull; Lancaster; Leeds Metropolitan; Liverpool John Moores; London South Bank; Manchester Metropolitan; Middlesex; Newcastle; Northumbria; Nottingham; Oxford Brookes; Plymouth; Portsmouth; Royal Agricultural College; Sheffield Hallam; Staffordshire; Sunderland; Swansea IHE; Swansea Met; Teesside; Ulster; Westminster; West Scotland; Wolverhampton; Worcester.

MATERIALS SCIENCE
Bradford; Loughborough; Portsmouth.

MATHEMATICS
Aston; Bath; Bradford, Bristol UWE; Brighton; Brunel; Cardiff; Coventry; East Anglia; Glamorgan; Greenwich; Hertfordshire; Kingston; Liverpool John Moores; Loughborough; Manchester Metropolitan; Northumbria; Nottingham Trent; Portsmouth; Reading; Staffordshire; Surrey; Wolverhampton; York.

MEDIA STUDIES
Bournemouth; Bradford; Brighton; Brunel; City; De Montfort; Gloucestershire; Greenwich; Hertfordshire; Huddersfield; Kingston; Leeds Met; Lincoln; Liverpool John Moores; Plymouth; Sheffield Hallam; Staffordshire; Surrey; Ulster; Worcester, York.

MICROBIOLOGY
Bristol; Bristol UWE; Cardiff; De Montfort; Glamorgan; Leeds; Liverpool John Moores; London South Bank; Manchester; Middlesex; Nottingham Trent; West Scotland.

MUSIC
Birmingham City; Bournemouth; Bristol UWE; City; Coventry; Glamorgan; Gloucestershire; Hertfordshire; Huddersfield; Leeds Metropolitan; London Metropolitan; Portsmouth; Staffordshire; Surrey; Teesside.

NUTRITION
CAFRE; Coventry; Glamorgan; Glasgow Caledonian; Harper Adams UC; Huddersfield; Kingston; Lancaster; Leeds Metropolitan; Manchester Metropolitan; Newcastle; Northumbria; Queen's Belfast; Reading; Sheffield Hallam; Surrey; Teesside; Ulster.

PHARMACOLOGY AND PHARMACEUTICAL SCIENCES
Bath; Bristol; Bristol UWE; Coventry; De Montfort; East London; Hertfordshire; Huddersfield; Kingston; London Met; Manchester; Manchester Metropolitan; Nottingham Trent; Sheffield Hallam; Southampton; Sunderland.

PHOTOGRAPHY
Birmingham City; Portsmouth; Staffordshire.

PHYSICS
Bath; Bristol; Brunel; Hertfordshire; London South Bank; Loughborough; Nottingham Trent; Surrey; West Scotland.

PHYSIOLOGY
Bristol UWE; Cardiff; Greenwich; Manchester; Manchester Met; Nottingham Trent; Portsmouth; Salford; Southampton; Wolverhampton.

PLANT SCIENCES
Manchester; Plymouth.

POLITICS (INCLUDING INTERNATIONAL RELATIONS AND PUBLIC POLICY)
Aston; Bath; Brunel; Coventry; De Montfort; Huddersfield; Lancaster; Leeds Met; Loughborough; Nottingham Trent; Oxford Brookes; Portsmouth; Plymouth; Surrey; Westminster.

PROPERTY MANAGEMENT
Bradford; Bristol UWE; Kingston; Northumbria; Ulster.

PSYCHOLOGY
Aston; Bath; Bedfordshire; Bournemouth; Bradford; Bristol UWE; Brunel; Cardiff; De Montfort; Hertfordshire; Huddersfield; Kent; Lancaster; Liverpool John Moores; London Metropolitan; Loughborough; Manchester; Manchester Metropolitan; Middlesex; Portsmouth; Sheffield Hallam; Surrey; Swansea Met; Ulster; Westminster; Wolverhampton.

QUANTITY SURVEYING
Bristol UWE; Coventry; Glamorgan; London South Bank; Loughborough; Nottingham Trent; Plymouth; Sheffield Hallam; Ulster.

RETAIL MANAGEMENT
Birmingham UC; Bournemouth; Bradford, Brighton; Cardiff (UWIC); Central Lancashire; De Montfort; Gloucestershire; Huddersfield; Manchester Metropolitan; Northampton; Oxford Brookes; Queen Margaret; Robert Gordon; Roehampton; Southampton Solent; Stirling; Surrey; Teesside; Ulster; Westminster; Wolverhampton.

SOCIAL POLICY AND ADMINISTRATION
Aston; Bath; Central Lancashire; De Montfort; Loughborough; Middlesex; Northampton; Surrey.

SOCIAL STUDIES
Bath; Gloucestershire.

SOCIAL WORK
Bath.

SOCIOLOGY
Aston; Bath; Brunel; Middlesex; Northumbria; Nottingham Trent; Surrey.

SPORTS SCIENCE/STUDIES (INCLUDING SPORTS ENGINEERING AND TECHNOLOGY)
Bath; Bournemouth; Brighton; Bristol UWE; Brunel; Coventry; Glamorgan; Gloucestershire; Hertfordshire; Huddersfield; Kingston; London Metropolitan; London South Bank; Loughborough; Nottingham Trent; Sheffield Hallam; Swansea Met; Ulster; Warwickshire College; Writtle College; Wolverhampton.

STATISTICS
Bath; Bristol UWE; Coventry; Kingston; Portsmouth; Reading; Staffordshire; Surrey; Wolverhampton.

TECHNOLOGY
Aston; Bradford; Brunel; De Montfort; Glamorgan; Huddersfield; Sheffield Hallam; Surrey; Teesside; Ulster; West Scotland.

TOURISM
Aberystwyth; Bedfordshire; Birmingham UC; Bournemouth; Brighton; Bristol UWE; Cardiff (UWIC); Central Lancashire; Coventry; Glamorgan; Gloucestershire; Greenwich, Harper Adams University College; Hertfordshire; Huddersfield; Leeds Metropolitan; Llandrillo Coll; London Metropolitan; London South Bank; Manchester Metropolitan; Middlesex; Northumbria; Oxford Brookes; Plymouth; Portsmouth; Sheffield Hallam; Staffordshire; Sunderland; Surrey; Swansea Metropolitan; Teesside; Ulster; West Scotland; Writtle College; Wolverhampton.

TRANSPORT MANAGEMENT
Aston; Bristol UWE; City; Huddersfield; Liverpool John Moores; Loughborough; Plymouth; Sheffield Hallam; Staffordshire.

ZOOLOGY
Cardiff; Durham; Exeter; Manchester; Nottingham Trent; West Scotland.

6 | OTHER AWARDS AND REFERENCE SOURCES FOR NON-EU STUDENTS

AFRICAN EDUCATIONAL TRUST
The trust has many UK-based funding projects to support students of African descent. For details, see www.africaeducationaltrust.org/home.html.

AGA KHAN FOUNDATION
The Aga Khan Foundation provides a limited number of scholarships each year for postgraduate studies to outstanding students from developing countries who have no other means of financing their studies. Scholarships are awarded on a 50% grant: 50% loan basis through a competitive application process once a year in June. The foundation gives priority to requests for master's level courses but is also willing to consider applications for PhD programmes, when doctoral degrees are necessary for the career objectives of the student. For further information, see www.akdn.org/akfisp/HTML/#geo.

AIREY NEAVE TRUST
This trust gives grants to refugees (those with refugee status or exceptional leave to remain in the UK; asylum seekers are not eligible) undertaking postgraduate studies in the UK, primarily those who are doing a part-time degree and not in the first year of study. Applicants must have good oral and written English, have some work experience, and would ideally be engaged in part-time work to help fund themselves. The trust deals mainly with master's rather than MPhil/PhD students.

Interested applicants should telephone the trust on 01258 471444 for an informal interview to check their suitability. Grants are normally in the region of £1,500. New enquiries must be made before 1 May in the proposed year of study.

Contact the Airey Neave Trust, Calshoot Cottage, Church Street, Sturminster Newton, Dorset DT10 1DB.

ARAB–BRITISH CHAMBER OF COMMERCE
Scholarships and student grants are offered to Arab nationals under the age of 40 with citizenship in a Member State of the Arab league studying in the UK at postgraduate level. These are top-up awards and total funding must have been secured. See www.abcc.org.uk.

ARTS AND HUMANITIES RESEARCH COUNCIL (AHRC)
The AHRC is concerned with the support of institutionally based project research and administers two schemes of postgraduate awards: postgraduate studentships in the humanities and postgraduate professional and vocational awards.

Awards for postgraduate studentships are offered in two schemes: Competition A and Competition B. Competition A is for one-year or two-year studentships, for full-time study towards master's degrees, or for training in research. Competition B is for up to three years' full-time or five years' part-time study for a doctorate. All applications require the support of your supervisor and faculty and the AHRC's closing date of 1 May is strictly enforced. Application forms are available from the research officer in the Academic Quality and Support Department.

Contact the Postgraduate Studentships Office, Arts and Humanities Research Council, 10 Carlton House Terrace, London SW1Y 5AH; tel: 0171 969 5212; www.ahrc.ac.uk.

BEIT TRUST
Postgraduate fellowships are available to support postgraduate study or research in the UK. Applicants must be under 30 years of age (35 in the case of medical doctors) and university graduates domiciled in Zambia (four fellowships), Zimbabwe (four) or Malawi (two). For further information, contact fellowships@beittrust.org.uk.

BRITISH CHEVENING SCHOLARSHIPS
Important changes are taking place in the administration of this scheme. Contact www.chevening.com.

BRITISH COUNCIL FELLOWSHIP PROGRAMME
This provides study in the UK for professionals in fields that the council considers particularly important in the country concerned. Subsidiary schemes are the exchange programmes with Eastern Europe, China and Russia, which each form part of a wider bilateral cultural agreement or programme. About 900 awards are provided annually.

Eligible subjects are determined by council directors overseas. The awards are for periods from two months to three years, for short attachments and courses through to postgraduate taught courses and PhD research. They generally cover fares to and from the UK, tuition fees, living expenses, and allowances for books, clothing and approved travel within the UK.

In the countries in which the scheme operates the local British Council director publicises the awards and is responsible for the selection of candidates. Students must apply to the British Council office in their own country for a fellowship and usually need to be a national and a resident of the country where they are applying. Students being considered for a grant will be interviewed in their own country.

Details are available in the UK from Development and Training Services, British Council Fellowship Section, The British Council, Bridgewater House, 58 Whitworth Street, Manchester M1 6BB; www.britishcouncil.org.

BRITISH FEDERATION OF WOMEN GRADUATES (BFWG)
The BFWG has national awards for the final year of PhD research. Women of any nationality may apply. The closing date for these awards is April.

The BFWG has awards for study, learning and training in various countries including America, Australia, Japan, Norway, South Africa and Switzerland. There are various closing dates for the international awards.

Contact: BFWG, 4 Mandeville Courtyard, 142 Battersea Park Road, London SW11 4NB.

BRITISH INFORMATION SERVICES
American students can consult the British Information Services, 845 Third Avenue, New York, NY 10022, or the Institute of International Education, 809 United Nations Plaza, New York, NY 10017. Enquiries about Rhodes Scholarships for Oxford can be addressed to the Office of the American Secretary, Rhodes Scholarship Trust, Pomona College, Claremont, CA 91711.

American students already in the UK can consult the US/UK Advisory Service, 62 Doughty Street, London WC1N 2LS; tel: 020 7404 6994.

Students from overseas are advised that the best source of information about awards is the British Council, which has 228 offices in 108 countries. Students should contact the British Council Office, or British embassies and high commissions.

The main UK offices are located at:

The British Council
10 Spring Gardens
London SW1A 2BN
Tel: 020 7930 8466

The British Council (ECS)
58 Whitworth Street
Manchester M1 6BB
Tel: 0161 957 7755

British Council awards and scholarships are available to certain international students. Details of the award schemes should be obtained from the British Council's representative in the candidate's own country or from www.britishcouncil.org/education/funding_index.htm or through www.ukcosa.org.uk or by email to education.enquiries@britishcouncil.org.

BRITISH LEBANESE ASSOCIATION
A small number of scholarships are awarded annually in October to Lebanese students of outstanding merit who wish to pursue one-year postgraduate courses in the UK. Contact the website www.britishlebanese.org.

BRITISH MARSHALL SCHOLARSHIPS
This scheme was set up by the British government as a practical expression of the British people's appreciation of the aid given by the USA under the Marshall Plan. Up to 40 new awards are offered each year. Each scholarship is held for two years and is available in any subject discipline.

Awards are open to US citizens under 26, who are graduates of US universities, to undertake study in any subject leading to a degree at a UK university. Selection is by regional committee in the USA. Awards are made on a competitive basis and are for two years in the first instance, renewable for a third year in certain circumstances. The awards cover fares, tuition fees, maintenance, books, thesis and travel allowances.

Contact in the USA: universities or colleges, British Consulates-General in the USA, or British Information Services, 845 Third Avenue, New York, NY 10022, who will issue application forms.

Contact in the UK: Marshall Aid Commemoration Commission, John Foster House, 36 Gordon Square, London WC1H 0PF; www.marshallscholarship.org.

CANADIAN SCHOLARSHIP FUND
There is funding available to Canadian citizens studying in the UK. Awards range from £500 to £2,500 and are for students who have already commenced their postgraduate studies in the UK. For further information and application forms, visit www.canadianscholarshipfund.co.uk.

CANON COLLINS EDUCATIONAL TRUST
The Canon Collins Educational Trust for Southern Africa (CCETSA) provides scholarships to students from/in the countries of Southern Africa who wish to pursue a postgraduate degree (normally a one-year master's degree) in the UK. Both partial and full scholarships are awarded annually. For further information see www.canoncollins.org.uk.

CENTRAL EUROPEAN UNIVERSITY FELLOWSHIP PROGRAMME
Each academic year, the Central European University, a US degree awarding institution of postgraduate study and research located in Central Europe (Budapest and Warsaw), awards 700 tuition and stipend packages in the form of a full CEU fellowship or partial financial aid. For more information about these opportunities, email admissions@ceu.hu or telephone +36 1 327 3009.

CHARLES WALLACE TRUSTS
Awards are offered to citizens of India, Pakistan, Burma and Bangladesh who intend to follow a postgraduate programme. For details, see www.britishcouncil.org/india-scholarships-cwit or www.wallace-trusts.org.uk.

CHURCHES COMMISSION FOR INTERNATIONAL STUDENTS

Assistance is only given to students who are currently enrolled on a programme of study, and not to prospective students.

This Hardship Fund was set up in 1990 by the Churches to assist international students, irrespective of their race, sex or religion, who face unexpected financial problems during the final stages of their degree course. Awards are normally made to those who can clearly show that a small grant will enable them to complete their course, normally those who are within six months of finishing.

Potential candidates should contact Mr David Philpot, Grants Secretary, CCIS Hardship Fund, 121 George Street, Edinburgh EH2 4YN.

COMMONWEALTH NASSAU FELLOWSHIP

A scheme for non-white South African students to study in Britain. Preference is given to postgraduate students who have not already obtained a first degree. Contact the Department for International Development (DfID), 94 Victoria Street, London SW1E 5TL.

DEPARTMENT FOR INTERNATIONAL DEVELOPMENT

The UK Department for International Development offers scholarships to candidates from Commonwealth countries. Candidates for schemes such as the Technical Cooperation and Training Programme (TCTP) are nominated by their own government. Details are available from the British Council's representative in the candidate's own country or contact ACU, John Foster House, 36 Gordon Square, London WC1H 0PF.

ECONOMIC AND SOCIAL RESEARCH COUNCIL (ESRC)

The ESRC funds research across a broad range of social sciences including area studies, economic and social history, economics, education, linguistics, management and business studies, media studies, politics, psychology, social policy, social statistics and socio-legal studies.

It allocates the majority of its research studentships directly to students through an annual competition (closing date is 1 May). As with the AHRC, students apply to ESRC through a single university school or department that has offered them a place. Applications are judged according to the student's academic record. See www.esrc.ac.uk for details.

ENGINEERING AND PHYSICAL SCIENCES RESEARCH COUNCIL (EPSRC)

The EPSRC funds research in the engineering and physical sciences, including Chemistry, Engineering, Information Technology, Materials Science, Mathematics and Physics. EPSRC funds standard research studentships, CASE (Computer-Aided Software Engineering) studentships and Engineering doctorate studentships. It does not make awards directly to students but allocates money to a university school or department (Doctoral Training Accounts) on the basis of the amount of EPSRC grant income held by that school/department. Schools and departments then advertise for, and select, candidates. See www.epsrc.ac.uk for details.

ENTENTE CORDIALE SCHOLARSHIPS

The Entente Cordiale Scholarships are awarded to British postgraduates to study arts, humanities, business and sciences in France for one year. Candidates should also be able to study in French. The scholarship covers maintenance, registration, study fees and student support services. For further information and application forms visit www.entente-cordiale.org.

EUROPEAN UNIVERSITY INSTITUTE, FLORENCE

The European University Institute in Florence, Italy is offering four-year postgraduate grants leading to a doctorate recognised in the EU Member States. The grants are for those studying in the following disciplines: Law, Economics, History, Social and Political Sciences. For information and conditions visit www.iue.it.

FOREIGN AND COMMONWEALTH OFFICE AWARDS
Awards varying in value are offered to overseas students through a number of different schemes. There are special schemes for students from certain overseas countries. Further details are available from British missions in the candidate's own country or from the Overseas Students Policy Section, Foreign and Commonwealth Office, Old Admiralty Buildings, Whitehall, London SW1A 2AF.

FULBRIGHT SCHOLARSHIPS
The British government contributes to the Fulbright Programme, which aims to further understanding between the USA and Britain. About 50 awards a year are available under the programme.

Awards are open to US graduate students for pre-doctoral study in the UK. There are no restrictions on subject or age. Awards are made on a competitive basis for nine months, but renewals for one year can be offered to a limited number of students. The awards cover round-trip travel, a maintenance allowance, approved tuition fees where applicable and an incidental expense allowance. The scheme is advertised in US institutions, which conduct preliminary reviews of applicants.

Scholars' Awards are also available for lecturing or advanced research for a minimum of three months. There are two types of award: programmed awards in response to specific requests from UK institutions; and grant-in-aid made on a competitive basis. Awards are also available under a Faculty Exchange Programme to enable faculty members to undertake an exchange of posts for teaching purposes.

Fellowships are offered for research librarians and academic administrators to spend three months gaining relevant experience in the UK. Arts fellowships and professional fellowships are awarded to individuals in a variety of fields to enable them to spend a period of six to nine months in the UK.

Contact details: Graduate students: The Institute of International Education (IIE), 809 United Nations Plaza, New York, NY 10017, USA; Scholars: The Council for International Exchange of Scholars (CIES), 3400 International Drive NW, Suite M,500, Washington DC 2,0008-3097, USA; arts and professional fellowships, research librarians and academic administrations, Faculty Exchange Programme (by the British participant in the exchange) and UK enquiries: Programme Director, The Fulbright Commission, Fulbright House, 62 Doughty Street, London WC1N 2LS, UK; tel: 020 7404 6994; www.fulbright.co.uk.

GILMAN INTERNATIONAL SCHOLARSHIP PROGRAMME
The Benjamin A Gilman International Scholarship Programme reduces barriers to study abroad by providing assistance to those undergraduate students in two-year or four-year institutions who demonstrate financial need. This programme is offered through the Bureau of Educational and Cultural Affairs of the US Department of State and is administered by the Institute of International Education. Selected recipients are awarded up to $5,000, depending on the length of their programme, to defray the costs associated with studying abroad.

For more information about this programme, eligibility requirements and the application procedure, visit www.iie.org/programs/gilman.

GREAT BRITAIN–CHINA EDUCATIONAL TRUST (GBCET)
This trust makes awards to British and Chinese students studying at PhD level. Awards of up to £5,000 are available. Only students who have completed the first year of their PhD programme are eligible to apply. For further information and application forms visit www.gbcc.org.uk/edtrust.htm or email trust@gbcc.org.uk.

INSTITUTE OF LATIN AMERICAN STUDIES
The School of Advanced Study has the largest postgraduate programme on Latin America in the UK. Student funding is available in the form of bursaries, fieldwork grants and hardship grants.

For further information contact the Postgraduate Administrator, Institute of Latin American Studies, 31 Tavistock Square, London WC1H 9HA; www.sas.ac.uk/ilas.

INSTITUTO LING FELLOWSHIP
This is an annual fellowship programme for Brazilian citizens with entrepreneurial spirit and leadership skills to contribute to the Brazilian economic, social and cultural development. To be eligible applicants must have Brazilian citizenship and be able to demonstrate financial need. The fellowships can be used for full-time MBA courses, and consist of a partial fellowship covering up to one third of the course costs. The fellowships are only available for the beginning of the second half of the course.

Application information can be found at www.institutoling.org.br or via email at instituto.ling@petropar.com.br.

INTERNATIONAL STUDENT HOUSE
Residential scholarships are offered to students from developing countries excluding North America, Japan, Israel, Australasia and all countries in the European Economic Area. Preference is given to students undertaking a master's degree or final-year students taking bachelor's or PhD degrees. Contact www.ish.org.uk for details.

JAPAN FOUNDATION
The Japan Foundation was founded in 1972 as a non-profit, special legal entity in order to further international mutual understanding through the promotion of cultural exchange between Japan and other countries. To this end, the foundation offers a range of scholarship programmes. For further information visit www.jpf.go.jp or contact the Japan Foundation London Office, 17 Old Park Lane, London W1Y 3LG; tel: 020 7499 4726.

KYUNG HEE UNIVERSITY (KOREA) SCHOLARSHIPS
Kyung Hee University offers three types of scholarships to its students:

* **Class A:** a full scholarship covering tuition fees, room and board
* **Class B:** a scholarship covering tuition fees
* **Class C:** a scholarship covering half of the tuition fees.

For further information about applying to Kyung Hee University and its scholarship programme, contact the Graduate School of Pan-Pacific International Studies (GSP), Kyung Hee, University at Suwon Campus, 1 Seochun-ri, Kiheung-eup, Yongin-si, Kyunggi-do 449-701, Korea; gsp@nms.kyunghee.ac.kr.

LADY DAVIS FELLOWSHIP TRUST
Lady Davis Fellowships are awarded at the Hebrew University and Technion, on the basis of excellence in achievement and promise of further distinction. They are open to candidates of every race, creed, nationality and sex. For further information visit http://ldft.huji.ac.il.

LANEKASSEN NORWEGIAN SCHOLARSHIP
An educational grant and loan is offered for a 10-month academic year. For further details see www.lanekassen.no or www.scholarships.ed.ac.uk/lanekassen.

LEVERHULME TRADE CHARITIES TRUST UNDERGRADUATE BURSARIES
To be eligible for one of these awards, you must:

* Normally be a resident of the UK; and
* Be the son, daughter, spouse, widow or widower of a commercial traveller, chemist or grocer.

The bursaries are intended for those in financial hardship, eg requiring funds for maintenance, tuition and examination fees, travel costs, study materials, accommodation or childcare costs etc.

The maximum value for any bursary is £3,000. Full details are available from the Leverhulme Trade Charities Trust, 1 Pemberton Row, London EC4A 3BG; tel: 020 7822 5227.

MARJORIE DEAN FINANCIAL JOURNALISM FOUNDATION

The foundation offers one or two studentships, worth roughly £10,000 each, to students who have been accepted to do a master's degree in Economics or Finance at a top British university.

Preference will be given to applicants who can write well and who will produce a piece of research (probably based on their dissertation) that is suitable for publication.

For further information visit www.mdfjf.co.uk. Candidates should send a CV, a proposed research topic and proof of entry to a master's degree programme to Martin Giles, c/o Elana Herron, The Economist, 15 Regent Street, London SW1Y 4LR.

MEDICAL RESEARCH COUNCIL (MRC)

The MRC funds research in all areas of medical and related science, with the aim of improving human health. The council does not make awards directly to students, but rather operates a quota system similar to that of BBSRC. Schools and departments bid to MRC for quota studentships every two or three years, and allocations are made on the basis of a number of criteria, including the research standing of the school/department and the strength of its research training programme. See www.mrc.ac.uk for details.

MONASH UNIVERSITY POSTGRADUATE RESEARCH SCHOLARSHIPS

Monash University offers a number of postgraduate research scholarships. Closing date each year is normally 31 October. For further information visit www.mrgs.monash.edu.au.

NATURAL ENVIRONMENT RESEARCH COUNCIL (NERC)

NERC funds research in terrestrial, marine and freshwater biology and earth, atmospherical, hydro-logical, oceanographic and polar sciences, and earth observation. As with MRC, NERC only funds students through university schools and departments. The majority of its studentships are awarded through its studentship algorithm, which takes account of the amount of NERC research funding awarded to the department over the previous three years. If schools and departments are allo-cated one or more studentships through this scheme they advertise for, and select, students, who then work on projects that fall within NERC's and the department's remit. See www.nerc.ac.uk.

OVERSEAS DEVELOPMENT INSTITUTE (ODI) FELLOWSHIP SCHEME

Each year the ODI Fellowship Scheme recruits up to 20 young postgraduate economists to work for two years in the public sectors of countries in Africa, the Caribbean and the Pacific.

Students will need:

* An excellent degree and postgraduate qualifications in economics or an economics specialism (one of which must be from a British or Irish university)
* A sound grasp of economic theory and its application
* Good communication skills
* A genuine interest in development.

Some work experience would be an advantage.

For further information and an application form, contact the Fellowship Scheme, Overseas Development Institute, 111 Westminster Bridge Road, London SE1 7JD; tel: 020 7922 0356; www.odi.org.uk.

OVERSEAS RESEARCH STUDENTS AWARDS SCHEME (ORSAS)

These awards are designed to ensure a continued supply of high-quality research students to UK universities. Up to 850 new awards are made each year.

These grants are for postgraduate students intending to undertake full-time study for a higher degree as registered research students at a British higher education institution and who are liable to pay the higher fees chargeable to overseas students. Academic merit and research potential are the sole criteria governing the selection of candidates. No account is taken of means, nationality or subject field. The awards meet the difference between the home and overseas level of tuition fees only, and do not cover maintenance costs. They are initially made for one year but, subject to the satisfactory progress of the award-holder, are renewable for a second or third year. Most but not all universities and many other higher education institutions hold awards under the scheme – a full list is available at www.orsas.ac.uk.

Apply through the UK higher education institution at which you wish to study. Alternatively, contact the ORS office at the Committee of Vice-Chancellors and Principals (CVCP), 29 Tavistock Square, London WC1H 9EZ; www.orsas.ac.uk.

PROGRAMME ALβAN

Programme Alβan aims at the reinforcement of European Union–Latin America cooperation in the area of higher education. The scholarships cover studies for postgraduates as well as higher level training for Latin American professionals/future decision-makers, in institutions or centres in the EU. It is open to Latin-American citizens living in one of the following Latin American countries: Argentina; Bolivia; Brazil; Chile; Colombia; Costa Rica; Cuba; Ecuador; El Salvador; Guatemala; Honduras; Mexico; Nicaragua; Panama; Paraguay; Peru; Uruguay; Venezuela.

For further information contact the Alβan Office, Asociación Grupo Santander, Universidade do Porto, Rua de Ceuta 118, 5º s/35, 4050-190 Porto, Portugal; Fax: +351 22 2046 159; www.programalban.org.

ROYAL SCOTTISH CORPORATION

If you are a Scottish student, resident in London for at least two years, there are funds available to help with tuition fees and course costs. Advice, information and application forms can be obtained by phoning Ms Finn Mackay on 0800 652 2989.

SAMSTAG AWARDS

An award is offered to Australian students wishing to study visual arts at an overseas institution. See www.unisa.edu.au/samstag for further details.

SCOTTISH INTERNATIONAL SCHOLARSHIP PROGRAMME

The Scottish Executive offers scholarships for students who are residents of China, India, South Africa, Australia, New Zealand or Singapore and who would like to study for a master's degree in Scotland. The scholarships are available for courses at any Scottish higher education institution and applications for science and technology and creative industries will be given priority. For further information see www.scotlandscholarship.com.

SINO-BRITISH SCHOLARSHIP SCHEME

These scholarships are for students from the People's Republic of China who are resident in China at the time of application. Awards are for postgraduate studies in the UK. Applications are channelled through the State Education Commission in Beijing. The British Council administers the scheme in the UK. Apply to your home institution or work unit.

SIR EDWARD YOUDE MEMORIAL FELLOWSHIPS FOR OVERSEAS STUDIES

Outstanding Hong Kong students, intending to study postgraduate courses overseas, are eligible to apply for this award. Candidates must have a strong commitment and intention to return to Hong

Kong following completion of their studies, where they will be expected to work for a minimum of three years.

Contact: The Secretary, Sir Edward Youde Memorial Fund Council, Queensway Government Offices, Low Block, G/F 66 Queensway, Hong Kong.

SIR RICHARD STAPLEY EDUCATIONAL TRUST
The trust was established in 1919 and has been a registered charity (no 313812) since 1974.

Applicants for grants (normally from £300 to £1,000 in value) must be:

* Over the age of 24 on 1 October of the proposed year of study;
* Graduates with a first or 2(i), studying for a degree in Medicine, Dentistry or Veterinary Science, or for a higher degree or equivalent academic qualification in any subject at a university in the UK;
* Already resident in the UK at the time of application.

For more information contact the Administrator, Sir Richard Stapley Educational Trust, North Street Farmhouse, Sheldwich, Faversham ME13 0LN; www.stapleytrust.org.

Application forms are available from 1 January each year. The annual closing date for applications is 28 February. Awards are announced in late June.

UK 9/11 SCHOLARSHIPS
The UK 9/11 Scholarships Fund provides awards for study in higher or further education in the United Kingdom to children or dependants of victims of the terrorist attacks on the United States on 11 September 2001. See www.britishcouncil.org/911scholarships for further information.

UNIVERSITY OF LONDON - CENTRAL RESEARCH FUND GRANTS
Applications are invited for research grants to assist specific projects of research with the provision of expenses such as materials, apparatus and travel costs. For application forms and further information, contact the Secretary to the Academic Trust Funds Committee, University of London, Senate House - Room 230, Malet Street, London WC1E 7HU; www.lon.ac.uk/crf.

US-UK FULBRIGHT COMMISSION
The US–UK Fulbright Commission provides scholarships to qualified US citizens who wish to study at master's or doctoral level at an educational institution in the UK. There are approximately 20 awards each year. The commission looks for evidence of academic excellence, leadership, outstanding references and strong reasons for coming to the UK. Consult www.fulbright.co.uk for further information.

WINSTON CHURCHILL MEMORIAL TRUST FUND
Fellowships are offered to cover study expenses. www.wcmt.org.uk.

7 | SUBJECT-SPECIFIC AWARDS FOR HOME/EU STUDENTS

Most universities and colleges offer large numbers of scholarships, bursaries and prizes in a wide range of subjects and applicants and current students should check with the Faculty or Departmental Heads for information of any awards on offer. However in Chapter 2, the institutions listed below provide details of *specific named awards* as shown below. Some of these awards are open to EU students.

ACCOUNTING
Dundee, Hertfordshire, Manchester

ACOUSTICS AND SOUND RECORDING
Southampton, Surrey

ACTING
Central School of Speech and Drama, Mountview. See also **Chapter 4,** under Drama

ACTUARIAL STUDIES
Southampton. See also **Chapter 4,** under Insurance.

AGRICULTURE
Aberdeen, Aberystwyth, Bristol UWE, CAFRE, Harper Adams Univ Coll, Imperial College London, Leicester, Newcastle Royal, Royal Agric Coll

AMERICAN STUDIES
Leicester

ANCIENT HISTORY
Lampeter, Leicester

ANIMAL SCIENCE
Plymouth

ANIMATION
Newport

ANTHROPOLOGY
Southampton, St Andrews

ARABIC/ISLAMIC STUDIES
Exeter

ARCHAEOLOGY
Cardiff, Leicester, Manchester, Southampton

ARCHITECTURE
AA School, Cardiff, Greenwich, Plymouth, Queen's Belfast

ART AND DESIGN
Cleveland CAD, Coventry, Newport, Plymouth, Portsmouth. See also **Chapter 4.**

ARTS
Newcastle, Queen's Belfast

BIOCHEMISTRY
Plymouth, Southampton, Surrey. See also **Chapter 4** under Science

BIOLOGICAL SCIENCES
Bath Spa, Cardiff, Essex, Leicester, Plymouth, Queen's Belfast, Royal Holloway College London, Southampton, St George's London. See also **Chapter 4** under Science

BUILDING/CONSTRUCTION
Glasgow Caledonian, Greenwich, Plymouth, Reading. See also **Chapter 4.**

BUSINESS/MANAGEMENT
Bedfordshire, Buckingham, Central Lancashire, Hertfordshire, Kingston, Regents Business School, Swansea, Trinity University College (Carmarthen). See also **Chapter 4.**

CHEMISTRY
Bath, Edinburgh, Imperial College London, Leicester, Manchester, Newcastle, Nottingham, Sheffield, Sheffield, Surrey, York. See also **Chapter 4** under Science

CHORAL
Aberdeen, Bangor, Bath, Bishop Grosseteste Coll, Bristol, Cambridge, Cardiff, Chester, Durham, Greenwich, Hertfordshire, Leicester, Newcastle, Nottingham, Royal Holloway College London, Sheffield, Surrey, York. See also **Chapter 4**

CLASSICS
Lampeter

COMMUNICATION STUDIES
Leicester

COMPUTER SCIENCE
Bangor, Birmingham, Bristol UWE, Cardiff, Dundee, Exeter, Hertfordshire, Huddersfield, Kingston, Leicester, Manchester, Northumbria, Oxford, Reading, Royal Holloway College London, Salford, Swansea, Trinity University College

CRICKET
Bradford, Cardiff, Glamorgan, Worcester

CRIMINOLOGY
Leicester, Southampton

DANCE
Leeds Coll Mus. See also **Chapter 4** under Drama

DENTISTRY
Dundee

DESIGN TECHNOLOGY
Central Lancashire

DIETETICS
Bath Spa

DRAMA
Central School of Speech and Drama, GSA Conservatoire, Imperial College, Mountview, Rose Bruford College. See also **Chapter 4.**

ECONOMICS
Aberdeen, Birmingham, Buckingham, Leicester, Oxford, Southampton

EDUCATION
Southampton, Trinity University College (Carmarthen)

ENGINEERING
Aberdeen, Abertay Dundee, Aston, Bangor, Bath, Brimingham, Bradford, Cardiff, Central Lancashire, Coventry, Dundee, Edinburgh, Exeter, Glamorgan, Harper Adams Univ Coll, Heriot-Watt, Hertfordshire, Kingston, Leicester, Lincoln, Liverpool, Loughborough, Manchester, Newcastle, Northumbria, Nottingham, Oxford, Queen's Belfast, Reading, Robert Gordon, Salford, Southampton, Surrey, Sussex, York. See also **Chapter 4**.

ENGLISH
Southampton, York

ENVIRONMENTAL SCIENCE/STUDIES
Bath Spa, Harper Adams Univ Coll, Manchester, Plymouth

EUROPEAN STUDIES
Bath, Southampton

FILM STUDIES
Leicester, Newport, St Andrews, Southampton, Univ of the Arts

FOOD SCIENCE
Cardiff (UWIC), Nottingham, Thames Valley. See also **Chapter 4.**

FRENCH
Southampton

GENETICS
Leicester

GEOGRAPHY
Bath Spa, Exeter, Leicester, Liverpool, Southampton, Swansea

GEOLOGY (INC. EARTH SCIENCES)
Aberystwyth, Imperial College London, Oxford, Royal Holloway College London, Southampton

GERMAN
Cardiff, Southampton

GOLF
Aberdeen, Exeter, Royal Holloway College London, St Andrews, York

HEALTH SCIENCES
Bath spa, Kings's College London, Queen's Belfast. NHS Bursaries for health professionals at all universities. See also **Chapter 4**

HISTORY
Leicester, Southampton, Swansea

HISTORY OF ART
Leicester, Manchester

HORTICULTURE
See also **Chapter 4**

HOSPITALITY MANAGEMENT
Thames Valley

HUMANITIES
Dundee, Newcastle, Queen's Balfast

HUMAN RESOURCES MANAGEMENT
Hertfordshire

HUMAN SCIENCES
Loughborough

INFORMATICS
Edinburgh, Manchester, Salford, Sussex

INFORMATION SCIENCE
Loughborough, Northumbria

ITALIAN
Cardiff. See also **Chapter 3** under Scottish Italian Scholarships

JAZZ
Leeds Coll. Mus

JOURNALISM
See **Chapter 4**

LANGUAGES
Bath, Liverpool, Manchester, Salford, Southampton. See also **Chapter 3** under Stevenson Exchange Scholarships

LATIN AMERICAN STUDIES
Southampton

LAW
Buckingham, Cardiff, Central Lancashire, Dundee, Hertfordshire, Kingston, Surrey

LEISURE
Manchester

LINGUISTICS
Manchester, York

MANAGEMENT
Leicester, Manchester

MARKETING
Hertfordshire

MATERIALS SCIENCE
Liverpool, Loughborough, Manchester, Newcastle, Nottingham, Oxford, Surrey. See also **Chapter 4**

MATHEMATICS
Brimingham, Cardiff, Coventry, Dundee, Edinburgh, Essex, Kingston, Loughborough, Newcastle, Nottingham, Oxford, Queen's Belfast, St Andrews, Sussex, Swansea

MEDIA STUDIES
Bournemouth

MEDICAL BIOCHEMISTRY
Leicester

MEDICINE
Dundee, Imperial College, Hull York Med. Sch., Keele, Newcastle, Queen Mary College London, St George's London. See also **Chapter 4.**

METALLURGY AND MATERIALS
Birmingham

MIDWIFERY
Southampton. See also **Chapter 4** under Medical and Related Courses

MINING
Exeter CSM

MUSIC
Aberdeen, Aberystwyth, Bangor, Birmingham, Brunel, Cambridge, Canterbury Christ Church, Cardiff, City, Durham, Exeter, Gloucestershire, Goldsmiths College London, Keele, Kent, Leeds Coll Mus, Leicester, LIPA, Nottingham, Oxford, Reading, Royal Holloway College London, Royal Northern Coll. Mus, Royal Scottish Academy Mus. Dr, Royal Welsh Coll Mus Dr, St Andrews, Sheffied, Southampton, Thames Valley, Warwick, York. See also **Chapter 4.**

NURSING
Southampton. See also **Chapter 4**

NUTRITION
Bath Spa.

OCCUPATIONAL THERAPY
See **Chapter 4** under Medical and Related Courses

ORGAN
Aberdeen, Bishop Grosseteste Coll, Bristol, Cambridge, Cardiff, Chester, Exeter, King's College London, Nottingham, Queen's Belfast, Royal Holloway College London, Sheffield, Surrey

PERFORMING ARTS
Durham, Newport, Trinity University College (Carmarthen). See also **Chapter 4** under Drama

PHARMACY
Nottingham

PHILOSOPHY
Lampeter, Southampton, St Andrews

PHOTOGRAPHY
Newport

PHYSICAL EDUCATION
Plymouth

PHYSICS
Bath, Birmingham, Edinburgh, Imperial College London, Loughborough, Queen's Belfast, Royal Holloway College, Sussex, Swansea, York. See also **Chapter 4**

PHYSIOLOGY
Leicester

PHYSIOTHERAPY
See **Chapter 4** under Medical and Related Courses

PLANT AND SOIL SCIENCE
Aberdeen

PODIATRY
See **Chapter 4** under Medical and Related Courses

POLITICS
Southampton

POLYMER TECHNOLOGY
Loughborough

POPULATION SCIENCE
Southampton

PORTUGUESE
Southampton

PRINTING
Univ of the Arts

PSYCHOLOGY
Southampton

PUBLIC POLICY
Birmingham

RELIGIOUS STUDIES
Bangor, St Andrews, Trinity University College (Carmarthen)

RENEWABLE ENERGY
Exeter

RUGBY
Exeter, Greenwich, Harper Adams Univ Coll, Huddersfield, Imperial College London, Kent

SCIENCE
Coventry, Lincoln

SOCIAL POLICY
Southampton

SOCIAL SCIENCES
Birmingham, Newcastle, Southampton

SOCIAL WORK
Southampton

SPORT
Aberdeen, Aberystwyth, Anglia Ruskin, Bangor, Bath, Bedfordshire, Birmingham, Brighton, Bristol UWE, Brunel, Cambridge, Canterbury Christ Church, Chichester, Coventry, Dundee, Durham, East Anglia, Edinburgh, Essex, Glamorgan, Glasgow, Glasgow Caledonian, Gloucestershire, Glyndwr, Heriot-Watt, Hertfordshire, Imperial College London, Leeds, Leeds Metropolitan, Leicester, Lincoln, London South Bank, Manchester, Marjon, Newcastle, Newport, Nottingham, Oxford, Plymouth, Portsmouth, Queen's Belfast, Reading, Roehampton, Royal Holloway College London, Sheffield, Southampton, Stirling, Strathclyde, Sussex, Swansea, Teesside, Trinity University College (Carmarthen), Ulster, Warwick, Wolverhampton, Worcester

STATISTICS
Essex

TEACHING
See **Chapter 4**

TECHNOLOGY
Coventry, Heriot-Watt, Lincoln

TEXTILES
Manchester

THEOLOGY
Lampeter

TOURISM
Glasgow Caledonian, London Metropolitan

TOWN PLANNING
Manchester. See also **Chapter 4**

TRANSPORT AND LOGISTICS
Huddersfield

TROMBONE
Leeds Coll Mus

VETERINARY SCIENCE
Royal Veterinary College London

WELSH
Cardiff, Trinity University College (Carmarthen)

ZOOLOGY
Southampton

8 | SUBJECT-SPECIFIC AWARDS FOR NON-EU STUDENTS

Many universities offer scholarships and bursaries in a wide range of subjects. Those institutions in the following list offer specific awards in the subjects as shown. See **Chapter 2.**

ACOUSTICS
Salford

AGRICULTURE
Hartpury College

AMERICAN STUDIES
Nottingham

ANATOMY
Bristol

ARTS SUBJECTS
Nottingham. See also **Chapter 6** under Arts and under Entente Cordiale

ASTRONOMY
Southampton

BIOCHEMISTRY
Bristol

BIOSCIENCES
Aston, Birmingham, Hull, Nottingham, Oxford, Southampton

BUILT ENVIRONMENT
Glasgow Caledonian

BUSINESS
Bristol, Southampton, Sussex. See also **Chapter 6** under Entente Cordiale

CHEMISTRY
Aston, Hull

CLASSICS
Nottingham, Oxford

COMPUTING
Aston, Birmingham, Bournemouth, Hull, Salford

CONSERVATION
Bournemouth

DENTISTRY
Liverpool

DRAMA
Rose Bruford College

EARTH SCIENCES
Birmingham

ECONOMICS
Bristol. See also **Chapter 6** under Marjorie Dean

EDUCATION
Southampton

ENGINEERING
Aston, Bath, Birmingham, Bournemouth, Hull, Nottingham, Salford. See also **Chapter 6** under Engineering

ENVIRONMENTAL STUDIES
Aston

FILM STUDIES
Nottingham

FRENCH
Nottingham

GEOGRAPHY
Aston, Hull, Southampton

GERMAN
Nottingham

HEALTH SCIENCES
Nottingham, Southampton

HISPANIC STUDIES
Nottingham

HISTORY
Nottingham, Oxford

HOSPITALITY
Birmingham Univ Coll

HUMANITIES
See **Chapter 6** under Entente Cordiale

INTERNATIONAL RELATIONS
Nottingham

LANGUAGES
Oxford

LAW
Birmingham, Liverpool, Nottingham, Oxford

LIFE SCIENCES
Nottingham

MATERIALS SCIENCE
See **Chapter 6** under Engineering

MATHEMATICS
Aston, Manchester, Oxford, Southampton. See **Chapter 6** under Engineering

MEDIA STUDIES
Bournemouth

MEDICINE
Southampton

MUSIC
Aberdeen, Nottingham

NANOSCIENCE
Nottingham

NURSING
Southampton

PHARMACOLOGY
Brunel

PHARMACY
Nottingham

PHILOSOPHY
Nottingham

PHYSICS
Hull, Oxford, Southampton. See also **Chapter 6** under Engineering

POLITICS
Oxford

PSYCHOLOGY
Hull, Southampton

PUBLIC POLICY
Nottingham

RUSSIAN
Nottingham

SCIENCES
See **Chapter 6** under Entente Cordiale

SOCIAL SCIENCE
Southampton. See also **Chapter 6** under Economic and Social Research Council and under European University

SPORT SCIENCE
Birmingham, Hull

TEACHING
Trinity University College (Carmarthen)

THEOLOGY
Trinity University College (Carmarthen)

TOURISM
Trinity University College (Carmarthen)

VETERINARY SCIENCE
Liverpool

VISUAL ARTS
See **Chapter 6** under Samstag Awards

9 | COUNTRY SPECIFIC AWARDS FOR NON-EU STUDENTS

Some awards listed under countries of residence, which are made to Non-EU students. These awards include postgraduate opportunities. See **Chapter 2.**

AFGHANISTAN
London Metropolitan

AFRICA
Aston, Hull, Salford

ANGOLA
Hartpury College, London Metropolitan

ARGENTINA
Bath

ARMENIA
London Metropolitan

AUSTRALIA
See **Chapter 6** under Samstag Awards and Scottish International

BAHRAIN
Keele

BELARUS
Nottingham, Oxford

BHUTAN
Liverpool Hope, London Metropolitan

BOTSWANA
Aston, Bradford, Greenwich, Hartpury College, London South Bank

BRAZIL
Aston, Bath. See also **Chapter 6** under Instituto Ling

BRUNEI
Durham, Keele

BULGARIA
Oxford

BURMA
See **Chapter 6** under Charles Wallace Trusts

CAMEROON
Aston, London Metropolitan

CANADA
King's College London, St Andrews. See **Chapter 6** under Canadian Scholarship Fund

CARIBBEAN
Southampton Solent

CHILE
Aston, Bath

CHINA
Abertay Dundee, Bath, Birmingham, Bradford, Greenwich, Keele, Hull, King's College London, Liverpool, Liverpool Hope, London South Bank, Nottingham, Roehampton, Sheffield. See also **Chapter 6** under Great Britain–China, Scottish International, Sino-British

COLOMBIA
Aston, Bath

COSTA RICA
Essex

CUBA
London Metropolitan

CYPRUS
London Metropolitan

DUBAI
Keele

EAST AFRICA
Aston

EAST ASIA
Hull, Salford

EAST TIMOR
London Metropolitan, Westminster

EASTERN EUROPE
Nottingham

EGYPT
Greenwich

ESTONIA
Essex

GAMBIA
Aston, London Metropolitan, Westminster

GHANA
Bradford, Greenwich, London South Bank, Southampton Solent

GREECE
King's College London

GULF STATES
Hull

HONG KONG
Aberdeen, Abertay, Birmingham, Cambridge, Durham, East Anglia, Edinburgh, Greenwich, Keele, King's College London, Liverpool, Sheffield, University College London. See also **Chapter 6** under Sir Edward Youde

ICELAND
Westminster

INDIA
Abertay Dundee, Birmingham, Bristol, Edinburgh, Exeter, Greenwich, Keele, Liverpool Hope, London South Bank, Sheffield, Southampton Solent. See also **Chapter 6** under Scottish International

IRAN
London Metropolitan

IRAQ
Nottingham

JAMAICA
London South Bank

JAPAN
Aston, Durham, East Anglia, Edinburgh, Greenwich, Liverpool Hope, Roehampton

JORDAN
London Metropolitan, Nottingham

KAZAKHSTAN
Glamorgan, London Metropolitan

KENYA
Birmingham, Bradford, Bristol, Glamorgan, Greenwich, Keele, London South Bank

KUWAIT
Keele

LATIN AMERICA
Bristol, Salford, University College London. See also **Chapter 6** under Programme Alban

LATVIA
Essex

LEBANON
London Metropolitan, Nottingham

LESOTHO
Hartpury College

LIBYA
Aston

LIECHTENSTEIN
Westminster

MACAO
Aberdeen, Greenwich

MALAWI
Aston, Hartpury College

MALAYSIA
Abertay Dundee, Bristol, Durham, East Anglia, Edinburgh, Keele, Liverpool Hope, Roehampton, Salford, Sheffield, Sheffield Hallam, Southampton Solent

MALDIVES
Birmingham

MAURITIUS
Brimingham, Bristol, Greenwich, London South Bank

MEXICO
Bath, Glamorgan

MIDDLE EAST/NORTH AFRICA
Salford

MONGOLIA
Glamorgan

MOZAMBIQUE
Hartpury College

NAMIBIA
Aston, London Metropolitan

NEPAL
Abertay Dundee, Glamorgan, Liverpool Hope, London Metropolitan

NEW ZEALAND
See **Chapter 6** under Scottish International

NIGERIA
Bradford, Greenwich, London South Bank, Southampton Solent

NORTH AFRICA
Aston

NORTH AMERICA
Abertay Dundee

NORWAY
Roehampton, Westminster

OMAN
Abertay Dundee

PAKISTAN
Greenwich, Liverpool Hope, London South Bank, Oxford, Sheffield, Southampton Solent. See also **Chapter 6** under Charles Wallace Trusts

PERU
Aston, Bath

PHILIPPINES
Greenwich

PORTUGAL
Bath

PUERTO RICO
Bath

RUSSIAN FEDERATION
Aston, Bristol, Glamorgan, Greenwich

SAUDI ARABIA
Keele

SINGAPORE
Abertay Dundee, Birmingham, Bristol, Durham, East Anglia, Edinburgh, Keele, Liverpool, Roehampton, Sheffield. See also **Chapter 6** under Scottish International

SOUTH AFRICA
Aston, Edinburgh, Greenwich, Hartpury College. See also **Chapter 6** under Canon Collins Trust and Commonwealth Nassau fellowship.

SOUTH ASIA
Hull

SOUTH EAST ASIA
Hull

SRI LANKA
Abertay Dundee, Birmingham, Bristol, Glamorgan, Keele, Liverpool Hope, London South Bank, Sheffield

SUB-SAHARAN AFRICA
Aston

SWAZILAND
Hartpury College

SWITZERLAND
Westminster

SYRIA
Nottingham

TAIWAN
Aberdeen, Abertay Dundee, Bournemouth, Greenwich, Keele, King's College London, Liverpool Hope, Roehampton

TANZANIA
Bradford, Glamorgan, Greenwich, London Metropolitan, Southampton Solent

THAILAND
Bristol, Durham, East Anglia, Edinburgh, Glamorgan, Greenwich, Keele, London South Bank, Roehampton, Southampton Solent

TIBET
London Metropolitan

TRINIDAD AND TOBAGO
London South Bank

TURKEY
Greenwich, London South Bank, Nottingham, Roehampton, Westminster

UGANDA
Bradford, Glamorgan, London Metropolitan, London South Bank

UKRAINE
Glamorgan

UNITED ARAB EMIRATES/OMAN
Keele

USA
Bath, Bristol, East Anglia, Edinburgh, King's College London, Salford, Sheffield, St Andrews. See also **Chapter 6** under British Marshall Scholarships

URUGUAY
Bath

UZBEKISTAN
Greenwich, London Metropolitan

VENEZUELA
Bath

VIETNAM
Brighton, Bristol, East Anglia, Glamorgan, Keele London Metropolitan, London South Bank, Nottingham

ZAMBIA
Aston, Hartpury College. See also **Chapter 6** under Beit Trust

ZIMBABWE
Aston, Glamorgan, Greenwich, Hartpury College, London Metropolitan

ZULU LANDS
Aberdeen, Aston

10 | USEFUL ADDRESSES, PUBLICATIONS AND WEBSITES

USEFUL ADDRESSES

Department for Children, Schools and Families (DCSF)
Sanctuary Buildings
Great Smith Street
London SW1P 3BT
Tel: 0870 000 2288
www.dfes.gov.uk

National Assembly for Wales
FHE1 Division
4th floor
Welsh Office
Cathays Park
Cardiff CF1 3NQ
Tel: 029 2082 5111
www.wales.gov.uk

Student Awards Agency for Scotland (SAAS)
Gyleview House
3 Redheughs Rigg
South Gyle
Edinburgh EH12 9HH
Tel: 08451 111711
www.saas.gov.uk

Department for Employment and Learning (Northern Ireland)
Adelaide House
39–49 Adelaide Street
Belfast BT2 8FD
Tel: 028 9025 7777
www.delni.gov.uk

NHS Bursaries in England
NHS Student Grants Unit
Hesketh House
200–220 Broadway
Fleetwood
Lancs FY7 8SS
Tel: 0845 358 6655
www.nhsstudentgrants.co.uk

NHS Bursaries in Wales
NHS Wales Student Awards Unit
National Leadership and Innovation Agency for Healthcare (NLIAH)
2nd floor, Golate House
101 St Mary Street
Cardiff CF10 1DX
Tel: 029 2026 1495
www.nliah.wales.nhs.uk

NHS Bursaries in Scotland
See the **Student Awards Agency for Scotland** on the previous page.

NHS Bursaries in Northern Ireland
Department for Employment and Learning
Student Support
4th floor, Adelaide House
39–49 Adelaide Street
Belfast BT2 8FD
Tel: 028 9025 7777
www.delni.gov.uk

Educational Grants Advisory Service
501–505 Kingsland Road
London E8 4AU
Tel: 020 7254 6251
www.egas-online.org

National Union of Students
2nd floor
Centro 3
Mandela Street
London NW1 0DU
Tel: 08712 218221
www.nusonline.co.uk

USEFUL PUBLICATIONS

Directory of Grant Making Trusts (Directory of Social Change in association with CAF); £95.00. Provides information on 2,500 grant-making trusts. Available from www.careers-portal.co.uk.

Grants Register (Palgrave Macmillan); £175.00. Includes information on a variety of scholarships, fellowships and research grants, exchange and vacation study opportunities, professional and vocational grants. Available from www.palgrave.com/reference.

Guide to the Major Trusts, Volumes 1 and 2 (Directory of Social Change); £34.95 each. Provide information on 1,600 of the largest grant-making organisations in Britain. Available from www.dsc.org.uk/acatalog/grant_making_trusts.html.

International Awards 2001+ (Association of Commonwealth Universities); £40.00. Guide to funding opportunities for international students and researchers – those wishing to study abroad in a country other than their own. The 950 detailed entries will help you match your requirements with the award schemes offered by international, US and European sponsors, and by many Commonwealth universities. Available from www.acu.ac.uk.

Guide to Student Money; Gwenda Thomas (Trotman Publishing); 16.99. Covers every aspect of the student financial scene. Available from www.careers-portal.co.uk.

Study Abroad; UNESCO, 7 Place de Fontenoy, 75700 Paris, France; also available from HMSO, PO Box 569, London SE1 9NH. Country-by-country lists of grants for studying in over 100 countries worldwide, including the UK.

'**Higher education tuition fees: non-European Union Students'** and '**Higher education tuition fees from 2006: EU students'** (British Council). Available from www.britishcouncil.org/learning-education-information-sheets.

USEFUL WEBSITES

www.acf.org.uk (Association of Charitable Foundations)

http://bursarymap.direct.gov.uk

www.educationuk.org/scholarships (British Council)

www.fundersonline.org

www.grantsforindividuals.org.uk

www.rcuk.ac.uk (Research Councils UK)

www.scholarship-search.org.uk

www.scholarships.ac.uk/financial/hardship/index

www.trustfunding.org.uk

www.ukcosa.org.uk (information about funding for overseas students).